Published by

ATLANTIC

PUBLISHERS & DISTRIBUTORS (P) LTD

7/22, Ansari Road, Darya Ganj,
New Delhi-110002
Phones : +91-11-40775252, 23273880, 23275880, 23280451
Fax : +91-11-23285873
Web : www.atlanticbooks.com
E-mail : orders@atlanticbooks.com

Branch Office
5, Nallathambi Street, Wallajah Road,
Chennai-600002
Phones : +91-44-64611085, 32413319
E-mail : chennai@atlanticbooks.com

Printed in India at Nice Printing Press, A-33/3A, Site-IV,
Industrial Area, Sahibabad, Ghaziabad, U.P.

For
WILLIAM MULDER
with
profound reverence

Sir, the objective correlative is love.
It vapourizes not inside the heart
Like fogs of happiness or despair, it is
Of mass, space, energy, composited

And touchable. What vagaries the heart
Turns feeling to, their object turns to love
Round, square, and tall as any classical stone
As any human form, correlative.

PREFACE

This book is the sweet fruit of my research in American Poetry with which I fell virtually in love for more than a decade. The memory of those halcyon days spent in the quiet of Libraries in the company of great books radiating the spirit of great hearts and minds continue to haunt and thrill me. I hope, it will do so forever.

I have chosen to study the poetry of Robert Frost and William Carlos Williams, two major poets of our time, for the very simple reason that they have successfully taken poetry to celebrate the "cry of its occasion."

My gratitude is recorded separately to all those who have in one way or other shown appreciation of and interest in my academic pursuit.

HARIHAR RATH

ACKNOWLEDGMENTS

To Prabhat Nalini Das, former Professor and Head of the Department of English, Utkal University, Bhubaneswar, who supervised my work with a great critical insight and intellectual acumen. No words can suffice to express my gratitude to her.

To Nirmal Mukerji, former Professor of English, Panjab University, Chandigarh (Punjab) for those memorable moments of interaction at Hyderabad.

To Bidhubhusan Das, former Director of Public Instruction, Orissa and Professor of English at Ravenshaw College, Cuttack, and Tribhuvan University, Nepal, for boosting my morale and inspiring me all along to work hard and complete the work.

To V.Y. Kantak, former Professor of English Literature, Central Institute of English and Foreign Languages, Hyderabad, for those memorable evenings I spent with him at Hyderabad but for which my understanding of Frost and Williams would have been poorer.

To Sisir Kumar Ghose, former Professor and Head of the Department of English, Visva-Bharati, Santiniketan, for the repartees with which he viewed my work, and for the continuous encouragement that I received from him to complete it.

To P.S. Sastri, former Professor and Head of the Department of English, Nagpur University, Nagpur, for his advice and encouragement.

To P.S. Chauhan, former Professor of English, Beaver College, U.S., for the affection and love with which he held me during his visit to the ASRC, Hyderabad.

To J. Birje-Patil, former Professor and Head of the Department of English, M.S. University, Baroda, for his affectionate queries regarding the progress of my work.

To Guru Prasad Thakur, former Professor and Head, Department of English, Birla Constituent College, Garhwal University, Uttar Pradesh, for initiating me into the mysterious world of American Poetry.

To Isaac Sequeira, former Professor of English, Osmania University, Hyderabad, and former Academic Associate, ASRC, Hyderabad, for advising me on my study.

To Amritjit Singh, former Professor of English, University of Rajasthan, Jaipur, and former Academic Associate, ASRC, Hyderabad, for the pains he took to advise me on the problems of my study.

To M.R. Satyanarayana, former Professor of English, Osmania University, Hyderabad, for the encouragement I received from him during my visits to the ASRC, Hyderabad.

To (Miss) Dorothy L. Clark, former Acting Librarian, and Mr. M. Vishnu Kumar, former Library Assistant (Acquisition), ASRC, Hyderabad for locating rare materials necessary for my work.

To Dr. K.R. Gupta, Managing Director, Atlantic Publishers and Distributors, New Delhi, for readily accepting to publish this work, and for bestowing loving regards on me.

And last but not the least to my wife and children whose unbounded love, and encouragement helped me to complete this work.

HARIHAR RATH

CONTENTS

1

Toward A Definition: The Adamic Mode in Poetry as A Creative Process

AN ATTEMPT has been made in this book to evaluate some important facets in which "the Adamic Mode" as a poetic process operates in the poetry of two important poets of our time: Robert Frost and William Carlos Williams. To study them together, and to discover levels of analogy in their poetry is not the purpose of this study, for it is well-known that between Frost and Williams there is a good deal of difference. Though more popular, Frost had little to do with the "modern trends" in the twentieth-century poetry, whereas the appeal of Williams, a quiet and unassuming man who led the uneventful life of a doctor, is perhaps more in tune with the demands of "modernity" in poetry today. Robert Frost who died slightly earlier than Williams had no lessons to learn as a poet from the "manifesto" of the *avant-garde* group of writers. Neither a *vers-librist via* "imagism" that gradually died into "Amygism," nor a lover of that innovation called "the period style" set space by the success of *The Waste Land,* Robert Frost's "pasture" lay elsewhere. He found a way different from that of Eliot, Yeats or Williams to write poetry in the twentieth century. He neither turned to Eliot's ultimate devotion to the "Prayer of the one Annunciation," nor to Yeats's prophetic vision "of some rough beast, its hour come round at last," nor to Williams's finding of the cause with people who "die also incommunicado." Frost turned to the real life of New England to build the rock-foundation of his poetry, and to work out "a practical *modus vivendi,* a way of making something out of the facts that life presented him with."[1]

To one who understands the poetry of the 'Seventies in terms of discarding the mask, of exposing intimate experiences with a tonal intensity that bears little or no trace of irony, say in the pattern of a John Berryman or James Dickey, Frost's poetry would appear to be made of a foreign stuff, although he may not totally reject Williams. Reserving, however, for the concluding chapter a brief comparative study of the two poets, this thesis proposes to begin with judging the meaning of "the Adamic Mode" as understood by poets, critics and historians, and to bring into focus its important facets which would form the background for a proper study of themes in the poetry of Frost and Williams. The present study of their poetry is selective, taking into account, as it does, only those poems which allow the kind of treatment proposed above because it is felt that such poems often suggest a consistent pattern functioning in their poetry. The justification for testing these two poets on a theory used fruitfully by Roy Harvey Pearce in *The Continuity of American Poetry*[2] lies very much in the fact that the theory has been applied more consistently to fictional works, and there are only negligible examples of its application to major poets of our time. What is true of fiction is more or less true of poetry. Mark Schorer has aptly remarked that "the two genres have moved closer together..., until it sometimes seems as if one is about to disappear into the other."[3]

Borrowing a pedagogically useful term from the historians of the Edenic Myth who considered America as the New World, and the American as the first Adam recreated, Roy Harvey Pearce made use of the word "Adamic" in *The Continuity of American Poetry* to describe trends opposed to the "mythic" which came up as a "counter-current" to its mainstream. A distinction between the Adamic faith in personality and the mythic faith in culture is also, broadly speaking, a distinction between such opposing points of view as self and society, ego and superego, humanism and religion and the like.[4] The two terms—"Adamic" and "mythic"—have been used to imply two radically opposed ways of life open to modern man. What is more important, Pearce is conscious that the terms are not his but the poets' being "their means of sorting out in the American poet's work the components of innocence and experience, past and present, self and other, freedom and limitation—in all his capacity to give and to take."[5] More cogently stated, the matrix of Adamic poetry is indeed "bound up in the fact of that insistent opposition: the egocentric as against the theocentric, man without history as against history without man, the antinomian as against the orthodox, personality as against culture...."[6] The Adamic poet's celebration of Adam in his various guises as the "inevitable culture hero"[7]of the twentieth century has to be understood with reservations. The statement of Pearce that the Adamic poem is involved with the operation of the creative imagination as an act of self-definition brings us face to face with one of the basic problems of creativity in art. If "the operation of the creative imagination" means a movement of the psychic life, its freedom then lies beyond consciousness or, as Brewster Ghiselin has stated, "in some degree of dissociation from consciousness."[8] At first, there is that "aspect of adventurous departure from the known, insofar as it has any aspects of which we can be aware, insofar as it is not altogether subliminal."[9] In other words, the fundamentals of this creative process lie embedded in an ability to be free of the "established," which again requires an understanding that "the established is not the absolute, but is only the instrumentality of life, is justified only by the service it renders to life and has no meaning apart from vital needs."[10]

The "mythic" poet has no occasion to suspect the sanctity of the "established," particularly, all that is gloriously associated with history, culture, and religion. Making, as he does, a recurring attempt to achieve grace through God, the "mythic" poet is, of course, not entirely "mythic." John Crowe Ransom's "stance" is of particular importance here to understand the implication of this statement. Ransom who has been rightly acclaimed as "the sage of the counter-current"[11] was a little too uncomfortable while noting "the urgent orthodoxy" of Elict which was achieved at the cost of a certain "gentleness."[12] He was of the opinion that the poet's faith is first of all ingrained in this world "inasmuch as it is not possible for imagination to acquaint us with any other world. It is a horrid as well as a beautiful world, but without the horror we should never focus the beauty, without death there would be no relish for life, without danger, no courage, without savagery, no gentleness, and without the background of our frequent ignominy, no human dignity and pride.... To the theologian the poet might want to say, *One world at a time*"[13] [Italics Mine]. As critic and teacher, though not as poet, Ransom sought to find out the subtle points of contact between the mythic and the Adamic poem, and wanted to justify his conviction that "the mainstream and the counter-current" are one. In other words, the continuity of American poetry should not be one or the other, but both.[14] Comparing Tate's "Death of Little Boys" with Remson's "Dead Boy," one is struck by the manner in which Ransom keeps to the vantage point between the mythic and the Adamic connotation of the "death theme." Tate is "mythic" as he avoids to seize upon the particularity involved in the emotions of the "episode," making the whole issue mysteriously *allusive*, so that death here is more or less, as Pearce would like to put it, "an apocalyptic sign of man's ultimate fate."[15] In Ransom's poetry, death takes on a different colour, making it a memento of man's earthly limitations. What pleases a reader of common denomination is the poet's condescension to hold to "a sense of the integrity of the occasion as something of value in and of itself, and to a sense of the particular way in which the past is implicated in the occasion."[16] What is of significance for the present study is Pearce's just noting of a parallel attitude in Ransom and Frost. "Frost takes stock of the present, as it is coloured by our deeds in the past, yet looks to the future (Freedom, so he has said, as "departure"). Ransom takes stock of the present, as it is coloured by our hopes for the future, yet looks to the past (Freedom as responsibility)."[17] Though Pearce misses it, another parallel could have been drawn, that between Ransom and Williams. Ransom's Phi Beta Kappa poem of 1939 bids Harvard man to take stock of the unseemlier world which is here and now,[18] instead of pendulating between two impossible longings—the New Englander's for the pure Idea, and the Southerner's for the Thing and its Myth. Ransom's concept of poetry lies ultimately in the poet's ability to return to the "unseemlier world," just as Williams's exhortation to dip into "the filthy Passaic" is a fitting "motto" for poets to remain fascinatingly alive by viewing the familiar, banal world with a "fresh eye."

"The Adamic Mode" as a poetic process has also its own paradoxes which should be carefully noted. The continuity of American Poetry lies in the manner in which American poetry freed itself, time and again, from the bondage of the traditional Puritan idea of poetry,[19] expressive of God's way with man, and went on to project a poetry expressive of "man's way with himself and with the God which his sense of himself reveals."[20] Thus, poetry in "the Adamic Mode" is a kind of egocentric creativity where the poet's "self" consciously or unconsciously gets associated with the "authentic autobiography" of the plain old Adam—the first man's experience of ever-lasting innocence, and its loss. It is also the same as Emerson's "simple genuine self against the whole world" which involves a basic confrontation with the anti-poetic world. For Thoreau, too, "The frontiers are not east or west, north or south; but wherever a man *fronts* a fact,...."[21] [Thoreau's Italics]. This is also to say that there is no end to the frontier of the wilderness of facts, or in other words, the wilderness of the antipoetic which, queerly enough, is an excellent *via media* for the poet to view the world afresh with the "innocent" eyes of Adam in the Garden of Eden. This is "the Adamic Mode" opposed so much to "the mythic Mode," but no one should be blind to a certain amount of inconsistency in its operation. This is so because most poetic processes are not "watertight compartments." They often admit of loopholes. The one possible loophole in "the Adamic Mode," for one trying to make it entirely distinct from "the mythic Mode," lies in the fact that the Adamic poet's mind is, to a certain degree, a mythologizing one, particularly in its basic concern with the various components of the Edenic Myth. The adjective "Adamic" is, therefore, to suggest a complex experience—one of innocence of Adam in the Garden of Eden before his Fall and the other of Original Sin that led to Adam's Fall and his ultimate expulsion from the Garden of Eden. The Adamic poet's insistence on recapturing "the lost Eden" through an imaginative process in his poetry is basically speaking "a mythic process" minus, of course, its religious connotation. Frost and Williams, placed rightly in the gallery of Adamic poets, reveal a desire in most of their representative poems to recapture an "innocent freshness" in "things" and "facts" of Nature and man which, in the face of the sophisticated nature of our mechanised and mechanical civilization, have been unfortunately dimmed, or even lost to our vision. The moment of such a vision is sacred for the poets. In a way, it is also "a mythic process." The summary formula for understanding the Adamic poet's vision of "unspoilt innocence" in "things" and "facts" is to know that by "living" the Edenic Myth, the poet "emerges from profane chronological time" and enters a time that is of a different quality, a "sacred Time at once primordial and indefinitely recoverable."[22] However, one basic distinction has to be drawn. Unlike the mythic poet, the Adamic poet does not involve himself with any "narrative resurrection of a primeval reality, told in satisfaction of deep religious wants...."[23] Keeping himself at a safe distance from "deep religious wants," the Adamic poet's recapturing of *innocence via experience* is not a regressus obtained by ritual means but a kind of "going back" "accomplished by an effort of thought."[24] In Frost this "going back" lies in his "strategic withdrawal" to "mountain and farm," to, what he has called, "wholeness beyond confusion." Frost would like to call this freedom "departure," but while departing, Frost's look, as Pearce has put it, is "backward, not forward." We shall indicate in Chapter IV that this "backward motion" is cyclic, not linear. With Williams, too, the "going back" is accomplished in the "Circular Time of the Eternal Return"[25] by which "things" are presented as purified, regenerated and restored to their original glory. In our study of Williams which appears in Chapter V we shall indicate how he, out of several ways of "going back," chooses the one of "rapid and direct re-establishment of the first situation."[26]

"The mainstream and the counter-current," that is, "the Adamic" and "the mythic" modes in American poetry, form a basic conflict in spite of a certain measure of identity between them which we have attempted to demonstrate briefly in the preceding paragraphs. This conflict, it may be suggested, is born out of the very "conflicting nature" of America's culture and history. The major tendency in such "polemical works" as Van Wyck Brooks's *America's Coming-of-Age* (1915), Waldo Frank's *Our America* (1919), D.H. Lawrence's *Studies in Classic American Literature* (1923) and Lewis Mumford's *The Golden Day* (1926) is to see "American history as developing out of a Freudian conflict between repression and liberation, between will and body' ...."[27] Also, there has been all along a "need for a biological adjustment to place,"[28] most successfully demonstrated in the masterful individualism of the Indians, the early possessors of the land, and the white invaders who thought the Indians as obstacles to their "pioneering mind," and yet recognized them as symbols of "the nobility man could achieve by living openly with nature."[29] Wildly dedicated to the charm of "unpath'd waters, undreamed shores," Columbus, Ulysses-like in his exploration of the unknown, chanced upon the discovery of the New World—"a spring field of flowers–wild, thorned, gardened flowers that riot their inharmonious songs under a mystic sky...."[30] Later on, the first settlers of this New World on the Massachusetts Bay, beginning with their "pact" that followed the anchoring of the Mayflower, went on to establish the colonies, form the confederation, and help themselves with confidence to finally break from the mother-country to herald the birth of a new nation. On a new soil, with a longing to become a true society they had their "pangs of maturation, of a *rite de passage* from innocence to knowledge...."[31] Their theocratic lineage, with its insistence on searching God's scriptures for evidence of His way with them and living accordingly, came, in fact, from Isreal *via* the holy Rome.[32] The Puritan's metamorphosis in American life from religiosity to acquisition, and his relation with "pioneer ideals" have received ample attention.[33] It can only be briefly stated here that the whole process has been ironical with a basic conflict involved. Patterned after St. Augustine's City of God [De Civitate Dei] to start with, the actual city they created rapidly degenerated into a necropolis *via* the metropolis and megalopolis. Frost's "pastoral ideals," or Williams's emphasis on a *communitas* between "the male and the female principles of life" do indeed indicate a positive reaction against this "American jungle" as Waldo Frank would put it.

One might say, those were the years of "transformation," but the most critical time in the history of the United States was the period 1855-1870. A breaking point was reached just as, out of so many, only three fundamentally opposed and opposing issues came into a positive clash. It was mainly a conflict between "the agrarian ideal of Jefferson and the industrial ideal of Hamilton," "the plantation gentility of the South and the commercial gentility of the North," and last but not the least, "a culturally mature East and a raw and expanding West."[34] This needs clarification of a sort. The Southern history, as Faulkner's story "The Bear" symbolically reveals, indicates a providential loss of Adamic innocence, but the story's *drive* draws our attention to how it can also be successfully recaptured. Further, though Thoreau and Emerson belonged to the East, they were, in spirit, obviously with the promise of Adamic innocence guaranteed by the rising consciousness of a South which no longer thought its predicament providential, but considered it retrievable by an effort to restore innocence. The opening of the Westward expansion beginning with Jefferson's Louisiana purchase is a case in point in the context of the Southern agrarianism with which, we believe, the rugged West has a large connection. The "Virgin Land" as Henry Nash Smith calls the American West has features of the South—in spirit, geography, and values, and hence the Adamic myth which is largely applied to the South can be very well extended to encompass the entire American West which opposes, like the South, the technology of the North. The Northern States, to some extent, continued the mythic tradition of Europe, and technology provided some kind of basis for the use of myth as a way of salvaging some human values from a technological environment. However, one could see the gradual and steady progress of "an epoch of achieved nationality."[35] What is important for the present study is not only to note the conflict but also to understand that in such moments of "fulfilment," life's tragedy is heroically confronted. The challenge was taken up, and in a way answered by Emerson in a radically revolutionary manner. He emphasized a need for "introspection" in an age of pioneering, the emphasis of which was on the glorification of "matter." Van Wyck Brooks defined in *America's Coming-of-Age* (1915) the nature of this cleavage whose tensional vibration "cut through all layers of American Culture"[36] and resulted in a dichotomy between the "high brow" and "low brow"[37] which is again related to the distinction made between the "redskin" and "paleface"[38] literature. George Santayana's reiteration of the conflict is more telling. "America is not simply," he says, "a young country with an old mentality: it is a country of two mentalities, one a survival of the beliefs and standards of the fathers, the other, an expression of the instincts, practices and discoveries of the younger generations. In all higher things of the mind—in religions, in literature, in the moral emotions—it is the hereditary spirit that shall prevail. ...the one is all aggressive enterprise, the other is all genteel tradition."[39] The confrontation of the two counterforces had also its deep impact on literature. James Russell Lowell's condemnation of Swinburne is a significant point to be noted. Lowell, emphatically putting forth his support for "the true church of Literature," as against the Adamic and other heresies, says:

> I have not seen Swinburne's new volume—but a poem or two which I have seen shocked me, and I am not

> squeamish.... Why should a man by choice go down to live in his cellar, instead of mounting to those fair upper chambers which look towards the Sunrise of that Easter which shall greet the resurrection of that soul from this body of this death? *Virginibus puerisque*? To be sure.... But I have outlived many heresies, and shall outlive this new Adamite one of Swinburne. The true Church of poetry is founded on a rock, and I have no fear that these smutchy backdoors of hell shall prevail against her.[40]

To draw another parallel example of animosity of this kind, one can recall the incident of Yeats paying scarce attention to Hopkins's talk, because Hopkins was carrying in his pocket a copy of Whitman's *Leaves of Grass*.[41] The jealousy of the Adamic poets for those in the "mythic" group is also well known. Robert Frost's puckish remark, "Let Eliot recite, I'll write one" has already become associated with one of the classic incidents of our time. What is enlightening here is to find that Eliot had certain levels of analogy in his poetry which came astonishingly closer to those found in Whitman, the most centrally recognized poet in "the Adamic Mode" in American poetry. Musgrove's *T.S. Eliot and Walt Whitman*[42] treats this point judiciously keeping in view its possibilities and limitations. Whitman is likened to a "demon" whose "ferocity" lies in his intention to see that all succeeding generations of poets *do* write after him. Whether these poets like it or not, they have been either aware of Whitman's "stature" without emulating him, or have been influenced consciously or unconsciously by his poetic themes and techniques.[43] Good points of analogy emerge when some specifically selected lines from Eliot's "East Coker" are compared with some specifically selected lines from Whitman's "Song of the Open Road." While comparing the following lines from the "Song of the Open Road,"

> To look up or down no road but it stretches and waits for you,
> however long but it stretches and waits for you,
> To see no being, not God's or any, but you also go thither,

To see no possession but you may possess it,
enjoying all without labour or purchase, abstracting
the feast yet not abstracting one particle of it, ...[44]

with some from "East Coker,"

In order to possess what you do not possess
You must go by a way of dispossession.
In order to arrive at what you are not
You must go through the way in which you are not.
And what you do not know is the only thing you know
And what you own is what you do not own
And where you are is where you are not[45]

one is struck by an obviously similar drive in syntax, and a subtle use of an extraordinarily varied "technique of parallelism and repetition." Of course, the Whitmanesque style is used by Eliot "to deny the truth and cogency of what Whitman would say."[46] More such examples can be cited from *Four Quartets,* acknowledged to be Eliot's greatest poem, to bring about "Whitmanian echoes and recollections."[47] However, Eliot, condemning the moon-mist ideas of Whitman, dismisses him as an "outdated" poet. An "originator" no doubt, Whitman had unfortunately, says Eliot, no "genuine originality" as a poet, though he may be rated as "a prose writer" of considerable import. In this he was inferior to Pound, Eliot's "poetic god-father."[48] Of course, Pound, having freed himself from the oppressively "antipoetic milieu" of his times, did acknowledge his debt to Whitman with some surliness, though. He writes:

I make a pact with you, Walt Whitmen
I have detested you long enough.
I come to you as a grown child
Who has had a pig-headed father;
I am old enough now to make friends
It was you that broke the new wood,
Now is a time for carving. [Italics Mine].

("A Pact")[49]

The tone of these lines is one of compromise, though dislike for Whitman's poetry is evident. Pound considers Whitman his "father-figure" from whom be must free himself even while acknowledging that it is his "father" who has taught him that "freedom" is not only possible but necessary.[50] Pound went on "for carving a new kind of poetry," "most notably in the middle of the *Pisan Cantos*, in which he identifies his role with Whitman's: making the modern world possible for poetry."[51] Pound's reconstitution of poetic sensibility to write a "*new tale of the tribe*" lay in the tenacity in which he rediscovered some of the surest elements in culture. For Whitman, however, life's central paradigm was discoverable in the release of the tremendous forces of the human self.[52] Such an "egocentrisn" was "horizontal, democratic and extroverted" and "it does not admit of any gap between the inner and the outer, self and the world, the individual and the collective and, therefore, unfolds itself without any resistance."[53] Professor Gargills's appreciation of Whitman as "the natural voice of breeding and prolific America, as the Priapus of the new continent"[54] suggests that Whitman's egocentric mask, or more pertinently speaking, the Adamic role, is an "existential choice" made out of a confrontation with the new economic and social realities of a Frontier society. For the purpose of this discussion, two clusters (first included in the 1860 edition of *Leaves of Grass*)—"Children of Adam" and "Calamus"—are highly important. James E. Miller rightly says that they "move the personality created in 'Song of Myself' from his self-imposed, imaginative isolation and provide him with lovers and comrades."[55] The ideal of sexual innocence and pleasure of Adam before the Fall is invoked:

> To the Garden the world a new ascending
> Potent mates, daughters, sons, preluding,
> The love, the life of their bodies, meaning and being.
>
> ("Children of Adam")[56]

This way the personality in the "New World Garden" is "To recreate the original garden [of Eden] in his relationship with women, and all the elements of nature are to participate in phallic and procreative celebration: "[57]

Bridegroom night of love working surely and softly into
the prostrate dawn,
Undulating into the willing and yielding day,
Lost in the cleave of the clasping and sweet-flush'd day.
This the nucleus—after the child is born of women, man
is born of woman,
This the bath of birth, this the merge of small and the
large, outlet again.
("Children of Adam")[58]

What is significantly striking in Whitman is the other aspiration, as reflected in "Calamus," for a "continent indissoluble" based on a spiritual, passionate and intense attachment of *man to man*. "Thus the spiritual comradeship of democracy fused with the sexual innocence of the Garden make up the New World society of the freshly created Personality."[59]

We would like to suggest that some such tone of "comradeship of democracy" and "sexual innocence" is also traceable in the poetry of Williams. In *Paterson,* Williams's *motif* lies in enunciating a need for communication, a basic proposition for democracy. The failure of communication is the problem:

The language is missing then
they die also
incommunicado.[60]

As a corrective to this failure he sets the primary symbolism of a primitive, pastoral culture, where "sexual innocence," not its "whorishness," is one of the main features of life:

...the 9 women
of some African chief semi-naked
astraddle a log....[61]

M.L. Rosenthal sees "the organic relationship of natural and social orders, ...communication and wholeness"[62] in the following lines:

Behind her, packed tight up
in a descending scale of freshness
stiffened the others
and then...

the last, the first wife,
present! supporting all the rest growing
up from her—whose careworn eyes
serious, menacing—but unabashed breasts
sagging from hard use...

Whereas the uppointed breasts
of that other, tense, charged with
pressures unrelieved
and the rekindling they bespoke
was evident.[63]

Williams's emphasis here is to plead for "freshness" which would "rekindle" or revitalise our "careworn" lives. Such a "freshness" is born by establishing a rapport with the natural order as opposed to the artificial *mores* of our social hierarchy.

In fact, Williams, in spite of his anti-Whitmanianism which will be indicated in Chapter V, recognized that Whitman was the pioneer who cleared the way for modern poetry, specifically "American" poetry of Williams's "free-wheeling sort."[64] Whitman's difference with Robert Frost, particularly in his "free-wheeling sort" of verse, is obvious, though certain identical features in treatment of themes can be noted.

Philip L. Gerber, however, remarks that with Walt Whitman "Frost has more affinity then appears on the surface."[65] Frost's direct and first-hand perception of man's communication with environment, or to put it in an Emersonian language, an "original relation to the Universe" is the same as Whitman's recognition that the soul perceives the world of things, space, light, and time to be an integral part of itself. A definitive statement in regard to Whitman's position in "the Adamic Mode" of American poetry is made by Pearce. Pearce concludes that Whitman worked "toward a new Paideuma: one entirely of process, of guiding, strengthening, energizing, and redefining the sensible self by putting it into direct contact with the world wherein it could be free, creative, and whole—a self proper to the American democrat."[66] Eliot's distrust of such a philosophy needs no explication. With a shyness for self-exposure which may perhaps be attributed to his religious training Eliot's basic style in poetry is to ostentatiously remove himself from his poem. To him, the egocentric, private world of man is so "straitjacketd" that it has to be transcended for giving it grace through God. Therefore, the *principle of being* does not lie in man's ability to achieve grace by his own humanistic efforts, but by conceiving "Truth," *the myth beyond myth* which is the same as conceiving "Love" as equated with "God." Eliot's rejection of the principle of personality and the acceptance of the principle of culture owes its origin to certain assumptions about the nature of experience that he imbibed from his early "dabbling" in F.H. Bradley's monism which, as indicated by Kristian Smidt, impressed its permanent mould on Eliot's life.[67]

Bradley's monism elucidates the point that the human self is not to be viewed as self-sufficient. A mere cluster of imperfections and delusions, our soul lacks unity in spite of its timeless finite centre of feeling where perceptions can verily occur.[68] Hence, the necessity for order, and for the poet to renounce his world by renouncing the demands of his "self" in favour of those of the Kingdom of God. In contrast, the Adamic poet's belief is strongly grounded in a humanism so powerful that even God comes under its sway: it is not from God that the poet's language emanates.[69] While equating the theory of poetry with the theory of life with "a significant humanity," Wallace Stevens writes in his "Adagia" of man: "This happy creature— It is he that invented the Gods. It is he that put into their months the only words they have ever spoken!"[70] Thus, the emphasis is shifted from God to the essence of poetry "as life's redemption."[71] In this essence is involved the predicament of man's "self," and its interaction with "reality." The Adamic poet glorifies the predicament, and gives us the poem itself—its "particularised reality," celebrating his belief from moment to moment in the very flux and disorder of reality. Thus, even the "damage of a life-time,"[72] may act as a celebrated back-ground for his poetry wherein he, "with the cumulative force of a whole life's cultivation"[73] invokes his "experiences" to bear deeply on his art. To him history is "individual history or must remain words."[74] He is also aware of our "limitations" here and now which is like that of "a diminished thing,"[75] but he must draw on his art to "...give us pleasure in the orchard white,/Like nothing else by day, like ghosts by night,/And make us happy in the happy bees,/The swarm dilating round the perfect trees."[76]

Again, he may sing softly to himself: "I am lonely, lonely,/ I was born to be lonely," and yet will take pleasure in recognising "I am best so."[77] The mythic poet's centre of "awareness," however, lies elsewhere. For him, "The knowledge imposes a pattern, and falsifies,/For the pattern is new in every moment/ And every moment is a new and shocking/Valuation of all we have been."[78] Hence, in poetry, as in life, the necessity for discipline of action, of patience, of renunciation by surrendering "the appetitive self" to God.

The rigorous discipline of art to which Eliot draws our attention in his introduction to Paul Valery's *Le Serpent* lies in an ability to cease to be interested in one's own emotions and experiences except as material.[79] Another statement of Eliot's that the essence of poetry lies in an "escape from emotions"[80] needs clarification, for it has often been read inaccurately. One suspects that some of the best critical canons of the aestheticians of our time have been turned lopsided under its impact. Particularly, the emphasis on "the cognitive aspects" of literature, and the failure to consider its "affective tonalities" has been responsible for creating a "position of stasis." Some such statements like the one made by Van O'Connor that Whitman's followers like "Robinson Jaffers, Vachel Lindsay, Edgar Lee Masters, Carl Sandburg, Stephen Vincent Benet and William Rose Benet and later Paul Engle, August Derleth, Muriel Rukeyser, Ben Neddow, and Alfred Hayes...are not in the line of American writers who have deepened our knowledge of human motivation or action"[81] have also added much to the confusion of common readers whose response to literature, we suppose, is more guided by "emotional participation" than "intellectual cooperation."All these have led to certain important discussions in judging literature. Robert Penn

Warren's essay "Pure and Impure poetry"[82] indicated the revolution that occurred since the Imagists banished ideas, since George Moore's anthology of pure poetry maintained that thought seeped into poetry is an adulteration. The nucleus of such a revolution lay in a shift from "the idea of images and images alone, or images and music of verse together"[83] to a growing tendency toward abstraction. The shift is, of course discernible in some of the most acclaimed Adamic poets as in the later poetry of Stevens or Williams. However, Stevens's two lectures "The Irrational Element in Poetry"[84] and "A Collect of Philosophy"[85] point to a kind of synthesis between "idea and image," "cognition and affection" or more plainly speaking "intellect and emotion."

Differentiating between "the true subjects" and "the poetry of the subject," Stevens enunciates that "the true subject" is the idea, an element of thought implicit in the poem, and "the poetry of the subject" is the essence of the poem, its inherently imaginative vision, its concentration of feeling, the tone and quality of its language. His eventual analysis pointed to a recognition that poetry could be inherent in idea just as much in image and incident.[86] Eliot's later modification of his extreme notions of impersonality in art is also important as it helps in giving critical sanction to the Adamic poet's passionate exploration of feelings and emotions.

In a lecture entitled "The Poetry of W.B. Yeats,"[87] Eliot relaxes his rigidity, and contends that a poet may, however, transform his personal experiences into a "general symbol," and use the same in his poetry. Thus, in "A Note on War Poetry"(1942), Eliot speaks of

> the point at which the merely individual
> Explosion breaks
> In the path of an action merely typical
> To create the Universal, originate a symbol
> Out of the impact, ...

and testifies to the possibility of

private experience at its greatest intensity
Becoming universal, which we call "poetry"....[88]

Grover Smith aptly comments that "this view is not incompatible with his earlier view, but, in the light of *Four Quartets* (1935-42), it implies, as the other does not, that *experience requires little masking*"[Italics Mine]. Though Eliot has not learnt either by action or by accidental experience "to bring into his craft proper the passions of all sorts and conditions of man," it is satisfying to note for enlarging our understanding of "the Adamic Mode" in poetry that "Eliot's strange, private vision, still faces inward to the isolated self."[89]Accordingly, the Adamic poet would insist that the essence of the creative process does not merely lie in cognitively seizing the subject, but by deeply feeling, almost with excitement, the subject so seized. The brilliant example is the way "Stopping by Woods" was composed by Robert Frost. While working on his long poem entitled "New Hampshire," Frost, to relieve his tiredness, went outside to look at the Sun, and the poem "came" to him.[90] To quote him: "I always thought it was the *product of autointoxication....*"[91] [Italics Mine]. The endless manner in which Williams's *Paterson* seemed to continue[92] is not due to a mere cognizing of the subject, but a strong feeling about it,—so strong indeed that the purely cognitive struggles which followed upon the original seizure, and which extended over a period of years, often had a compulsive character.[93]

Within this compulsion lies the Adamic poet's selfconsciousness to "test" his own "origin as an artist and a person in a way radically different from that of the mythic poet's. The Adamic poet, like an American, or as it is put, "A United Stateser,"[94] is an "eternal beginner" for whom the quest for "new beginnings" is a cyclic process that goes on forever. Frost and Williams both belong to this tradition, and like Whitman, they can be taken as "doubly fallen." Firstly, they wrote in a time and of a time when the old gods were "annihilated" which obviously created a feeling of dispossession, leaving most of us "alone in a solitude like children without parents."[95] Secondly, in the context of modern man's life encompassed by the machine and its artificial gadgets, they must have seen a society based on mere "factical existence" gradually losing its contact with life's "primordial" and "authentic" origins.[96]

The Adamic poet, going beyond the "Hegelian formulas," does not repeat the past, and unlike the theocentric mythic poet, he has the bravado of re-interpreting it to have a state of consciousness that creates his own time. It is like an endless movement out of time to seize one's own "authentic" origins. The paradox lies in reorienting the myths of the community of man to suit his purpose of creating a "primary myth"[97] based on his private, and peculiar "idea" that coincides with the things—the flora and fauna—immediately perceived in the georgraphical topography of his locality. Though "All men hunger for Alpha...,"[98] the Adamic poet has a particular fascination for the same. In extreme cases he may partake of the Melvillean "reaching back through time until he got pushed back so far he turned time into space."[99] A seeker after "origins," that is, the ground of creation, the Adamic poet is more concerned with basic emotions unlike the mythic poet's dramatic structuring of emotions with such "floating feelings"[100] added to it as are culturally, and historically pertinent and relevant. These basic emotions act as a pointer to his own complex ground of "origins"—his self-definition. This may also necessitate a commitment to do "violence to the very things he loves, the romance of his native history, in order to reveal the ground of his own historicity."[101] Since the Adamic poet's recapturing of his innocence or his "primary myth" lies in "the Adamic act of naming," he is also obviously involved with the process of "mediation," or what we might call, "interpretation." Ironically, this "throws him once more into history."[102] This may, of course, function as a sort of awareness in him, but what he is after is to enact a rapport with the "origins" so as to repeat a new "beginning." As a "beginner," the Adamic poet challenges the "myth of presence," that is, any meaning that may be assigned to anything by a process of disconnection from the contextuality of his own "place"—from where alone his words start, and move from their peculiar particularity to a universality of appeal. Judged from this angle any attempt to interpret American history from the point of view of embracing tradition would boil down to an act of perpetuating "the myth of the Idea" lying ingrained at the very centre of the Western Christianity. The Adamic poet does not accept the myth of such a "presence,"[103] and tends to reject the "onto-theological thought" of considering "the idea of presence or of the center, or the idea of structure or system" whose centre lies simultaneously "outside and inside the system."[104]

Thus, the Adamic poet attempts to free himself from the "myth of centered structurality" which means that he does not cut himself away from the "centre" but from the "centre's tyranny" only. In fact, the concept of history as a structure has undergone several changes in attempting to substitute one "centre" for another:

> Successively, and in a regulated fashion, the centre received different forms or names. The history of metaphysics, like the history of the West, is the history of these metaphors and metonymics. Its matrix...is the determination of being as *presence* in all the senses of the word. It would be possible to show that all the names related to fundamentals, to principles, or to the centre have always designated the constant of a presence... essence, existence, substance, subject... transcendentality, consciousness, or conscience, God, man, and so forth[105] [Derrida's Italics].

The history of Adamic poetry in America shows that the poets under this banner were all along engaged in the free-play of the game of substitution of "centres," and in doing so the very pattern underlies a series of "discontinuities" which form the very basis of its "continuity" as Pearce's appropriately insistant metaphor would reveal. The concept of "old centres" gave in to make room for "new centres" until the only believable "centre," that is, "self" was found as the basis to work in and through. Thus, we find a successive progression of substituting one thing for another: "...the Puritan's wrathful God for the Anglican Word, the Deist's Reason for the Puritan God, the Transcendental Spirit for Deity; Self for Spirit; self for Self."[106] In such a "renaissance of attention"[107] the radical change lies in ultimately freeing the poetic self from the impact of "Idea." It becomes, then, an "idea" of deprivation and dispossession which for the Adamic poets of our times may be "the last believable centre."[108] As these poets fall into the buzz and confusion of empirical experience, the old aesthetic of emphasizing imagination as the basis of creative process does not hold good for them.[109] This development, strange and unexpected as it might appear, has been described as the "double-consciousness" of the modern poet's Adamism as it is opposed to the "Transcendental Adamism" of an Emerson or a Whitman.[110] It has been thus a persistence to see, as it were, the vision of "a world with an *absence* rather than a *presence* at its centre"[111] [Riddel's Italics]. It only means that the Adamic poet, being under the provocation of a sense of "metaphysical deprivation" in our times, questions the very valence of what has been called man's "finite self." He imagines, as Stevens did, "an increasingly human self" since the whole "mythology of self" must be made free from "old nostalgias."[112]

History and language may in such cases be totally re-invented as it were at their origins. Between Emerson's concept of the "central man" and Stevens's concept of the "fictive central man," the Nietzschean question of the "death of God" strikes a note of discordance. However, the emphasis of continuity in the great effort of self-transformation leading to a state of knowledge, freedom and peace must remain in the limitless ability of the "central man." He alone could achieve the returning of the Word into words as Hart Crane did in that famous Whitmanesque tradition of going "beyond desire" unlike an Eliot whose means lay in liberating himself from the "time-event-complex" to reach an ineffable "still-point"—the ultimate silence in evoking the Word [God as Shantih, "The Peace that passeth understanding."]. What should be noted here is that the Admic poet is involved with a "free-play" of his will which incorporates in him a nostalgia for the loss of disappearance of the centre of innocence. The moment of redemption in him does not heavily burden his poetry with tradition and history. On the other hand, he is happy in "pursuing" to restore the loss of the centre, though he may be aware that such a restoration may be a fiction. Speaking of post-Modern poetry as a step ahead of Modern poetry it may be noted that the poet therein has become rather a sophisticated Adam for whom the immediacy of all experiences must be asserted through a language which, forming the very basis of his "game of art,"[113] establishes the co-existence of words with things, with their innocence. While the mythic poet's self-consciousness is inhered in a logocentrism that forever tries to bridge the gap between the words of his poetry and the Word, the Adamic poet shows his intensity in celebrating the energy and light of his imagination. He does not lament as an Eliot would do "the ruptured immediacy words suffer in relation to the absent still-point."[114]

Of course, poets in both the "modes" have a dream to recover an "origin." The difference lies, however, in the fact that the mythic poet senses the purity of such an "origin" strictly from the angle of a "morality" deduced, more or less, from certain previous notions of moral and religious precepts and preconceptions whereas the Adamic poet undertakes the quest for the plenitude of such a "lost origin" essentializing its peculiar moral tone directly from his own experiences. Eliot and Hart Grane, with their different means of approach to encapsulate the "lost origin," are suitable examples to illustrate this point. Eliot's poetry, particularly as we find it in the *Four Quartets*, has its own paradox well known in its perambulation between a process of ceaseless exploration and a visualization of an "end of all exploring" in that desire for "stillness" which shall quieten "desire's" restlessness ["...itself is movement/Not in itself desirable."][115]

To Crane the exploration as we find it in "The Bridge" starts from the very centre of the reality of his personal, empirical experiences, its buzz and confusion. It then proceeds through unknown areas of thoughts and feelings, making the restlessness of "desire," and its complex, convoluted "movement," the very object of exploration. For him the process is surcharged with a Dionysiac rhythm that shifts grounds relentlessly between "fragmentation or individuation" on one hand, and "ecstatic reunion" on the other. The act of achieving the reunion or possessing the object of desire was to annihilate the "object," and by doing so, to annihilate his own self. Thus, Grane's ecstasy, as Riddel puts it, is a kind of Adamic self-sacrifice, "a frenetic violence"[116] engaged in a form of deliberate myth-making "born of a desperate personal need...."[117] Even matter is "made into human action," and acts as an "instrument of spirit."[118] It becomes an "Everpresence, beyond time":

> So to thine Everpresence, beyond time,
> Like spears ensanguined of one tolling star
> That bleeds infinity—the orphic strings,
> Sidereal phalanxes, leap and converge:
> One Song, one Bridge of Fire! Is it Cathay
> Now pity steeps the grass and rainbows sing,
> The serpent with the eagle in the leaves...?
> Whispers antiphonal in azure swing.[119]

These lines are characterised by a consciousness of the poet's self which is in perfect union with life—its variegated world of sense experience. The bridge itself becomes "one Bridge of Fire," and "One Song," suggesting its ability to "purify" us through the power of an "ecstatic utterance." The "Sidereal phalanxes" of the bridge are to Crane a symbol of "orphic strings" which recalls the Orphic myth—the myth of the poet's unmediated vision of innocence of a "lost plenitude." The Bridge is absorbed by the poet's consciousness and becomes the new "word"—the *logos* in man's search for the Absolute. Thus, it "lends a myth to God," and enables the Almighty to make Himself understood in the modern world. There is here an obvious movement "toward a state of...innocence" that gives "a single, new *word,* never before spoken and impossible to actually enumerate, but self-evident as an active principle in the reader's consciousness henceforward."[120] [Weber's Italics]. Such an approach involves an intense principle of Adamic liberation of human spirit. It is opposed to the ideal of encapsulating man in the limitations of religion, and its perpetual invocation of the Word for his bliss just as we find, for example, in Eliot's *Four Quartets.* There the silent Word—the very Incarnation of "a presence of presence" in the theological sense—is the ultimate desire of the poet's "thematic." The self is thus tied to a "parent" existing either before or beyond the world. Without accepting the myth of such "a presence," the Adamic poet rejects the very idea "of meaning given from outside one's 'place.'"[121] In this there is no deliberate reaching after sanctioning an "autotelic" status to the poem composed, for poetry conceived Adamically provides a new, and sometimes a revolutionary aesthetic wherein "the point of view [is] that of an intenser humanity."[122] We may cite, for example, Stevens's attempt to put an emphasis in his poetry on the evolution of man's self, so that it can convincingly engage itself in the task of changing "the word to man" when someone keeps"...speaking, of God."[123] As a substitute for the mythic poet's consciously chosen theological stance, the Adamic poet's self has a "primordial pleasure" arising mainly from the truer, and perhaps nicer knowledge of sustaining itself through a humanistic ideal—a presumption that one can "believe without belief, beyond belief" ["the nicer knowledge of/Belief, that what it believes in is not true."[124] Stevens has made it clear in the following words:

> The final belief is to believe in a fiction, which you know to be a fiction, there being nothing else.[125]

This "willingness to believe beyond belief"[126] enables the Adamic poet to fix the "centre" in reality. In him, therefore, the "centre" is not a "focus" as in the mythic poet but a "force" that enables him to shape his spirit in a multifaceted manner, so that the self can not only think and feel beyond itself, but also become "other in the presence of Other."[127] As Riddel puts it, such a poet "never quite escapes the ultimate Cartesian cleavage."[128] For him Adam was "the father of Descartes" ["Adam/In Eden was the father of Descartes"].[129]

The myth of history, and its continuing emphasis on the linear progression of time gets demythologised when the Adamic poet tries to participate in a self-sustaining pleasure of "removing from the field of history, art, and myth the privilege of presence or center."[130] It means that the poet's imagination gets freely involved in a "game of chess"—a sort of joy in endlessly substituting the "centre." Thus, considered in this light, history, particularly for the American Adam, is a blockage that must be overthrown as it violates the American "effort" to begin "again." The poet who composes poems with this belief must have to rely on his own "self" and "sensibility" affirming "reality" which manifests itself through an "inventiveness" based on his own "individual experience of the communal" as opposed to the mythic poet's sacramental "celebration of the communal experience of the individual."[131]

Without any consideration of antecedents, and without any thought of possible consequences, such poetry, as Wallace Stevens's later poems reveal, may appear almost naked. Even then it is sufficient in itself, particularly in its humanistic possibilities, that is, in its special appeal to man that he is at liberty to invent his own world. Being in such a world, the poet, as Wallace Stevens wrote in 1954, endeavours "to find out whether it is possible to formulate a theory of poetry that would make poetry a *significant humanity* of such a nature and scope that it could be established as a normal vital field for all comers"[132] [Italics Mine].

The ultimate role of such a poet with his "passion for yes" is to be Adam—the Adam whose expulsion from Paradise led him to rely on that "terrible force" called mind which is perhaps "the only force that can defend us"[133] in the face of the world's horror. The Adamic poet would thus play in America the role of Emerson's American Scholar who confronts "reality"—"the varitable *ding an sich*" as Stevens puts it in the "The Comedian as the Letter C"—and dedicates himself to it in order that what he calls "reality" becomes his own version of an indomitable autocracy of the human self where man instead of God rules the roost. This may be a limitation, and yet this has also the possibilities of a limitless triumph. Moreover, this also accounts for the inherent strength of the Adamic poet's "simple, separating self" whose radical interaction with reality like that of the botanist-protagonist's in Stevens's poem "Botanist on Alp" may not motivate him to undertake a quest for heavenly things, but may entail upon him the persistent pleasure of "rich perceptions of earthly things."[134] Notice, for example, the Dionysiac charm that the rider in Frost's "Stopping by Woods on a Snowy Evening" feels while confronting the woods. It is his rich perception of a common phenomenon that makes him realize the lovely qualities of the woods. Randall Jarrell also places Williams in the same perspective. He notes, in analyzing Williams's poem "To a Solitary Disciple," that to Williams what matters is the subtle way in which the landscape's contours, colours, and surfaces reveal a pattern of "analogical, anthropomorphised life."[134a] Thus, the Adamic poet, being a highly sensitized individual, tries "to satisfy simultaneously the claims of reality and the imagination."[135] It means that he can easily contain ambiguities, and make an undifferentiated single vision out of them. It may be an impossibility, but the secret of the Adamic poet's success lies in sustaining his belief in playing the role of, what Stevens has so aptly stated, the "...impossible possible philosophers' man." Having time to think enough, he is not only the "central man" but also the "human globe" whose responsiveness makes him almost like "a mirror with a voice."[136] In one of his famous later poems, "Chocorua to Its Neighbour," Stevens contemplates the possibility of such a future in Jesus Christ who appears as the very image of man, and recreating himself imaginatively, touches the very deepest core, and farthest reach of humanity:

> To say more than human things with human voice,
> That cannot be; to say human things with more
> Than human voice, that, also, cannot be;

To speak humanly from the height or from the depth
Of human things, that is acutest speech.[137]

In Robert Frost's two *Masques* we also find a somewhat similar approach in the portrayal of the character of God. God is denuded of the closed aura of myth, and is presented as a humanised figure pondering over deeper meta-physical problems humanely. Moreover, the Adamic poet's venture in this context takes him to work *contra* the tradition of appropriating *mere myth* as poetic form. He rather works under the assumption that the intrinsic and "inherent form of experience," and even of language is, in fact, "the author of the myth, past and present manifestations, and it is this form poetry seeks to release from historical language."[138] Thus, the Adamic poet tends to sing the everlasting glory of the "single self" of man which, in its uniqueness, gathers qualities of harmony and proportion in being unitary and selfsufficient in the face of all that smacks of the mass and its generic culture. Optimistic American poets like Walt Whitman may, of course, imagine that the single self and the democratic mass might produce an electrifying force if they complemented each other fruitfully and suitably. This apart, the Adamic poet's "sovereign self" may contain in itself a deeper level of self-assertion which in its very condition of isolation and separateness may develop an elementary and realistic sense of honour just as we find, for example, in Thoreau's self-chosen retirement from the community to carry on a kind of experiment with life beside Walden Pond.

The main thrust of the argument of this dissertation springs out of a distinction between the Adamic strain in American poetry initiating itself from "the Antinomianism of the early Puritans through Emerson and Whitman to such Moderns as Stevens and Williams, and the reactionary or traditional strain which denies the priority of the Adamic (and latterly, the Romantic) self and takes as its model poets in the classical and English (*logos*) formalist tradition."[139] It only means that the view that we take in the succeeding Chapters is to a large degree opposed to the fundaments of the Puritan arthodoxy in America, and the anti-individualist tradition created and perpetrated by the Fireside Poets of the Nineteenth century which in our times culminated in the suspicion raised against the transcendent unity of self by such Moderns like Eliot and the Southern Agrarians.[140]

Various factors such as the theory propounded by the psychologists, and the stand taken by the logicians and physical scientists in addition to the work of Darwin and the early anthropologists may have contributed largely to the view that not only man's Ego is a poor and paltry shelter against "the rage in outer reality," but also this "I" on which we tend to make so much fuss is no more than a mere grammatical expression. Even then, it is worthwhile to see in our explication of the poems of Frost and Williams in the Chapters devoted to them in this study how they, with their triumphant Adamism and with their own allegiance to this "mode" in poetry, carry on an active and ceaseless campaign on this "shrinking front against self." In Frost this campaign consists in driving himself almost relentlessly to a life simplified, to a sort of "wholeness beyond confusion" ["Me for the hills where I don't have to choose"]. So also in Williams we find an affirmative spirit which, while rejecting the past and future and embracing the potentiality ingrained in the present moment, reveals that our quest for beginnings is "To begin to begin again,"[141] and to imitate the very "dynamic" of Nature—her seminal adventure, and freeplay.

NOTES

1. Elaine Barry, *Robert Frost* (New York: Frederick Unger Publishing Co., 1973), p. 101. See also Lloyd Nash Dendinger, "Robert Frost: Popular Image of a Poet," Dissertation. Louisiana State Univ., 1966, p. 85.
2. Roy Harvey Pearce, *The Continuity of American Poetry* (Princeton, N.J.: Princeton Univ. Press, 1961).
3. Mark Schorer, *The Literature of America: Twentieth Century* (New York: McGraw-Hill Book Company, 1960), pp. 11-12.
4. See Pearce, *The Continuity of American Poetry,* p. 291.
5. *Ibid.*, p. 42.
6. *Ibid.*, p. 423.
7. *Ibid.*, p. 187.

8. Brewster Ghiselin, ed. "Introduction," *The Creative Process: A Symposium* (New York: The New American Library, 1955), p. 19.
9. *Ibid.*
10. *Ibid.*
11. While understanding "the mythic Mode" in the context of the continuity of American poetry, *it has always to be evaluated as a "counter-current" to the mainstream.* Cf. John Jenkins Espey, *Ezra Pound's Mauberley: A Study in Composition* (London: Faber & Faber, 1955), p. 25. The word was first used by Pound in a 1932 *Criterion* essay.
12. For Ransom's critical dualism see John M. Bradbury, *The Fugitives: A Critical Account* (Chapel Hill: Univ. of North Carolina Press, 1958), pp. 22-23 and Louise Cowan, *The Fugitive Group: A Literary History* (Baton Rouge, La.: Louisiana State Univ. Press, 1950), pp. 123-125. Cowan expresses succinctly how Tate condemns "the 'theory of inspiration' that Ransom had built up and charged that he had offered 'only an abstract restatement of superannuate theories of consciousness'." p. 124.
13. John Crowe Ransom, "The Concrete Universal: Observations on the Understanding of Poetry," in *Poems and Essays* (New York: Vintage Books, 1955), pp. 183-84.
14. Pearce, *The Continuity of American Poetry,* p. 333.
15. *Ibid.,* p. 327.
16. *Ibid.*
17. *Ibid.*, p. 329.
18. See also Ransom's poem "Old Mansion," in *Poems and Essays,* p. 37, where he "...went with courage shaken/To dip, alas, into some unseemlier world."
19. It's a common misconception to think that the Puritanic culture was antipathic to literature, and arts in general in America. Cf. Kenneth Murdock, "Introduction," *Handkerchiefs from Paul* (Cambridge: Harvard Univ. Press, 1927), pp. lxvii-lxviii.
20. Pearce, *The Continuity of American Poetry,* p. 9.
21. Henry Thoreau, *A Week on the Concord and Merrimack Rivers,* ed. Walter Harding (New York: Holt, Rinehart & Winston, Inc., 1963), pp. 257-58.
22. Mircea Eliade, *Myth and Reality,* trans Willard R. Trask (New York: Harper & Row, 1963), p. 18.
23. B. Malinowski, *Myth in Primitive Psychology* (1926), reprinted in *Magic, Science and Religion* (New York: Doubleday & Co., Inc., 1955), p. 101. See also Eliade, *Myth and Reality,* p. 20.
24. Eliade, *Myth and Reality*, p. 112. Eliade, of course, indicates it as "damythicization."

25. See Mircea Eliade, *Myth of the Eternal Return: Cosmos & History,* trans. Willard R. Trask (Princeton, N.J.: Princeton Univ. Press, 1971).
26. Eliade, *Myth and Reality,* p. 88.
27. James E. Breslin, *William Carlos Williams: An American Artist* (New York: Oxford Univ. Press, 1970), p. 88.
28. *Ibid.*
29. Robert E. Spiller, *The Cycle of American Literature: An Essay in Historical Criticism* (New York: The Macmillan Company, 1955), p. 4.
30. Waldo Frank, *The Re-Discovery of America: An Introduction to a Philosophy of American Life* (New York: Charles Scribner's & Sons, 1929), p. 5.
31. Issac Sequeira, *The Theme of Initiation in Modern American Fiction* (Mysore: Geetha Book House, 1975), p. 10.
32. Frank, *The Rediscovery of America,* p. 214.
33. For a definitive account of the decline from high Puritanism, see Perry Miller, *The New England Mind: From Colony to Province* (Cambridge, Mass.: Harvard Univ. Press, 1953). Talking of hypocrisy Miller writes: "It was not a confession of failure, but a discovery of uses to which an unforeseen development could be put. The city on the hill quickly began to prove one in which hypocrisy itself could be employed for the benefit of society." p. 81.
34. Spiller, *The Cycle of American Literature,* p. 111.
35. *Ibid.*, p. 212.
36. *Ibid.*, p. 213.
37. Later on Brooks, of course, recaptured the American past in "a series of volumes of exquisite artistry," and found it "both palatable and exciting." For a lively discussion on this see Henry Steele Commager, *The American Mind: An Interpretation of American Thought and Character Since the 1880's* (New Haven: Yale Univ. Press, 1950), pp. 437-38.
38. Philip Rahv, "Paleface and Redskin," in Harold Beaver, ed. *American Critical Essays: Twentieth Century* (London: Oxford Univ. Press, 1959), pp. 280-86. Hereafter cited as Beaver, ed. *ACE.* Rahv's comments are: "The paleface continually hankers after religious norms, tending towards a refined estrangement from reality. The redskin, on the other hand, accepts his environment, at times to a degree of fusion with it, even when rebelling against one or another of its manifestations."
39. George Santayana, "The Genteel Tradition in American Literature," in *Winds of Doctrine and Platonism and the Spiritual Life* (New York: Harper & Brothers, 1957), pp. 187-88.
40. Quoted in Vernon Louis Parrington, *Main Currents in Amarican Thought: An Interpretation of American Literature from the Beginnings to 1920* (3 vols. in 1; New York: Harcourt, 1937), II, 436-37.

41. Leslie A. Fiedler, *An End to Innocence: Essays on Culture and Politics* (Boston: The Bescon Press, 1955), p. 171.
42. S. Musgrove, *T.S. Eliot and Walt Whitman* (New York: Baskell House Publishers Ltd., 1970).
43. *Ibid.*, p. 84. Musgrove puts: "Perhaps Eliot's contest with this 'monstrous anthropoid' has left such permanent traces in his work just because he was an American not a European...."
44. Louis Untermeyer, ed. *The Poetry and Prose of Walt Whitman* (New York: Simon & Schuster, 1949), p. 191. Hereafter cited as *Poetry & Prose of Walt Whitman.*
45. T.S. Eliot, *The Complete Poems and Plays* (New York: Harcourt, Brace and Co., 1952), p. 127.
46. Pearce, *The Continuity of American Poetry,* p. 304. For a detailed discussion on this point see also Musgrove, *T.S. Eliot & Walt Whitman,* pp. 48-55.
47. Roy Harvey Pearce, ed. "Introduction," *Whitman* (New Jersey: Prentice-Hall, Inc., 1962), p. 3. Hereafter cited as *Whitman.*
48. T.S. Eliot, ed. "Introduction," *Ezra Pound: Selected Poems* (London: Faber & Faber, 1928), p. 10.
49. Ezra Pound, *Personae: The Collected Short Poems* (New York: New Directions, 1926), p. 89.
50. *Whitman,* p. 3.
51. *Ibid.*
52. See V.K. Chari, *Whitman in the Light of Vedantic Mysticism* (Lincoln: Univ. of Nebraska Press, 1964), p. 65. Chari aptly comments that "With this self-expression Whitman felt that the ubiquitous soul of man enters into all existence and bestows reality on it."
53. Som P. Ranchan, *Walt Whitman and the Great Adventure with Self* (Bombay: Nanaktalas, 1967), p. 10.
54. Oscar Gargill, *Intellectual America: Ideas on the March* (New York: Macmillan & Co., 1941), p. 541.
55. James E. Miller, Jr., *Walt Whitman* [1962; rpt. Allahabad: A.H. Wheeler & Co. (P) Ltd., 1971], p. 79.
56. *Poetry & Prose of Walt Whitman,* p. 144.
57. Miller, *Walt Whitman,* p. 79.
58. *Poetry & Prose of Walt Whitman,* p. 148.
59. Miller, *Walt Whitman,* p. 80.
60. William Carlos Williams, *Paterson* (New York: New Directions, 1963), p. 20. Hereafter cited as *Paterson.*
61. *Ibid.*, p. 22.

62. M.L. Rosenthal, ed. "Introduction," *The William Carlos Williams Reader* (New York: New Directions, 1966), p. xxix. Hereafter cited as *William Carlos Williams Reader.*
63. *Ibid.,* pp. 21-22.
64. *Whitman,* p. 3.
65. Philip L. Gerber, *Robert Frost* (New York: Twayne Publishers, Inc., 1966), p. 57.
66. Pearce, *The Continuity of American Poetry,* p. 75.
67. Kristian Smidt, *Poetry and Belief in the Work of T.S. Eliot* (London: Routledge and Kegan Paul, 1961), pp. 129-137.
68. Grover Smith, *T.S. Eliot's Poetry and Plays: A Study in Sources and Meaning* (Chicago: Univ. of Chicago Press, 1956), p. 4.
69. Cf. S. Radhakrishnan, Trans., *The Bhagavadgita* (London: George Allen & Unwin Ltd., 1967), p. 215. Unlike the Adamic connotation of language, the *Gita* reiterates God's supremacy as the formulating spirit behind all language: "I am the syllable Aum in all the Vedas; I am the sound in ether and manhood in men."
70. "Adagia," *Opus Posthumous* ed. S.F. Morse (New York: Alfred A. Knopf, 1957), p. 167.
71. *Ibid.,* p. 168.
72. Hugh Kenner, ed. *T.S. Eliot: A Collection of Critical Essays* (Englewood Cliffs, N.J.: Prentice-Hall, 1962), p. 137.
73. Ralph Waldo Emerson, *Essays* (New York: Carlton House, n.d.), p. 50.
74. *Ibid.,* p. 12.
75. Robert Frost, "The Oven Bird," in *Complete Poems of Robert Frost* (New York: Holt, Rinehart & Winston, 1960), p. 150. Hereafter cited as *Complete Poems of Robert Frost.*
76. Frost, "A Prayer in Spring," *Complet Poems of Robert Frost,* p. 17.
77. William Carlos Williams, "Danse Russe," in *The Collected Earlier Poems of William Carlos Williams* (New York: A New Directions Book, 1951), p. 148. Hereafter cited as *CFP.* Cf. Eliot's note to *The Waste Land* on the horror of solitude.
78. Eliot, *The Complete Poems and Plays,* p. 125.
79. See T.S. Eliot, "Introduction," in Paul Valery, *The Art of Poetry,* trans. Denise Folliot (London: Routledge & Kegan Paul, 1958), p. xii.
80. T.S. Eliot, *Selected Essays* (New York: Harcourt Brace, 1960), p. 21.
81. Quoted in Fiedler, *An End to Innocence: Essays on Culture and Politics,* p. 170.
82. First published in the *Kenyon Review* (Spring 1943), 228-254. Delivered as one of the Measures lectures at Princeton in 1942.
83. *Letters of Wallace Stevens,* ed. Holly Stevens (New York: Alfred A. Knopf, 1966), p. 288.

84. A lecture delivered at Harvard in Dec. 1936, and published in Morse ed. *Opus Posthumous,* pp. 216-229.
85. A lecture delivered at the Univ. of Chicago in Nov. 1951, and published in Morse ed. *Opus Posthumous,* pp. 183-202.
86. See Joseph N. Riddel, *The Clairvoyanı Eye: The Poetry & Poetics of Wallace Stevens* (Beton Rouge, La.: Louisiana State Univ. Press, 1965), pp. 109-120. Quoting from a statement by Stevens that appeared on the dust jacket of *Ideas of Order,* and from Stevens' "The Irrational Element in Poetry," Riddel throws much light on the various aspects of the term "pure poetry." The poems of Stevens in *Ideas of Order* as indicated by Stevens himself are "pure poetry" as they are void of any economic, political or social theory. However, Stevens recognized the intricate operation of ideas even in some pure poems. Riddel's definitive statement on this issue is revealing: "Poetry, which emerges from animal rage, is the containment of experience in the order of word or in the order of an imaginative self whose words attach to the world but are forms of his mind. If poetry searches the fragrant portals of the incurable, extending our horizons and creating our ideas of order or our heavens, the outline or abstraction of those portals is flooded by things of this world." p. 120.
87. The First Annual Yeats lecture, delivered to the Friends of the Irish Academy at the Abbey Theater, June, 1940, published in *Southern Review,*7 (Winter 1941), 446.
88. Eliot quoted in Smith, *T.S. Eliot's Poetry and Plays,* p. 5.
89. *Ibid.*, p. 6.
90. See Reginald L. Cook, "Frost on Frost: The Making of Poems," *American Literature,* 28 (March 1956), 66.
91. *Ibid.*
92. Schorer, *The Literature of America,* p. 150.
93. For a detailed discussion of the cognitive value of Literature see Wayne Shumaker, *Literature and the Irrational* (Englewood Cliffs, N.J.: Prentice-Hall, Inc., 1960), pp. 7ff.
94. William Carlos Williams, *Imaginations* (New York: New Directions, 1970), p. 175.
95. Morse, ed. *sOpus Posthumous,* pp. 206-7.
96. See Martin Heidegger, *An Introduction to Metaphysics,* trans. Ralph Manheim (New York: Anchot Books, 1961), pp. 48-49.
97. Joseph N. Riddel, *The Inverted Bell: Modernism and the Counter-Poetics of William Carlos Williams* (Baton Rouge: Louisiana State Univ. Press, 1974), p. 44.
98. Edward Dahlberg, *The Sorrows of Priapus* (Norfolk, Conn.: New Directions, 1957), p. 59.
99. Charles Olson, *Call Me Ishmael* (San Francisco: City Lights Books, 1947), p. 14.

100. See T.S. Eliot, "Tradition and the Individual Talent," in John Hayward, ed. *Selected Prose* (1953; rpt. Harmondsworth: Penguin Books Ltd., 1953), pp. 29ff.
101. Riddel, *The Inverted Bell,* p. 45.
102. *Ibid.*
103. See Jacques Derrida, "Structure, Sign and Play in the Discourse of the Human Species," in Richard Macksey and Eugenio Donato, eds. *The Language of Criticism and the Sciences of Man: The Structuralist Controversy* (Baltimore: The Johns Hopkins Univ. Press, 1970.)
104. Riddel, *The Inverted Bell,* p. 45.
105. Derrida, "Structure, Sign, and Play," p. 249.
106. Riddel, *The Inverted Bell,* p. 46.
107. Hugh Kenner, *The Pound Era* (Berkeley: Univ. of California Press, 1972), p. 69.
108. Riddel, *The Inverted Bell,* p. 46.
109. See Morse, ed. *Opus Posthumous,* p. 212.
110. For a good discussion on this point see Riddel, *The Inverted Bell,* pp. 46 ff.
111. Ibid., p. 46.
112. Morse, ed. *Opus Posthumous,* pp. 212-13. Also see *The Collected Poems of Wallace Stevens* (New York: Alfred A. Knopf, 1957), p. 503, p. 245.
113. Riddel, *The Inverted Bell,* p. 208.
114. *Ibid.*,
115. Eliot, *The Complete Poems and Plays,* p. 122.
116. Riddel, *The Inverted Bell,* p. 272.
117. Waldo Frank, ed. *The Collected Poems of Hart Crene* (New York: Liveright Inc. Publishers, 1933), p. xxii.
118. *Ibid.*, p. xxviii.
119. *Ibid.*, p. 58.
120. See Brom Weber, ed. *The Complete Poems and Selected Letters and Prose of Hart Crane* (New York: Anchor Books, 1966), pp. 220-21.
121. Riddel, *The Inverted Bell,* p. 45.
122. See Morse, ed. *Opus Posthumous,* pp. 212-13.
123. *The Collected Poems of Wallace Stevens,* p. 245.
124. *Ibid.*, p. 336, p. 332.
125. See Morse, ed. *Opus Posthumous,* p. 163.
126. See *Ibid.*, p. 202.
127. Riddel, *The Inverted Bell,* p. 48.
128. *Ibid.*
129. *The Collected Poems of Wallace Stevens,* p. 383.
130. Riddel, *The Inverted Bell,* p. 274.

131. Pearce, *The Continuity of American Poetry,* p. 377.
132. Letter to Archibald MacLeish. See Morse, ed. *Opus Posthumous,* p. xvi.
133. Pearce, *The Continuity of American Poetry,* p. 385.
134. Randall Jarrell, *Poetry and the Age* (New York: Vintage Books, 1953), p. 219.
134a. *Ibid.*, p. 219.
135. Pearce, *The Continuity of American Poetry,* p. 391.
136. See "Asides on the Oboe" in *Poems by Wallace Stevens* (New York: Vintage Books, 1959), p. 103.
137. *The Collected Poems of Wallace Stevens,* p. 300.
138. Riddel, *The Inverted Bell,* p. 104. See also for its opposite view "T.S. Eliot, 'Ulysees' Order, and Myth," *The Dial* 75 (Nov. 1923), 380-83, Eliot, of course, later on repudiated the concept that myth could or should give a sort of allegorical frame-work to reiterate order for the Modern artist. What is also significant is that in spite of Eliot's overplus rhetorical divestations of his American roots, his stand highlights his nostalgia all the more.
139. Riddel, *The Inverted Bell,* p. 262.
140. See the main drift of argument in Hyatt Waggoner, *American Poets: From the Puritans to the Present* (Boston: Houghton Mifflin, 1968). Hereafter cited as *American Poets.*
141. *Ibid.*, p. 53.

2

The Continuity of the Mode: American Poetry

BRIEFLY FOCUSING the critical counterpoints between "the Adamic Mode" and "the Mythic Mode" in poetry, we have made an attempt in the last Chapter to indicate how the world is confronted by the poet, more particularly, by the Adamic poet. This Chapter, while indicating the main contribution of Emerson, Thoreau and Whitman in creating the necessary atmosphere for the growth of poetry in "the Adamic Mode," attempts a cursory survey of American Poetry in that mode by tracing its major lines of development in some of the representative poems of poets like Edward Taylor, Joel Barlow, William Cullen Bryant, Edgar Allan Poe, Emily Dickinson, James Russell Lowell, Henry Wadsworth Longfellow, Oliver Wendell Holmes, John Greenleaf Whittier, Henry Timrod and Sidney Lenier. Their poetry, we believe, has created the tradition necessary for the continuity of America's poetry in "the Adamic Mode" which culminated, as Pearce says, in the poetry of Wallace Stevens. Though it might be useful and enlightening to mark how consciously or unconsciously the poetry of the two poets selected for special attention, Frost and Williams, carries echoes of the thematic preoccupation, or even in some cases, the linguistic pattern of the earlier poets, such an attempt would be outside the scope of the present study. But as the Chapter goes on to reveal the intricacies of America's poetry in "the Adamic Mode" it will be easier to place Frost and Williams in that tradition.

Emerson's words written in "The American Scholar" as far back as 1837 are relevant to begin with:

> The scholar of the first age received into him the world around; brooded thereon; gave it the new arrangement of his own mind, and uttered it again. It came into him life; it went out from him immortal thoughts. It came to him business; it went out from him poetry.[1]

If what the American Scholar received from the world around would mean a feeling of man's limitless freedom to make his own destiny free from the "deathtraps" of history, culture, and tradition, then, such a feeling had its independent life in the innocent beauty of Nature in her abundance in the New World. The function of the scholar who happened to be also a poet, as Emerson would put it, was therefore, to capture this antinomianism, and to convey it with "the received form" of poetry to his fellow beings, so that they could act accordingly with greater force. Such an attitude was perhaps a threat from the manifestly traditional Puritanic point of view that emphasised the Christian recognition of God as an end. In the face of this expansiveness of the age that partook of the antinomianism latent in the environment, even Shakespeare had to face Emerson's critical comments for his inadequacy to portray the human condition with truthful amplitude: "As long as the question is of talent and mental power, the world of man has not his equal to show. But when the question is, *to life and its materials and auxiliaries* how does he profit me?"[2] [Emerson's Italics].

It may be added here that during the Puritanic Age the poet was more of a priest and less of a "maker" in the sense suggested above. The "objects of the world" were there imbued with a simple, innocent beauty, and to quote Barlow:

> Here springs indeed the day, since time began,
> The brightest, broadest, happiest morn of man.[3]

But, for the poet-priest-prophet, say one like Taylor in the Puritanic Age, even the "daylight so brave" is "benighted" as we are sinful men:

> Looke till thy looks look wan, my Soule; here's ground
> The World's Bright Eye's dash't out: Day-light so brave

Benighted: the Sparking sun, pald round
With flouring Rayes, lies buri'de in its grave
The candle of the World blown out, down fall
Life knocked a: *Heaven by Hell*[4] [Taylor's Italics].

Under the circumstances, as Emerson has so brillantly outlined, "the beauty straightaway vanished," and "they read commandments all-excluding mountainous duty." Thus, "life became ghastly, joyless, a pilgrim's progress, a probation, beleagured round with doleful histories of Adam's fall and curse behind us, with doomsday and purgatorial and penal fires before us, and the heart of the seer and the heart of the listener sank in them."[5] Even the death of another may be viewed as caused by our sins. Notice, for example, the forty-seventh stanza in Urian Oakes' elegy on Thomas Shepard, 1677:

See what our sins have done! what ruines wrought
And how they have pluck'd out our very eyes!
Our sins have slain our Sheperd we have bought,
And dearly paid for, our Enormities.
Ah, Cursed sins that strike at God and kill
His servants, and the blood of prophets spill.[6]

Everything was ultimately referred back to God and His wisdom. Thus, both in life and in the "little recreation" called poetry, the poet was to find the "wisdom of God in the world, and not to be idle; for the world, and the creatures therein are like a book wherein God's wisdom is written, and there must we seek it out."[7] In other words, the poet's function was "a dialogic mode of communication," or specifically speaking, a kind of "I-Thou" relationship between him and God. Such a function was the reflection of the Puritan's orthodox attitude of limiting the freedom of the human self.

In a literary scene of this kind, Emerson's essay, eulogizing "self-reliance" instead of "God-reliance" would have appeared heretical. Had he written thus in 1634, he would have been tried as Mrs. Anne Hutchinson was for sedition and heresy. The nature of the concept of radical freedom in the antinomian controversy is that man is "subject to no laws or institutions except those which [are] in accord with their own consciences."[8] This is the basic attitude beneath all Adamic poetry. In opposition, Puritanism [has] all along assumed the primary function of art to be, not the discovery of truth, but the elaboration of doctrines already known. The basic style for such a mode of art, or for that matter, of poetry had to be plain, as "it encouraged the widest possible comprehension"[9] of the Puritanic ideas for all and sundry keeping society free from chaos born out of extreme individualism. Such a social "more" along with a growing greed for possession of "matter," created petty, insipid and paltry interests. Alexis de Tocqueville makes the correct assessment of the mood prevailing in the United States then:

> Nothing conceivable is so petty, so insipid, so crowded with paltry interests—in one word so anti-poetic—as the life of a man in the United States.[10]

However, it is heartening to note that de Tocqueville could discover a silver lining in the black clouds. "But among the thought which it suggests," he said, "there is always one which is full of poetry, and that is the hidden nerve which gives vigor to the whole frame."[11]

Emerson's declaration in 1851 "to resist the anti-poetic influences of Nassachusetts "that retarded the poetic sensibility of the time was, in fact, a product of his "spiritual egalitarianism" which was a challenge to the factional, impolite and mercenary elements in society. Advocating equality on the ground that all are connected with the Oversoul, Emerson said that "the free man is he who heeds the true nature of his own spirit and defies the inheritance of error which our institutions perpetuate."[12] In tune with this stand, Whitman's bardic boast in the preface to *Leaves of Grass* that "the Americans of all nations at any time upon the earth have probably the fullest poetical nature [and that] the United States themselves are essentially the greatest poem,"[13] broke through the antipoetic to the putatively poetic idea of man—a basic tenet of Adamic poetry. Of course, this ultimately helped in transforming the anti-poetic into poetic, but it was not the same stand as we find later in William Carlos Williams's specific contention for making the antipoetic translatable into, or congruent with the concept of "self." In other words, the anti-poetic came up as a process of his Adamic "naming" of things only while the nucleus of his ideas lay in his "self." To a degree this was a mutilating conception of reality as opposed to Williams's dictum: "No ideas but in things." However, Whitman "was never tempted to obliterate the actual to get at the real...."[14] For him "the externals, the catalog of concrete details, are transcendental symbols of what he might call spiritual truths."[15]

In fact, Emerson's *modus operandi* in poetry anticipated this earlier, particularly in its transcendentalist hopes and presuppositions. Rejecting the Puritanic Super-ego as a censoring agency, Emerson was cautious enough to see that his poetic egocentrism did not slip back into complete inwardness to be trapped in the Ego's interaction with the Id. Referring to a collection of verses a friend had sent him, he writes to Elizabeth Dodge Kinnay in 1850: "My quarrel with it, if I have any, is what is almost a national quality, the inwardness or 'subjectiveness' as they call it of our lyrics...."[16] This is important in reminding us that too much subjectivity in a poem may disable the Adamic poet to "externize" himself into the anti-poetic world and make it a part of his idea of himself, keeping his identity as a man intact. The poet's theme, Emerson would say, is the biography of the authentic men—"...the plain old Adam, the simple genuine self against the whole world."[17] This "self" as it looks into the sky, into the ocean, upon the Valleys and the mountains is capable of transmuting the scenery into something freshly seen and fully found as Adam felt in his exploration of the Garden of Eden. This is also a lesson for the common readers to re-inforce a renaissance of their senses. Thus, with the help of the poet, they are able to experience that "the world is not painted or adorned, but is from the beginning beautiful; and God has not made some beautiful things, but Beauty is the creator of things."[18]

With a total freedom of thought and emotion, the poet's expression—"not metre, but a metre-making argument that makes a poem"[19]—is the most important factor. The creative imagination of the poet acts more through "inspiration," and technical skill is kept in the background, so that it does not hamper the poetic act. "The poet knows that he speaks adequately then when he speaks wildly, or 'with the flower of the mind', not with the intellect used as an organ, but with the intellect released from all service and suffered to take its direction from its celestial life, or as the ancients were wont to express themselves, not with intellect alone but with the intellect inebriated with nectar."[20] This appears to be the same process of "cognizing the feelings," "but any attempt to create sharp distinctions between materialism and spiritualism, between intellect and intuition, is likely to give one an erroneous idea of Emerson's basic attitude."[21] Though he distrusted materialism and pure intellect, he did not champion the cause of any abstract idealism if it was unrelated to problems of actual human existence. This accounts for his "skeptic" and "pragmatic" outlook, which, we shall see later, deeply influenced Frost. Emerson's transcendental literary theory is behind his conviction that the poet, receiving the symbols of nature, has to transform them to the single, decisive experience of the One, the Oversoul or God. This may mystify us into believing that his poetry is all revelation and no creation. However, the creativity lies in the "unvatic" way in which his poetry functions with its subtle undercurrent of "irony"—an important factor in Adamic poetry. Avoiding to be a priestly ontologist in the traditional sense of the term and a mystagogue, he worked hard to create his own poetry as an artist.

For example, in "Each and All," Emerson yields no doubt to "the perfect whole," but the egocentrically subtle way in which he renders the natural scenes becomes ultimately *his* discovery alone, and no one else's:

I inhaled the violet's breath;
Around me stood the oaks and firs;
Pine-cones and acorns lay on the ground;
Over me soared the eternal sky;

Full of light and of deity,
Again I saw, again I heard,
The rolling river, the morning bird;—

Beauty through my senses stole;
I yielded myself to the perfect, whole.[22]

("Each and All")

An attempt is made here to synthesise polarities, for Emerson, while indicating "the eternal sky" as "full of light"—a naturalist's note—is not oblivious of the spirit of "deity" permeating it—a spiritualist's concern.

We have given so much emphasis to Emerson here, because we feel that in spite of, and to a considerable degree, because of his specific stand as a transcendentalist theorist of poetry he happens to be almost the central force behind the evolution of the basic tenets of Adamic poetry. He gave the idea of breaking through the ante-bellum culture of nineteenth-century America, and to emphasize the importance of man in our letters. He went a step further to the idea of God—but no other poet-philosopher has championed so convincingly the cause of secularism and humanism in life and literature. Whitman went on to demonstrate this as it were in answer to Emerson's call that America awaits the poet who, freeing himself from the barbarism and materialism of the times, shall sing gloriously on "Our log-rolling, our stumps and their politics, our fisheries, our Negroes and Indians, our boats and our repudiations, the wrath of rogues and the pusillanimity of honest men, the northern trade, the southern planting, the Western clearing, Oregon and Texas..."[23]

Expanding his Ego to the extent of making it generic, Whitman's pantheistic and mystical embracing of the phenomenal world with an insight into its oneness[24] was motivated by a "cause" similar to that of Shelley's in "A Defence of Poetry":

> The cultivation of poetry is never more to be desired than at periods when, from an excess of the selfish and calculating principle, the accumulation of the materials of

> external life exceed the quantity of the power of assimilating them to the internal laws of human nature.[25]

To the absolutist, Whitman's expanding ego, and its constant motion to embrace the "gliding wonders" of the world in one unified whole, may mean sheer confusion and disintegration. To the relativist it may mean, however, the very essence of poetry in a modern sense of the term as it clearly anticipates such radical literary concepts like "Expressionism," where the function of the Ego is predominant. One of the important elements of Expressionism" as noted by Dahlstrom[26] is the concept of the *Aussatrachlungen des Ichs*—the radiation, expression, and unfolding of the Ego. The Expressionist's Ego is a kind of unifying instrument that moulds oneness of the countless items poured into it. Hence the justification for discovering expressionistic elements in Whitman's poetic style. For Whitman—the Adamic poet *par excellence*—the Ego is the predominant element in our universe; it is indeed the very heart of the world's reality. In this "magic crystal," one can see the absolute in constant play. More important is its function as a "subject" that ably registers the eternal *state of becoming.* Functionally speaking, its antipole—the object—may assign meaning to it. But it is this Ego—the subject—which is the deciding factor in gathering reality in its ultimate character.

While discussing the subject-object equation in Adamic poetry, mention should be made how some poets belonging to that poetic mode view reality. Poe, to begin with, will serve our purpose. His conception of "reality" was a characteristic sense of the unreal—the Coleridgean fanciful. Evaluated by Rod W. Horton "as a somewhat late and localised manifestation of the European romantic movement,"[27] Poe saved American poetry from its repetitiveness—its being tied to the stock themes of Man and Democracy and National aspiration—paving, as he did, the way for poetry as an unconventional, organic art. His phantasmagoric, hypnagogic imagination was a positive reaction against the pioneering New World's emphasis on factors of common-sense behind all material growth and success. The

American Idea was the Idea of Man without history, with which "the Adamic Mode" of poetry is so deeply connected. Logically speaking, the Idea of Man is ultimately the Idea of Life which, in each poet's case, had a different connotation. With Poe the idea of Life was an evolution of his deep-rooted convictions about art. Radical in sensibility, Poe, who James Russell Lowell felt lacked elements of manhood or character,[28] had yet that wonderful wizardry of letters that enabled him to have intimations of "immortal truths." Without any sense of place, which is an American concern according to D.H. Lawrence,[29] Poe's poetry had the originality of a fecundatory imagination. For him poetry is not a purpose, but a passion—"a rhythmical creation of beauty." With its evocation of feelings that often border on the irrational, Poe's poetry is a good example of what we have earlier shown to be characteristic of the creative imagination of the Adamic poet and his peculiar self-definition. However, Poe's self-definition was a sort of self-limitation, too:

> His mind, walking in a vain show, was taught nothing by experience of suffering....His intellectual enjoyment was in the power of his mind over literature as an art; his skill, in forcing the mere letters of the alphabet, the dry elements of the dictionary, to take forms of beauty and apparent life which would command the admiration of the world...Hence his delight in the exercise of his powers as a destructive critic, and his favorite proposition that literature was all a trick, and that he could construct another Paradise Lost....[30]

To comment on this, one would say, it is a preoposterous method of diffusing truth if reality is supplanted by fiction and more so when "the shows of things" are accommodated to "the desire of the mind," rather than to "the reality of sober fact."[31] Hence, Poe's artistic creed illustrated in nearly everything he wrote that the end of all art is pleasure, not truth, that in poetry the proper means of arousing pleasure is the creation of beauty. Music, too, is an indispensable element in poetry, and is especially valuable in the poet's straining towards the supernal, since music comes nearer this goal than any other art. This accounts for Poe's world being significantly created out of the "music of words," and not very much by virtue of what the words "really" mean. Roger Sessions, a composer, says that words in music can "reproduce for us, both qualitatively and dynamically certain gestures of the spirit...."[32] Here is the legend of Israfel "whose heart-strings are a lute," and "who has the sweetest voice of all God's creatures" as the Koran would put it:

> In Heaven a spirit doth dwell
> "Whose heart-strings are a lute;"
> None sing so wildly well
> As the angel Israfel,
> And the giddy stars (so legends tell),
> Ceasing their hymns, attend the spell
>   Of his voice, all mute.[33]
>
> ("Israfel")

Or

> If I could dwell
> Where Israfel
>   Hath dwelt, and he where I,
> He might not sing so wildly well
>   A mortal melody,
> While a bolder note than his might swell
>   From my lyre within the Sky.[34]

Poe's unfailing conviction in the above lines about his ability to "sing a mortal melody wildly well"—even a bolder one than that of Israfel's—proves his Adamic asserting of a romantic egocentrism so pervadingly artificial that he appears to be largely "a figment of his own restless imagination."[35] What is significant is the way he recreates for us the world of Israfel by a careful choice of imaginatively suggestive words. Truth, one is eager to say, is sacrificed here at the expense of a world of supernal beauty. The words of Poe on truth are the measure of what he would do about truth when faced with it:

> In enforcing a truth we need severity rather than afflorescence of language. We must be simple, precise, terse. We must be cool, calm, unimpassioned. In a word, we must be in that mood which as nearly as possible, is

> the exact converse of the poetical. He must be blind indeed who does not perceive the radical and chasmal differences between the truthful and the poetical modes of inculcation. He must be theory-mad beyond redemption who, in spite of these differences, shall still persist in attempting to reconcile the obstinate oils and waters of Poetry and Truth.[36]

Two of his poems, "Dreams" (1827), and "Dream-Land" (1844), prove the practical applicability of this theory in the actual writing of poems. For example, no one relishes the idea of being happy in a dream only, and not very much in life. But notice Poe:

> I *have been* happy, tho' in a dream.
> I have been happy-and I love the theme....[37]
> [Poe's Italics].
> ("Dreams")

Again, the value of place, of being rooted to the soil, is relegated to the background:

> By a route obscure and lonely,
> Haunted by ill angels only,
> Where an Eidolon, named NIGHT,
> On a black throne reigns upright,
> I have reached these lands but newly
> From an ultimate dim Thule—[38] ("Dream-Land")

In all these poems, it is the subject or the Ego that Adamically asserts itself on the object, giving it new areas of meaning, opening up speculations which are unprecedented. To be true to imagination at all costs, is to disintegrate the knowable world no doubt, but no one but Poe, in the whole range of American poetry, had that superb megalomaniac pre-occupation with lyrical self-indulgence, a factor that goes well with poetry in "the Adamic Mode." There is no space here in our brief background study of "the Adamic Mode" in American poetry, for a consideration of the two contrasting roles which Poe played that of the romantic poet and that of the calculating intellectual. However, recent criticism describes Poe as a sort of "emotional engineer," and creates a second parallel Poe myth—the myth of "an intuitive Philosopher, a dealer in hypotheses which anticipated Einstein's, whose literary art and critical theories represent a particular application of his universal theories." Intangible and nebulous as Poe's "real" personality was, it is better to say that both the Poe myths "represent an imaginative reality created for himself by a brilliantly talented but intellectually untrained and socially displaced person who found no ground in life sufficiently solid to provide firm support to his genius."[39]

In contrast with Poe's craving for a land of dreams, of tempests, of fantastic terrors, ashen skies, croaking ravens, ghosts and crawling figures, Emily Dickinson wrote poetry with a much humbler conviction—the one of discovering "infinity in a little room." Yet hers has the hallmark of great achievement, one of the surest, in American poetry. How to place Emily Dickinson in the study of "the great experiment" in American literature had been a problem for some time,[40] but in the twentieth-century evaluation of writers, past and present, she has occupied "a central position."

Temperamentally different from John Donne, and others of "the English metaphysical group so much championed in our times, she had yet many striking similarities with them, particularly in her interest in strange and occult resemblances as well as her constant deviation from regularity in meter and rhyme." This accounts for her popularity with modern readers who, while reading a piece of poetry, do not merely exclaim—"Imagination is a wonderful thing!" but want to see the poet getting involved with a particular kind of technique to discover, and subject to explore, developing his subject, conveying its meaning, and finally evaluating it.[41]

For her, "Muses are not a set of sentimental fine ladies who are frightened at the free and open face of real life. Real life...is the element in which they live and move, and have their being."[42] In her poetry, she does not give any indication of having been influenced by Emerson's "transcendental sacramentalism," as that would have certainly made her lose her identity. However, she had undoubtedly read Emerson's essay "The Poet," and was very comfortably reassured in his recommendations that "the poet's habit of living should be set in a key so low, that common influences should delight him."

Again, the poet should be cheered by the sunlight, and inspired by the air, and be made "tipsy with water."[43] Here is Emerson's "Bachhus" in the hands of Emily Dickinson:

I taste a liquor never brewed—
From Tankards scooped in Pearl—
Nor all the Frankfort
Yield such an Alcohol!

Inebriate of Air am I—
And Debauchee of Dew—
Reeling—through endless summer days—
From inns of Molten Blue.—

When "Landlords" turn the drunken Bee
Out of the Foxglove's door—
When Butterflies—renounce their "drams"—
I shall but drink the more!

Till Seraphs swing their snowy Hats—
And Saints—to windows run—
To see the little Tippler
Leaning against the—Sun—[44]

The Adamic innocence of her sense of herself is reflected through her sense of nature. She encapsulates in this brief but telling poem the beauty of common things like the "blue of the sky" or the "dewdrops on the grass" in pleasant summer days when the air itself is "inebriating" like "liquor." Also, this shows her famous ability to see infinity in small commonplace "things" of nature, and that, too, in the seclusion of a small room. It is, therefore, obvious, as George Whicher remarks that "her poems are demonstrations that the simplest commonplace of life in practical America could be vitalized and made precious to the mind."[45]

With a fancy remarkably rich, this New England "nun" wrote down in her poems the record of her egocentric predicament as revealed through her own "passionate thinkings" and "thoughtful passions." She wanted to contain this chaos—"the white heat of feelings"—by streamlining them with passionately felt thoughts. With a tendency to curb her calvinistic leanings by considering it to be a burden,[46] she threw herself back on her own innocent self, and created poems, the final vision of which lies in a belief that man is ultimately responsible to his own conscience, and grace lies in his own humanism alone.[47] In fact, "Emily's most characteristic difficulties are with the morals of the Bible especially of the Old Testament—which in her time and place had not been subjected to 'Higher Criticism.'"[48] Not approaching traditionally the Christian Myth as exemplified in the Puritan temper during her times, she, through human action, was "able to grasp the terms of the myth directly...."[49] This is evident in the manner she faces the utmost implications in a particular experience. Making her cosmic background shrink to her individual conscience in a manner of "recoil," her ruminations about problems are not a process of reasoning out, and finding easy solutions, but one of looking at the *situations,* directly fusing sensibility with thought.[50] Emily Dickinson's relevance to the present study lies in the fact of her evoking certain perceptions in us that call up parallel examples both from Frost and Williams. Frost's continual withdrawal to "mountain and farm," and so also Williams's impulse to lead the secluded life of a doctor as "the great world did not interest [him],"[51] and yet their ability to write some of the greatest poems of the twentieth century, making their private, intimate experiences symbols of man's ultimate destiny, do call to our mind the parallel situation in Dickinson who jotted her "letters to the world" on scraps of paper innocently, without knowing that her "humble act," like that of Saint Francis' preaching to the birds at Alviano, Lincoln's writing the second insugural "with malice toward none," *or* Galileo's dropping weights from the Tower of Pisa, will one day become an example of "human excellence." Dickinson's dislike for "conventional rhymes," her "imagism," her "casual whimsies" along with serious abstraction, her ability to absorb the local environment and make it meaningful with universal implications, constitute the secret of her appeal to the modern readers. Emily Dickinson's greatness lies in the manner in which "she exemplified in life the truth which the local colour writers discovered in literature: the narrow limits of a single house and garden could provide infinite room for the workings of the imagination and supply it with materials for some of the most striking verse written in nineteenth century America."[52]

The ideological centre in the full-throated expressions of the antinomian "self" of the Adamic poet in America lies in championing the idea of Man and in making a continuous attempt for fulfilling the American Dream. This necessitated a cultivation of a national literature which would not merely look up to European cultural scenes for its "materials," but will make the most of "the present, immediate ground" in America. In other words, it will be an American literature in the true sense of the term. Though initiated in the poetry of Emerson and Whitman, the necessity to carry this point of view to its climax was particularly felt in the years between the Civil War and the end of the nineteenth century. Publishing a series of essays in 1838-1839 Orestes Brownson puts his argument thus: "...the national literature could only be enriched if American 'scholars' could abandon their 'lone reveries' and 'scholastic asceticism' and rather seek their inspiration...in the 'really living, moving, toiling and sweating, joying and sorrowing people around them.'"[53] Though more realistic in its tenor, these words doubtless echo Emerson's notes in 1837 on the American Scholar's opinions on the kind of literature America needs:

> The literature of the poor, the feelings of the child, the philosophy of the street, the meaning of house-hold life, are the topics of the time. It is a great stride. It is a sign...of new vigour when the extremeties are made active, when currents of warm life run into the hands and feet. I ask not for the great, the remote, the romantic, what is doing in Italy or Arabia, what is Greek art, or Provencal ministrelsy; *I embrace the common, I explore and sit at the feet of the familiar, the low*[54] [Italics Mine].

Immediately after the Civil War, the cultural development of the United States took a different turn. A growing concern to discard the past was discerned, and it was indeed a time of precious, and in a way, premature flowering of a concept in which the *real* was considered to be noble and beautiful. To add to that, the practical tendency of the time was to raise Man to an inconceivably higher and more liberal position in the context of society and State.[55]

Sweet, tender, and thoughtful, Bryant in the poet who, in the words of Whitman, pulsed "the first interior verse throbs of a mighty world...." He was the "...bard of the river and of the wood, ever conveying a taste of open air, with scents as from hayfields, grapes, birch-borders...."[56] Of course, in a serious poem like "Thanatopsis"—be is the moralist *par excellence,* but the readers are apt to find in it the vanity and impermanence of much of his Puritanic temper. The poet here seems unwilling "to leave his effect to the emotion conveyed in the poem itself..."[57] and not being interested in emotion, or the expression of personality in this poem he keeps before him the moral of "salvation" as the essential issue, and relegates the demands of "life" to the background. "For this reason," Van Wyck Brooks has accurately observed, "Bryant was never a '*personality*'"[58] [Italics Mine]. However, Bryant's Nature poems like the "Green River," "A Forest Hymn," "To a Waterfowl" or "Inscription for the Entrance to a Wood" are full of a certain kind of excellence that makes us enjoy and love the scenes for what they are, and not for the "moral endings" attached to them. "Real poetry springs from the assumption that the spectacle is its own reward, that feeling happy or unhappy is final: it is concerned as Shelley pointed out, not with effect and applications, which are temporary, but with causes, which are permanent. The moral ending is simply a rigid and impersonal intellectualisation of life, which is, consequently, out of touch with the motives that really determine men."[59] One may almost find the Adamic poet's conception of poetry sounded in these words, for he, unlike the mythic poet is *more likely* to believe that the secret of Man lies in the "motives and causes" of life's experiences, and *not every much* in the effects of idealism or the intellectual application of principles of "being" formulated from the evolution of history and culture.

"The poet's office," James Russell Lowell said, "is to be a voice, not of one crying in the wilderness to a knot of already magnetised acolytes, but singing amid the throng of men, and lifting their common aspirations and sympathies...on the wings of his song to a purer and a wider reach of view."[60] With Longfellow the "purer ether" and the "wider reach of view" are reached in and through a "domesticated certitude" of Nature's function.[61]Though reprimanded as a plagiarist, Longfellow's secret of originality as a poet lay in the Adamically innocent manner in which he handled the theme of Nature and Man. It recalls and confirms our own unvalued sensations and perceptions, and gives "classic shape to our nebulous, over-shifting, amorphous imaginings":

> As a fond mother, when the day is o'er,
> Leads by the hand her little child to bed.
> Half willing, half reluctant to be led,
> and leave his broken playthings on the floor,
> Still gazing at them through the open door,
> Nor wholly reassured and comforted
> By promises of others in their stead,
> Which, though more splendid, may not
> please him more;
> So Nature deals with us, and takes away
> Our playthings one by one, and by the hand
> Leads as to rest so gently, that we go
> Scarce knowing if we wish to go or stay,
> Being too full of sleep to understand
> How far the unknown transcends
> the what we know.[62] ("Nature")

It is a rest-giving, calm, and quiet "mother-figure" that we find in Nature. Though the poem gives an impression of the imagery being somewhat laboriously accumulated, we are, however, reassured of the warm security that Nature can offer man. It becomes more "relevant" when the concept of the American as

Adam is taken into account, for this Adam can only retain his innocence by the smooth but impetuous rush of unmistakable inspiration from "Nature's grand simplicities."

Unlike William Carlos Williams who in our times would argue in favour of attaining "the universal" through "the particular," Longfellow desired "the universal" no doubt but strangely enough neglected "the particular," so much so that his imagistics in "Hawthorne" and "Divina Commedia" fail to get Hawthorne and Dante "rooted to the particular soil" from which they "grow like plants" to attain universal glory. Even then it would be wrong to say that Longfellow had not "gauged the temperature" of the American soil. For example, while in Europe, he never forgot "that he was on leave of absence, and that in gathering specimens he was to bear in mind the soil to which they were to be transplanted.[63] Though he "transplanted" a lot, it is primarily his belief in the creative imagination as an act of self-definition as indicated in poems like "L'Envoi: The Poet and His Songs" that bring his poetry so close to the "Adamic Mode."

For James Russell Lowell, a poet's creative imagination in an age devoted to "matter and commonsense," should function in converting the antipoetic as the basis for all poetry. This is as relevant to-day as it was in Lowell's time. Lowell believed that the office of the poet must needs be revered, because he comes to terms with the miracles of science and structures his theme on the basis of his understanding in poetic sensibility. Again, Lowell argues, we are taught by the lives of the grest poets "that they were the men of their generation who felt most deeply the meaning of the present."[64] All these words anticipate some very cogent statements in twentieth-century critical canons. Take, for example, Eliot's admiration for the Metaphysicals, and in the light of that his insistence on "a unified sensibility" to broaden the concept of poetry, or William Carlos Williams's saying that the poet's duty is:

> to lift, by use of his imagination...the material conditions

> and appearances of his environment to the sphere of the intelligence where they will have new currency.[65]

In fact, the poet's function, like that of Adam's after the fall, is to discover and possess the environment so as to know the *inherent* nature of its innocence and beauty in the face of all horror. In other words, the ablest poet and by far the best is he who can look beneath the antipoetically trivial, and ordinary features of the environment, and see "the ideal," and reiterate it in his poetry. For him, as it is also for the readers, the discovery of "the ideal" is an inspiring moment of higher aspiration and attainment. Lowell is perhaps one of the earliest examples of such as aspiration for the status of poet. A study of the motif in "The Vision of Sir Launfel" reveals his genuine concern for searching out themes for "poetry in the homeground." Sir Launfal's quest for the Holy Grail, it is well known, led him to the startling discovery that it is to be sought at home alone, that is, in and through the American Experience and Dream. Of course, Sir Launfal's "startling discovery" was in a dream vision for which Lowell"s pleading in favour of "Reality" in poetry appears to be a little too paradoxical. Nonetheless, the importance of "place" in American poetry and its realisation, whether through "Fantasy" or "Reality," is unquestionable. This accounts for Lowell's commodious sense of "Community" which is a corollary to his sense of "place." *The Biglow Papers,* and pointedly enough his "Commemoration Ode," like many of his other later odes, testify to this. "Never did poesy appear/So full of heaven..."[66] to Lowell as when he celebrated America "in widest commonalty spread," as, for example, in the following lines:

> Bow down, dear Land, for thou hast found release!
> Thy God, in these distempered days,
> Hath taught thee the sure wisdom of His ways,
> And through thine enemies hath wrought thy peace!
> Bow down in prayer and praise!
>
> No poorest in thy borders but may now
> Lift to the juster skies a man's enfrenchised brow.
> O Beautiful! my country! Ours once more!

Smoothing thy gold of War-dishevelled hair
O'er such sweet brows as never other wore...[67]

Lowell hears "the Voice of a higher and invisible power," and like a "real prophet takes up the word again and speaks as one divinely inspired."[68] This is the goal outside of self—not the Song of Myself, but of God realised through one's land and her people. Thus, the people's poet, as Lowell's demanding reiterations show, is to work through "an exquisite sensibility both of soul and sense that sympathises like gossamer sea mass with every moment of the element in which it floats, but which is rooted on the solid rock of our common sympathies."[69] These "common sympathies" are to be perceived through common man's attachment to Nature. This is Lowell's achievement as a poet, but his failure lies elsewhere—in his failure to follow consistently his "manifesto" originally declared in "The Function of a Poet." Accordingly, poems making the antipoetic world of commonsense and materialism poetic are few and far between. Even then, Lowell's was an example of a poet who tried his best to possess his environment Adamically with an emphasis on men. "In outward nature it is still man that interests us, and we care far less for the things seen than the way in which they are seen by poetic eyes like Wordsworth's or Thoreau's, and the reflections they cast there."[70] Lowell, of course, looked upon "a great deal of modern sentimentalism about Nature as a mark of disease."

Witty and urbane, Oliver Wendell Holmes, the famous New England Brahmin, was a crusader whose writings in general exemplify a major concern for the freedom of the mind from terror—Adam's first reaction, we suppose, when he "died into life." Combining humour and sentiment in graceful verses, Holmes in a certain "neo-classical" fashion, reiterated his belief that there is a sense common to all men which can be made the basis of republicanism. He thought it a "high-falutin ideal" to carry republicanism like Whitman, through the whole world of created objects.[71] Aristocratic to the tip of his tongue, it is indeed "great" to note that Holmes fixed his faith in the creative ability of common folks: "lusty men,—the bristly, pachydermatous fellows that hew out the highways for material progress of society, and the broad-shouldered, out-of-door men that fight for the great prizes of life."[72] In fact, these are the fearless people, the self-made men. "It is a great deal better to be made in that way then not to be made at all."[73] The tenor is Emersonian minus Emerson's transcendental preoccupation.

His Tennysonian faith in the "Climbing soul of creeping men" found expression in "The Secret of the Stars," from which he developed a figure of speech into the popular allegory of "The Chambered Nautilus." The uniqueness of the American Experience, and the metaphor of the American as Adam, free from the old shackles of a traditional Europe, find ample expression in the allegorical implication of the lines from "The Chambered Nautilus":

Year after year beheld the silent toil
That spread his lustrous coil;
Still, as the spiral grew,
He left the past year's dwelling for the new
Stole with soft step its shining archway through,
Built up its idle door,
Stretched in his last-found home, and
knew the old no more.[74]

From the "Nautilus" to "Man" the shift is quick, and Holmes interprets and views Nature in terms of human experience and values.

Anthropocentrism which is an important factor in poetry in "the Adamic Mode" has been prominent, one way or the other, in almost all nineteenth-century poets in varying degrees. In Emerson man is not merely the creature of Nature but also its creator; in Bryant, Longfellow and Lowell man's relationship with Nature gives him greater perspective to understand his own inmost recesses of heart and mind. In short, man's view of himself as man is a view *via* his own reactions to and deliberations over Nature. Holmes would give us a similar view but with certain modifications. "Holmes goes one step beyond even the Lowell of the Thoreau essay.... He cannot realize even what it might be somehow to lose oneself in Nature, so as to find oneself in that man who is at once in Nature and, in the depths of his selfconsciousness, above it"[75] [Pearce's Italics].

"None of our great poets," said James Russel Lowell, "can be called *popular* in any exact sense of the word, for the highest poetry deals with thoughts and emotions which inhabit, like rarest sea-mosses, the doubtful limits of that shore between our abiding divine and our fluctuating human nature, rooted in the one, but living in the other, seldom laid bare, and otherwise visible only at exceptional moments of entire calm and clearness"[76] [Lowell's Italics]. Having at bottom his Quaker faith on one hand, and his ability to portray "reality" for an emerging people on the other, Whittier, of all the Fireside Poets, satisfies the strict standards of "popularity" enunciated in these lines by one of his contemporaries. Some of his basically religious poems like "What the Voice Said" fill us with a "fellow-feeling" for others in society. Therefore, the poems do not ultimately stand on a strict religious plane, but happen to bear a testimony to a national programme of sweet and elevating emotions:

Cease not, Voice of holy speaking,
Teacher sent of God, be near,
Whispering through the day's cool silence,
Let my spirit hear!

So, when thoughts of evil-doers
Waken scorn, or hatred move,
Shall a mournful fellow-feeling
Temper all with love.[77]

Though his religious belief in "the inner light" has made him akin to the Trenscendentalists, he did not lose his interest, and, in fact, his genuine love for the "Ordinary World"—the world of New England about him. For example, in "The Shoemakers" while talking of "beauty" and "Crystal Mountains," Whittier is not forgetting the social role of common folks—the shoemakers:

Rap, rap!—Your stout and bluff brogan,
With footsteps slow and weary,

May wander where the sky's blue span
Shuts down upon the prairie.
On Beauty's foot your slippers glance,
By Saratoga's fountains,
Or twinkle down the summer dance
Beneath the Crystal Mountains![78]

In such lines Fantasy is accommodated to the requirements of reality. What makes him a true poet in "the Adamic Mode" is the manner in which he depicted scenes."..So rich and picturesque and free,/(The Common unrimed poetry/Of simple life and country ways,)...."[79]

The impact is one of innocence of past events, like that of "Our uncle, innocent of books,/was rich in lore of fields and books/The ancient teachers never dumb/Of Nature's unhoused lyceum...." Next is, of course, "...the dear aunt, whose smile of cheer/And voice in dreams I see and hear,...."[80] Thus, the "hands of memory" are "stretched forth" not only for warming them in the onset of the snow-storm "at the woodfire's blaze," but also to have a grateful sense of sweetness and benediction in the face of all "graver fears" of life.[81] Without stretching himself too much to search wistfully for intimations of immortality in the recollections of early childhood, Whittier went on to feel like a common man the "loss in all familiar things" of an innocence that once permeated them, and was conscious of "something gone which should be nigh." Stirred by "the birth of a nation" in Montgomery in 1861 poets of the South who had been feeling neglected till then[82] convincingly stated that the Southern way of life was not a mere "local" episode in the history of America, but that it might set a beneficent example to the world as a whole if it were allowed to develop in its own fashion. This is Adamic egocentrism, but the focus is on transcending its limitations by making it expansive. Here is Henry Timrod, the most lyrical of the Southern poets, celebrating the concept of nationhood:

Hath not the morning dawned with added light?
And shall not evening call another star
Out of the infinite region of the night,
To mark this day in Heaven?[83]

Agrarian in cultural set-up, the South has its own message—the message of what has been called a "natural" economy. In this, Timrod fixed his faith even while dreaming of the destruction of the United States as a Commercial nation. He considered "the Cotton Boll" as the symbol of his own land, and of the interdependence of nations in the old "agrarian vision" so much disapprovingly viewed by Alexander Hamilton whose main contention was that the "...manufacturing establishments not only occasion a positive augmentation of the produce and revenue of the society, but that they contribute essentially to rendering them greater than they could possibly be without such establishments."[84] Timrod called for a poet who, like Emerson's American Scholar, while answering to the present needs, would also create a poetry with local themes but with universal implications:

> Where sleeps the poet who shall fitly sing
> The source where from doth spring
> That mighty commerce which, confined
> To the mean channels of no selfish mart,
> Goes out to every shore....[85]

To sing the "source where from doth spring/That mighty commerce..." is not only to free commerce from its "selfish channels," but also to celebrate the Adamic freedom of innocence which is at the root of all things. Evoking a sense of the South's unravaged beauty of Nature was all the more necessary under such a contingency:

> Spring, with that nameless pathos in the air
> Which dwells with all things fair,
> Spring, with her golden suns and silver rain,
> Is with us once again.
> Out in the lonely woods the jasmine burns
> Its fragrant lamps, and turns
> Into a royal court with green festoons
> The banks of dark lagoons.[86]

With Sidney Lanier we enter the Post-Civil-War era of reconstruction. An agricultural theorist, he knew that the plantation system was gone. As a poet, he readjusted himself to view the economic problems of the new South with greater sympathy, and sometimes even with humour. He knew where the shoes pinched. "He realized that back of the economic problems of the new South lay the materialistic disease which Wordsworth had diagnosed in 'The World Is Too Much with Us' and against which such New England poets as Emerson and Lowell had protested and Walt Whitman...was protesting at the time."[87]

Hence, Lanier's Adamic preoccupation with and a search for innocence lay in the manner he championed the cause of life and man, and condemned the unnaturalness implicit in the consciousness of a society primarily devoted to trade and commerce. Nature's sanctity is gone, and the "monstrous foul air" is the death-trap for man's sense of love. Lanier records his outcry:

> Thou Trade; thou king of the modern days!
> Change thy ways,
> Change thy ways...[88]

Hence, the time is an occasion for heart's loving feelings and divine instincts:

> "...The Time needs heart —' tis tired of head:
> We're all for love," the violins said.[89]

Tired of the "getting and spending" of "trade," Lanier is all out for deep humanitarian feelings. He strongly felt that "the cure for the ills of the world was to be found in greater love of nature and one's fellow man...." With Lowell he bore something in common, particularly in his revealing recognition that man's thoughts begin with feelings, and that they live by rationalizing their sentiments only. Lanier's poetry is also a record of this belief. One of his most ambitious poems, "The Symphony," admits the cogency of reasons for accepting the value of one of the greatest of abiding human sentiments—love—which, as the poem shows, has not had so far its adequate verbal expression. Lanier's career shows a steady moving away from a kind of poetry written for the public in an attempt to solve the peculiar problems of Southern community life, towards a poetry of a private kind in which the dignity and stature of the individual self is increasingly felt to be established. This he did for the very obvious reason that "his Community's values, once so self-evident as to issue into simplistic public pronouncements, no longer guaranteed that a specifically Southern Culture might furnish all necessary indices for measuring and celebrating human achievement."[90] Ultimately he had to fall back on the integrity of his own art with its universality as poetry. His art's "beautiful forms" as created by him were not at all nebulous but, verily controlled by life, they were there as testimony "to the satisfaction of our human needs."[91]

Thus, the implicit Southern nature myth of "Corn" gets transformed, and becomes an explicit religion of nature for the whole of mankind to follow. He attained the Adamic freedom of spirit by following assiduously the tenets of this new religion. Notice, for example, the release of his inhibitions while contemplating "The Marshes of Glynn":

> Oh, What is abroad in the marsh and the terminal sea?
> Somehow my soul seems suddenly free
> From the weighing of fate and the sad discussion of sin,
> By the length and the breadth and the sweep of the
> marshes of Glynn.[92]

For gaining ascendancy to a sense of innocence, and freedom Adam must free himself from "the sad discussion of sin." But Lanier could not quite trust his own awful freedom. In fact, he wanted to know what the Lord knew:

> And now from the vast of the Lord will the waters of
> sleep
> Roll in on the souls of man,
> But who will reveal to our waking ken
> The forms that swim and the shapes that creep
> Under the waters of sleep?[93]

Lanier's inquisitiveness as an artist "to know the unknown" has taken him into the realm of what has been called "pure art," making him a sort of latter-day Poe, though unlike Poe, he has been unable to free himself completely from his pre-occupation with "public poetry."

More than any other poet in the post-bellum South, Lanier showed definite signs of making his antinomian self flourish in his poetry, though he could not move as far as Emerson, Whitman or Emily Dickinson did in that direction. If the world of art is created by a mysterious union of reality and imagination, Lanier's meditative poetry which is the "act of his mind" is a fitting example of that mystery. He "mystifies" us by inviting our attention to look into the tangled, involuted forms of Nature operating in the Marshes. It is almost like challenging us to take stock of our own complex psychological tissues of thoughts and feelings:

> But no: it is made: list! somewhere,—mystery, where?
> In the leaves? in the air?
> In my heart? is a motion made: ...[94]

Our intention for bringing in a discussion of these poets beginning with Emerson down to Lanier *via* Whitman, Poe, Dickinson, Bryant, Longfellow, Lowell, Holmes, Whittier, etc., has been not so much to evaluate them as to place in perspective the chief elements of their poetry, particularly those that closely connect them with the Adamic Mode in American Poetry. The findings, we feel, are significant enough to form the background for the present study. Their preoccupation, more or less, has been with the American Idea which is the Idea of Man in search of Edenic innocence. Consequently, they have written poems, avoiding as they did, "the sad discussion of sin." They have not been mere plagiarists imitating the poetry of their counterparts in England. They have made the most, as is evident, of "the present, immediate ground." In fact, they, by writing of man in relation to the American "flora and fauna," have fittingly answered the demand made by Emerson that the American poet need not write about "the great, the remote, the romantic..." but should devote his time to "the familiar, the low." Whether they see "infinity" in the isolation of a little room like Emily Dickinson, or see the mysterious "motion" of the heart in the face of the tangled, involuted forms of Nature manifesting in the Marshes like Lanier, they have been conscious, with a wonderful "personal sincerity," of the value of their roles as "poets taking off their masks."

To them America is a poem, and they have sung the glory of its "Green River,"its "Prairies," its "Corn," its "Hills," its "Waterfowls," even its "Nautilus." Some have written like Holmes "by request of friends," but once they have recorded their "passionate thinkings," and "thoughtful passions" like Emily Dickinson they have indeed written their "letters to the world," singing their "Songs of Myself" with a "local pride" that takes on a universal implication. Whether their egocentricism *recoils* like that of Emily Dickinson's or *expands* like that of Whitman's, the quest is after giving a "name and habitation" to the American Dream—the dream of going back to the primal innocence of "things" in Life, Nature and Man *per se.* They have also, like Timrod, suggested the necessity of love—the most abiding of human sentiments—as the factor that can resurrect man in the face of all death-like hollowness and emptiness of the modern world. Their attraction for the American wilderness with its hills, prairies, rivers, and trees, indicates a poetic awareness that undisturbed Nature can enable man to experience mysteries transcending his daily life. It can also enable him to recapture almost directly the electrifying touch of forces from which he emerged. To add to this, the emphasis of these poets on *emotions as the operating material for their creative imagination* cannot be lost sight of.

In the light of these "findings" the poems of Robert Frost and William Carlos Williams take on meaningful dimensions. It is well known that the most recurrent and most popular image in American literature is that of the solitary man confronting the natural world, usually the great American wilderness. Frost's characters get morally rejuvenated whenever they are close to American wilderness knowing full well the impact of birch trees, axe-helves, rock walls, pasture lands or snow-storms, of man's sense of himself and the Earth he lives in.[95] The poetry of Williams too, particularly his *Paterson,* brings into limelight the innocent, simple and unspoilt elements in American "flora and fauna" by contrasting them with man-made "*artificialities.*" The way Williams looks at the Passaic River and presents the surrounding mountains and trees does, indeed, point to a bygone time in history when like Adam, man was able to look on Nature with fresh and curious eyes.[96] For him, every morning was a rebirth of the Universe. We have perhaps lost that sensibility in the face of the artificialities created by a technocratic society. Love, too, has gone dry in the human heart. Frost's definition that "Home is the place where, when you have to go there,/They have to take you in"[97] shows the need of "loving attention" as the beginning of all genuine human relationship. For Williams too it has primary significance:

It was the love of love
    The love that swallows up all else,
    a grateful love,
A love of nature, of people,
    animals
    a love engendering
gentleness and goodness
    that moved me
        and *that* I saw in you[98] [Williams's Italics].

As poets in "the Adamic Mode" both Frost and Williams knew the sharp distinction between the man who acts with genuine feeling and the one who denies emotion. In Frost such figures are well known appearing as they do in such poems as "Home Burial," "The Death of the Hired Man," etc. Coming to Williams one also finds some of the best portraits of "simple people who live naturally" as in "Canthara," "Portrait of a Woman in Bed," "To Mark Anthony in Heaven," etc.[99] The poems show how man may be man in an anti-imaginative world. Frost's belief that a poem is in the process of making "if *you felt* it as it is *making* in your mind"...[100] [Italics Mine] connect him with our discussion earlier in this chapter on "the affective tonalities" that evidently act within the creative imagination of "the Adamic Poet" and define his self. Williams also had all along tempered his deep belief in what he termed "an essential part of poetic process, the imaginative quota, the unbridled, mad-sound basis of all poems."[101] In his essay "How to write," Williams hints that the artist's function is to touch his own "primitive profoundity [sic] of [the] personality."[102] The artist's "faculties, untied, proceed backward through the night of our unconscious past. It goes down to the ritualistic, amoral past of the race, to fetish, to dream to wherever the 'genius' of the particular writer finds itself able to go."[103] As indicated at the beginning of this chapter Frost's look is also backward even while going forward. The look is directed to mountains and farms, to forests and their deep darkness. It is another way of proceeding backward through the night of our unconscious racial past. In Williams the concept of "No ideas but in things" enables him to present life and Nature with their "primitive profundity" or "primal innocence." The American Adam's search is to recapture this. His belief in what has been called "the Edenic Myth" is well-known.

NOTES

1. Carl Bode, Leon Howard and Louis B. Wright, eds. *American Literature* (New York: Washington Square Press, Inc., 1966), II, 244. Hereafter cited as *AL*.
2. Ralph Waldo Emerson, "V. Shakespeare; Or the Poet," in *English Traits, Representative Men, Other Essays* (1908; rpt. New York: K.P. Dutton & Co., Inc., 1951, p. 25.
3. Joel Barlow, *The Columbiad: A Poem* (Philadelphia: C & A Conrad & Co.,1809), I, 145.
4. Edward Taylor, "Meditation Nineteen," in Donald E. Stanford, ed. *The Poems of Edward Taylor* (New Haven: Yale Univ. Press, 1960), p. 32.
5. Emerson, *English Traits, Representative Men, Other Essays,* p. 259. See also Miller, *The New England Mind from Colony to Province.*
6. Edmund Clarence Stedman & Ellen Macay Hutchinson, eds. *A Library of American Literature from the Earliest Settlement to the Present Time* (New York: Charles L. Webster & Co., 1890), II, 42.
7. Alexander Richardson quoted in Perry Miller, *The New England Mind: The Seventeenth Century* (Cambridge: Harvard Univ. Press, 1967), p. 162.
8. Pearce, *The Continuity of American Poetry,* p. 40.
9. Daniel G. Hoffman, ed. "Tradition and Invention in American Poetry," *American Poetry and Poetics* (New York: Doubleday, 1962), p. xxiii.
10. Phillips Bradley, ed. Alexis de Tocqueville, *Democracy in America* (New York: Alfred A. Knopf, 1963), II, 74.

11. *Ibid.*
12. Daniel G. Hoffman, ed. *American Poetry and Poetics,* pp. xxviii-xxix.
13. Walt Whitman, "Preface, 'Leaves of Grass' (1855)," in Norman Forester ed. *American Critical Essays:* XIXth and XXth Centuries (London: Oxford Univ. Press, 1930), p. 106. Hereafter cited as Forester, ed. *ACE.*
14. Hyatt H. Waggoner, *American Poets,* p. 160.
15. Gay Wilson Allen, *Walt Whitman Handbook* (New York: Hendricks House, 1962), p. 384.
16. Ralph L. Rusk, ed. *The Letters of Ralph Waldo Emerson* (New York: Columbia Univ. Press, 1939), IV, 196-197.
17. Ralph Waldo Emerson, *Journals & Miscellaneous Notebooks of Ralph Waldo Emerson,* ed. William H. Gilman, et al. (Cambridge, Mass.: Harvard Univ. Press, 1964), p. 141.
18. Ralph Waldo Emerson, "The Poet," *Essays First and Second Series* (New Delhi: Eurasia Publishing House (P) Ltd., 1972), p. 229.
19. *Ibid.*, p. 231.
20. *Ibid.*, p. 240.
21. Shiv Kumar, "Introduction," Ibid., p. xi.
22. *AL* II, 303.
23. Emerson, *Essays: First and Second Series,* p. 246.
24. See Allen, *Walt Whitman Handbook* p. 382. See also Henry B. Reed, "The Heraclitan Obsession of Walt Whitman," *The Personalist* XV (April 1934), 125-36.
25. Shelley, "A Defence of Poetry," in Russell Noyes, ed. *English Romantic Poetry and Prose* (New York: Oxford Univ. Press, 1956), p. 1109.
26. Carl E. Dahlstrom, "Introduction," in *Strindberg's Dramatic Expressionisms* (1930; rpt. New York: Arno Press, 1978), pp. 49-50.
27. Rod W. Horton and Herbert W. Edward, *Background of American Literary Thoughts* (New York: Appleton-Century-Crofts, Inc., 1952), p. 112.
28. Letter to C.F. Briggs, 21 August, 1845. See *Letters of James Russell Lowell,* ed. C.E. Norton (New York: Harpers & Brothers, 1894), I, 99.
29. See D.H. Lawrence, *Studies in Classic American Literature* (London: Heinemann, 1964).
30. *Cyclopaedia of American Literature* [1855] (New York: Charles Scribner, 1866), II, 537-38. See also Perry Miller, *The Haven and the Whale: The War of Words and Wits in the Era of Poe and Melville* (New York: Harcourt, Brace & Co., 1956), p. 326.
31. William Charvat, *Origins of American Critical Thought, 1810-1833* (New York: A.S. Barnes & Co., Inc., 1961), pp. 84-85.
32. Ghiselin, *Creative Process,* p. 46.

33. Louis Untermeyer, ed. *Complete Poems of Edgar Allan Poe* (New York: The Heritage Press, 1943), p. 63. Hereafter cited as *Complete Poems of Edgar Allan Poe.*
34. *Ibid.*, p. 64.
35. Editorial Commentary, in *AL.* I, 6.
36. Poe, "The Poetic Principle," *Ibid.*, II, 101.
37. *Complete Poems of Edgar Allan Poe,* p. 13.
38. *Ibid.*, p. 136.
39. Both quotations from Editorial Commentary, "Decadent Romanticism," in *AL* II, 6.
40. Carl Bode, ed. *The Great Experiment in American Literature* (New York: Frederick A. Praseger, Publishers, 1961), p. 53.
41. Mark Schorer, "Technique as Discovery," *Hudson Review,* I (Spring 1948), 67.
42. Evorett quoted in B.T. Spencer, *The Quest for Nationality* (Syracuse: Syracuse Univ. Press, 1957), p. 209.
43. See Emerson, *Essays: First and Second Series,* p. 241.
44. Emily Dickinson, "214" in Thomas H. Johnson, ed. *The Complete Poems of Emily Dickinson* (Boston: Little, Brown & Co., 1960), pp. 96-99.
45. George Frisbie Whicher, *This was a Poet: Emily Dickinson* (New York: Charles Soribner's Sons, 1938), p. 159.
46. Thomas H. Johnson, *Emily Dickinson: An Interpretative Biography* (Cambridge: Harvard Univ., Press, 1966), pp. 232-59.
47. Cf. Emily Dickinson, "976," "324" in Johnson, ed. *The Complete Poems of Emily Dickinson,* p. 456, pp. 153-54.
48. Austin Warren, "Emily Dickinson," in Beaver, ed. *ACE.*
49. Allen Tate, "Emily Dickinson," Egbert S. Oliver, ed. *American Literature 1890-1965* [New Delhi: Eurasia Publishing House (P) Ltd., 1970], p. 167.
50. *Ibid.*, p. 169.
51. *William Carlos Williams Reader,* p. 308.
52. Editorial Commentary, "Infinity in a Little Room," in *AL* III, 295.
53. Quoted in Spencer, *The Quest for Nationality,* pp. 113-14.
54. Emerson, "The American Scholar" in *AL* II, 256.
55. See Arthur Hobson Quinn, ed. *The Literature of the American People: An Historical and Critical Survey* (New York: Appleton-Century-Crofts, Inc., 1951), p. 813. Also Charles Godfrey Leland, *Sunshine in Thought* (New York: C.T. Evens, 1862), p. 144.
56. Walt Whitman, *Specimen Days* (Philadelphia: David Mckay, 1863), p. 181. See also William Aspinwall Bradley, *Williams Cullen Bryant* (New York: The Macmillan Co., 1905), p. 210. Bryant's conception of

Nature as sinless, forming a part of the aesthetic appeal of his poetry is summarised thus: "Man brought evil into the world, but it came from the hands of its creator."

57. Van Wyck Brooks, "Our Poets," in Forester, ed. *ACE,* p. 488.
58. *Ibid.*
59. *Ibid.*
60. James Russell Lowell, "Wordsworth," in Forester, ed. *ACE,* pp. 85-86.
61. Pearce, *The Continuity of American Poetry,* p. 211.
62. Henry Wadsworth Longfellow, "Nature" in *The Complete Poetical Works of Longfellow*, Craige Edn. (Boston: Houghton Hifflin Co., 1922), p. 318. Hereafter cited as *Complete Poetical Works of Longfellow.*
63. Van Wyck Brooks, "Our Poets," in Forester, ed. *ACE,* p. 485.
64. James Russell Lowell, "The Function of a Poet (1855)," in *Lowall Essays, Poems & Letters,* ed. William Smith Clark II (New York: The Odyssey Press, 1948), p. 69. Hereafter cited as *LEPL.*
65. Williams quoted in Norman Holmes Pearson, "Williams, New Jersey," *The Saturday Review*, I (Autumn 1957), 36. Cf. Lowell, "The Function of a Poet," *LEPL.* p. 67.
66. James Russell Lowell, "An Incident in a Railroad Car," in *The Complete Poetical Works,* Cambridge Edn. (Boston: Houghton Mifflin Co., 1897), p. 45. Hereafter cited as *Complete Poetical Works.*
67. *Ibid.*, p. 347.
68. Lowell, "Wordsworth," in Forester, ed. *ACE*, p. 98.
69. *Ibid.*, p. 103.
70. Lowell, "Thoreau," *Ibid.*, pp. 622-623.
71. Howard Mumford Jones and S.I. Hayakawe, eds. *Oliver Wendell Holmes: Representative Selections* (New York: American Book Co., 1939), pp. lxiii ff.
72. *Ibid.* Holmes had two views of poetry: one that "poetic sense" is universal, that is to say "all people are poets," and the other that poetry is "divine" "to which human beings attain only by some sort of miracle ...." p. lxxiv.
73. Holmes, "Album Verses," in *AL,* II, 576.
74. Holmes, "The Chambered Nautilus," in *The Complete Poetical Works of Cliver Wendell Holmes*, Cambridge Edn. (Boston: Houghton, Mifflin & Co., 1895), p. 149.
75. Pearce, *The Continuity of American Poetry,* p. 224.
76. Lowell, "Wordsworth," in Forester, ed. *ACE,* p. 104.
77. John Greenleaf Whittier, "What the Voice said," in *The Complete Poetical Works of Whittier,* Cambridge Edn. (Boston: Houghton Mifflin Co., 1894), p. 425. Hereafter cited as *Complete Poetical Works of Whittier.*

78. *Ibid.*, p. 358.
79. "Snow-Bound," *Ibid.*, p. 401.
80. *Ibid.*, p. 402.
81. *Ibid.*, p. 406.
82. See E.W. Parks, ed. *The Essays of Henry Timrod* (Athens: Univ. of Georgia Press, 1942), p. 84. Timrod states in his essay "Literatures in the South:" "It is the equally firm conviction of the South that genius literary genius, at least is an exotic that will not flower in a Southern soil."
83. Timrod, "Ethnogenesis," *AL* III, 25.
84. Quoted in John N. Blum, *et al.*, *The National Experience: A History of the United States* (New York: Hercourt, Brace & World, Inc., 1963), p. 142.
85. Timrod, "The Cotton Boll," *AL*, III, 31.
86. Timrod, "Spring," *Ibid.*, 34.
87. Timrod, "Civil War and Reconstruction," *Ibid.*, 6.
88. Sidney Lanier, *Poems of Sidney Lanier,* ed. by his wife [Mary D. Lanier] (New York: Charles Scribner's Sons, 1906), p. 65. Hereafter cited as *Poems of Sidney Lanier.*
89. *Poems of Sidney Lanier,* p. 60.
90. Pearce, *The Continuity of American Poetry,* p. 241.
91. C.R. Anderson, ed. *Centennial Edition* (Baltimore: The Johns Hopkins Press, 1945), IV, 27.
92. *Poems of Sidney Lanier,* p. 16.
93. *Ibid.*, p. 18.
94. *Ibid.*, p. 6.
95. *Complete Poems of Robert Frost,* p. 153.

    ...Earth's the right place for love:
    I don't know where it's likely to go better.
    I'd like to go by climbing a birch tree,
    And climb black branches up a snow-white trunk
    Toward heaven, till the tree could bear no more,
    But dripped its top and set me down again. (Frost's Italics]
96. See *Paterson*, p. 71

    Stand at the rampart (use a metronome
    if your ear is deficient, on made in Hungary
    if you prefer)
    and look away north by east where the church
    spires still spend their wits against
    the sky to the bell park
    in the hollow with its minute figures running
    beyond the gap where the river
    plunges into the narrow gorge, unseen

—and the imagination soars, as a voice
beckons, a thundrous voice, endless
—as sleep the voice
that has ineluctably called them
that unmoving roar!

97. "The Death of the Hired Man," *Complete Poems of Robert Frost,* p. 53.
98. Williams, "Asphodel, That Greeny Flower," in *William Carlos Williams Reader,* p. 72.
99. See Linda Welshimer Wagner, *The Poems of Williams's Carlos Williams* (Middletown: Wesleyan Univ. Press, 1964), pp. 22-23. Wagner's emphasis is on Williams's ethic of linking love and its emotion with Nature and its dignity.
100. Quoted in Graham Munson, *Making Poems for America: Robert Frost* (Chicago: Encyclopaedia Britannica Press, 1962), p. 143.
101. Letter to Harvey Breit, March 18, 1942, in John C. Thirlwell, ed. *The Selected Letters of William Carlos Williams* (New York: McDowell, Obolensky Inc., 1957), p. 194.
102. See Appendix: "How to write" by William Carlos Williams in Wagner, *The Poems of William Carlos Williams,* p. 145.
103. *Ibid.*

3

Edenic Dream and Reality: The Cycle of History in American Poetry

THE CONCLUSION drawn in the previous Chapter leads us to discuss the traditional belief that America was once a Paradise on Earth, the Garden of Eden rediscovered, and that the American man incorporated the innocence, youth and beauty of the original Adam. Keeping this discussion as a backdrop, we have also to consider "the Adamic Mode" in the poetry of Frost and Williams in consequence of which the tangle involved can be unravelled for a better assessment of the position of these two poets in American poetry.

It is well known that the concept of a Paradise on earth is essentially Utopian. However, in spite of the impossibility of actualizing this Utopia, a quest or craving for the "lost" Eden goes on. In Frost's poetry this craving takes the form of a kind of "retreat" from civilization to mountains and farms, and in Williams it manifests itself, among others, in his extraordinary ability to see objects through the pious eyes of an American Adam, giving them the necessary freshness of "design" that seems to have been spoilt by the "technological basis" of our thinking. This connects those poets with the Myth of Adam, or for that matter, Edenic possibilities, which reflects the hope of creating a second Paradise, not in the next world and not outside time, but in the bright New World of the American continent "here and now."[1] Beginning with its first settlement, America was considered by the Europeans "a land of boundless opportunity, a place where man, after centuries of poverty, misery, and corruption, could have a second chance to fulfil, in reality, his mythic yearnings for a return to Paradise."[2] Captain Edward Johnson announced the following in 1654 to the Old-World-weary people of England:

> All you the people of Christ that are here Oppressed, Imprisoned and scurrilously divided, gather yourselves together...as you shall be shipped for His service, in the Western World, and more especially for planting the United Colonies of New England.... Know this is the place where the Lord will create a new Heaven, and a new Earth in new churches, and a new Commonwealth together.[3]

However, the desire to reject the inhibited "past" and to embrace the "present" with a hope for fulfilment of life's many-splendoured promises is as old as man. The new Protestant movement did, of course, give a definite direction to it with a change of emphasis from a spiritual to an earthly Kingdom of God. Richard Niebuhr in a brilliant analysis of the religious credo involving the whole gamut of the movement rightly remarks that "the new movement was impatient...with the deferment of the fulfilment of life's promise. Its word was 'now.'"[4] The Edenic Dream, is "as old as the mind of man," but the idea that "this is the place" was uniquely American. Keeping this as the main "drive" of his discussion Frederic I. Carpenter goes on to expound the idea:

> Earlier versions had placed it in Eden or in Heaven, in Atlantis or in Utopia; but always in some country of the imagination. Then the discovery of the new world gave substance to the old myth, and suggested the realization of it on actual earth. America became "the place" where the religious prophecies of Isaih and the Republican ideals of Plato might be realized.[5]

Under the circumstances, we might add, the mythic longings of primitive man, his continual approach to the innocent source of "things" in life and Nature could also be realised by modern man[6] in all the glory of what has been called, "primal innocence." Charles L. Sanford, while tracing out in detail the pros and cons of the history of this belief that doubtless linked the discovery of America to the founding of a second Eden, makes out the case in understandable terms:

> Colonists were often explicit and detailed in developing the imagery of planting, especially since many of them were an agricultural people familiar with nature. They were planting the seed of the posterity of a new Adam and Eve in the rich, virgin soil of a new Eden, warmed by the sun of Righteousness.[7]

The themes of such bright expectations, which derive from the Edenic myth of Adam's quest for innocence, form a major thread in the fabric of American literature. It can be traced from Crevecoeur's *Letters from an American Farmer*[8] through the works of Emerson, Thoreau, and Whitman to such modern writers as Hart Crane and Thomas Wolfe. Thoreau's adventures at Walden pond, Emerson's insistence of the natural man in a natural setting, and Whitman's well-known chantings of Adamic songs, do indeed point to a new Adam—liberated, innocent, and heroic—in the New World Garden of America. Though the concept of "garden" in relation to our thinkings of America might mean the garden as a Darwinian jungle, a waste-land or a life-killing garden of poisonous trees and plants, it would primarily stand for an agrarian heaven in a pastoral landscape. But the tension does not lie here: it is only felt when an individual, nurtured in this belief, confronts the "counterforce" that seems to emanate from a painful initiation into an awareness of evil. Thus, there appears to have been two states of consciousness giving rise to two typical figures in the Myth of Edenic possibilities: one is without tension and the other, as indicated by D.H. Lawrence in his *Studies in Classic American Literature,* is filled with a "dark suspense" latent in the American Dream.[9] There is a basic opposition between the two "types." Lewis' analysis of the former is apt. He rates him as "a radically new personality, the hero of the new adventure: an individual emancipated from history, happily bereft of ancestry, untouched and undefiled by the usual inheritances of family and race; an individual standing alone, self-reliant and self-propelling, ready to confront whatever awaited him with the aid of his own unique and inherent resources."[10] It may be indicated here that this type appeared time and again as a heroic figure, more particularly in the novels embodying the Leatherstocking Saga. The nature of the impact can be better understood in relation to Fenimoore Cooper's Natty Bumpo, the central figure of the Leatherstocking Saga. He has his moral purity, and social innocence. Being a child of the wilderness, forever in flight before the corrupting influence of civilization, he is the explicit version of Adam before the Fall, free from the moral compromises of Eve. He is what Lewis calls the "hero in space," and Lewis goes on to remark that it is so in "two senses of the word":

> First, the hero seems to take his start outside time, or on the very outer edges of it, so that his location is essentially in space alone; and, second, his initial habitat is space as spaciousness, as the unbounded, the area of total possibility.[11]

However, in opposition to this uncorrupted Adam, the other American hero, with all his complexity of character during and after the Fall, has to be understood while considering the American people's frantic determination to slough off the old skin of European tradition and "evil," in the face of the more tight constriction by their New World heritage of Puritan conscience and inhibition. This brings us to what has been called the symbolic loss of Edenic innocence and the painful initiation into an awareness of evil. This darker thread in America's literary fabric is more successfully woven in the works of novelists like Hawthorne and Melville through Mark Twain and Henry James to Hemingway and Faulkner. The import of both the categories under discussion has been also present in one form or another in what has been called the "antinomian strain in American poetry" to which reference has been made earlier in this study. "Once having achieved its mastery" it "has made for only iterated and reiterated songs of oneself,"[12] which in a major way has excluded the God-fearing Puritanic temper while asserting the ego. The form has been confessional, though "confession in itself is nothing, but without the confession there can be no understanding, and without the understanding..., we will not be able to move forward from a liberalism of innocence to a liberalism of responsibility."[13] This forms the very basis of the American Experience in which the close proximity of Dream and Nightmare cannot be underrated. To quote David Madden,

> It appears that there are two major American dream myths: the Old Testament idea of a paradise hopelessly lost, followed by endless nightmare suffering; and the New Testament idea of a paradise that the New American Adam will eventually regain.[14]

Madden explains that there has been a slanting in American literature against the New Testament vision, and that "the hope for the clear vision lies in the ambiguous area between Paradise Lost and Paradise Regained."[15] Thus the implications are complex and manysided. Several themes do obviously derive directly from it. First, there is the theme of Arcadia, the traditional belief that Nature has been a constant source of plenty and bliss. Consequently, the "garden" imagery and pastoralism as representative of a perfect life have been present in American writings from the beginning. Coming to Frost, it is easy to find his preoccupation with pastoralism that evokes the sense of Adamic peace and tranquillity, and above all, the sense of the leisure of a rural life. Though not a pastoral poet in the manner of Frost, Williams as a poet, also uses images of innocence and beauty connected with mountains, flowers, and women. However, in both of them there is that consistent "reference to the great world beyond"[16] as a challenging counterforce, and its impact is sometimes obvious as in Frost's "Mending Wall" where "a surrender to the natural forces which draw human beings together" is sharply contrasted with "the conservatism which persists in keeping up the distinctions separating them,"[17] or in Williams's *Paterson* where the Garrett mountain as the feminine figure symbolising faith and innocence is juxtaposed with Paterson, the city, as the masculine figure[18] symbolising the horrors of a technocratic industrial society where,

> The language is missing them
>   they die also
>   incommunicado.[19]

This evidently explains the transmutation of the "garden" image into the master metaphor of the Wasteland.

The historians of the Edenic Myth which is the basic postulate of "the Adamic Mode" in literature have produced a substantial corpus of challenging scholarship. They are the authors who have written about "Virgin Land," the "American Adam," the "Arcadian" and the "Agrarian" myths, and have fortunately fashioned their methods of analysis after the myth and symbol analyses of modern literary critics, so that we can make use of their findings in studying the creative pattern functioning in the poetry of Frost and Williams.

The Edenic Myth has no doubt its different variants, but it has been proved to have formed the archetypal American cultural pattern based on the faith in America as a New World Garden. As a symbol it has also interpreted the American Experience. And accordingly most Americans have sought, in one manner or the other, to order their lives.[20] As it appears the American version of "the Adamic Mode" of existence had its origin in the cultural and political traditions of Western civilization. Its antecedents are traceable to the Bible. It is also contained in the pastoral tradition of Western literature, and in the Gnostic perfectionism that has punctuated the history of Europe since the late middle ages. There has been, of course, good evidence, as Rosenmeir has argued of its presence in the work of the founders of the Massachusetts Bay Colony.[21] Robert Payne's remark that "America is Europe with all the walls down"[22] is important while defining the American civilization which "emerged as an offshoot from the larger entity of the West which was seeking a New World form." As such, "the American is... the concentrated embodiment of Western man, more sharply delineated, developed under more urgent conditions, but with most of the essential traits present."[23] This is the basic formulation of the American Dream, a "dream" which has been the most important national experience of America. Therefore, it is much too difficult on the part of any American writer of importance to escape the almost certain confrontation with it. Thus, difficulty is always felt by critics to find any other meaning of the New World as the Garden excepting the one so firmly defined by the first European pioneers, that the New World as the Garden would redeem man of the Old World.[24] There have been clear warnings against this. The enterprise has been thought "impossible" "which twists the heart, blights the mind, and results in social sterility...."[25] But loyalty to this "antique faith" has been discernible in most American intellectuals who, with Fitzgerald, have, more often than not, chosen, to "beat on, boats against the current, borne back ceaselessly into the past."[26] This is obviously an effort at recapturing "the primal innocence" of things.[27]

Also, one of the more breath-taking suggestions has been "that every individual was in spirit and in fact a perfectly new man, as new as Adam, each the first man, each the new man fallen."[28] Thus, in spite of the nineteenth-century split between the yea-saying and nay-saying intellectuals, the dominant element of American culture in the early twentieth century was its "innocence" which consisted of a belief in the eternity and universality of moral values like truth, patriotism, and decency, a belief in the inevitability of American and world progress, and lastly a belief in the traditional culture based on idealism, refinement, and a view of materialism—what Santayana called "the genteel tradition," to which reference has been made in the previous Chapter.[29] This innocence which comprises the clear absence of guilt and gives rise to some kind of doubt and complexity of thought seem to have ended with the onset of World War I which, for the Americans, had its own cycle of hope, hatred and disillusionment.[30] But like all basic human qualities "innocence" would never come to an end, as after each shock or initiation into the complex tangle of human experience, there is always a rebirth of "innocence."[31] The historians who are concerned with the rise and fall of "innocence" in America very much agree that it reached the acme of its influence in the nineteenth century, the heroic age of American expansion when, as is well known, settlers burst through the Appalachian barrier to reclaim millions of acres of wilderness and virgin land from

Kentucky to California for "nature's new nation." John Locke's proclamation that "in the beginning, all the world was America..." does not appear to be a difficult philosophical formulation when this new expansionism, along with its vast opportunities for freedom and innocence, is taken into consideration.[32] For a time, the American Indian was viewed as the noble savage in "nature's new nation," an aboriginal Adam, an innocent flower in the New World Garden till the image of nature's noble men was transferred from the Indian to the pioneers at the cutting edge of civilization on the frontier. However, achievement of progress in the New World Garden meant that the civilized man would also have to regress to savagery, because the road to the "Garden" ran through perilous wilderness where the barbarous alone could survive. Again, the seeking of a golden mean between the extremes of civilization and savagery has been discernible in the American Adam's magnificent effort to create an "agrarian republic" based on what has been called a "new nation of yeo-men farmers." As opposed to this, some went on to dream of a higher civilization whose achievements would, by all means dwarf those of its predecessors. Thus, the situation involves an egocentric predicament that evidently engenders contradictions or contraries. American History is filled with "characters" underlying the two distinct reactions to the New World as mentioned above. On one side there are those like Rasles, Boone or De Soto who submitted with a mood of acceptance to the larger, and perhaps more immaculate spirit of the New World. They, as Williams has so remarkably indicated in his book *In the American Grain,*[33] experienced the particulars of the New World's environment as though it were "a voyage of *discovery.*"[34] [Breslin's Italics]. In this "voyage" their "mythic descent to origins"[35] of "things" gave them the opportunities for delicate and perhaps sudden discovery of meanings of Adamic innocence, and for an exploration of instinctual forces in human nature which are perennial, and therefore inevitable. They can, for example, be best understood if we consider the motif of the following oracular utterances of a "she" who, as depicted by Williams, symbolises the spirit of the new continent:

> But you are mine and I will strip you naked—jealous of everything that touches you. Down, down to me—in and under and down, unbeaten, the white kernel, the flame—the flame burning under the water, that I cannot quench.
>
> I will cause it to be known that you are a brute. Now it is no sea-ringed island, now it is no city in a lake: come, here is room for search and counter search. Come, blackbeard, tireless rider, with an arrow in the thigh. I wait for you—beyond the river. Follow me – if you can.[36]

Breslin's analysis of the "motif" of this passage not only indicates its prophetic tone, but also stresses the importance "to see that this prophetess is not looking down from above, like Eliot's Tiresias; her knowledge comes from the earth and she looks upward, fiercely seductive...."[37] This evidently brings us to a point of realization, as Frost would like to put it, that

> ...Earth's the right place for love:
> I don't know where it's likely to go better.[38]

It is quite likely that our "continuous identity with the ground itself, where everything is fixed in darkness"[39] may lead us to accept man's darker side, his wilder instincts and moods. But acknowledgement of the earth as "primal source" may also enable man's spirit to have a firm grasp and to begin to awaken. However, there were those like the great Franklin and Washington who, instead of submitting with a mood of "lover's acceptance" to the passionate, implacable call of the New World, imposed upon it a ready-made culture. Though these men have been idealised and idolized in American History as the bearers of civilization, they appear somewhat empty and hollow when compared with the massive strength of a Rasles, a Boone or a De Soto who "boldly leapt into the chaos—to be made new men..."[40] These are the ambiguities with which America had her national beginning, and even in our times it is felt that these ambiguities have continued to exercise their impact of tension in many major policies of the century where the "montage" of "counterforces" is involved. All these considerations would make the students of American culture understand that the central question here is not "what then is the American, this new man?"[41] but rather "How has this man, the American, viewed himself?"

First, the American was the eternal innocent, freed from tradition, and bereft of the knowledge of good and evil. He was also, as we have realized, unaware of his kinship with the rest of mankind. Liberated from history, he lived in, through and beyond time in a condition of perpetual perfection, oblivious of the complex tangle of tragedy and irony of human experience. Thus, totally autonomous, the American Adam not only stood both outside space and time, but also he was without ancestors, relations or progeny.

Second, the American Adam was only the European Man in a different guise fighting for his existence at a difficult crossroad of history, and he ceased to be "Adamic" at a certain time, and he joined "a perfect community" in the end which, incidentally and ironically enough, has proved in our times the perfectibility of the saying that the end of progress is an end to progress.[42] In the face of those "historical tensions" in the American Experience, it has been more and more difficult on the part of most writers in America to escape being, as Fiedler said, "the recorder of the encounter of the dream of innocence and the fact of guilt" as America seems to be "the only part of the world where the reality of that conflict can still be recognized."[43] The debate in some cases as in the nineteenth century took on complex dimensions, so that any nimble generalization over the issue raised becomes difficult.[44] Carpenter couches the debate in candid terms by arguing that "the great writers of the American Renaissance carried on a kind of imaginary debate—Emerson, Thoreau and Whitman affirming the beauty of the dream, while Hawthorne and Melville denounced its falsity." He goes on to expound the contention that "the Civil War seemed to establish the final victory of the ideals of democracy and freedom, and to end the matter....[But] the rise of realism in literature and of pragmatism in philosophy emphasized that the problem still existed....”[45] This proves that “myopia is indeed the most profound trait of utopian vision...” and the vital matter lies in the nature of human self which “in action and reaction, in stress and freedom, in assent and denial” confronts experience or recoils from it as the case may be to preserve its sanity in a reiteration of innocence.[46] Despite America’s Puritan inheritance which came to be thought of as “the skeleton in the closet,” America evolved her doctrine of salvation and emancipation through progress. This came to be considered, as Santayana points out, to be the mainstay of her moral optimism.[47] It has been, therefore, obviously difficult for the critics and historians of the Edenic Myth to reconcile it with the numerous offshoots of the Protestant ethic, *viz.,* the success cult, the achievement fetish, and the work mystique. All these are well known to have “condemned” the Americans to labour in order that they would achieve and sustain material well-being.[48] As far back as 1831, de Tocqueville, while visiting the United States, had also a glimpse of this American penchant for “Other-direction” as opposed to “inner-direction” as a mode of conformity.[49] Tocqueville went on to note that the people seemed to “care but little for what has been, but they are haunted by visions of what will be if this their unbounded imagination grows and dilates beyond all measure.”[50] Of course, one must not unthinkingly value the inner-directed person over the other-directed one on the grounds of his independence only. In fact, the inner-directed person is “no less a conformist to others than the other-directed person, but the voices to which he listens are more distant, of an older generation, internalized in his childhood.”[51] The dislocations caused in the American cultural scene due to the notion of progress that adapted all events past and present for its use was doubtless a threat to visions of innocence which the inner-directed person had all along nurtured. For him there were several courses open. To quote Susman: “They might reject history in its currently accepted sense and seek beyond it or apart from it some sense of the importance and meaning of life.”[52] This was the path of Emerson and Thoreau who consistently, in their life and letters, refused to allow rational historical analysis to take away from them the transcendental visions of such basic myths like the one of Adamic or Edenic possibilities for man in the New World Garden. "If history did have a value," Susman emphasizes, "it was not the history as on-going process but rather the study of what might be abstracted from the past as a standard in the present—exactly those transcedent virtues and ideas that were unaffected by the relativities of the historical process itself."[53] It is worthwhile to note that American history had its historic struggle within itself, and that it was basically one between the concept of "the useless past" and the concept of "the usable past."[54] For the Adamic poet it was not so much the pastness of the past but its presentness that matters most, for he had to make a continual effort to regain the lost paradise in the face of all horrors of a world fast degrading into the complexities of an industrial society. This accounts also for the story of the Antinomian controversy which, as it appears, was only meant for setting the record right in America. The leaders who set the ball of this debate rolling in and across America considered that any defense of Puritan America would not only mean the reiteration of the "so-called" official creed with its perpetuation of intolerable social and cultural values and attitudes, but would ultimately thwart the development of the America of their dreams. Thus, it was necessary to find "a useful past, a version of American history and of the nature of history..."[55] so that America would be propelled on to achieve a desirable culture, and thereby "provide the critical tools with which to overthrow the official view..."[56] which, Van Wyck Brooks suggests, put a "talmudic seal" on institutions, values and policies so obviously repellent to the intellectuals in the period after 1890.[57] The area of tension lay somewhere between history and myth, inasmuch as it has been found, as Susman has argued, that much of the story behind the American Experience lies in the confrontation "between established myths and developing ideologies, between the efforts of converting history to mythic ends and of using history in its more traditionally ideological way...."[58] The true nature of the American tradition and the special promise of American life are known to have been exposed to one or the other of the above two approaches to the culture, and for that matter, to the literature of America. The mythic poet as opposed to the Adamic one is more conscious of portraying history as full of "cunning passages, contrived corridors" which, according to the Eliot of *Four Quartets,* presents dangerous traps from which man must escape to achieve freedom in the true sense of the term. This freedom lay in a glorification of faith in God—the myth beyond myth. In the opposite camp, on the other hand, there appears to have been a persistent effort to make the past alive and important in the present, and to insist on a special treatment of America's history in a unique mythopoeic way. Williams, for example, says that the past is made meaningful by the imagination of the artist, and such a past, as he envisages is "our greatest will of inspiration, our greatest hope of freedom...."[59] One may take Frost's poem "The Need of Being Versed in Country Things" as an illustration of this concept. There the scene evokes man's inherent "primal perfection" as exemplified in the innocently simple approach that he can make in viewing himself and his environs in the face of all sophistication of civilization. Thus, the whole situation "is pictured as a community of human and country things in which the light of the fire has become a sunset-glow, the house a flower-like ruin, in which the barn 'would have joined the house in flame,' and the birds seem to sigh for 'what has been.'"[60] This not only shows the poet's consciousness of the beauty of the natural, but also shows his intrinsic love of life. Above all, the poet's insistence on the centrality of man is obvious, for "the need to be versed in country things" is *man's need.* This also proves the validity of Whitman's declaration: "In the centre of all, and object of all, stands the Human Being, towards whose heroic and spiritual evolution poems and everything directly or indirectly tend, Old World or New."[61] The past can, therefore, be recreated not very much by mere retrospection but by re-living it. For the Adamic poet the consciousness of an initiation into the complexities of experience is also a reminder that man's lost innocence after his "fall" need also to be recaptured for creating a balanced state of existence. In fact, the two "counter-forces"and their interaction supply the very essence and vitality so much necessary for poetry if it has to become alive. Rightly here we may refer to Emerson's "History" which starts with the basic premise that human character in all ages has "something" identical in it. It's not the same thing to say that there is a need for being "history-ridden" though we may have the desire "to translate the Then into Now"[62] and to believe in the dictum that "the use of history is to give value to the present hour."[63] The point lies in the necessity, as Emerson would again put it, to achieve "an original relation with the Universe."[64] This is the basic tenet on which "the Adamic Mode" in American poetry appears to have based itself. The Edenic Myth with which this kind of poetry associates itself celebrates life in a particular manner "whereby the moment becomes infinitely larger than itself, and the individual existence escapes from its narrow bounds and finds sanction and consecration."[65] To add to this, the Edenic Myth with "the Adamic Mode" of existence as its basic posture, took on a new dimension as the chosen people of the American colonies had the occasion to look upon "their mission in the wilderness not merely as the continuation of something old, but as the beginning of something new: they were to usher in the final stage of history."[66] The new world was, of course, inherited in a physical sense, but the necessity the colonists felt to see that the most rigorous ideal of the reformation is vindicated, motivated them to begin a new world in a "spiritual sense" as Jonathan Edwards would put it.[67] They engineered themselves to associate the intensity of the drama of their moral and spiritual regeneration with the American "virgin land" which was untouched by the mistakes of the past, and where failure was not only intolerable but also inexcusable. Thus, America was hailed as the "new Canaan," the "second Paradise," the "promised land," or more simply speaking, the "new heaven on earth." In response to a frontier environment and also to a cyclical theory of history, the Americans found that the process of moral regeneration to which they subjected themselves made them capable enough to oppose the corrupt urban culture of Europe, and thereby to see the rising of a civilisation with an agrarian basis that celebrated the simple virtues of the saw and the axe. Ironically enough, the desire to establish a new heaven on earth or to tie spiritual hopes to a plot of land gave rise to a process of dismantling the celestial heaven in favour of the earthly one, so much so that it ultimately meant the death of the "Cultivators of the Earth" with their "glorious public virtue," and the gradual but sure rise of the urban dwellers who fashioned their colonial cities after the European metropolis. This would explain the reasons behind two emergent ways of thinking and feeling among the American writers. If one group demanded freedom from European forms, and emphasized confidence in emotion and spontaneity by preaching in general the necessity for democratic optimism in the Whitman tradition, another championed the cause of discipline by calling for concentration, the rejection of irrelevant moral and political purposes, and the development of conscious intellectual aristocracy. If the former sought "the seeds of literary spring time" in the American soil itself in spite of her crass materialism, vulgarity and hopelessness, the latter believed in the necessity of being an expatriate to seek those "seeds" in the European soil. Among the expatriates some like Ezra Pourd and T.S. Eliot did not only leave America for ever, but also looked on America from a distance with ironic reservations while specifically championing the love of European and other traditions.[68] Others like Robert Frost and William Carlos Williams who went on short visits to European countries might have had the occasion for gaining an insight into, and thereby a love of European tradition, but ultimately they nostalgically turned towards American vitality.[69] Van Wyck Brooks, struggling seriously with this problem as far back as 1914, appealed for a literary renaissance in America. Also, as a corollary to this appeal, Brooks launched his famous attack on the Genteel Tradition so laboriously expounded in his classic book, *America's Coming-of-Age.*[70] All this would clearly show why, time and again, the American poet has chanted his

Adamic songs of innocence in the face of all devastations of human intuition that science with its emphasis on pragmatism and progressivism so rapidly engendered. For him, reality *via* man and Nature has to be apprehended through intuition. In the succeeding Chapters on Frost and Williams it will be demonstrated how their poetry, by and large, incubates this spirit of intuitive apprehension of reality to a major extent.

It is worthwhile to explain here the ambiguous nature of what has been called the myth of America with which "the Adamic Mode" in American literature has been so closely connected. One may begin with Henry Nash Smith who in 1950 differentiated for the first time three separate myths of America. In his book *Virgin Land* he contrasted "the wild west" and its traditional romanticism of "the noble savage" with "the agrarian west" and its cult of utopianism.[71] Smith not only showed the logical conflicts between the two myths, but also explained how and why neither of them could adequately expound the idea behind "the modern myth of America as a new industrial civilization and the colossus of the Western world."[72] The old myths might have affirmed an admirable set of values, but "...they ceased very early to be useful, because they offered no intellectual apparatus for taking account of the industrial revolution."[73] More important is Smith's emphasis that the old "frontier" ideals have continued, perhaps illogically, in the industrial America of to-day. This doubtless gives us a clue to a better understanding of the fact about Frost's choice at various times to lead the secluded life of a "literate farmer,"[74] or of Williams's choice to remain "rooted" to New Jersey, the landscape of which had its idyllic character from the beginning, though it was fast disappearing under the impact of growing industrialism.[75] A further improvement on the thesis of Henry Nash Smith is to be found in R.W.B. Lewis' book *The American Adam.* In that book Lewis does a wonderful job in successfully subsuming the frontiersmen of "the Wild West," and the homesteads who tilled and possessed "the New World Garden," into the master figure of Adam before his fall leading life hopefully and innocently in the balmy days of a peaceful America of the nineteenth century. The "Epilogue" of the book does, however, suggest the American Adam's confrontation of evil which, considered from a broader scale, also indicates the dilemma whether the contemporary Americans can ever find the hopeful sense of life that has become not only difficult to attain but also scarce to find in the technocratic world around them. Lewis' emphasis is, therefore, on "the dichotomy between the agrarian America of a century ago and the industrialised giant of the modern world, even while suggesting the image of Adam to unify the two."[76] The centrality of the fact lies in the American Adam's outgrowing of all hopeful innocence, and his experience of evil. Lewis considers the "fall" to have been partly fortunate, and thereby brings in his thesis to keep in line with ideas that go back to Milton.[77] The old hopefulness being lost, the American Adam had his painful *rite de passage* to maturity that brought a sort of sad wisdom to him, and also a felt consciousness of the ironic nature of all experiences.

To add to this, Leslie A. Fiedler's contribution to a better understanding of the myth of Adamic innocence cannot be lost sight of. In his collection of essays entitled *An End to Innocence* Fiedler takes the myth a step farther by applying it to the modern American world, and thereby giving it a broader area to function. Fiedler attributes the popular success of MacCarthysim to a recognition of the naivete of America's traditional innocence in the face of communist double-dealing which, as is well known, sufficiently disillusioned the liberal idealists of the times. In fact, the "discovery" of America," Fiedler contended, enabled the Europeans to actualise their dream of "unspoilt innocence" in a state of "primal perfection."[78] To them it was a successful condition that projected the image of Rousseau's "noble savage." More so when it got merged and mingled with the concept of "the American farmer" living innocently, and in a way, in an uncultured manner in the New World Garden of America. However, he concludes his thesis with a critical slant by deploring the naive immaturity of those who, by favouring the cult of "unspoilt innocence," do certainly mistake the "ideal" for "reality." It is, therefore, necessary for a writer to praise maturity which comes through a realisation of life's desperate reality. The ideal of primitive innocence and purity which gained literary currency in the nineteenth century has its own inconsistencies as a result of which, said Fiedler, it is inadequate to cope with the trials and tribulations of life. Hence, the maturity of Adam after the "fall," Adam who "died into life," should be the motto for all writers.

If this is taken as a background study of American Experience, it is easier to distinguish, as Robert E. Spiller does in his book *The Cycle of American Literature,* the two distinct though basically interrelated "cycles" of literature in America. The first deals with the well-known romantic and agrarian experience which sprang from the peculiar American condition prevailing in the frontier settlements. The second one is marked with the sense of disintegration, dislocation and disillusion that was caused by the Industrial Revolution, and the subsequent closure of the physical frontier. The cogency of Spiller's argument, giving as it does a section of the two "cycles," lies in suggesting a pattern on the basis of "continuity" which is not entirely inconsistent with the concept of the American Adam as developed by Smith and Lewis. The end of the "first cycle" of American innocence was punctuated with the closing of "the first frontier," and the "second cycle" was marked with an initiation into tragic disillusion that has continued to focus on America's "second frontier" of what has been called "continental industrialism." Significantly enough, Spiller asserts that the old frontier ideals, instead of dying out, have, gained relevance and effectiveness in America's Industrial Civilization. Thus, the concept of innocence has found a fresh pulpit for expression in the "second cycle" of literature in America.

Max Lerner's publication in 1957 of his book *America as a Civilisation* is also important as it gives a similar evolution of the American Adam's "position." The work was incisive in that it emphasized, even more forcefully than Spiller's, the underlying unity of the American spirit and dream pervading the country's literature. He went on to reject the possibility of its discontinuity, and also indicated, not unlike his predecessors, that the old "frontier" ideals have persisted in modern America. His was, however, an improvement on this old thesis of Turner as he transformed it into a new theory of "Extended Genesis." The dominant "motif" in the American experience, he said, lies in a love of perpetual change and renewal giving rise to a nation of "dynamism." Along with the "moving frontier" and the "moving technology" there has been also a furtherance of an American sense of democracy with its emphasis on liberation and freedom from conservatism. What should be stressed here is not the "ecstatic condition" that might have been created by the nation's involvement with the American Dream, but the later disillusionment that converted the old "dream" into "nightmare." As stated by Kenneth S. Lynn,[79] one particular aspect of the American Dream is the "dream of success" which may be grand but, as we see, certainly difficult to attain and realize. And so, the modern impossibility of satisfactorily realizing it has also produced a mood of disillusion.

Several strands of rivalling arguments emerge out of all these considerations on the American Adam's "position" though similarities of approach in some cases cannot be overlooked. Firstly, the American Adam may be imagined as living before the "fall" in the New World Garden of America, and then subsequently to have been exiled to the "East of Eden." Secondly, it may be stated that the American Adam's life in a new land where he eagerly sought to regain a lost paradise by an attempt at purifying a way of life was essentially religious. Thirdly, it is possible to feel that this new Adam was naively innocent, and was consequently immature. Fourthly, the American Adam has perhaps attempted to achieve the highest ideal of Christian innocence[80] which has greater maturity in comparison with cultivating "mere worldly sophistication." Lastly, this mythical figure may have had the occasion to live in a state of noble primitivism seeking to recreate a "primal perfection" in life and Nature.

However, whatever be the nature of the structure of this myth, it is true that it has served certain important functions. It is stated that such a view of man in America may have given solace to people whose lives got consumed by an endless drive for success. It surely gave them rest by inviting them to imagine a world full of peace, harmony and tranquillity.[81] Again the myth has been, to a great extent, a poetic expression of Western man's antique faith in the workability of natural law that clearly validated moral standards which, as conceived by man, seem to have been a bunch of categorical imperatives out-side the periphery of history that provided clear ethical systems with an objective and immutable base.[82] Beginning their poetry with a reverence for "things,"[83] Frost as well as Williams had a belief in the impact of the "natural law" on man, and so they have consistently depicted the innocence of man in a natural, unsophisticated state of life. Learning his own art as a poet from some of the rarest poems of Emerson like "Uriel," Frost taught us the art of seizing a "vantage point" from which one could easily perceive *the natural* without forgetting *the human*. Williams, too, had not only his eye on "things" ["—Say it, no ideas but in things—"],[84] but often by shifting the direction of his poems characteristically expressed "...a love of nature, of people,/ animals,...."[85] It should also be made clear here that neither Frost nor Williams was all out for innocence. In fact, the central situation of a number of their poems bears testimony to the fact that they were aware of "the Danger of Innocence." With the elderly Frost, the defensive mechanism lay in the form of an ironic attitude "against too much love or too boundless a vision of physical or human nature,"[86] which is at the root of all Adamic innocence. When it comes to Williams, particularly his magnum opus *Paterson,* one is also at once aware how the hero is pulled in opposite directions. There is a nostalgia for the beauties of given structures, but there is also an earthward thrust, "toward the flux of raw experience."[87] There is, therefore, a "basic ambiguity" in their quest for an innocence which must be somewhere "hidden," but seem to have been hopelessly "lost." In fact, theirs is a kind of philosopher's style of living which is outwardly simple but inwardly complex. Thoreau wrote: "There are two kinds of simplicity,—one that is akin to foolishness, the other to wisdom. The philosopher's style of living is outwardly simple but inwardly complex. The savage's style of living is both outwardly and inwardly simple."[88] Thus, the "ambiguity" appears both in the language used by Thoreau as indicated above and the imagery of the American Adam as discussed earlier in this Chapter. Though Thoreau preached the ideal of "a wise simplicity," it was perhaps impossible on his part to achieve it as he did not live long enough. More plausibly, he failed to anchor it in the complex economy of his times which he was, in all likelihood, beginning to accept. Both Frost and Williams, who lived considerably longer, came under the impact of the complex economy of our times, though it did not change the basic tenor of their life. After all, Frost spent a valuable period of his life as "poet in residence," and Williams also wrote poetry in the midst of his busy life as a doctor. In fact, they were not oblivious of an alien world encroaching upon their simple pleasures. With Frost, the innocence lay in a craving for the natural surrounding, and for Williams, in a preoccupation with the unspoilt beauty of the American landscape. It is, therefore, evident that the pastoral ideal which is seemingly unpopular to-day has not yet lost its hold upon the native American imagination, and surely enough it has been used to define the meaning of the American ever since the age of discovery. As Ortega Y. Gasset indicated in his book *The Revolt of the Masses,*[89] the whole drive towards agrarianism, and its impact on the national consciousness may have been considered as an impediment to clarity of thought and social progress. Nevertheless, agrarianism, partaking as it does of "primitivism" of a sort, has obviously helped in the growth of "a Nature myth rising up in the midst of a civilized world." Freud's view on a similar state of man in his book *General Introduction to Psychoanalysis*[90] is worth mentioning here. As Leo Marx comments: "...he [Freud] takes up the nostalgic feeling we often attach to the unspoiled landscape as an illustration of our chronic yearning to enjoy 'freedom from the grip of the external world.'"[91] This impulse is also behind all our fantasy-making as the mental realm of "phantasy" reserves the rights to liberate ourselves from the encroaches, of what Freud would call the "reality-principle." Freud refers back again to this in *Civilization and its Discontents*[92] and examines how civilized men, amazingly enough, tend to idealize simple and often primitive conditions of life. Perhaps symptomatic of a "collective neurosis" this tendency is generated by an inherent pastoral desire of man to escape the growing complexity of civilization. Leo Marx's views are worth quoting in full:

> Evidently it is generated by an urge to withdraw from civilization's growing power and complexity. What is attractive in pastoralism is the felicity representated by an image of a natural landscape, a terrain either unspoiled or, if cultivated, rural. Movement toward such a symbolic landscape also may be understood as movement away from an "artificial" world, a world identified with "art," using this word in its broadest sense to mean, the disciplined habits of mind or arts developed by organized communities. In other words, this impulse gives rise to a symbolic motion away from centers of civilization toward their opposite, nature, away from sophistication toward simplicity, or, to introduce the cardinal metaphor of the literary mode, away from the city toward the country.[93]

If this impulse is not properly checked, it may lead to what has been called "a simple-minded wistfulness, a romantic perversion of thought and feeling."[94] Whether the technological-materialist society is condemned by way of a suggestion of "blockage" it creates for the freedom of the "primitivist" is a different question, but the pastoral poet is able to seek a resolution of the conflict between the country and the city by being able to indicate that he is fully conscious of the city's organised power, authority, restraint, and even of its suffering and disorder. Both Frost and Williams have chosen neither an extreme affinity with the country nor with the city. In fact, their ideal has been what Lovejoy calls an embodiment of "semi-primitivism." Locating themselves somewhere "between" the opposing forces of civilization and nature, they were yet in a state of mind to get transcendentally related to both.[95] For example, in some of his poems Frost has the habit of juxtaposing the pastoral element with its "counterforce," and by a process of coaxing the reader, at most without his awareness, extends the implication of a particular idea far beyond its plain presentation. Thus, it achieves philosophic dimension. The poem "A Passing Glimpse" is an illustration of this where "I often see flowers from a passing car/ That are gone before I can tell what they are." He even wants "...to get out of the train and go back/To see what they were beside the track." This leads him to conclude that "Heaven gives its glimpses only to those/Not in position to look too close."[96] The car or the train here disturbs the poet's desire to enjoy the sight of the flowers at close quarters just as Hawthorne, sitting near woods in Concord, Mass., and attending to "pleasing sounds," was not only disturbed, but also, in a way, "alienated" from his immediate source of joy in The Sleepy Hollow when he heard the noise of a passing train. This is not to say that there was "a sense of bifurcation" in Frost or Hawthorne. In fact, the intrusion of the "counterforce" in their pastoral experience enabled them to coherently realize that the character of society has undergone a radical change. It swings to-day between two states of feeling: one partaking of the tranquillity of the Arcadian vision, and the other of the awareness of "reality" in a technocratic materialist society which, to quote Wordsworth, is a token of the "fever of The World." Take, for example, the following lines from Williams's *Paterson* where the pastoral landscape, symbolising some kind of a wild fecundity, is treated as a mythical "figure" lying not only face to face, but also linked in a lover's embrace with the bedraggled and frangmented industrial landscape of the city:

> And there, against him, stretches the low mountain.
> The Park's her head, carved, above The Falls, by the
> quiet river,

> Colored crystals the secret of those rocks;
> farms and ponds, laurel and the temperate wild cactus,
> yallow flowered...facing him, his
>   arm supporting her by the *Valley of the Rocks*, asleep.
> Pearls at her ankles, her monstrous hair spangled with apple-blossoms is scattered about into the back country, waking their dreams—where the deer run and the wood-duck nests protecting his gallant plumage.[97]

In fact, the role of America had its own duality. It seemed to promise all that man had ever wanted, but its ironic counterpoint lay in that it also threatened to obliterate much of what the country already had achieved. Not that this was anything very much "special" about America and her literature. The point is that the discovery of the New World invented such a "tension." And rightly speaking, its relevance as a tradition had its origins in the very basic posture behind such ancient writings as Virgil's first Eclogue where the idea of chaos in the complex life of the countryside people is amply suggested, compelling the attention of the readers away from the quietude of the green, lush surroundings of the countryside. It, is, therefore, obvious that a mature poet's function lies neither in the praise of Nature nor civilization. He strikes a proper balance between them. Particularly important is his ability to strip away the superfluities and defenses of man's everyday life, and to make an endeavour to regain the lost context with the innocent essentials of life, and like Emerson, to make man ask questions for which man was made. In this connection it can be said that the close affinities between magic and modern science are well known, and it is quite relevant to say that

> ...the artificial is but a special, human category of the natural. Mind and nature are in essence one. Nature is all.[98]

Rousseau was, therefore, justified in remarking that neither the savage nor the civilized model can be fully endorsed as an ideal, and that the proper "stance" for mankind would lie in departing from the state of Nature, but never too far into the canyons of commercially motivated life's din and bustle. In other words, all proclivities towards wishful thinking, as Jefferson suggested in his *Notes on Virginia,*[99] should be properly held within the bounds of control by a judicious use of facts pertaining to power. Hence the need for what has been called a "syntax of the middle landscape" which, as suggested by Marx, will not only affirm the primitive values but also will cut itself "loose from an easy acceptance of established ideas and institutions."[100] This "doubleness" of approach that forms the bedrock on which the pastoral ideal stands explains by itself the complex motivations at work in the writings of such pastoralists as Henry Thoreau and Robert Frost. The "simplicity" of American manners is embodied in their works in a peculiarly native language. The style, therefore, becomes distinctively American insofar as its manner of use of idiom and syntax is concerned. A ready example is that of Walt Whitman's poetry which, while absorbing the industrial landscape, and assimilating the forces represented by the machine, takes us back to the origin of things in a simplified, stripped-down natural environs. Take, for example, his main concern in "A Passage to India" in which "the speaker's sense of separation from the past, his fear that he will forget his origins...is dissolved by the familiar, all-assuming logic of *first things first.*"[101] [Italics Mine]. Bringing himself to a point where all manner of doubt in regard to the circular pattern of historical time is dispelled, Whitman envisions the process through which mankind is carried back to realise the innocence in "primal thought." Nature and Man are no longer "disjoined and diffused:"

> ...the voyage of his mind's return,
> To reason's early paradise,
> Back, back to wisdom's birth, to innocent intuitions,
> Again with their creation.[102]

In this "reason's early paradise" and the mind's return to "innocent intuitions," there appears to be no necessity to submit the ego to history and to God to achieve a modicum of "true" definition of one's life. In fact, life's definition may very well lie in life itself. Frost and Williams did not, however, as their poetry would demonstrate, believe that "...the voyage of...mind's return, /To reason's early paradise," is completely achievable or desirable. Thus we find their belief very much rooted in certain ambiguities and contraries which account for a basic "tension" in their poetry. With Frost the process of recognising the "contraries" starts with what he would like to regard as a "swinging" between heaven and the earth. And yet he would also like to compose his "line" of choice: "Me for the hills where I don't have to choose." Williams's startling discovery that poetry is a process of "release" against all "blockage" shows its "Adamic" bias and inclination to accept the "primal innocence" of simple intuitions of the primitive mind. What is important in Williams's belief is best expressed in these lines:

> I cannot stay here
> to spend my life looking into the past: the future is
> no answer[103]...

The emphasis is, therefore, on a personal order with a necessity for renewing the moment by its present potential. No less important is the contrast Williams posed in *Paterson* between the city and the Wilderness, calling the former the male and the latter the female principle of life. A true communication between the two will enable us to make our lives meaningful, releasing for ourselves forces for building a new world. This is how a resolution is arrived at by the two poets, and the objective is more or less set in "a society of the middle landscape, a...nation exhibiting a happy balance of art and nature."[104] Though a tilting of the balance is always imminent and might be expected at any time, and progress may cease to be progress, writers, more or less, have been trying to get the meaning inherent in this contradiction. For the Adamic poet, the very process of exploring the contradiction involves an Odyssey of wonder. Frost's enunciation that "Fact is the sweetest dream that labour knows" or Williams's dictum that the thing precedes the idea become meaningful when analysed with reference to certain variations of meaning associated with the word "Adam." Its early Yahwaist source traces its origin to the Hebrew word *adamah,* meaning "ground" that can again be compared with the Arcadian word *adamu,* meaning "make" or "produce," or *admu,* meaning "child." These details of the origin of the word "Adam,"[105] when connected with one another form into a pattern of thought Adam had thus the sense of wonder of a child with which he viewed Eden's flora and fauna. He was also deeply associated, particularly after his Fall, with the ground—the source of all fecundity. Plausibly enough, he viewed the commonplace facts with an uncommon ardour as does Williams in "The Red Wheelbarrow" or Frost in "Birches" and gave them names for the first time with a child's sense of wonder. This is how the perception of "facts and things" assumed the role of a ritual for them. Imaginative perception of reality transforms the real into the ideal by a process of "loosening and inclusion." The innocent but sub-human, animalistic condition of man could be extremely intolerable without such a perception, which, in one way or the other, emphasizes the need of simple, undelegated experience of life's complexities. Williams, in absorbing the technological landscape, and not forgetting the natural, and Frost, in describing the natural as a "strategic retreat" from civilization, indicate how Nature is one of the chief conditions for the physical and moral well-being of man. A sense of Nature's physical splendour, and idyllic bliss helped articulate the main characteristics of the New Eden concept of America. For quite some time, Norman Foerster says, "the distinction of America, the newness of the New World, was simply Nature."[106] Though Frost and Williams were very much conscious of the sanctity of Nature, and wanted a natural way of life as a cure for modern maladies, they were characteristically different, and did not make the Romantic commitment of accepting "a benign spirit behind the forms of nature through which it manifests itself."[107] Speaking of Frost, V.Y. Kantak elaborates this difference:

> The Wordsworthian affirmation of the Wisdom and Spirit of the universe is alien to his mode. The kindly Genius implicit in nature which plants in man those impulses that

> grow and bring to fullness man's moral and spiritual powers, the instructress whose presence Wordsworth senses as she overlooks his doings over his shoulder or Shelley's 'Plastic Stress' which runs through all the inward impulsion that produces the great magnificence of nature's forms—such convictions are not Frost's.[108]

With Williams, the natural mainly appears as life's "female principle" and its "marriage" with life's "male principle" makes life whole and perfect. In most cases, however, the simple, unsophisticated way of looking at *things as things,* reducing them to their rudiments, is what gives Williams the thrill of the natural. This is how "the plain, old Adam" must have viewed Nature. As indicated earlier in this study, Thoreau, Emerson and Whitman grounded their faith on the conviction that life's emancipation from the trammels of hypocrisy lay in rejecting the Puritan doctrine of inherited sin, and in having a specifically oriented view of man as a noble creature of unlimited potentialities. Belonging as they did to what Lewis has called "the party of hope," the key-term of their "moral vocabulary," including that of their followers and imitators, was "innocence."[109] Though the influence of this group, in one way or the other (as of Emerson on Frost, and of Whitman on Williams), has been considerable, it is significant to note how the two poets under study freed themselves from its impact, and wrote poetry of a different kind.[110] The poetic ambiguity in their poetry, particularly their involvement with "the syntax of the middle landscape," joins them with the tradition of dualism in American thought. Their seeing of "evil" in Nature, and also in human nature would indicate their recognition of the sinful, weak, and "fallen" condition of man. However, thematically speaking, their poetry is not without its quest for "innocence" in certain areas. It has been said, of course, that "the American as Adam has been replaced by the American as Laocoon." and that the Emersonian figure—"the plain old Adam, the simple genuine self"—has been frowned out of existence.[111] But it is equally worthwhile to note that man's attempt to recapture "innocence" is never-ending, and as indicated by us earlier in this Chapter, there is always a rebirth of innocence after every shock, though the struggle for it may appear hopeless and even impossible. Adam's expulsion from the Garden of Eden, and God's placing of the angel of the flaming sword to keep vigil on the Tree of Life is allegorically complicated with the hurdles that man has to face in his undertaking to regain Edenic "innocence." Hence the justification for calling this quest "ambiguous," and, after all, what is important is the quest, and not the possibility or impossibility of achieving "innocence." No doubt, it is a representative situation, and we should note, as suggested by Heilman "the discrepancy between dream and actuality, between the ideal we can visualize, and the instinctive and the habitual ways of life that yield only partly to the ideas."[112] Thomas A. Krueger's "critique" on the Adamic myth of "innocence" reveals that "the myth's historians have focussed primarily on its content and on its relation to major historical development."[113] What is required is a satisfactory exploration and description of "its relation to the history of American society."[114] In other words, apart from the evidence for its existence that can be collected from the rambling, and often cursory writings of American intellectuals, there is a great necessity "for recovering the Judaeo-Christian tradition into an evocative story for widespread distribution"[115] among the masses of people. Christopher Lasch in his book *The New Radicalism in America,* 1889-1963: *The Intellectual as a Social Type* (1965) makes some such attempt to study the response of the intellectuals to the myth so as to work out a "tradition" which can be wholesomely accepted by the public. Though interesting, the work appears to be unsystematic, which makes it difficult to find any proof whether or not the ordinary men and women could share the intricacies of the intellectual exercises involved in the deliberations. It is, therefore, more plausible, that the myth was the intellectuals' own creation. "Ordinary men and women," Krueger makes a sweeping observation, "may have showed the self images of the poets, novelists, and other publicists who entertained Edenic [Adamic] visions about America or they may not have."[116] Pertinent questions may, therefore, be asked in general whether at one time or the other immigrants, workers, the proletariat, blacks in slavery or in ghettos, Orientals and Puerto Ricans crowding themselves in slums, Chicanes and Indians on reservations did ever have even a glimpse of that vision of a second paradise in America. It has been said that in New England, "it [the Edenic Myth] ran into competing myths and it never fully adapted [itself] to the area's rugged terrain and harsh climate."[117] Standing outside of heirarchically organised "uptight," "straight" society, the American Adam, in spite of all his innocence and beauty, seems to fit less into some of the conflicting issues of our time, particularly, for example, the one of South's black subordination and white supremacy, though themes of innocence and perfection appear in Southern literature from time to time to indicate the existence, of what may be called a society of classless harmony.[118] Of course, the myth seems to have a greater, and more dominant cultural impact in the Mississippi Ohio Valley and in the Far West.[119] Moreover, the gynophobia of the myth can hardly endear it to conscientious American women, excepting to those who believe in some kind of "a sanctity in easy sexual *mores*" as the revitalizing force of life. The aged people's reaction to it is also sharply different from that of the young people's. For example, it is common to find that those who are old get stricken with fear in the face of impending death, though the young may cling to the idea of death with expectation of "dreams of bliss." All these have therefore, led quite a considerable number of historians of the Edenic Myth to express deep discontent over its failure to interpret American Experience, beginning with Peter Schmitt's "gentle mockery" through R.W.B. Lewis' evidently "ambivalent attitude," to David Noble's "shrill, uncompromising hostility." Moreover to describe the Edenic experience as a phenomenon of "myth" is like giving it a sort of negative connotation of falsehood. The critics are, therefore, inclined to believe that the Edenic Myth may not possibly guide the twentieth-century man through his search for truth in a period of crisis. However, Henry

Nash Smith's paper "Virgin Land Revisited," presented before the American Literature Section of the Modern Language Association in December 1972,[120] reconsiders this point in an intellectually pertinent manner. Drawing heavily on Edwin Fussell's thesis in *Frontier: American Literature and the American West* (1965) and also that of Leslie Fiedler's in *The Return of the Vanishing American* (1968), he concludes that there ought to be a new intellectual system which he had earlier declared to be necessary at the end of his book *Virgin Land*. One may venture the opinion that a *via media* could help us, that is, we might hope fruitfully to attain Edenic bliss if we cultivated the habit of dynamically interplaying in our life the counterpoints of law—freedom, society—solitude, Nature—civilization, etc. This is, of course, done by a huge number of Americans. Their "mystique" of "camping out" enables them to dedicate no less than two Summer weeks to eking out subsistence in a quasi frontier situation. This is done, as is well known, not for any financial gains but for forming character, achieving identity and creating a system of value by a positive response to the wilderness.

There may be historical evidence against the Edenic Myth, but it must be noted for the purpose of our present study that the myth's "operational field" is not totally lost, though there seems to have been a disjunction between modern and primitive societies. One may take, for example, the new born child to be an Adamic figure. It is "outside tradition, history, and society...," though all its innocence will be lost when it gradually but steadily gets accultured to our community's collective memory and social hierarchy.[121] So also our memories of various facets of early childhood evoke blissful expectations of an Edenic kind. Moreover, most of us after having our *rite de passage* to maturation in mind and heart formulate our own form of "retreat" from the grim realities of life. This "internal expatriation" may turn itself on any "decision," beginning with the one of Richard Hoffstader's to lead an academic life in the isolation of libraries, to Frost's decision to stay on in farms and with poetry resigning coveted "teaching positions," and to

Williams's life-long devotion to Rutherford in an attempt to get at "the universal through the particular." So long as men seek a state of perfection beyond the impurities, complexities and horrendous situations around them, they are just enacting the role of the American Adam to seek "innocent bliss" in isolation from the tortures of what has been called "tripartrite time."

NOTES

1. Narinder Singh Pradhan, "Edenic Themes in Modern American Drama," Dissertation. Univ. of Utah, 1972, p. iv.
2. Wilfred L. Querin, Earle G. Labor, Lee Morgan, John R. Willingham, *A Handbook of Critical Approaches to Literature* (New York: Harper & Row, 1966), p. 144.
3. Quoted *ibid.*
4. Richard Niebuhr, *The Kingdom of God in America* (New York: Hapre r & Brothers, 1937), p. 26.
5. Frederic T. Carpenter, *American Literature and the Dream* (New York: Philosophical Library, 1955), p. 6.
6. See Charles Roberts Aldrich, *The Primitive Mind and Modern Civilization* (London: Kegan Paul, Trench, Trubner & Co. Ltd., 1931), p. 21. From Aldrich's study it can be concluded that at birth, no essential difference can be marked between modern man and his primitive ancestors. His education is a sort of coating, beneath which he remains simply man—the same kind of creature as his remote forebears who wore skins or leaves and, for want of sophisticated knowledge, read his own consciousness into natural phenomena.
7. Charles L. Sanford, *The Quest for Paradise: Europe and the American Moral Imagination* (Urbana: Univ. of Illinois Press, 1961), p. 104.
8. J. Hector St. John de Crevecoeur, *Letters from an American Farmer* (1782; rpt. New York: Fox, Auffield & Company, 1904).
9. See Lawrence, *Studies in Classic American Literature,* p. 5. Lawrence states: "America has never been easy, and is not easy to-day. Their liberty is a thing of sheer will, sheer tension: a liberty of THOU SHALT NOT. And it has been so from the first. The land of THOU SHALT NOT."
10. R.W.B. Lewis, *The American Adam* (Chicago: Univ. of Chicago Press 1955), p. 5.
11. *Ibid.*, p. 91.
12. Pearce, *The Continuity of American Poetry,* p. 430.
13. Fiedler, *An End to Innocence: Essays on Culture and Politics*, p. 24.
14. David Madden, "True Believers, Atheists and Agnostics," in *American*

Dreams, American Nightmares, ed. David Madden (Carbondale: Southern Illinois Univ. Press, 1970), p. xxxix.

15. *Ibid.*
16. John F. Lynen, *The Pastoral Art of Robert Frost* (New Haven: Yale Univ. Press, 1960), p. 20.
17. *Ibid.*, p. 29.
18. See Sister M. Bernetta Quinn, *The Metamorphic Tradition in Modern Poetry* (New Brunswick, N.J.: Rutgers Univ. Press, 1955), pp 89-106.
19. *Paterson*, p. 20.
20. In the twentieth century the myth has taken on different dimensions. It has lived on in wilderness and outdoor cults, in the popular faith in the essential innocence of American foreign policy, in periodic but timely renewals of belief in the promise of American life. Roderick Nash, *Wilderness and the American Mind* (New Haven: Yale Univ. Press, 1967), pp. 141 ff. Peter J. Schmitt, *Back to Nature: The Arcadian Myth in Urban America* (New York: Oxford Univ. Press, 1969), pp. 169-89. Also see Sanford *Quest for Paradise,* pp. 228 ff.
21. See Jesper Rosenmeir, "New England's Perfection: The Image of Adam and the Image of Christ in the Antinomian Crisis, 1634 to 1638," *The William and Mary Quarterly,* 26 (Spring 1953), 361-382.
22. Quoted in Max Lerner, *America as a Civilization: Life and Thought in the United States To-day* (New York: Simon and Schuster, 1957), p. 62.
23. Quoted *ibid.*, p. 62.
24. See David W. Noble, *The Eternal Adam and the New World Garden: The Central Myth in the American Novel since* 1830) (New York: George Braziller, 1968), p. 225.
25. *Ibid.*
26. Quoted *ibid.*
27. See Lewis, *The American Adam,* p. 183.
28. *Ibid.*
29. See Henry F. May, *The End of American Innocence* (New York: Alfred A. Knopff, 1959), pp. 9ff.
30. See *Ibid.*, pp. 387ff.
31. Though some have celebrated and glorified this "innocence," others have found fault with it, and have depicted its gradual destruction caused either by man's rejection of life and God, or by the machinations of an evil Universe.
32. See John Locke, "An Essay concerning the True Original, Extent and End of Civil Government: Second Treatise on Civil Government," in *Social Contract: Essays by Locke, Hume and Rousseau,* introd. by Sir Ernest Barker (New York: Oxford Univ. Press, 1960), p. 29.

33. William Carlos Williams, *In The American Grain* (Norfolk, Conn.: New Directions, 1956), pp. 45-58, 105-29, 130-39.
34. James E. Breslin, *William Carlos Williams: An American Artist* (New York: Oxford Univ. Press, 1970), p. 115.
35. *Ibid.*
36. Williams, *In the American Grain,* p. 53.
37. Breslin, *William Carlos Williams,* p. 114.
38. "Birches," *Complete Poems of Robert Frost,* p. 153.
39. Williams, *In the American Grain,* p. 33.
40. Breslin, *William Carlos Williams,* p. 99.
41. Crevecoeur, *Letters,* p. 54. Also the letter entitled "What is an American," pp. 48-91.
42. See David W. Noble, *The Paradox of Progressive Thought* (Minneapolis: Univ. of Minnesota Press, 1958), pp. 3-33.
43. Fiedler, *An End to Innocence,* p. 128.
44. See Ihab H. Hassan, "The Idea of Adolescence in American Fiction," *American Quarterly,* 10, No. 3 (Fall 1958), 312-324.
45. Frederick I. Carpenter, *American Literature and the Dream,* p. 9.
46. Ihab H. Hassan, *Radical Innocence: Studies in the Contemporary Novel* (Princeton, N.J.: Princeton Univ. Press, 1961), p. 4.
47. George Santayana, *Character and Opinion in the United States* (New York: George Braziller, 1955), p. 116.
48. See Irvin G. Wyllie, *The Self-made Man in America: The Myth of Rags to Riches* (New York: The Free Press, 1954), pp. 87ff.
49. See Chapters 3, 4 and 5 of David Riesman, Nathan Glazer and Reuel Denney, *The Lonely Crowd: A Study of the Changing American Character.* (New Haven: Yale Univ. Press, 1950), p. 492. Also Carl N. Degler, "The Sociologist as Historian: Riesman's *The Lonely Crowd.*" *American Quarterly,* 15, No. 4 (Winter 1963), 483-497.
50. Quoted in F.O. Mathiessen, *The Responsibilities of the Critic* (New York: Oxford Univ. Press, 1952), p. 142.
51. Riesman, *The Lonely Crowd* p. 48.
52. Warren I. Susman, "History and the American Intellectual: Uses of a usable Past," *American Quarterly,* 16, No. 2, pt. 2 (Summer 1964), 251.
53. *Ibid.*
54. See Warren I. Susman, "The Useless Past: American Intellectuals and the Frontier Thesis, 1910-1930," *Bucknell Review,* 11 (March 1963), 1-20.
55. See Susman, "History of the American Intellectual: Uses of a Usable Past," p. 258.

56. *Ibid.*
57. *Ibid.*
58. *Ibid.*, 247.
59. Williams, *In the American Grain,* p. 189.
60. Reuben A. Brower, *The Poetry of Robert Frost: Constellations of Intention* (New York: Oxford Univ. Press, 1963), p. 79.
61. Quoted in F.O. Mathiessen, *American Rensissance: Art and Expression in the Age of Emerson and Whitman* (Delhi: Oxford Univ. Press, 1973), pp. 587-88.
62. *Ibid.*, pp. 626-27.
63. *Essays: First and Second Series,* p. 11.
64. *Ibid.*
65. Mathiessen, *American Renaissance,* p. 629.
66. Charles L. Sanford, "An American *Pilgrim's Progress,*" *American Quarterly,* 6, No. 4 (Winter 1954), 301. See also Chapters 3 and 7 of Sanford, *The Quest for Paradise.*
67. See Jonathan Edwards, *The Works of Jonathan Edwards,* ed. John E. Smith (1843; rpt. New Haven: Tale Univ. Press, 1959), II, 206. Edwards puts: "...this spiritual sense is immensely the most noble and excellent...without which all other principles of perception...are useless and vain..."
68. See Chapters 11 and 12 of Van Wyck Brooks, *Scenes and Portraits: Memories of Childhood and Youth* (New York: E.P. Dutton & Company, Inc., 1954). For a more comprehensive account of this, see also James M. Cox, ed. *Robert Frost: A Collection of Critical Essays* (Englewood Cliffs, N.J.: Prentice-Hall, Inc., 1962), pp. 54-57.
69. For a better "over-view" of this necessity, see Malcolm Cowley, *Exile's Return: A Literary Odyssey of the 1920s* (New York: The Viking Press, 1951), pp. 289ff. Cowley remarks tellingly: "A generation of American writers went out into the world like the children in Grimm's fairy tales who ran away from a cruel step-mother. They wandered for years in search of treasure and then came back like the grown children to dig for it at home." p. 289.
70. See Van Wyck Brooks *America's Coming-of-Age* (Garden City, N.Y.: Double day, 1958), pp. 20 ff.
71. See Henry Nash Smith, *Virgin Land: The American West as Symbol and Myth* (Cambridge: Harvard Univ. Press, 1950), Chapt. I.
72. Frederick I. Carpenter, " 'The American Myth': Paradise (To Be) Regained," *PMLA,* 74 (1959), 599.
73. *Ibid.*
74. The Robert Frosts had known isolation and privacy in Derry, Plymouth and Franconia, and even during their English sojourn. See Elizabeth

Shepley Sergeant, *Robert Frost: The Trial by Existence* (New York: Holt, Rinehart and Winston, 1960), p. 169.

75. See James Guimond, *The Art of William Carlos Williams: A Discovery and Possession of America* (Urbana: Univ. of Illinois Press, 1968), p. 169.
76. Carpenter, "'The American Myth': Paradise (To Be) Regained," 599.
77. See Pradhan, "Edenic Thomas in Modern American Drams, pp. 103 ff.
78. See Fiedler, *An End to Innocence, pp. 208-10.*
79. See Kenneth S. Lynn. *The Dream of Success: A Study of the Modern American Imagination* (1955; rpt. West Port, Conn.: Greenwood Press, Inc., 1972).
80. "Harmless as doves and wise as serpents," *The Bible.*
81. See Arthur P. Dudden, "Nostalgia and the American," *Journal of the History of Ideas* (Oct.–Dec. 196), 515-530.
82. Frank R. Kramer, *Voices in the Valley: Mythmaking and Folk Belief in the Shaping of the Middle East* (Madison: Univ. of Wisconsin Press, 1964), pp. 176-77.
83. Frost's attention to "facts," which make him the Thoreauian naturalist that he was, is well known. For a broader idea on this subject see Brower, *Constellations of Intention,* pp. 83ff.

    A majority of Williams's poems do also show consistently how he wanted to have an unmediated encounter with "things." For a better grasp on the subject, see Breslin, *William Carlos Williams,* pp. 51ff.
84. *Paterson,* p. 14.
85. Williams, "Asphodel, That Greeny Flower," *William Carlos Williams Reader,* p. 72.
86. Brower, *Constellations of Intention,* p. 110.
87. Breslin, *William Carlos Williams,* p. 171.
88. Quoted from Thoreau, *Works,* 11, 420, by Leo Stoller, "Thoreau's Doctrine of Simplicity," *N.E.Q.,* 29 (Dec. 1956), 457. See also Leo Stoller, *After Walden: Thoreau's Changing Views on Economic Man* (Stanford, Calif: Stanford Univ. Press, 1957).
89. Jose Ortega Y. Gasset, *The Revolt of the Masses,* trans. anon (London: Allen & Unwin Ltd., 1932), p. 44.
90. Sigmund Freud, *A General Introduction to Psychoanalysis* trans. Joan Riviere (New York: Washington Square Press, 1952), p. 325.
91. Leo Marx, *The Machine in the Garden: Technology and the Pastoral Ideal in America* (New York: Oxford Univ. Press, 1964), p. 8.
92. Sigmund Freud, *Civilisation and its Discontents,* trans. Joan Riviere (New York: J. Cape & H. Smith, 1930), p. 44.
93. Marx, *The Machine in the Garden,* pp. 9-10.

94. *Ibid.*, p. 10.
95. Arthur O. Lovejoy, *et al.*, *A Documentary History of Primitivism and Related Ideas* (Baltimore: Johns Hopkins Press, 1935), p. 369.
96. "A Passing Glimpse," *Complete Poems of Robert Frost,* p. 311.
97. *Paterson,* p. 17.
98. Marx, *The Machine in the Garden,* p. 67.
99. William Peden, ed. *Thomas Jefferson, Notes on the State of Virginia* (Chapel Hill: Univ. of North Carolina Press, 1955), pp. 111 ff.
100. Marx, *The Machine in the Garden,* p. 121.
101. *Ibid.*, p. 224.
102. "A Passage to India," in *The Poetry & Prose of Walt Whitman,* p. 384.
103. *Paterson,* pp. 172-173.
104. Marx, *The Machine in the Garden,* p. 226.
105. See James Muilenberg, "Adam and Second Adam," in *A Handbook of Christian Theology* (New York: Living Age Books, 1958), p. 11.
106. Norman Foerster, *Nature in American Literature* (New York: Macmillan, 1923), p. 5.
107. V.Y. Kantak, "Poetic Ambiguity in Frost," *Western Humanities Review,* 28, No. 1 (Winter 1974), 36.
108. *Ibid.*
109. Lewis, *The American Adam,* p. 7.
110. See Lawrence Thomson, "Robert Frost" & John Malcolm Brinnin "William Carlos Williams," in Leonard Unger, ed. *Seven Modern Poets* (1967; rpt. Allahabad: A.H. Wheeler & Co. Pvt. Ltd., 1971), pp. 42-43, 88.
111. Lewis, *The American Adam,* p. 195.
112. Robert B. Heilman, "The Dream Mctaphor," in *American Dreams and American Nightmares,* p. 17.
113. Thomas A. Krueger, "The Historians and the Edenic Myth: A Critique,"*The Canadian Review of American Studies,* 4, No. 1 (Spring 1973), 8.
114. *Ibid.*
115. *Ibid.*
116. Krueger, "The Historians and the Edenic Myth," 8. See also Rush Walter, "The History of Ideas in Europe: An essay in Redifinition," *The Journal of American History,* 51, No. 4 (March 1965), 603. Walter Observes: "Yet they have also treated them as ideas, in that they have neither reduced them to byproducts of historic events nor submerged them in the spirit of their age," & Fred Matthews, "The 'Myth' and 'Value' approaches to American Studies," *The Canadian Review of American Studies,* 3, No. 2 (Fall 1972), 114-15. Matthews comments: "The

assumption that literature does express cultural values reliably was then used, without much overt discussion, to resolve the problem of representativeness, allowing us to proceed on the *unanalysed assumption* that selected literature embodies essential sociology, that it was possible to extrapolate from literature to literary myths to values to direct statements about the society in which the literature was created." [Italics Mine] & Bruce Kuklick "Myth and Symbol in American Studies," *American Quarterly,* 24 (October 1972), 444-45. Kuklick states: "...We are left with a second large question—the relation of 'popular culture' to ordinary life. The 'literate public' that reads popular books is much larger in number than the intellectuals whose behaviour we initially wanted to explain. Nonetheless, this public is by no means everyone, and without hesitation American studies scholarship has jumped from the 'literate public' to everyone."

117. Krueger, "The Historians and the Edenic Myth," 9.

118. See Louis Martz. *The Liberal Tradition in America: An Interpretation of American Political Thought Since the Revolution* (New York: Harcourt, Brace & World, Inc., 1955). Hart says: "If the trouble with Southern slave society had merely been that it did not fit the American liberal formula, as historians have often noted, its ideologists might not have had so hard a time. But the real trouble with it was that it did not fit any formula, any basic categories of Western social theory," p. 147, and F. Carven Davenport, Jr., *The Myth of Southern History: Historical Consciousness in Twentieth-Century Southern Literature* (Nashville: Vanderbilt Univ. Press, 1967), pp. 11-12. "Furthermore, Southerners who have explored this theme have incorporated into it a suggestion that because of this peculiar uniqueness the South has a peculiar vital contribution to make to the national life," p. 11.

119. See Smith, *Virgin Land* & Arthur K. Moore, *The Frontier Mind: A Cultural Analysis of Kentucky Frontiersman* (Lexington: Univ. of Lexington Press, 1957).

120. "Virgin Land Revisited," *Indian Journal of American Studies,* 3, No. 1 (June 1973), 83-90.

121. Krueger, "The Historians and the Edenic Myth," 11.

4

Frost: "Directive" to the Wilderness and Innocence

THE ANALYSES in the last three Chapters have not only posed significant questions, but also have enabled us to seek answers in our evaluation of "the Adamic Mode" as a poetic process in relation to its history and nature of operation in American poetry. It has been observed that it is a special kind of creative act as opposed to "the mythic Mode" in poetry. In it the poet, while defining his own self in a peculiarly egocentric way, finds no specific necessity to test his poem's subject-matter by a reference to God, religion or culture in the traditional manner. In the other hand his reference to God, religion or culture may be highly "personal" and what is, perhaps, unacceptable from the point of view of traditional Christianity, it may be at times ironical also. Like Robert Frost or William Carlos Williams, he may feel the importance of a "primitive charm" inherent in the basic innocence of "things" and "facts," though their "terrifying aspect" is not totally forgotten. Celebrating America as an independent country—a New World Garden—free from the social sins and shackles of Europe these poets have not only catalogued and given local habitation and a name to their own land's flora and fauna, but also have emphasized that an Adamic simplicity, innocence and naturalness lie embedded at the source of all "things" and "facts," and our failure to seize it, to go back to it at least temporarily from the centre of civilization, is the root-cause of most conflicting situations. This may be one of the reasons why Williams at one period of his career as a poet wanted to present "still" lives in their own right to create a vision of "first things first," as Whitman would have put it. Frost's insistence on facts as the source of sweetest dreams of labouring men reminds us of Adam whose condemnation to a life of labour after being expelled from paradise turned, in fact, to "a labour of love" as it engendered in him the desire not only to work for his living, but also to achieve grace through his own "natural capacity."[1] Also, it has been pointed out that the Adamic figure is a figure in isolation, perhaps often in love with it; and yet isolation does not mean total and complete separation from the world of man.

In the light of these findings we propose here to evaluate Robert Frost, the poet and man who, it is felt, falls into a larger pattern of American consciousness, untarnished by the growing industrialism of our time. First, one may try to clarify the definition of an American, for such a definition will help us in our evaluation of Frost and his poetry in a more definite manner.

An amalgamation of all nations, the American, as Crevecoeur put it in 1782, was a "new man" who left behind him "all his ancient prejudices and manners" in order to enable himself to make a new beginning in human existence. There has been no stopping in this desire to attain a condition of innocence. As we have seen in our discussion in the last Chapter, it culminated in the American desire for a Westward movement till the last Frontier was explored. Thoreau wished to "start now on that farthest western way which does not pause at the Mississippi…."[2] Whitman's open road theme of manifest destiny gave also an imaginative expression to how the "society and literature of the United States…. must turn away from the feudal past of Europe to build a new order founded upon nature…."[3] It had the same motif as is found in the romantic heritage of restoring man's lost harmony with Nature. In fact, the Atlantic sea-board represented the sophistication of a city-civilization under the shadow of Europe, and the geographical mass of the continent beyond the Mississippi towards the Pacific symbolized not only man's democratic spirit, but also human existence at its most innocent—unspoilt by the artificial *mores* of civilization.

All civilization, as Freud put it, begins with a desire to subdue the instinctive nature of man. In extreme cases this gives rise to highly "uptight" cultures. The Americans, as history reveals, have been the "pioneers" in our time in creating the twentieth—century technocratic society that believes in human enlightenment through science, but it was evident from the nature, and perhaps, the manner of the progress of their history that they would be the first to revolt and emphasize a new liberated life-style based on a blunt affirmation that the natural state of man is the secret of "life's ecstasy," as Allan Watts has put it in an incisive article entitled "The Future of Ecstasy." More pointed is, of course, Lewis Mumford's *The Pentagon of Power* (1970) that shows how in our days different social institutions have precipitated in the undermining of the dignity of man instead of raising it. Milton R. Konvitz puts it more eloquently in drawing our attention to how this "dirty job" is done variously by industry with dull work, scholarship with deadening bureaucracy, and lastly, art, literature and music with their cults of "anti-life."[4] This has, therefore, given rise to a rapid growth of certain "sub-cultures" in America where one discovers a changing attitude in man's life to pass from power to plenitude, from mere affluence to the fullness of life. In the face of the complexities of America's industrialized , science-based society, this appears to be an apt modulation of the very basic pattern of what has been stated from time to time in the earlier Chapters as the Americans' quest for lost innocence—the Edenic Paradise. Such a pattern of culture is no mere self-indulgence. It explores an ego that is all within, such an ego, to quote Pearce, as "guarantees its own continuing existence; and it reveals its meaning to itself in the creative acts it performs out of its rock-bound faith in its own ability…."[5] The American has thus a faith in himself. His "fecund power" to know himself, to see, hear or feel every moment of his life, even the evil in reality, has enabled him to sing his twentieth-century Adamic song:

> So many selves, so many sensuous worlds,
> As if the air, the midday air, was swarming

> With the metaphysical changes that occur,
> Merely in living as and where we live.[6]

Robert Frost who preferred to be rooted in the American culture, unlike expatriates like Ezra Pound and T.S. Eliot,[7] created a universal art with a high "locative" bias, and singularities of place. Lawrence's statement that "all creative art must rise out of a specific soil and flicker with a spirit of place"[8] becomes highly relevant when we underscore Frost's dependence on New England for evolving the subject-matter of his poems.

With these ideas in mind a consideration of Frost's poetry with a knowledge of his critical canons will bear testimony, as it shall be shown in the succeeding lines, that Frost is consistently pre-occupied with "the Adamic Mode" in American poetry. A knowledge of what he has to say on poetry *vis-a-vis* his own experimentation in that field will be helpful as a starting-point for our enquiry.

Though quite akin to Eliot in his distrust of sentimentality, feeling for conservatism and a belief in the "necessity for objectivity in art, and of the artist's interaction with the past."[9] Frost held opinions on the artist's "creative moment" that connect him with our view of "the Adamic Mode" in poetry as discussed in Chapter I.

Frost talked of "enthusiasm" in poetry, but was also one who sincerely meant to force it through the "prism" of metaphor. For that matter, as he wrote to Sidney Cox, "a subject must be an object"[10] as the poet holds it clearly outside of himself. This way Frost may seem to be reiterating the mythic poet's emphasis on poetry as "an escape from emotion."[11] Though there is always a necessity for this, as Frost's approach to themes in his poetry would show, Frost is, perhaps, a little too uncomfortable when a poet makes a cause of it. Commenting on a poem by John Erskine, Frost concludes:

> But why to objectify the idea and put it far enough away from yourself must you put it away off in antiquity and say it in heroes and gods. Why must you every time, I mean. All right for this poem; but why not next time say

> it in modern people. It is like diffidence, shyness, this remoteness in time and space. Get over it and you can break in on the age with your strength and insight.[12]

These comments on Erskine's unpublished poem "Metaneira" shows Frost's concern for giving a stamp of individuality to poems while attributing to their themes a local habitation and a name. It is also a clear indication of his dislike for some of the convictions of the mythic poet, particularly the one of using mythical heroes and gods to expound a potential poetic theme. He is, therefore, Adamically determined to have his own way of thinking great thoughts. There is, no doubt, something innocent about it as he bothers in the least whether he was in a historical position to feel that his artistic purpose established a contact with any urgency of cause, or for that matter, "grievances," deeply felt and championed by the *avant-garde* group of twentieth-century writers. More concerned with human "griefs," and avoiding very much the social and political credos of the 1920's, Frost, unlike Eliot and a host of his followers, thought that "we have no way of knowing that this age is one of the worst in the world's history." It will not be, therefore, modest enough for a man "to think of himself as going down before the worst forces ever mobilized by God."[13] The tone in the lines just quoted is one of Adamic individuality as Frost prescribes what should be man's self-defence in the face of God's machinations and even those of man's. It may be "humour," but preferably it should be "irony," for any form of "humour" goes on to show a touch of fear and inferiority, and even a good amount of cowardice.[14]

A judicious reference to Frost's self-definition through his creative imagination would mean, first of all, and particularly from about 1925 on, a growing interest in establishing a certain kind of correspondence between poetry and life. While talking of belief in God, Frost is also interested in fixing confidence in the self-belief, the belief of love and literary belief.[15] This again shows his Adamic freedom of choice in entertaining an ambiguous attitude towards the problem of existence because such an attitude is the *only thing* possible in a mysterious universe. This is how "his *will* braved alien entanglements." [Italics Mine]. The ease with which he liberated "form" from its traditional "constrictions" gives us an impression that "form" is indeed the road to "freedom," which, for him, is "nothing but departure." Thus, "the creative possibilities were staggering," and "what mattered, as he came more and more to extract himself from his material, was 'performance,' the self-definition achieved by means of technical mastery."[16]

However, Frost's "poetic impulse" that enabled him to define himself as an individual cannot be generalized. Lawrance Thompson notes its ambiguity and emphasizes its operational interaction of opposites. Sometimes, his emotional reaction to an experience is worked out into a provoking thought *via* a telling metaphor as he does, for example, in "Stopping by Woods on a Snowy Evening." At other times, he begins with a sudden perception that smacks of intellectuality, but working it out through analogy, he reaches an emotionally vibrating afterglow.[17] This is particularly applicable to poems like "For Once, then, Something." Though Frost never wanted to "worry a poem into existence," he never forgot the value of "working out a poem" which he would have been delighted to name as the "facility of performance in an act of clarification."

Judging Frost's poetry in the light of the Adamic poet's emphasis on "the operation of the creative imagination as an act of self-definition,"[18] one is struck by Frost's manner of discussion on the nature of poetic creation. The "mood" or "moment" that accompanies poetic creation would act as the initial inspirations, for a poet's "performance" would not operate in a state of vacuum. Frost's clarification of this point in a latter to Louis Untermeyer establishes the importance of the "creative moment"—the moment of grace or intuition:

> A poem is never a put-up job so to speak. It begins as a lump in the throat, a sense of wrong, a homesickness, a lovesickness. It is never a thought to begin with. It is at its best when it is a tantalizing vagueness.[19]

A close analysis of the lines stated above will reveal that a poet's creative act begins with a tantalising perception of something, may be, "a sense of wrong," "a homesickness" or "a love-sickness." As such, it may also be equated with the basic style in which the Adamic poem is conceived and created—a style that "portrays the simple, separating inwardness of man as that which at once forms and is formed by the vision of the world in which it has its being."[20] "The simple, separating inwardness" begins with a tantalising perception and matures, while the poem is created, into a vision of the world. Concerned with the nature of poetic communication, Frost has his most famous and sustained metaphor for poetry carefully stated and fully developed in "The Figure a Poem Makes." Adam's perception of the flora and fauna in the Garden of Eden must have begun in delight, but surely enough it ended in wisdom. Here is Frost on what a poem must begin with, and to what a poem should aspire:

> It begins in delight and ends in wisdom. The figure is the same as for love. No one can really hold that the ecstasy should be static and still in one place. It begins in delight, it inclines to the impulse, it assumes direction with the first line laid down, it runs a course of lucky events, and ends in a clarification of life—not necessarily a great clarification, such as sects and cults are founded on, but in a momentary stay against confusion.[21]

This is, then, Frost's lyrical description of the nature of poetic creation. However, he also expounds "his almost existential concept of the way a poem transcends its original idea and creates itself through the very struggle with the discipline of form."[22] Even then, Frost is not oblivious of the poet's fate of being entranced to an "exact premonition" of "something" that touches him emotionally to begin with:

> The freshness of a poem belongs absolutely to its not having been thought out and then set to verse as the verse in turn might be set to music. A poem is the emotion of having a thought while the reader waits a little anxiously for the success of dawn. The only discipline to begin with

> is the inner mood that at worst may give the poet a false start or two like the almost microscopic filament of cotton that goes before the blunt thread-end and must be picked up finest by the eye of the needle. He must be entranced to the exact premonition.[23]

This way in writing poetry it might seem that Frost was only conscious of "the inner mood" that determines the creative act in any art. But his assertion of the uncertain nature of the poet's "creative act" is obvious when we mark how the language with which he talked about his poetry changed over the years. When he put his emphasis on "tones," "voice-posture" and "metrics," he was preoccupied with the technical aspect. Once again, when he referred to "belief" "commitment," "courage" and "prowess," it was the moral and psychological side of poetry that gave him the desired satisfaction. Lastly, when we find him dabbling in such terms as "meaning," "metaphor" and "naming," he was clearly mentioning what can be said to be the linguistic pattern in poetry. This thesis does not intend to exhaust all these three points in the form and growth of Frost's poetry. However, a brief discussion on all the three aspects would make us aware that Frost was basically an Adamic poet insofar as his critical theories and their application to his poetry were concerned. We may begin with the first of his critical stands: "Voice-posture" or "tones." The primitive, or the Adamically innocent aspect of "Voice-posture" meant for him "the most volatile and at the same time important part of poetry."[24] The ability to capture the sentence tones of everyday talk, and to use them in poetry is the first qualification of a good poet. In Frost's critical canons, the common man is a poet, a "maker" of poetry who is forever conscious of "cave things":

> No one makes them or adds to them. They are always there—living in the cave of the mouth. They are real cave things: they were before words were. And they are as definitely things as any image of sight. The most creative imagination is only their summoner. But summoning them is not all. They are only lovely when thrown and drawn and displayed across spaces of the footed line.[25]

Here the emphasis is on a sort of primitivist or, for that matter, Adamic instinct born out of a desire for understanding the sense behind the speaking voice and for employing it to attain poetic effects of drama. "Intonation" that naturally occurs is meaningful, and following the meaning of the words is not necessary as "the voice.... add[s] connotative to denotative meaning."[26] Referring to language as a living entity with an extra "zing" of drama, Frost notes its communicative aspect thus:

> Words exist in the mouth not in books. You can't fix them and you dont [sic] want to fix them. You want them to adapt their sounds to persons and places and times. You want them to change and be different.[27]

Frost makes a shy hint here at the primitivity of the origin of language which started with a certain kind of articulation of sounds in the mouth ["words exist in the mouth..."].

Thus, it can be deduced that Adam and Eve, the first man and woman, must have communicated by what might be called "the ACTION of the Voice, sound-posturing, gesture"[28] and this was all the more necessary in the absence of language in its logical, scientific sense. "There was speech in their dumbness; language in their very gesture."[29]

When it comes to literature, Frost says that one should gather one's sentences by ear, and imagine them again while writing. This, in poetry, would guarantee not only an "escape from dry rhetoric,"[30] but also an ability to "get the *stuff* of life into the technique of your writing"[31] [Frost's Italics]. Frost's most favourite example was how a variety of meaning can be almost endlessly attributed to the manner of uttering the simple word "Oh." He asserts as follows:

> 'Take, for instance, the expression 'oh.' The American poets use it in practically one tone, that of grandeur. 'Oh Soul!' 'Oh Hills!'—'Oh Anything!' That's the way they go. But think of what 'oh' is really capable: the 'oh' of surprise, the 'oh' of doubt—and there are many more.'[32]

It is the situation, and its element of drama that will determine the tone chosen in its particularity. The poet's function is not, therefore, to see things only. In a letter to John Cournos, Frost took great pride in indicating his own special kind of achievement as a poet:

> I also think of those four 'don'ts' in Home Burial. They would be good in prose and they gain something from the way they are placed in the verse....
>
> It is that particular kind of imagination that I cultivate rather than the kind that merely sees things, the hearing imagination rather than the seeing imagination though I should not want to be without the latter.[33]

It is in this "hearing or audial imagination" that Frost anchors his fame as a poet. The old rhetorical tradition that emphasises "unity" and "coherence" in grammatical sentences should be discarded, and the poet, he says, is to recognize, and assimilate in his poetry "sentence sounds" which he catches "fresh from the mouths of people."[34] Frost is insistent in asking us to remember that "the sentence sound often says more than the words."[35] In fact, such a poetic "stance" would exhort a reader to look for affective or sensory grasp of the meaning of language through its sound. This appears to be a kind of regression to earlier psychic patterns of the primitive.[36] In our times, too, some of the primitive cultures do still practice certain signalling systems of sound which forms an important place in the genesis and psychology of their language development.[37] William G. Moulton's comments on "the nature of language" are also helpful in this connection. While noting that human language as a system of communication is to be understood in terms of "human experience" at one end, and "the audible sound" at the other, he insists that "the best we can do is to note the correlation between experience and sound—and try, from this, to deduce something of the inner workings of this most enigmatic, ingenious, flexible, productive, and elegant of all human communication systems."[38] Relating sound to sense was one of the media by which Frost preserved, or rather endeavoured to keep intact, the innocent, normal look of things. V.Y. Kantak expounds this "lyric technique" with great precision:

> It is what may be called the Roman element in him, that solid Epicurean—Lucretian universe, the firm ground he likes to feel below his feet; and he employs a technique based on the 'sound of sense' and the dramatic voice tones of the language to embody the vividly identified object. Here is a language addressed to bringing out what is common in experience—the very nature and essence of things—a language which, as has been suggested, may properly be regarded as a sort of *Lingua Adamica*.[39]

Apart from this "linguistic consideration" that reveals him as an Adamic poet, a discussion on the moral and psychological "undercurrent" in Frost's poetry would also indicate an Adamically human relevance as its object is to achieve "form" that is "true to any chance bit of true life."[40] Thus, his kind of poetry becomes a yardstick for discipline that liberates itself to a broader, more authentic Adamic freedom — "the almost incredible freedom of the soul enslaved to the hard faats of experience."[41] In fact, Frost's sense of "realism" begins with an acceptance of the crudity of life. This is also the stepping stone to conquering new areas of innocence. Wanting the world to remain as it was, he "wouldn't give a cent to see the world... made better."[42] Behind this so-called orthodoxy there is that proud affirmation of the way the modern Adam should confront the world around him:

> Except as a hard place to save his soul in,
> A trial ground where he can try himself
> And find out whether he is any good,
> It would be meaningless. It might as well
> Be Heaven at once and have it over with.[43]

Terminologically speaking these lines recognize artistic creativity as a process of the artist's ability to capture the meaning of life through a sense of "trial," being neither too romantic nor "false-realistic,"[44] but forever trying to create the "form" of art by means of a confrontation with the "threat" of "formlessness." In that "breathless swing between the subject-matter and form" lies Frost's moral and psychological "commitment." The search for Adamic innocence is obvious:

> The most exciting movement in nature is not progress, advance but expansion and contraction, the opening and shutting of the eye, the hand, the heart, the mind. We throw our arms wide with a gesture of religion to the universe; we close them around a person. We explore and adventure for a while and then we draw in to consolidate our gains.[45]

This indicates that in Frost's opinion "poetic impulse," among others, is a process of "recoil" by means of which the poet gets to the "source" of his "inspiration." This very much corresponds with the world of Nature where all "growth" is from the "source." Frost, while working out the central image of the waterspout to explain the point, expounds the intricacies of the poet's creative act:

> No one given to looking underground in spring can have failed to notice how a bean starts its growth from the seed. Now the manner of a poet's germination is less like that of a bean in the ground than of a waterspout at sea. He has to begin as a cloud of all the other poets he ever read. That can't be helped. And first the cloud reaches down toward the water from above and then the water reaches up toward the cloud from below and finally cloud and water join together to roll as one pillar between heaven and earth. The base of water he picks up from below is of course all the life he even lived outside of books.[46]

This in how the poet's "style" begins to take shape, and as hinted in a letter to Louis Untermeyer, it is "that which indicates how the writer takes himself and what he is saying.... It is the mind, skating circles round itself as it moves forward."[47] Obviously, therefore, Frost's emphasis is on seeing the poet recognise his "own voice" in his poetry. Wherever and whenever its authenticity strikes a false note, Frost is all out to criticize. Here is his verdict on Amy Lowell:

> How completely outside of herself she gets and how completely outside of everybody she keeps. She executes a frightfulness.[48]

On the other hand, the best writer for Frost is one who takes one's own beliefs seriously: "Belief is better than anything else, and it is best when rapt, above paying its respects to anybody's doubt whatsoever."[49] This "commitment" does indeed smack of a deep-rooted "prowess," the radical tone and temper of which is Emersonian in its Adamic egocentrism. Though Frost was prepared to accept his own age for "possibilities" it held out for him, he was deeply committed to the poet's task of finding a clue through his poems to the eternal verities of life—its central ebb and flow. The Faulknerian confusion and chaos of the world was fearlessly braved by him and his "belief" that life is a sort of "metaphysical struggle" led him to write in 1944 that "every poem is an epitome of the great predicament: a figure of the will braving alien entanglements."[50] This is how Frost succeeded in relating life to poetry.

The most intriguing of his critical developments does, however, lie in his increasing fascination for such complicated questions as the "meaning of meaning" in poetry. This gave him an opportunity for analysing the problem of "communication" for the poet. While evaluating the poem's effect, Frost hints at "a two-way traffic" for both the poet and the reader between whom the common bond is one of "recognition"—the "initial delight" of "remembering something I didn't know I knew."[51] All that Frost wanted to keep intact was his own feelings, and by doing so to strike the same tune in his readers. What he would keep for himself should be "the freedom of my material—the condition of body and mind now and then to summon aptly from the vast chaos of all I have lived through."[52] This may not be a very new idea, for it smacks of Whitmanesque overtone,[53] but all Adamic freedom, to be sure, begins with an attempt to allow the mind the luxury of new "feats of association." It means that all thinking is ultimately metaphoric and through "metaphor" a poet is invigorated to give new dimensions of meaning to old, worn-out words and themes. This way the poet's role is one of a "namer" for whom all revelations are meaningful that ultimately shape his experience. His experience in turn does also create its own impact of meaning. One of the preoccupations of Frost was with "poetry as the renewal of words."[54] The themes thus presented determine a meaning that often takes us to a point where we can very well visualise the " primal innocence" of "people and things." Frost's poetry becomes expansive as his native similes not only connect "people" with "things," but also make language a mode of discovering channels of new freedom. In fact Frost's kind of freedom is Adamic. It has its Emersonian heritage, for Frost goes on to champion the cause of liberty ignoring evil though evil's existence cannot be lost sight of. And so, his sense of freedom tends to reach "innocence" at its original, unspoilt source presenting life afresh. All this begins with what has been called "the relation of naming to meaning."[55] What is named is, of course, the "actual" for, as Thoreau indicated, "a true account of the actual is the rarest poetry."[56] Frost says, "I'm sure Im [sic.] glad of all the unversified poetry of Walden—and not merely nature-descriptive, but narrative as in the chapter on the play with the loon on the lake, and character-descriptive as in the beautiful passage about the French-Canadian wood-chopper."[57]

While placing himself in the same arena as Thoreau insofar as poetry's preoccupation with the "actual" is concerned Frost puts forth through poems like "Maple," "Truth," "Birches" that any truthful exposition of the "actual" is an interpretation, a discovery, an experience or a metaphor that deeply touches the central forces of life. More important is, of course, the understanding of Frost that what we mean by the central forces of life are ingrained in man's "profound and complex ideas about the nature of knowledge, language, and personality."[58] It's the meaning given to names that opened up the avenue of knowledge for all of us. This issue is the central one in a poem like "Maple" where Frost approaches it from various standpoints. Each one is valid, and gives us ample clues to discover for ourselves the whole history of man as a "namer" beginning from Adam downwards. The various questions that bothered Maple while she tried to locate the experience that gave rise to the meaning of her "name" may very well bother anyone who is after discovering the connotative aspects of "names" whether they are those of people or things. Who, for example, gave meaning to a particular "name"? If it is the previous generation, well, they must have had their own peculiar experience as a result of which the "name" created for them fresh metaphoric relevance. Whether meaning shapes experience or experience creates meaning, the problem of locating the innocent origin of the meaning of a "name" is an eternal one. It is the poet who may unravel the mystery behind the existence of a "name," and may again view it with the same freshness as Adam did while viewing the surrounding flora and fauna in the Garden of Eden. All that Frost did as a poet, as he told John Freeman, was due to what is implicit in his statement: "my theory was out of my practice."[59] Not that he made a consistent attempt to theorise as Eliot or Pound did.

In fact Robert Frost belongs to a different order of belief. His "optimism" is pagan in comparison with Eliot's Christianity that is smeared with "pessimism." Here is what he thinks of Eliot:

> [Eliot] is a pessimistic Christian; I am an optimistic pagan.[60] I play euchre. [Eliot] plays Eucharist. We both play.[61]

Frost's difference with Eliot as a man and poet need not be more emphasized, and also it is needless to describe his breaking away from Pound though Pound was one who by causing a consistent exposure of Frost's poetry to public appreciation helped establish Frost as an important poet of the twentieth country.

Robert Frost, unlike these two stalwarts of modern poetry, preferred to be rooted to the American soil, and his poems published in England smelt strongly of it. The American bias of Frost's poems was obvious, rooted as they were in the singularities of scenes in New England, and yet, in spite of their high "locativeness," the poems had a universal appeal. Very much like Boone, that great explorer, Frost's aspirations as an American poet lay in a tireless effort to be "filled with the wild beauty of the New World...."[62] Elizabeth Sergeant stresses the point well in *The Trial by Existence*. She says that Frost preferred keeping farm "less as a farmer than as a fugitive from the world."[63] This aspect of Frost's life must, first of all, be well contained in our mind before we start searching the "roots" of his pastoral poetry which emerged from a closer Thoreauvian understanding of the fairly "uninterrupted scene of pleasures"[64] of the wilderness—the original home of man where one can discover, given the willing suspension of disbelief, man's "aboriginal self"[65] with all its primal innocence and beauty. Belonging as he did to the Party of Hope, Frost, in his pastoral poetry, balances the two opposite and opposing forces that usually cover a major area in our literature—the force of civilization as against man's continual attempt to regain lost innocence in the face of its artificiality and sophistication. This leads the critic of Frost's poetry to believe that Frost had enough sense of hope not to sing of the effects of time as we often find in European Romanticism. A thematic study of Frost's poetry will reveal as we shall demonstrate later on in this Chapter that time's effect can be countered by a persistent effort to recapture innocence in the context of a present situation that may appear to be artificial and even seemingly spoilt and confused beyond all repair. One may say that there is an echo in his poetry of a Blakian "state of innocence set forth in symbols of pastoral life akin to those of the Twenty-third Psalm."[66] His poetry's preoccupation is not directly with childhood as in Vaughan, Traherne or Wordsworth, but with the childlike vision of innocent existence.

Take, for example, his poem "The Pasture" that serves as a suitable introduction to his recurring theme of innocent love which knows no death, and thrives ever-gloriously in Nature. However, Frost's emphasis is not every much on inviting us to escape from the complexities of modern life as on the cultivation of an Adamic sense of innocence. In fact, Frost's career as a poet shows many a time how he oscillated, not often without reason, between his profession as a teacher on one hand, and the self-styled, and perhaps deliberately chosen life of a "literate farmer" on the other. Moreover, "particularly during vacation months of seedtime, growth and harvest,"[67] he could manage to indulge in his intrinsic love for the life of a farmer. As Lawrance Thompson says, it is in such "contraries" that the drama of his life is implicit. Elizabeth Sergeant's apt enunciation of this side of Frost's life in *The Trial by Existence* is highly revealing as it draws attention to how the poet forever was electrified with a desire for cultivating a deep communion with a Nature manifesting herself in her inherent glory of primordially innocent beauty.[68] A poet in residence, Frost, during his sojourn in some of the university campuses, would seem positively averse to the very idea of getting "comfy" by staying indoors, and relaxing. One remembers, for example, how Frost discovered for himself "a subject.... in the wood-surrounded town of West Pelham, several miles from the campus"[69] he was scheduled to stay on. Thus, as a teacher and man, his Emersonian non-conformities, though sometimes irritating to some, had also its lure of "nineteenth-century beauty,"[70] and, therefore, appealed to the mind of anyone who came to him with an open mind. This sense of "nineteenth-century beauty," a positive Adamic trait in his character, enabled him to appreciate anything that is natural. To illustrate the point, one could note with appreciation the thrill he and his family felt when they lived under thatch at Ryton Dymock in Gloucestershire, England. Thematically speaking, a major area in his poetry is symptomatic of this characteristic. Take "The Road Not Taken," one of the most representative poems of Frost. Even though it is "more about Edward Thomas than about [Frost]"[71] it states clearly the existential choice he made to take to the road "less traveled by," and it's this that "has made all the difference" to Frost. Cecil Day Lewis has already indicated, while referring to the properties which Frost uses in his poetry, that they are big for the most part, but in a way they are also everyday ones like "snow, trees, animals, farm implements, stars and spiders...."[72] This was a strange choice indeed, particularly for one who was once a mill-hand. One would remember with pleasure how he wrote "My Butterfly" "all in one go." He "sensed that something was happening. It was like cutting along a nerve."[73] To put it more specifically, "it was the beginning of *me*" [Frost's Italics], and for him, poetry was, by and large, "like a blush—you can get something you didn't know you had."[74] A close observation of Frost's statements on poetry will reveal that he was no classicist as he often emphasized his allegiance to the qualitative aspect of poetry couching the same in such well-known phrases like "all in one go," "like a blush.... you didn't know you had," "....the beginning of me," etc. However, this did not merely give birth to a gush of inspired poetry as one might tend to believe. On the other hand, he had the wisdom of an Adam who "died into life." And so, he concluded poems like "The Road Not Taken" in that well-known Frostian ambiguity where fooling and seriousness go hand in hand:

> Two roads diverged in a wood, and I —
> I took the one less traveled by,
> And that has made all the difference.[75]

Beginning from the simple lyric "The Pasture" down to the two complicated "Masques" that give a sophisticated end to his *Complete Poems*, one is struck by the persistence with which this poet's Adamic figure emerges in strong outlines. It is the figure of Robert Frost in New England landscape, the elemental character of which is recaptured with a tantalizing sense of nostalgia. What is important, as James M. Cox puts it, is the final identification of the figure and the scene, for Robert Frost "personifies his region, making it an extension of himself and converting what was mere geographical space to personal property."[76]

The received logic of this inner conviction lay in creating his own myth—the myth of Robert Frost, while others like Eliot discovered "symbols for his age in the ancient myths of creation and fertility."[77] Frost rejected the transcendental machinery of his New England predecessors, and went forth to project his consciousness on to Nature. His was the existentialist emphasis on *being* rather than *doing* or *planning*. The poetic themes reveal this attitude as they go on to dispense with conceptual knowledge, and place a prime importance on "sensory experience" through the poet's participation in and involvement with the events of life and Nature. Thus, one of the major mechanics of Frostian imagery lies in the manner they "serve the demands of sensory experience before [serving] those of any symbolic scheme."[78] The Adamic principle behind all sensory experiences is, perhaps, deeper than what it ordinarily appears to be. The episode of Adam's eating of the apple at the behest of Eve in the Garden of Eden has been a time-worn articulation of the Christian consciousness of Original sin, and it can be described for our purpose as an example of sensory experience, the thrill of which is intensified by participation and involvement.

To consider a few poems in this light we are inclined to start with "The Pasture"—a well-contained, brief lyrical expression of the Frostian world of "innocent charm" where one would "stand in the good of senses.... in the perspective not of history...but of nature...."[79] In this simple, and authentic world of Nature the lover-hero who is a naturalist-cum-environmentalist, does not reveal any complicated desire for making nature participate in Gothic moods as Coleridge would like to do, or for reflecting a personal sense of guilt or joy as Wordsworth would like to do. On the other hand, there is a straightforward, open desire, in the midst of all isolation, for gaining contact and communication with Nature by delving deep into her "primal origin." To gain perspective Frost is prone to add to this the human drama that perpetually shifts ground to commandeer a modicum of rapport with Nature. This rapport may either fail, or succeed, but the whole edifice of all manner of human relationship depends on that. Though critics like Squires suggest that Frost is "no primitivist in the sense of admiring our dim.... origins," we are of the opinion that his primitivism is often obvious in the face of all his sophistication, wizardry of wit and fooling. Even beneath the simple, ordinary down-to-the-earth, domestic temperature of "The Pasture," there is a vista of meaning which proves the points just stated. The pasture spring is to be cleansed of the blocking leaves till its water becomes clear. The young tottering calf that is standing by its mother is also to be brought along. To this is given that suggestive refrain—"You come too"—which is a gentle urging to his partner in love to be initiated into the odd chores of realities of the physical world—the continuing task, for example, of cleansing the spring season after season. Gaily reaching into the wonders of the common place, the poem takes a symbolic dimension bringing into contrast the nature of "innocence" versus "experience."

We are conscious that Frost has expressed his dissatisfaction over any John Ciardi mode of analysis of his poems for fear it might read unnecessary meanings into them. However, it is not at all unwarranted, as Radcliffe, puts it, to say that in the poetry of Frost "the symbol, presented quite casually as an image, opens outward upon a vista of meaning."[80] With such a critical sanction, one is apt to say that by the very economy with which he uses the words that are so very intimately connected with "visible things,"[81] the impact is metaphoric. "Every poem is a new metaphor inside or is nothing."[82] Thus, the reference to spring—water in "The Pasture" is important enough to draw our attention to the principle of "first things first." Water, as the evolutionary scientists would say, is the source of all life, and by asking us to remember our Adamically "simple beginnings" through the poem's recreation of the water-imagery, Frost hints at our basic innocence. The fact is further reiterated by the introduction of the calf which symbolizes innocence that lies embedded in all "simple beginnings." However, "simple beginnings" do not remain as such, and they get complex as they get into touch with the reality of "experience." Thus, the calf, by its tottering, would suggest that it would not remain all along a calf. Its Arcadian state of beauty, would get appalled, and, in a way, helpless before the first appearance of reality as it gets growing. Though Cleanth Brooks has indicated that "Frost does not think through images; he requires statements,"[83] it is often seen that statements are not required as the images become so suggestive that they work as a form of "natural symbolism." The one oft-quoted example is, of course, the sleep/death equation in his poem "Stopping by Woods on a Snowy Evening." Though there are quite a few poems of "The Pasture" variety that condition our mind in a particular mood which we may like to term as Adamic, there are also some complicated poems where the "tooth and claw" of nature and man's precarious life in her bosom is laid bare. There Frost uses a broader canvas and juxtaposes "complexity" with "innocence" so that his poetry gains momentum in perspective, and functions significantly through imagery, allusion, simile, metaphor, symbol, myth etc. Unlike Eliot, he avoids overburdening the readers with these techniques as he uses them in a manner that is reasonably sparing and economical. What strikes us as important is that sometimes, if not always, even smaller poems that fall in line with "The Pasture" variety do evoke associations which open up vistas of meaningful surprise such as we come across in his magnificent long poems. One of the earliest in this category is "Into My Own." The poem leads us to a Pateresque invocation of the early world. "Fearless of ever finding open land,/Or highway where the slow wheel pours the sand,"[84] Frost, in the Emersonian—Thoreauvian tradition, seeks to steal away after the fashion of the Forester-hero "into the vastness" of "those dark trees."[85] To live with the trees and enter their precincts is not merely to leave behind the knapsack of custom, but also to find one's own being which lies hidden and unspoilt in "those dark trees;/So old and firm they scarcely show, the breeze,...." The meaning of Nature here appears to be hardly consoling. However, it is the same "meaning that troubled Wordsworth, though he managed to find grandeur in it."[86] To Frost as it has been to Thoreau "the whole dark side of the world was no more than another 'guaranty of the inexhaustible variety of nature.'"[87] That variety would console Frost no less than it would the modern man when civilization languishes in mechanical stereotypes.

Like Emerson, Frost's life and poetry bear testimony to the difficulty he had in "the private drama of his soul"[88] to rely on his relation to the universe in the face of a rough and surly world. As a cure he, like Hawthorne, is "responsive to...the appeal of the forest,"[89] and does not see reason why he "... should e'er turn back,/Or those should not set forth upon my track/To overtake me, who should miss me here/And long to know if still I held them dear."[90] It is in the benign forest and not in the genealogy of princes that one can find the history of liberty which, to quote Bancroft, is "the real history of man."[91] The deepest core of the poet's ego is not totally barred from participation in and involvement with other people's intentions. In fact, his egocentrism springs directly from all that is glorifying in his quotidian self as he does not mind others overtaking him in his journey and longing to know if he still held them dear. In fact, the protagonist talks like a "hero in space" locating himself "outside time, or on the very outer edges of it."[92] Frost's hero, we feel, is a sort of Natty Bumpo removed from the cities and placed in a solitary stance in the presence of the mystery of Nature. His glory lies in being discovered. Much has been said on this solitary stance of the poet himself in his own life, and the same posture that he was fond of attributing to the protagonists of his poems such as "A Dream Pang," "Come In," "Stopping by Woods on a Snowy Evening," "Desert Places," "Directive," to give only a few examples here. Such themes emphasize "a frontier myth" of some sorts expressed in a "microcosmic" manner which reflects, is a way, the "macrocosmic" experience of the American Adam's confrontation with the wilderness, his subtle interaction with it, and the completed, cohesive vision born out of comprehending civilization and Nature complementarily. "Into my Own," the poem that sets the tune of "A Boy's Will," is important enough as it unfolds the drama of the poet's basic desire, "one of my wishes" as he calls it, to slip into the vastness of "those dark trees" away from "open land" or "high way where the slow wheel pours the sand."[93] Thus a contact with the actual, "the primordial unity"[94] as Mircea Eliade puts it, or "primal innocence" for that matter, would give him an occasion to recognize himself. The last two lines suggest the maturation of experience in the wilderness:

> They would not find me changed from him they know —
> Only more sure of all I thought was true.[95]

The wilderness's ability to free man from civilization's "blockages" will make the poet realize, in perhaps a better manner, the eternal values of such moral questions like Truth, Love, etc.

Without considering here the two serious charges brought against Frost, namely, that he was a "spiritual drifter" and that he suffered from a "teleological uncertainty," which we shall consider later in this Chapter, we should point out at the moment that this "strategic retreat," to borrow the phrase from Hyatt H. Waggoner, was *significant* in the Frostian metaphysic of growth.[96] From Emersonian "self-reliance" to "a strategic retreat" there may have been something canny, but, all the same, one finds it difficult to agree with the critic who says that it was "a shrewdly calculated strategy, aimed at *survival*!" [Italics Mine] or a genuine "fear of experience,"[97] to face civilization squarely. A poet's world is his own, and must not be challenged on the ground that he should have approximated it to the vision of "modish" critics. What Lawrance Thompason said about the early years of Robert Frost—the formative period of an artist's growth—will give us a better perspective:

> For Frost the central problem of his life—artistic and non-artistic—was to find *orderly ways of dealing with dangerous conflicts* he found operative within himself and others.... Most of the time...he used his poems either as tools or as weapons for actually trying to bring under control and resolve those conflicts which he viewed as being so dangerous that they might otherwise engulf and destroy him[98] [Italics Mine].

To grapple with this problem, and to help brave "alien entanglements"[99] the poet's function is to summon up metaphors, and thereby to imitate "the original and divine creative act by fashioning order out of chaos."[100] With Frost, one of the major metaphors that seems to have served this purpose well is, to our mind, the metaphor of the American Adam grappling with the problem of innocence and experience. Nitchie draws our attention to this "deliberate intention on Frost's part."[101] He drops the hint that his poems "reveal elements of an Eden pattern—such elements as a condition of innocence, a fallen condition in which one may remember or desire that lost innocence and an attendant condition of melancholy engendered by such mixing of memory and desire, or a situation in which the relationship between two lovers...defines as it were, the entire operative universe."[102] Quite a number of poems in Frost evoke a "sense of lost paradise."[103] The cyclic pattern of memory and desire, growth and decay on which so much insistence is laid in these poems gives us a clue to study them together in the light of the American Adam's preoccupation with the Edenic myth. To our mind, this tendency towards "retreat" was, perhaps, infiltrated into Frost's poetry partly because of his habit of developing "imaginative ways of escaping from unpleasantness."[104] Certain incidents must have indeed geared up this tendency. His official biography shows that apart from writing a dream story in childhood, his first major attempt to escape from failure was by running away to the Dismal Swamp. Though no escapist in the traditional sense of the term,[105] Robert Frost has undoubtedly made a consistent attempt both in his life and poetry "to resolve his tension between his instinctive desire to escape, and his maturing desire to accept through confrontation."[106] This was all the more necessary to know his position between opposites or extremes of viewpoint.

The poems which we propose to analyse in the following paragraphs in the light of the above observations centre round an Adamic myth-making, though oftentimes such myth-making emerges out of a personal experience.

We may begin with "A Dream Pang," a seemingly simple lyric though charged with complicated overtones of meaning. The poem's autobiographical undercurrent—that concerns the achieving of a reconciliation through the poet's confession insofar as his relationship with Elinor was concerned—is not the point that needs expansion here. Thompson who suggests *that* does also himself allow the readers a free hand to work out any other meaning "through valid symbolic extension."[107] The theme is, of course, one of failure of communication or compatibility in conjugal love, and the pleasure in attaining the same. The reason why this communication gets into a trauma is dramatically offered in the poem itself. Though outwardly the problem of communication does not exist as the last two lines of the poem indicate, it is, however, significantly rehearsed in a dream that reveals a fear in the subconscious level of the poet's mind that, because of his wild nature, he may at any time fail to live up to certain "mysterious demands of love." The lady's sense of pique in love that is wronged is expressed in her desire that the lover should seek her out from wherever she may be instead of her seeking him out from the forest to which he has escaped. Another consideration for which she is also held up almost at the edge of the forest is contained in the line that reads—"I dare not too far in his footsteps stray..."[108] This she utters when she "...did not enter, though the wish was strong...."[109] Her reaction which acts almost as a "counter-force" echoes some such similar feeling as that of the rider in the poem "Stopping by Woods on a Snowy Evening." The mysterious charm of the forest has had no doubt its impact on the mind of the lady, but she is deterred from entering the precincts of the forest for fear of straying too far into it which means straying too far away from home and the society of man. The second consideration must have been that in the forest where the lover hides himself in an unknown place it is difficult to trace him out. Thus, it raises the problem of fixing a common ground for love. While hiding "Behind low boughs..." very much near the forest's edge, the poet would not call the lady in, though she was within his sight, and hence he felt the sweet pang of separation. All this was in the trance of a dream though in reality the lovers were very much together when the day broke.

Though the story of the poem is based on the facts of a drama, the images may help us in formulating the pattern of a myth around it. The images of escape to the forest, of the edge of clearing in it where the poet hides, and of the visitor who has a second thought in not submitting to the all-pervading charm of Nature, all these, while metaphorically suggesting in general the problem of innocence and experience, do also indicate the Adamic myth of a search for Edenic bliss in the midst of the wider, and more demanding cares and anxieties of living in society. The American Adam, bereft of the shackles of the old world, had his second chance to regain Paradise in the New World Garden of America. In this lyric, the poet as Adam is enacting that drama in a microcosmic manner. The lady, by her subtle machinations to tempt away the poet from the "closed bower" of Edenic bliss in the forest, is playing the Eve-like role of temptress *par excellence*. Since the poem has its subject-matter in the form of a dream the tendency to analyse it in Freudian terms is difficult to check. In fact, what George W. Nitchie said of some lines of "The Gift Outright" can be successfully applied to this poem as well, namely, that acceptance of reality in the context of the "here and now" is difficult until and unless earlier fixations in the mind's sub-conscious are replaced by other values.[110] The poet's sub-conscious attraction for the woods is there, for the woods symbolise for him artistic introspectiveness,[111] but too much obsession with it may ultimately hinder his role as an individual in society, particularly the one of being a partner in conjugal love with its greater demands for mastery over practical problems of life. There is, thus, the learned world of "experience" on one hand, and the intuitional world of "innocence" on the other, and the Edenic confrontation between the two ultimately points to the well-known philosophical stand of the poet—his "centrist" movement between intuitionalism and rational-empiricism.

The stand that Frost takes is obvious. He is affected by the tension between spiritual and material goals. His poem "The Trial by Existence" throws light on what God has made of man—"a flower of gold":

> And God has taken a flower of gold
> And broken it, and used therefrom
> The mystic link to bind and hold
> Spirit to matter till death come.[112]

The metaphor of loss of Paradise is again invoked by the image of man conceived as "a broken flower of gold." The mysterious way in which we are linked to matter till death snaps the tie is, perhaps, God's way of looking at man. The poet views man differently, and says that our "trial by existence" lies in the choice we somehow made—the existential choice-between spirit and matter. And that makes "all the difference" as he indicated in "The Road Not Taken." For Frost, however, as a poet and man, the choice was to keep to the "centre" and the forward and backward march between "Experience" and "Innocence" did not blind him either to the "complex" aspects or to the "simplex" aspects of life. It's not a compromise but a resolution that he wreaks out of the tension, and achieves, one feels, a completed vision of life. He, thus, takes "the vantage point" where "two roads diverge," and has an overview of man at the centre of the cosmos. Notice, for example, the image-pattern in the following:

If tired of trees I seek again mankind,
Well I know where to lie me—in the dawn,
To a slope where the cattle keep the lawn.
There amid juniper reclined,
Myself unseen, I see in white defined
Far off the homes of men, and farther still,
The graves of men on an opposing hill,
Living or dead, whichever are to mind.[113]

The images in their very juxtaposition work as the metaphor for a vision of life where the mysterious pulls of the wilderness and of mankind are held in balance, and partaking of the essence of the two, the poet feels whole and self-sufficient. The earthward thrust is there and at the same time the utilitarian world of man's society, the vanity of which ends in death ["The graves of man on an opposing hill..."][114] is perceived as an identical feature in the lives of all men. In an interview with Benson Y. Lendis, Frost clearly set out his habitual stance in the context of this predicament:

> "I should expect life to be back and forward—now more individual on the farm, now more social in the city—striving to get the balance."[115]

The American Adam's pioneering odyssey into the mysterious wilderness and the frontier myth that was born of it, were based on "a philosophy of balance"—a philosophy that banked upon solitude for the preservation of human personality, so that it is revitalized in its own inferiority that radiates its warmth in social life.[116] Thus, loneliness and isolation which form a major theme in Frost's poetry, poem after poem, is an essential part of human life. Adam who "died into life" had this burden to carry, so that he would be better equipped to understand the mysteries of this universe.

The paradise of "innocence" is something difficult to retain and in the onset of "reality," the feeble and the frail, however beautiful they may be, have been known to have fallen. All this may happen because of certain daemonic forces of destruction latent in Man and even in Nature. Nature by her own counter-action and man by his depredations may cause this drama of horror to take place. "My Butterfly," as well as "Nothing Gold can Stay," enact this drama, and give us a clue to the reasons behind all loss of innocence. The "butterfly" which is the poet's "own," for this was the butterfly that symbolized his possession of a sense of beauty as an artist, has died for two reasons:

> Thine emulous fond flowers are dead, too,
> And the daft sun-assaulter, he
> That freighted thee so oft, is fled or dead:
>
> ....
>
> Thou didst not know, who tottered, wandering on high,
> That fate had made thee for the pleasure of the wind,
> With those great careless wings, ...[117]

Just as the "sun-assaulter"—the "he" of the poem—by his sheer piece of casual work during his mad rush for fulfilling his ambitions as high as the sun, "frightened" the butterfly, so also the wind for its own pleasure "tottered" it, and consequently the butterfly died. Its "broken wing" is found now "....with the withered leaves/Under the eaves." The butterfly's "airy dalliance..."—"...the wild touch of any dye-dusty wing!..."—

consoled the poet when "a conspiracy was rife against the poet's life." The poem shows the tension of which we spoke earlier—the working of opposites in life and Nature. More important is its stress on the cyclic pattern of time which takes everything back to its origin—that point of innocence prior to the onset of the complex pattern of growth. The pride of the "sun-assaulter" is set at rest in the innocence of death or even in his "flight." So also the butterfly in dying goes back to the earth out of whose "elements" its throbbing, quivering heart of beauty was made. In this elegiac lamentation, the poet's "sense of acceptance" that "nothing gold can stay" is suggested. The poem "Nothing Gold Can Stay" brings out the theme in clearer categorical statements without making us belabour the difficult process of symbolic extension:

> Nature's first green is gold
> Her hardest hue to hold.
> Her early leaf's a flower;
> But only so an hour.
> Then leaf subsides to leaf.
> So Eden sank to grief,
> So dawn goes down to day,
> Nothing gold can stay.[118]

The image of "green" and "gold" both suggest the beauty of "innocence." For example, the "early leaf" is so beautiful in its simplicity that one may confuse it with "flower"—the very essence of beauty in a tree. Once the process of growth starts (just as the calf in "The Pasture" would not long remain a calf), the shiny shimmer of the leaf's tantalizing beauty will vanish once for all. Thomas Mann suggests in his book *The Magic Mountain* that the process of life of "oxidisation" as he puts it, penetrates and *questions* the very core of man's being. That is so indeed, and those who *can carry* this realisation to its logical end may even go to the extent of branding God an "absurd creator" as Camus maintains in *The Myth of Sisyphus*. For an absurdist philosophy of this kind Frost had no predilection, though one may suspect that some such doubts clouded his mind as we find, for example, in "The Masque of Reason" and "The Masque of

Mercy." Lastly, however, he gives "courage" and makes his final verdict: "Nothing can make injustice just but mercy."[119]

We shall return to the themes of the two "Masques" later, but what we have just stated about their message would, we suppose, give us a clue to the shortest route to "innocence." The "alien entanglements" in all these poems as analysed in the preceding pages are there for the poet's ability as an artist to tackle them as courageously as possible, for "courage" is all that is needed to bring about a satisfactory resolution of the conflicts involved. In fact, "Frost's symbols are hidden like children's Easter eggs—barely out of reach and easily found."[120] This is almost to reverse the well-known Eliotic technique in which "symbols lie in the open."[121] Telling the truth, but telling it slantly, a Frost poem, however simple it may be, may very well keep the reader going to unravel mysterious overtones of meaning in the images. John Ciardi reminds us that "a poem [by Frost] is never about what it seems to be about."[122] Thus, an attempt to extend symbolically the images used by Frost has given us so far a better opportunity to throw more light on him as an Adamic poet. The artistic premises of Frost do also show that he advocated the promotion of art for the sake of wisdom, as most symbolists do, and backed away from the concept of art for art's sake. Speaking in general, it any be stated that Frost was a symbolist in the Emersonian-American tradition. The two dominant symbolic themes in some of the earliest works, as shown by us, are the withdrawal and *sic transit* motifs. This is suggested by "the dark wood" image and others of similar import that help the readers attain a sort of "primordial unity" in the face of "other distractions." The artistic maturity comes *via* poems like "Mending Wall," "After Apple-Picking," "Stopping by Woods," "West-Running Brook" and "Directive." Most of the late poems grouped under *A Further Range, A Witness Tree* and *A Steeple Bush* indicate his concern for spiritual problems, more particularly his sense of the passage of time utilizing some of his earlier symbols so very dear to him. Thus, there again we face Frost's preoccupation with the resolving of opposites like "innocence" and "experience"—a theme dear to the poets in "the Adamic Mode" of poetry in America. To this a comprehensive answer, we suppose, was significantly offered by Frost in "Directive."

"Reason" is *sometimes* worthless whether dealing with day-to-day problems or with great moral and spiritual issues. This dictum—one that caused the fall of Adam—is applied to "Mending Wall." The phrase in the poem that "Good fences make good neighbors" stands for rational human relationship. The poet, however, reverses this dictum and invites us to look at the "other side," that is, the "mysterious forces" at work which break down these artificially thrust barriers between human beings. Such a view of Nature from whom these "mysterious forces" emerge is, in fact, American in tone and temper. Clark Griffith takes us to a broader analysis of this unique phenomenon:

> The American writer does not, by and large, participate in what I.A. Richards has called 'the neutralization of nature.' That is, unlike many of his European counterparts, he is not content to visualize the Natural as dumb and witless, as a force which 'neither knows or cares.' Rather, he is prone, in the manner of his American predecessors, to see Nature as a personality: a creature.[123]

Of course, Nature is not all benevolent as Frost would like us to believe: "she is likely to rebuff...and...the antagonism she harbors seem to emanate not from a clod, but are the expressions of a specific identity."[124] Thus, Frost's view of Nature is post-Emersonian, sharing, as he does, the ambivalent attitudes of a variety of writers like Faulkner, Steinbeck, Jeffers, Wallace Stevens and E.A. Robinson *via* Melville and Emily Dickinson. "Mending Wall" takes us to a kindlier view of Nature—the natural forces that help crumble artificially raised "formalities" of man in an organized society. The farmer's world, though less organized from that of his counterpart's in an industrial society, has its "ritual" chore of Springtime repairs. The poet's description of his neighbour who is a farmer like him makes this point clearer. The man and his ideas belong to stone-age savagery ("...like an old-stone savage armed...)[125] and Frost's reference is not merely to the darkness of the woods but to a primitive kind of "destructive force" which perhaps lurks in every man's heart as it is in that of the neighbour's ("He moves in darkness as it seems to me,/Not of woods only and the shade of trees."[126] This is a kind of mentality, formal and conventional, which does not test the "present validity" of a "ritual" which has been handed down from the past. In the context of a broader and more liberated sense of companionship, respect, love, or what we may call, the mystical togetherness of man who work "on common grounds," the repetition of the phrase "Good fences make good neighbours" may sound a little too incantatory. Though Frost is actually engaged in doing the same kind of work—an example of Frostian "ambiguity"—as his neighbour does, "theoretically" he does not agree with his neighbour's point of view ("Something there is that doesn't love a wall, ...").[127] In his independent and analytical attempt to find the cause and meaning of events that destroy the wall, Frost expresses his dissatisfaction over outmoded ideas and forms. Thus, he has no liking for the ritualistic, mythic origin of the Springtime repair, and without very much emphasizing the practical damage that may have been done by the hunters, his reference is to "Elves" which suggests, we suppose, the presence of mysterious forces in Nature that work secretly to break down "artificial barriers," thereby contributing to man's sense of human brotherhood, and camaraderie. Even though the poem gives us the problem of tackling the well-known "Frostian ambiguity of meaning," it is very much clear as to which side lies Frost's "sympathy." His doing the ritual of Springtime repair is indicative of the fact that living in society means doing certain types of work though, given freedom of choice, we would not like the work done, at all. On the whole, the poem is an enunciation, through an "objective correlative," of the paradoxical nature of man's life—"...the complexity of relations among men, institutions, and nature...."[128] This is the poet's inner world. As usual, he is seen travelling between two "opposites"—the obligations of living in society versus free choice. This is a delicate task, but it is achieved with a sense of "completed vision" born out of striking a balance "between the world he sees and works in and the processes of thought and emotion which he is keenly aware of in himself."[129] Even though "the contrarieties" in a Frost poem, as in this which we have studied, may for a while cause us concern in our search for a clue as to which side lies the poet's sympathy, for indeed this poet has an "element of reserve."[130] We can, however, safely conclude that Frost is not only fruitfully interplaying the counterpoints but by doing so he is gaining a perspective that amounts to a total vision of life. The readers may, however, "stumble," but Frost's poems which he calls "*everybody's poems*—are set to trip the reader head foremost into the boundless"[131] [Italics Mine]. The American Adam's "dying into life" was also a leap into the "boundless possibilities" of recapturing "innocence" in the face of the "destructive elements" of his society. In attempting this he must be a lone searcher. As such, he must face sometimes "the inevitable"—the reason's "darkling plane" where, before attaining equipoise that is born of a steadfast realisation of innocence, and mercy, he shall have to experience the pangs of loneliness ("An Old Man's Winter Night," "Lost in Heaven"), of melancholy, of resignation ("Bereft," "Desert Places"), and of emotional bi-polarity ("Stopping by Woods"). The tension is always there, and it is felt that Frost makes it all the more acute, especially because various elements in the American Experience, beginning from Puritanism and Transcendentalism down to contemporary existential philosophy, have made him conscious of the bi-polarity of American culture.[132] This would not, however, mean that he did nothing in his poetry to unite the polarities and contain the inconsistencies. Irony and understatement and a sense of "Puckish humour"[133] apart, he achieved a resolution by a consistent return to *his* way of tackling a poetically viable theme through the suggestivity of some basically paradoxical metaphors. Waltz says that "Paradox registers his concept of nature," and suggests that it combines an "intense personal interiority with exploitation of the common store of symbols in the collective unconscious."[134] For example, "woods," "water" and "barrier" images that recur so often in his poems may stand for one thing at one time, while the very "things" way suggest quite an opposite point of view on other occasions. If "woods" act as an image of "permanence" ("Stopping by Woods"), it may give us lessons on mutability, too ("In Hardwood Groves"). If "water" symbolizes life, that sustains, renews, and revitalizes us as a "restorative elixir" ("Directive," "West-Running Brook"), it may give us cause for concern as a destructive clement—an image of evil—that takes us so fast towards death ("Once by the Pacific"). The Frostian approach to images of "barrier" as in "Mending Wall" does also reveal truth paradoxically, for Nature as conceived there does not only unite but also divide (the neighbour, for example, lives "beyond the hill" and "in darkness.... not of woods only").[135] Though this kind of poetry may smack of "teleological uncertainty" as Nitchie puts it, or of "spiritual drifting" as Winters emphasizes, there still appears to be a validity in saying that the existence of "ambivalence" in "contraries" highlights a greater approximation to truth.

Though Frost insisted on "boundaries," unlike Thoreau who wanted the deepest possible immersion in Nature,[136] we feel that these "boundaries" were there for the sake of "boundaries only," lest we got inclined to take to "extremes." In one of his poems—"A Winter Eden"—Frost reverses the popular concept[137] that Spring alone can bring Edenic bliss, and establishes the fact that Winter, in its own right, does also contain elements of "certain kinds of happiness" for "certain kinds of creatures"—human and birds. Thus, the equation of Winter/Spring is solved: the "boundaries" vanish, though it may be for a short while ("An hour of winter day might seem too short/To make it worth life's while to wake and sport").[138] If this is how he carries on his dialogue with Nature it is obvious that the centre of his poetic vision is characterized by what we have called "ambivalence," which is the only "locus" on which we can stand in a confusing universe. However, our confusion will tend to become worse confounded if we failed to be convinced "that reality without distortion could be 'bound to no thesis.'"[139] Jean-Paul Sartre's appraisal of Hemingway is of some relevance here as the same could have been very well said of the Frostian *ars poetica*:

> When Hemingway writes his short, disjointed sentences, he is only obeying his temperament. He writes what he sees.[140]

Ezra Pound's verdict is there to support the point made. He praises Frost for "the good sense to speak naturally and to paint the thing...as he sees it."[141] Though obviously enough Frost avoided portraying the vast panorama of our modern metropolitan and commercial scene, he perhaps gained by it more than he lost. As a poet he was drawn to instinct and impulse, but denigrating, as Frost perhaps does, any rational approach to explore the human self, does not make him a second-rate poet as Winters has stated in one of his critical observations.[142] Frost's greatness lay in making the most of the "ambivalence" that he discovered in Nature and men. It gave him an opportunity to look into life's truth which would not ordinarily be possible by a mere rationalistic approach. In this sense he is a distinguished and valuable[143] poet—a point missed by Winters. Therefore, the chief complaint by Winters that his poems "do not lead toward intelligence,"[144] and as such do not comprehend human experience, appears hardly tenable. Moreover, it has been often observed by critics like Newton Arvin that Frost has all along kept up the high crescendo of dialogue between reason and thought nearly in all his poems, though it is most obvious in his dramatic monologues and briefer lyrics.[145]

Adam, to reiterate what has been said in an earlier Chapter, had to cling to earth after his fall from Paradise. This was "a fortunate fall" for "dying into life" he had his *rite de passage* to maturation—a condition brought on by his eating of the apples from the tree of knowledge. This enabled him to know himself. The "innocence" he had lost, and the aspirations he must have, make him conscious of a "tension" in his life. Since he had to remain confined to earth, and earn his bread by the sweat of his brow, earth is the place from where he has to begin, and earth is the place to which he must return. His world is, of course, a "dappled" one—"swift, slow, sweet, sour, adazzle, dim." Such a world, far form being a threat to Robert Frost, was much too welcome—a veritable place to interplay the counterpoints of "innocence" and "experience," and thereby to increase his joys of life. This is the message of "To Earthward"—a central poem in our understanding of the intricate functioning of "the Adamic Mode" in Frost's poetry. Wilbur S. Scott expresses his opinion that this poem, like many of Frost's poems, "is a parable, in terms of natural beauty and human love."[146] As a parable, therefore, the poem is an invitation to the readers to extend the metaphors with as much validity as possible. The poem begins with expounding two planes of experience one of pleasure "innocently separated from pain" in an area of "sensuous perception of nature" and the other of "joy of love for human nature which still stops short of that point where the entrance of pain makes experience a compound."[147] As we read the fourth and fifth stanzas of the poem we are aware of a maturer understanding in the poet which is announced in his not wanting any separation between joy and pain. In fact, our joys, he means to say, should also include their opposites like "weariness," and "tears," and even "fault" ["...The sweet of bitter bark/And burning Clove"]. This is how he understands experience—the amalgam of "sweets" and "bitters"—and that, too, he had his realisation "now," that is, in the context of his present "experience." What else, the readers may ask, was Adam's lot after he "died into life"? It was, to be sure, a fall from the joys of "innocence" to the pangs of "experience," but his individualized existence as a man bereft of God's grace meant his acceptance of his lot as it was. To make the most of it existentially, he is to accept extremes—the extremes of joy and the extremes of pain ("The hurt is not enough/I long for weight and strength/To feel the earth as rough/ To all my length").[148] Similar reconciliation of "opposites" in other poems like "A Tuft of Flowers," "Birches," "Stopping by Woods" and "West-Running Brook" take us to an area of consciousness where isolation and communion, heavenward swing and earthward coming back, appeal of the wilderness and obligations of promises in society, Time's flow toward the void and man's resistance to it, all combine to become a stepping-stone to a broad, full and comprehensive vision of life—something like a compensation for Adam's expulsion from the Garden of Eden, we suppose!

Such a view as the above has, of course, led Frost to concentrate on "the soul-in-present-action" as opposed to Browning's emphasis on the "nuances of past happenings."[149] The symbols, and metaphors that are dear to Frost have thus a vital flexibility as a result of which the truth of experience that they encompass do not escape us. In fact, the truth of experience lies in "ambivalence"—the very essence of life in which there is always a clash of impulses underlying the subconscious level of our mind. And, whether or not a total resolution is brought about, sheer attempt alone at resolving the opposites must remain for us our great satisfaction. It is quite true that our literature is full of "those images of pain and horror that often accompany," as Nitchic says, "the...ritual of the Eden archetype."[150] Nitchic draws our attention to Milton and Conrad in whose writings the quest for Paradise means a process of rebirth through initiation that brings on pain, horror and fantasy. To our mind, Frost, while avoiding such nightmarish pictures, is satisfied in giving us only the simple commonsense of accepting the "opposites" as a single entity. "To Earthward" makes a good attempt at this, and asks us to make "both our eyes a single sight."

When there is in any manner a feeling of alienation or estrangement from our sense of values deeply ingrained as a faith, particularly because there are "other considerations" foreign to the existing value-system, the only alternative then for our survival as sane human beings lies in what Sidney Cox says "dual conformity." We cannot, of course, call it non-conformity, though we can name it as the process of "Opening and shutting, throwing our arms wide and closing them, exploiting and adventuring, then drawing in to consolidate."[151] Robert Frost had also his words to describe this intricate psychological process. He writes in 1925:

> The most exciting movement in nature is not progress, advance, but the expansion and contraction, the opening and shutting of the eye, the hand, the heart, the mind. We throw our arms wide with a gesture of religion to the universe; we close them around a person. We explore and adventure for a while and then draw in to consolidate our gains.[152]

This simile of "swinging" is antipodal to our concept of twentieth-century progress—a concept that puts a premium on linear movement, as a result of which it becomes difficult for us, materialists as we are, to grasp the idea that if we keep our natural, simple self "completely down we shall discover it brooking out in us, ourselves."[153] It is, therefore, all the more necessary that to attain the "ultimate real" we must have a close relation with the "particular real," so that we can have a "clear perception of relationships."[154] When Frost is both attracted and repelled by darkness ("Come In," "Design," "The Draft House," "Stopping by Woods"), his psychology functions in some such pattern. Sidney Cox says that once when Frost was young he spent about three months alone on Ossipee Mountain in order to find out "where he was, and what he wanted…"[155] This habit continued in his adult life, and taking to the hills, he would always learn to "refuse offered choices between opposing goods." The hills would offer him, as Cox adds, an opportunity to "combine the good things, before he explores and adventures some more."[156] Of course, there is the enigmatic question—whether or not some "design of darkness" would not entrap us, as the beautiful proud woman in "The Lovely shall be Choosers" is entrapped, when we are too much obsessed with the idea of believing ourselves free. This may happen due to some chance misfortunes, and not very much due to our involvement in evil. The heart, of course, may not give up its desire to fight, but instead of fighting with violence, Frost offers us to play-act a gentle posture of "swinging" as we find in "Birches." It will keep us kicking down to the earth, and at the same time enable us to rise to the starry heights of ambition with balance:

> I'd like to go by climbing a birch tree,
> And climb back branches up a snow-white truth
> *Toward* heaven, till the tree could bear no more,
> But dipped its top and set me down again.
> That would be good both going and coming back.[157]
>
> [Frost's Italics]

Frost would like to keep himself in close communion with all that is natural in the face of his aspirations as a civilized being which, we may presume, might engender in him a breaking away from innocence to embrace a certain kind of mental sophistication. Again, by sheer "expansion" without the alternative recourse to "contraction" any thing will snap, break or even get disintegrated. Man's tendency to "recoil" is as much natural to him as his tendency to "expand." A motif of *regressus* may very well act as a cure for the mental imbalance born out of the excesses of progress that tend to kill the natural roots of human happiness. The pioneering ideals of the American Adam shall, of course, necessitate an effort to recapture "innocence," because "innocence" is often lost in the white heat of "experience." This is also another way of saying that Nature simplifies man's emotions. The glowing example is that of Robinson Crusoe's or Thoreau's particular way of dealing with life. We have seen how the speaker in the poem "Into My Own" would cultivate integrity by just stealing away into the wilderness. The "intellectual content" in such poems is suggested well, and it is obvious that Frost is not writing with any "preconceived theory" in such cases. Nitchie says that, "paradoxically or not, one of the cardinal errors according to Frost's scheme of values is going against nature or natural processes ...."[158] Man can only do so at his own peril. We have already seen this distrust of the unnatural in the poem "Mending Wall." The same theme with its emphasis on Adamic innocence is carried on through a number of poems of exquisite beauty. Wherever man's "artifices" or "devices" are seen, Frost casts his dice in the opposite direction. Whether he ponders over man's unnatural treatment of a brook in the city ("A Brook in the City") or thinks of what happens to peaches if they are grown in much too severe a climate ("There Are Roughly Zones") or reveals the truth that spontaneous response of our heart is a sublimer substitute for the rigidity of any principle ("A Hundred Collars") or tries to find the meaning of war by telling us the disaster unleashed by a bullet as it pierces cobweb, flower and butterfly ("Range-Finding"), Frost is only re-enacting a drama in which he, as the protagonist, emphasizes the point, as he did in "The Gift Outright," that our failure to respond to all that is natural, and our failure to give ourselves over to the land is the reason of our basic "weakness." Some of the poems that tell us about Frost's quarrel with science, do not, of course, have any clear-cut logical consistency which spells a total moratorium on man's tampering with Nature. The ambiguous area in the poems of this sort lies in Frost's use of paradox which neither fully justifies the preservation of "the natural," nor whole-heartedly condemns science's utilitarian motive to subdue Nature. The poem "The Line-gang" is a good example in which, to quote Nitchie, "it is not clear whether the bringing of telephone and telegraph does or does not justify the wanton slashing down of forests, whether it is more 'natural' to leave forests standing or to subdue them to man's purposes."[159] More positive response that expresses Frost's dissatisfaction with science, particularly with the recklessness of technological men, can be discovered in poems like "The Ax-helve" "The Egg and Machine," "The Master Speed," and "Out, Out...." Avoiding philosophically conceptualised definitions of Nature, Frost gives us only a series of "attitudes" which ultimately gives us sample occasion to believe in man and his intrinsic potentialities to recapture innocence. Though poems of "A Lone Striker" variety reveal pride in science, it is obvious that Frost has no sympathy for mindless and careless onslaught on Nature organized so callously sometimes at the very cost of man's Adamic pleasure and aesthetic satisfaction. Of course, Frost is conscious of man's ambivalent relation with Nature. For instance, "Acquainted with the Night" and "Desert Place" emphasise man's total isolation and predicament as no hints are given by "an indifferent nature for charting his course in an alien world."[160] Keeping himself at a safer distance from unsurer ground, Frost, who hardly used his poetic talent to capture the vatic or the prophetical, had his eye on *this* earth, as steadfastly as possible, and was "content to dwell [there] and accept his lot as poet-sampler...."[161] Loving Nature for the very fact of her creating a body of unsophisticated, simple "attitudes" for us to emulate an against science's complex ones, Frost was, however, no enemy of the machine itself. He only disapproved of any system of ethics that was mechanistic, or any state of mind that was materialistic.[162] This was perhaps one of the reasons why Frost did often feel the compulsion to "deliberately cut himself off from the modern, metropolitan and commercial scene."[163] Whether it is "strategic withdrawal" or "primarily an evasion according to plan,"[164] as Nitchie puts it while reviewing Frost criticism, the pastoral element in Frost has to be understood with certain reservations in the light of Arcadian tradition. Appearing to have involved himself with an idea of escape as a possible cure for his "jaded spirit," Frost as a pastoralist is actually exploring "upstream, past the city with its riverside factories and shipping, on against the current of time and change to the clear waters of the source."[165] It may be something akin to the dualistic attitude so fervently contained in the New Humanism of the 1930's championed by certain writers of the older generation like Irving Babbitt and Paul Elmer More. In fact, this New Humanism was old enough, and could very well be traced back to the Emersonian credo expressed in the following lines on the human law and the law for things:

> There are two laws discrete,
> Not reconciled, —
> Law for man, and law for thing;
> The last builds towns and fleet,
> But it runs wild,
> And doth the man unking.[166]

Such a doctrine of two laws—one for "man" and the other for "thing"—seems to have had its impact on Frost, though any particular "doctrinal label" is difficult to fix on him as it is wellknown that whatever he wrote had little to do with the critical opinions or rigid aesthetic systems current in his times. The important point is, however, that Frost was all along in search of finding "a golden mean" between the two laws, and without avoiding the extremes, he established a pattern of poetry quite consistently to indicate that the extremes could be successfully "enclosed and contained." The poem "Acquainted with the Night" which, an Randall Jarrell says, is cast in the mould of "Dante's own form and with some of Dante's own qualities,"[167] enables us to illustrate the argument:

> I have looked down the saddest city lane,
> I have passed by the watchmen on his beat
> And dropped my eyes, unwilling to expalin.[168]

Frost's dislike for "the saddest city lane" is obvious, particularly when his out walking "the furthest city light" is evaluated in the light of his preoccupation with isolation and withdrawal. The dropping of his "eyes, unwilling to explain" when he "passed by the watchman on his beat" indicates not only the recognition of man's society where obligations and duties run counter to one's deepest desire, but also the necessity of discarding such obligations and duties in the interest of an Adamically more free and socially more uninhibited life. This was Frost as we know him to have been at various times of his life, eager to enjoy the solace of isolation away from the heavy schedules of life. Thus, Frost was more or less like Nature, free to make his own existential choice.[169] What was perhaps more important, Frost had an "ability to dismiss the past and move along with the known, living present."[170] Not that the age of innocence for Frost's family was never over, for it is well known for any Frost biographer that "the world had compulsively and irresistibly broken through into the little family which Lesley, in her reminiscent vein, had compared to the unworldly, introverted Brontes."[171] However, Frost's one continuous battle has been to represent in his poem "a culture's hum and buzz of implication"[172]—the culture being that of New England's hard-bitten, everyday wisdom which cultivates simplicity almost effortlessly, and makes it a philosophy of life. Such a philosophy, we suppose, is obviously implied in "Acquainted with the Night," and it is Frost's reply to George Edward Russell's subtle statement that "The Time is not right."[173] Frost means to say that no time is right or wrong which is as well as realising that "calm" rests on ironically acknowledging or accepting "lostness, and by that action only, maintaining control."[174] The Adamic tone in this "stance" need not be overemphasized, for Frost takes the reader step by step "to a moment beyond good and evil, in which absence of design is faced and met."[175] Unlike Wordsworth in "Westminster Bridge," Frost moves away from brightness and serenity, and performs a Baudelairean autopsy upon himself, and attempts to look into the depths of his own heart's "unnerving darkness" through his realization of a city of dreadful night outside Nature:

> And further still at an unearthly height,
> One luminary clock against the sky
> Proclaimed the time was neither wrong nor right.[176]

Strategically retreating from civilization's dogmas and conditionings Frost believes that it is the "flight of the alone to the alone" that must act as a "momentary stay against the confusion" of the soul in its own turmoil of loneliness. This is how Frost, the New England sage, formulated "his sparse working morality,"[177] founding his staunch belief in country things, and like Herrick, raising them "for his own sly purposes."[178] As indicated in the flexibility, perception and naturalness in the composition of "Acquainted with the Night," Frost plays the role of the Puritan putting on Cavalier, and to be exact, Adamic airs, and forces a gay, worldly-wise tone of cultured simplicity to counteract the divisive and destroying impact of modern city life. The necessity of being aware of country things motivated, to a major extent, all manner of action in the Frostian world. This need has, of course, to be understood in the light of the American way of the "country knowledge" of a farmer whose "intellectual sophistication," and whose search for "new terms of worth" are recognized as modern.[179] The essence of such a modernity lies also in Frost who had the ability to contain the "opposites" by seizing "a vantage point," so that he could easily take in the overview of the city or the country, the human or the natural "whichever are to mind."[180] Without sharing the Emersonian credo of yielding himself "to the perfect whole," he was thus able to perform an "act of self assertion... in a place that is not quite a place and in a time that is no longer a time, but a memory of one."[181] This is Adamic freedom, to be sure, and through this he defined himself. Frost was driven to secure his own peculiar kind of "wholeness beyond confusion" and had his ineluctably poignant march through "ambiguities" to a life reconstituted and recovered in simplicities that might appear in the first instance to be a "failure," but on second thought, as Pearce puts it, is actually "a condition of strength—the strength in discovering oneself as a person, limited by the conditions which can be made clearly to define oneself as a person."[182] It may appear peculiar, and even a little too irrelevant insofar as the conditions of "modernity" and "science" are concerned. But that was the manner with which Frost wanted to come to grips with human problems. It was direct, and unmediated, and its "series of explanations of life" faded "off into horizons too swift for explanation."[183] Over and above this, man, "the diminished thing," to use a Frostian terminology, is made the most of. In fact, man, whether his freedom is limited, or whether he discovers evil in his own innocence, becomes the centre of the whole drama. He is, in fact, the modern man, though speaking from a purely regional point of view, he may appear in Frost in the guise of a New Englander. One may take, for example, a poem like "Desert Places" which, like "Acquainted with the Night," is also an exploration of a modern condition—the condition being one of knowing what one faces without invoking the absolutes like an Emerson or a Wordsworth. In this Frost was neither like Eliot whose implicit denial of the significance of nineteenth and twentieth-century science led him to reaffirm his belief in the validity of

Christianity in the modern waste-land, nor was he like Yeats and Wallace Stevens who, under the same conditions, went on to make an attempt to explain life through a creation of personal myths. Like Thomas Hardy and Robinson, to give some relevant examples in this context, Frost "attempted neither to deny the loss nor to replace it with personal myth but rather to make poetry out of the diminished thing itself [Man]."[184] If a Conrad in *The Heart of Darkness*, while anticipating the hollowness, emptiness and panic of our century, succeeds in his effort to present "the horror" as "an affirmation" and "a victory," and thus gives us the necessary defense not to be lost within ourselves, Frost on the other hand has in poems like "Desert Places" and "Design" his ironic attitude to bank upon, through which even the presence of "fear" and "loneliness" gets turned into an intense awareness of the soul experiencing a "ravishment of the fact":

> And lonely as it is that loneliness
> Will be more lonely ere it will be less —
> A blanker whiteness of benighted snow
> With no expression, nothing to express.
> They cannot scare me with their empty spaces
> Between stars—on stars where no human race is.
> I have it in me so much nearer home
> To scare myself with my own desert places.[185]

Explicitly rejecting the romantic response to Nature, Frost sees Nature through twentieth-century eyes, and as Dendinger puts it, "he reacts to the frighteningly expansive view with a stoic posture..."[186] This "posture" comes from an altogether different understanding of what a poem should mean to Frost. It does not, of course, mean a "spontaneous overflow of powerful feelings...recollected in tranquillity." The emphasis, as we have seen in our analyses of his poems, is more or less on "the present moment." In order to illustrate this point we may consider Frost's poem "The Tuft of Flowers" in which the poet, neither turning to the past, nor recollecting emotion in tranquillity, makes a surprising turn to capture "the uncommon" through "the common in experience." It is the tall tuft of flowers spared by the mower that makes all the difference:

> But he turned first, and led my eye to look
> At a tall tuft of flowers beside a brook,
> A leaping tongue of bloom the scythe had spared
> Beside a needy brook the scythe had bared.[187]

Apart from suggesting the spirit of human participation as the "rich and ripe philosophy" of universal understanding, the poem does record a still greater account of our work-a-day world where the instinct to preserve the natural and the innocent even for a moment may act as the real secret of joy and happiness in the face of all artificialities. In addition to it there is Frost's obvious appreciation of the worker who is also a dreamer. It is not a retreat to a fantastic dream world that he suggests. On the other hand, his aim is to capture the reality of experience that lapses into a sweet Adamic dream, be it even the banishment from the Garden of Eden with a curse to labour and die:

> The fact is the sweetest dream that labour knows.[188]

Thus, fact and fancy play together in which crystal ice may become heaps of broken glass, the arched tree may get transformed into girls on hands and knees or a country boy may become a mature poet to announce a deep philosophy ("Birches"). Therefore, in Frost one is able to feel the working of an "intellectual principle by which the 'tantalizing vagueness' of any creative intuition—be it scientific or artistic—finds its thought and takes communicable shape."[189] Though Frost never ceased to be preoccupied with the common elements of traditional prosody (rhyme, rhythm, meter, stanza pattern, etc.), it was indeed his seeing of 'form" as a deep, philosophical mental process that would cohere the loose ends of the technical elements of his poetry. Behind this, one finds Frost's pragmatic, and for that matter, an Adamic acceptance of life as it is, with its limitations of human knowledge and capacity. This does not, of course, mean that the human soul is devoid of qualities of heroism. In an earlier poem, "The Trial by Existence," Frost makes a clarification of this point. Similar to the theme in Blake's *Book of Thel*, this poem, too, chooses "pre-existence" as the state or condition from which human souls, as they are born, emerge "heroic, valiant, and above all, free."[190] "But," as Barry goes on to add, "there is a catch. Life would be too easy and conducive to pride if, at any moment of 'agony or strife,' the soul could comfort itself with the realization that it had freely chosen such an act of 'daring.'"[191] It is, therefore, worthwhile to mention here the action taken by God to nip pride in the bud by obliterating the "lasting memory..../That life has for us on the wrack/Nothing but what we some how chose."[192] Heroism has to be proved by reaffirming courage and self-definition through suffering, and this was Adam's lot, it might be remembered, in his fall from Paradise. On the basis of this, one could add that such a Fall "is always a rise, an ascent-descent."[193] Our assessment of Frost's poetry earlier in this Chapter touches this point at its fringe, only. It, therefore, needs a little more elaboration. It has to be stressed that Frost took the Edenic myth more as a metaphor for equipoise between good and evil or stasis and dynamism than something of a theological concern from the Christian point of view. Frost was a creative artist, and Adam's expulsion from the Garden of Eden had for him the possibilities of a theme to feed his artistic urge on. Frost wrote in March 1941 to Louis Untermeyer that he had the exciting experience of "good talk" on and about the complex "two-word phrase *Felix culpa.*"[194] That the fall is fortunate, and leads to a sense of high value is obvious as we go through poems such as "Kitty Hawk," "The Lesson for To-day," "Design," "The Oven Bird," "A-Wishing Well" "Spring Pools," "A Boundless Moment," "In Hardwood Groves," "Range-Finding," "On the Heart's Beginning to Cloud the Mind," "There Are Roughly Zones," etc., which thematically taken together, enables us to move in that twilight region between innocence and experience. This is not to say that innocence is kept at an arm's length, and is something that is forever lost as "...Eden sank to grief."[195] On the other hand, it is possible to retrieve it through life's loss, grief, and change. It is of great importance to expect "that dawn does not 'go down' to day, but comes up, as in Kipling's famous phrase, 'like thunder,' into the satisfying warmth of sunlight and full life."[196] Considering the bipolar nature of man's existence on earth, there is no denying the fact that evil may very well spring from good or vice versa. In fact, it is more often a quandary of intellect than that of emotions—"a risking of spirit in substantiation":

But God's own descent
Into flash was meant
As a demonstration
That the supreme merit
Lay in risking spirit
In substantiation.[197]

As we go through "Kitty Hawk," this idea, which makes the poem dependent on the metaphor of Fortunate Fall, and identifies Frost's problem in late age to maintain a delicate balance of thought, gains ascendancy, and culminates in a Jamesian emphasis on self-realization through "courage," "Will," "effort," "tussle," "risk" and "threat"—words which appear consistently throughout Frost's critical comments here and there. In the coming of the second Adam [the Christ], man had his hope for salvation. Adam's choice in the garden to eat of the apple may have been a sin which "pulpiteers will censure," but it laid the foundation of "Our instinctive venture/Into what they call/The material...."[198] This is Frost's Adamic acceptance of the human condition—the persistence to accept life as it is. "I wouldn't give a cent," he wrote to a young poet in 1930, "to see the world...made better." And so, he has "no quarrel with the material."[199] Our maturation teaches us to "love the things we love for what they are"[200] and yet, as we find in "A Boundless Moment," we may sometimes lapse into a vision of Paradise, and bring into our adult life a sudden glimpse of lost innocence:

'Oh, that's the Paradise-in-bloom,' I said;
And truly it was fair enough for flowers
Had we but in us to assume in March
Such white luxuriance of May for ours.[201]

The lovers walk in the March woods but obviously enough they have their mind on the magic May-flower called Paradise-in-

Bloom. However, it should not also be forgotten that Frost like Milton felt a little too uneasy in idealizing Nature, but, in our opinion, the poem is not an attempt to present Nature in her pastoral elements, but is a record of the lovers' way with the world. For them "meaning is transformed into a motive, a shaping force, and experience takes on the form of a quest—a search for discoveries that are self-reflexive in that they are not truths about things found, but truths about the process of seeking."[202]

Even though the lovers are in a mood of romantic nostalgia for a moment, Frost shows that this mood is only a transitory one, and they should lastly face the strange reality of this world:

> We stood a moment so in a strange world,
> Myself as one his own pretense deceives;
> And then I said the truth (and we moved on).
> A young beech clinging to its last year's leaves.[203]

Thus, the Adamic clinging to the earth with its cycle of birth and death in Nature and man becomes an existential choice for the lovers. "This whole commitment to earth," as Cox puts it, "is not idea, but act—act in the form of the colloquial poet who embodies the poems."[204] It must, therefore, be stressed that, unlike Emerson and Thoreau, Frost did not believe, regionalist as he was, in complete "retreat." "Here is flight that must not carry itself away; the fact must end securely on the ground; all metaphor is tentative rather than positive."[205] This has been already indicated in our analysis of Frost's "Miltonic" poem, "Trial by Existence." The brave souls that find their way to heaven find that it is their earthly courage and valour that "commits them once again to the heavenly act of choosing human rather than angelic existence."[206]

Some of the more well-known poems from the point of view of the receptivity of ordinary readers do also contain what critics have recognized "the depth of the actual in Frost's poetry."[207] For example, a poem like "After Apple-Picking" contains an "association pattern" which, once unravelled, would enable us to feel how deep even ordinary events could be in our life. Of course, there may be various strands of meaning just because symbols in a Frost poem do always point to a "vista," and not to a "terminus" as ordinarily encountered in the poetry of "the mythic Mode." An absorbed reading would indicate that the poem shows "something" other than the literal experience of a season's good and satisfying apple-picking harvest. For our purpose, we shall limit ourselves to an interpretation that falls in line with the central argument of this dissertation without, however, intending that other interpretations, if any would not add to a full awareness of the meaning of the poem. It is admitted by Condor that the poem is based on a rather shaky and "unsure knowledge" of the Edenic myth. Even then, Condor admits that the overtones of the Fall metaphor greatly enrich the poem's complex meaning.[208] A recent interpretation by William Bysshe Stein who studies "After Apple-Picking" as an "echoic parody" takes a bolder step to explore the possibility of associating it with the religious doctrine of the Fall.[209] Projecting itself out of the experience of picking apples—an ordinary day-to-day experience in the life of a farmer—the situation of this poem begins with what happens after the harvest of apple-picking, and its ritual chore of storage are formally over. It became, we may again emphasize here, man's lot to be condemned to labour by the sweat of his brow when he "picked the apple" in the Garden of Eden, and was consequently expelled by God from that veritable Paradise. This led in its turn to Adam's knowledge of good and evil—a circumstance that was opposed to the Christian doctrine of Original Sin if we would argue the case in terms of a "fall" that was "fortunate." Thus, the poem's speaker lives in a fallen world of tiresome labour ["...I am overtired/Of the great harvest I myself desired,"][210] and yet there are ample compensations for the speaker, not merely because he had a good harvest, but because he almost recovers his lost values by attempting to touch the core of all values, that is, "I myself"—the source of man's ascending desire. There is obviously no source outside man's self where values can get a fresh lease of life once desire is restored and refurbished. The poem sets in motion with the ladder pointing "Toward heaven still," and with "a barrel that I didn't fill/Beside it...."[211] Here is indication enough that the speaker is in a tension to polarise contrarieties or opposites—the heavenward movement and the earthward thrust. This recalls what Frost told during the years in England (1912-15) in regard to a man's art as something like "a bursting unity of opposites."[212] It, of course, refers to the kind of change that art is seen to have achieved through a process of movement from "form to content and back to form."[213] Frost as an artist liked to stay contented, "alive and in motion, between those two things...."[214] Argued differently, Frost's remarks would mean, from a broader point of view, the kind of attempt that everyone of us, like the speaker in "After Apple-Picking," is constantly making to polarize conflicting opposites in our life. This not only takes place in our eager attempt to recapture innocence after every crisis explodes it, but also in our desire to gain respite, peace and happiness after a spell of "willing labour." Such resources lie in ourselves given to us by Nature, and also it was so with Adam when he "died into life" after being expelled from Paradise. Having been "done with apple-picking," the speaker is thus naturally conscious that the "Essence of winter sleep is on the night..."[215] Sisyphus-like he snatches a moment of relief before the stone again rushes downhill, that is, before the next season of apple-picking harvest cyclically returns. That hour is "a breathing space," but not "a sheer vacuum," for it is also an hour of consciousness—a time that goes beyond "just some human sleep" to assume a larger dimension of refurbished values. For Frost's speaker the "ambiguity" involved in assessing his own "sleep" is full of its intrinsic complexity as a result of which he leaves the question on to the "woodchuck" for an answer:

> Were he not gone,
> The woodchuck could say whether it's like his
> Long sleep, as I describe its coming on,
> Or just some human sleep.[216]

Frost's attempt to synthesize the polarized tension between

one kind of sleep, and another lies in leading himself away from any Dantesque faith in a god-centred universe to an openended universe where, in the famous words of Emerson, life is viewed as activity, and an effervescence of power residing "in the moment of transition from a past to a new state, in the shooting of the gulf, in the darting to an aim." Before the speaker's "drowsing off" led to a "long sleep" like that of the woodchuck's or "just some human sleep," the dream that he dreamt of was in relation to the human activity associated with the harvest of apple-picking:

> Magnified apples appear and disappear,
> Stem end and blossom end,
> And every fleck of russet showing clear
> ....
> I feel the ladder away as the boughs bend.
> And I keep hearing from the cellar bin
> The rumbling sound
> Of load on load of apples coming in.

As in "Mowing" so also in this poem "It was no dream of the gift of idle hours..."[217] to which Frost draws our attention. Again it is "fact"— "the sweetest dream that labour knows."[218] Thus, in spite of man's "fall," his undefeated determination to live and to create provide him with a ground for values. And for this he must turn to his own self—the "I myself" of "After Apple-Picking." It is, as it were, that man must endeavour forever to attain a synthesis of polarizing opposites.

The one great criticism that might be levelled against such containment of forces, attitudes, impulses and concepts which are contradictory by nature is that it could very well be mistaken for "an apologia for a deeply entrenched evasiveness...."[219] Viewed correctly, this only could lead, for a poet like Frost, to an exemplary response to understand complex experience with unquestionable subtlety, and to refuse to accept a state of reconciliation with ease, and without mental compunction. Without an obscuration climaxing in dogmatic rigidity, Frost a life-long devotee of paradox, hold the contraries together, and through the alchemy of metaphor brought about a see-change in them to present endlessly new entities and unities. His unique feat in this regard has been well known among the readers of his poetry. No one can forget, for example, his oven-bird who treats us to the music of "talk-songs" in "singing not to sing,"[220] the countercurrent's "backward motion toward the source"[221] as Nature's and through Nature certainly man's persistent attempt at recapturing Adamic innocence from which we have travelled far away in our mad rush to go ahead either in the name of progress or civilization. Broadly speaking, all this is only Frost's commentary that man who is, and yet is not, involved in time's flux, may have his own limitations, but in his "free spirit" alone lies the force supreme to transcend the temporal and grasp a richness through and beyond matter. Frost thought it "immodest of a man to think of himself as going down before the worst forces ever mobilized by God."[222] The Adamic posture is clear enough, though critics like Whicher have labelled Frost as an "Imperfect Guru" which adds also to that other charge against Frost as a "a spiritual drifter." It is complained that "the withdrawal into and through the simpler past is a withdrawal into and through a fiction, a falsification."[223] What we go back to may be an earthly Paradise, but, as Auden records his statement to join the band of Frost's condemnators, "nothing of serious importance can occur in it."[224] Though statements of this kind born of great critical insight do have a good deal of basis about it, we should, however, do well by analysing a few more important poems to justify the point that in spite of the changing rural New England scene which forms the matrix of most Frost poems, the ulterior impact of such poetry lies in "something else"—in human imagination's perpetual response to satisfaction that one can get by relying on "old intuitive knowledge and the simple truths of the human heart."[225] In fact, Frost's poetry is for him a continuous process reaffirming his faith in life. Without relying on reason as critics such as Nitchie, Winters or Auden would have liked him to do, Frost's point of view lies in digging truth out of his own self by way of inspiration and intuition which may indeed be termed as "spiritual prospecting," and cannot simply be waived off as "spiritual drifting." If Frost often "chose for theme/Traditional sanctity and loveliness," he, as stated earlier in this Chapter, was also the poet who emphasized our alienation in an indifferent universe. Thus, Frost not only sings of man's departure and homelessness, but also of his desire to return home, to recapture the lost plenitude of innocence. To recapture innocence is not to permanently reside in it, but to keep it as something that we obtained on our way, so that we may rely on it as a counterforce for fighting the ordeal of initiation into experience. We may analyse a few more poems to illustrate the point that in Frost the invitation to a state of innocence is not a moral suicide, but a life-giving force which invigorates just as an elixir would to a sick man. It is almost like saying that however much we may forge ahead as civilized man we should be at proximate distance from the "place" of plentitude—the origin, the source of innocence.

"The Death of the Hired Man" is a case in point which enables us to illustrate the argument stated above. Plainly speaking, it is a poem on death, but its main thrust of emotions is also directed towards an understanding of the nature of home, and the cliams of justice and mercy on human life. We are initiated into the central situation of the poem just as Mary announces, almost unostensibly, to Warren the purpose of Silas' return in those silent but rather portentous words: "Warren,...he has come home to die...."[226] The return of Silas to a place which was to him more than a mere house is also his return to his "source"—a plaçe of innocence in the face of the growing complexities of his life in old age with no one to hire him in particular or look after him in tender care. His soul's "pilgrimage" to "eternal home," that is, death—a state of everlasting innocence—must precede as he views it, his return to a place where he had perhaps found a sanctuary. In fact, "home" is a temporary sanctuary for all of us, a place of sweet memories that renews us from time to time, and very rarely allows us to forget innocence which, ideally speaking, permeates its whole atmosphere. Hence the justification in Mary's argument that their home is also Silas' home. Mary knows what home is, or what it ought to be:

'Yes, what else but home?
It all depends on what you mean by home.
Of course he's nothing to us, any more
Than was the hound that came a stranger, to us
Out of the woods, worn out upon the trail,'
'Home is the place where, when you have to go there
They have to take you in.'
'I should have called it
Something you somehow haven't to deserve.[227]

This conversation between Mary and Warren, and its basic voice-posture reveal Mary's liberal and perhaps correct view of what a home is or should be in opposition to the recalcitrant, rather elliptical statement of her husband. Nothing is, however, said outright in Biblical terms of heaven and hell, but the whole thing is implied as Mary carries home the idea of home as home-coming ["you...haven't to deserve"], and with it a widening of meaning that refers to death as a kind of "eternal home." A critical Post Mortem performed to evaluate the dead Silas' character with reference to Mary's definition of home would enable us to understand that Mary's implication of "eternal home" is very much in the Christian tradition. Adam after his Fall did not deserve it, and so was it with all mankind in view of Adam's commitment of Original Sin. In the Bible, Cain protests, "Am I my brother's keeper ?" But Warren, by his wife's slow persuasion, may have been initially haunted by the very question asked by Cain, but immediately after his symbolic breaking of the stick at the porch step his hard-heartedness melts like ice, and he chooses to be his brother's keeper though the choice was too late as Silas was then dead [" 'Dead,' was all he answered."][228] It is an ultimate acknowledgement of the supremacy of mercy as opposed to justice—a theme which Frost would elaborately enunciate in his two *Masques*. Robert Frost, a self-styled "Old Testament Christian" was all out for tempering justice with mercy which is akin to innocence.[229]

Against this recommendation, Frost, the "terrifying poet" as Lionel Trilling put it, has his views about a kind of dark design, an evil, which mysteriously enough comes like a thief to steal away innocence, and cause disaster. We may take, for example, the much debated poem "Design" which takes for its theme the view of our universe as "The Darkling Plain." By now we are well acquainted with Frost's luxury of being "witched by sunlight...," but, then, in some of the poems as in this one under our scrutiny one feels as if the poet is intent upon showing us "the blackness of darkness beyond."[230] If there are poems like "A Cow in Apple Time" and "A Blue Ribbon at Amesbury" at one extreme, there are poems like "Acquainted with the Night," "Out, Out —" and "Design" at the other extreme of Frost's poetic spectrum. Of course, a poet who wrote "Design" has elsewhere in poems like "The Night Light" given us evidence that man cannot be totally gloomy-shut. In fact, gloom itself can also be a luxurious self-indulgence, though the poet refuses to be totally carried away by it:

She always had to burn a light
Beside her attic bed at night.
It gave bad dreams and broken sleep,
But helped the Lord her soul to keep.
Good gloom on her was thrown away.
It is on me by night or day,
Who have, as I suppose, ahead
The darkest of it still to dread.[231]

Thus, Frost would refuse to give us a total dichotomy of good and evil. On the other hand, his view of "the terribleness of things" is imbued with a sense of duality. It is a part of the very process of existence itself. Therefore, speaking from the point of view of man's postlapsarian condition and his persistent desire to possess prelapsarian innocence and then to depart from it for an ordeal of initiation into the complexities of experience, duality has to be accepted with grace as both a condition of negation and blessing. Though critics like Randall Jarrell [in *Poetry and the Age*], Isadore Traschen and Irving Howe [in *A World More Attractive*] had focused on the poem's speculative aspects, its exposition of a universe as "a design of darkness" and its representation of "a dumb-show of purposeless terror" respectively, it is Frost, we suppose, who in spite of his reticence to explicate the poem at any time, had given us rather in a casual statement the real clue to an understanding of it. Frost thought "Design" to be "a very special piece of observation," and would be, therefore, "never sure" of it.[232] We may not also be very sure of its implication, and should, therefore, approach to interpret the poem carefully noting in our mind Frost's kind of "fooling" which might twist the meaning in spite of the seriousness of the theme. First, it must be understood that the poet is putting forth an ironic interrogation with a mood to explore evidences whether tenderness, and for that matter, innocence is an operative factor in a universe where the ultimate design suggests that there is neither anything called "preordained evil" or "preordained goodness." The poem with this basic quest as its theme gives us at the beginning a situation as negligible as the humble phenomenon of a drama of interaction between a spider, a heal-all and a moth. The emphasis is on a colour pattern of "white" in the first three lines:

> I found a dimpled spider, fat and white
> On a white heal-all, holding up a moth
> Like a white piece of satin cloth.[233]

Though it may be noted that Frost's study of whiteness echoes Melville's "Whiteness of the whale," we should, however, be cautious and must try to find Frost's own observations in the sonnet itself. The heal-all which at wayside is blue is at "that height" white, and the "kindred" "snow-drop spider" which is "dimpled" kills the beautiful moth white as "satin cloth." Frost obviously reverses "terribleness" in ironic pleasantry, and means to imply that in a Darwinian universe of "organic evolution" "the killer and the killed are transformed from dreadfulness to innocence."[234] The innocence of the "dimpled" and "kindred" spider is not lost just because it eats the moth, for the moth is its natural food. So also the strange phenomenon of the heal-all getting blasted and losing its "blue" innocence is quite possible as an outcome of a mysterious natural process. The point is whether what happened in the macrocosmic world of Nature, that is, the killing and liquidation of the beautiful moth by an innocent spider, has its bearing within the microcosmic world of man. Though fall from innocence is not universal, it can very well be man's own invention as an attempt to explain the mysterious operation of evil in an openended universe. Frost does not, however, resolve this question: he only observes the operation of evil within the "design." We must then squarely face it, and have a spirit of existential acceptance of "evil" without putting it as a counterpoint to "good." Of course, there may be time when we have to show undefeated endurance so as not to be swept away by the merciless and hostile forces of a universe with dark design. We may take, for example, "Bereft" which leads us beyond solitude to the very verge of despair. But in spite of the evil design inhering the cosmic situation encountered by man—the fallen Adam—there is no reason why it should be doubted that solitude, isolation, bereftness, and desolation coming in gradual order one after another can lead him to utter despair. The poem initiates us to a hostile universe—a vanishing Eden—where the wind is no longer a wind but the roar of a wild animal let loose to molest and do its worst. The "sagging floor" of the porch, the end of summer, the "frothy shore" along with the gathering of "Somber clouds in the west..."[235] intensify the unleashing of evil forces. The dried leaves coming in the "coil" of a whirlwind do also assume the deadliness of poison. The metaphor of Adam's fall from Paradise is evoked through the intensely suggestive lines describing "how the Leaves got up in a *coil* and *Hissed....*"[236] [Italics Mine]. It is, as it were, the voice of the Serpent tempting Adam to do the forbidden thing of eating the apple ["Something sinister in the tone..."][237] This solitary man may have relied on God, but, as the poem shifts emphasis from his condition of God-dependence to God-forsakeness ["Word I was in my life alone,/Word I had no one left but God"],[238] we are conscious that the fall has been precipitated. And yet the resoluteness and determination that mark his character show that in spite of his aloneness he is capable enough to withstand and endure the evil design of the Universe. Such a design is ultimately inexplicable, and the motivation of evil with conjoining hatred, and its malevolence to destroy, remains a mystery, excepting that we can verily observe it and arm ourselves with confidence to endure it. Frost's "The Draft Horse" is a fitting commentary on the evil forces in the Universe insofar as an accounting for innocence and the motivation that tries to end it are concerned. The poem has been accepted as a parable. The "pitch-dark limitless grove" may very well stand for life, and the "lantern that wouldn't burn" with "a buggy" "too frail" may justly signify that our journey of life has to be undertaken in the face of dark forces. Such dark forces are anthropomorphized in the person of the man who "...came out of the trees/And took our horse by the head/And reaching back to his ribs/Deliberately stabbed him dead."[239] The poem in its very ambiguity is highly suggestive, and as Cook points out in drawing a certain comparison with Hemingway's "A Clean Well-Lighted Place," it may very well be taken as "a revealing parable *of* our time."[240] [Cook's Italics]. One of the meanings that might be wrested out of this ambiguity is that however innocent the "unquestioning path" of man and woman may be there are dark forces in Nature, and also hatred at large in the world, and, therefore, in society which may throw a challenge to their built-in innocence and comfort. What the poem means to imply is that we may have to submit to its forces without being able to defend ourselves. Also, the man who emerged from the trees may symbolise the very "strain of guilt" in ourselves that is capable of "killing" all innocence. It may even signify the action of an authoritarian God who purposelessly sacrifices us just as flies are killed by wanton boys. This second meaning is suggested by the phrase "to obey" if we put it in a Biblical context. God's imperiousness, His authoritarianism and dictatorial powers do sometimes fail to be rationally explained just as it is difficult to explain why the innocent pair suffered for no fault of theirs. It must be emphasized here that in the Judaeo-Christian version of history the situation of two lovers [Frost's "unquestioning pair"], constituting a world of their own, based on continued and continuing innocence of love existed but once, and in Paradise only. Since man's post-lapsarian degenerations are inherent in him he must fall into the tangled convolutions of fears and desires. In spite of a strength of character that we might gain from our preoccupation with theology, the very human condition may very well create situations where man is propelled by a sudden interaction of innocence and experience which may land him in utter helplessness. Such "...forces...do not lie directly open to thought, nor to the control of the will."[241] Frost's "Love and a Question," one of his earliest poems, reveals how difficult it becomes to deal even with the very simple intrusion of a harmless stranger in the idyllic isolation of two lovers. It even amounts to inflicting a woe, and raises questions of ethical complexities:

But whether or not a man was asked
    To mar the love of two
By harboring woe in the bridal house,
    The bridegroom wished he knew.[242]

Indeed, it is always the presence of a third person, like the voice of the Serpent in the Garden of Eden, that may work against the innocently simple isolation of two lovers. Sometimes the will of the innocent may become self-sufficient enough for the very simple reason that it is innocent, and thus capable to take risks. The character of brother Neserve in "Snow" is a case in point. His going out into the snow, and his dropping in at the Coles' are viewed with all its ambiguity:

'The whole to-do seems to have been for nothing.
What spoiled our night was to him just his fun.
What did he come in for ?—To take and visit ?
Though he'd just call to tell us it was snowing.
If he thinks he is going to make our house
A halfway coffee house 'twixt town and nowhere—'

'I thought you'd feel you'd been too much concerned.'

'You think you haven't been concerned yourself.'

'If you mean he was inconsiderate
To rout us out to think for him at midnight
And then take our advice no more than nothing,

Why, I agree with you. But let's forgive him,
We've had a share in one night of his life.
What'll you bet he ever calls again?'[243]

The conversation between Fred Cole and his wife here with its specific intonation shows the husband's grudging admiration, and the wife's contemptuous reaction born of a sense of duty and responsibility to family and home. Incidentally and by way of indirection, the poem does also throw light on Neserve's innocence of character which alone enables him to brave the risk of going out in a night of heavy snow. He has accepted the challenge of the dark forces of Nature not out of any iron-willed determination that may enable him to defend himself, but for the very simple reason that his innocence has made his will efficaciously defensive to withstand any contingencies. Such innocence has been forever the romantic's self-defense as it was, say, for a Shlley in braving the storm in the Mediterranean. Nitchie thinks that "This link between innocence and manageable environment is not peculiar to Frost, nor is it,...accidental; rather it had been one of the irreducible elements of the Eden myth since the time of Genesis and Hesoid."[244]

In "Blueberries," Loren, a prototype of Robinson Crusoe, has created his own world with thrift and caution, so that the members of his family and he himself do not starve, and do not have to depend upon others for their survival. The choice that he has made to subsist upon berries has its own clarity, and he has made it without passing through the pains of any psychic effort which only proves that his world is motivated, as it were, by the will of the unfallen infant. Mark, for example, the innocent lie that he utters when he was approached to tell the place where the berries grow. The reply has all the innocence of a child who has hidden his toy of love, and does not want to disclose the secret for fear of losing it:

'...The rascal, he said he'd be glad
To tell if he knew, But the year had been bad.
There *had* been some berries—but those were all gone.
He didn't say where they had been. He went on:

> 'E'm sure—I'm sure'—as polite as could be.
> ....'[245]

[Frost's Italics]

As opposed to "Bluebarries" we may put as a counterpoint the theme of postlapsarian melancholy in "Reluctance." If Adamic bliss lies in a state of innocence, it is with a great wrench that one feels the loss of it. And yet man has no alternative but to yield with grace to such a condition. The departure from Paradise is like the beginning of winter:

> The leaves are all dead on the ground,
> Save those that the oak is keeping
> To them one by one
> And let them go scraping and creeping
> Out over the crusted snow,
> When others are sleeping.[246]

But a fall from Paradise is also the beginning of Adam's lonely journey through life in search of new areas of values in the face of melancholy and desolation. Hence, in spite of "the dead leaves" lying "huddled and still," and the "flowers of the witch-hazel" withering, the speaker's "heart is still aching to seek."[247]

What should also be remembered, as Frost implies in "The Bear," is that too much of seeking may sometimes make a man so much engaged in sheer intellectual pursuits that he may lose touch with the innocent source of things in life. Drawing attention to this poem Yvor Winters aptly observes that Frost is only engaged in a satire against "the intelligent man from the point of view of the unintelligent...."[248] The poem draws a sharp contrast between a bear that freely romps, and a bear that is caged, and with that Frost carries home the basic difference between the simple man with his innocent pursuits and the modern intellectual with his obsession with the Library and the Laboratory. The latter's preoccupation may generally checkmate his incentive for partaking of simple joys and innocent happiness in life and Nature, and thereby limit his freedom in a way:

> The world has room to make a bear feel free;
> The universe seems cramped to you and me.

Man acts more like the poor bear in a cage
That all day fights a nervous inward rage,
His mood rejecting all his mind suggests.
He paces back and forth and never rests.
The toe-nail click and shuffle of his feet,
The telescope at one end of his beat,
And at the other end the microscope,
Two instruments of nearly equal hope,
And in conjunction giving quite a spread.[249]

Whether "sedentary" or "peripatetic," man with his desire for knowledge—a cause that brought about his expulsion from Paradise — appears to be a "pathetic" and "baggy" figure. His devotion to machine ["The telescope at one end of his beat,/And at the other end the microscope"], and his restless mobility in civilized society that takes him farther away from love of Nature ["The bear puts both arms around the tree above her/And draws it down as if it were a lover"],[250] have been the canker that eats into his happiness.

This again brings us to the question of containment of opposites or proper balance between contrarieties in Frost's poetry. A successful resolution of the problem would enable man to have a unified vision of life. And yet, as we read poems like "Build Soil" we are more or less conscious, in spite of Frost's "whimsy" and his kind of "fooling" that Frost is inclined to favour and give a rather great weightage on the cultivation of a rich and innocent individuality in man as the very basic precondition of significant human achievement fulfilling its own end of happiness in an inner abundance and exuberance of human spirit. This was so, as Lawrence Perrire says, "during the middle ages, when holy hermits lived in caves studying exclusively their own spiritual self-perfection."[251] As opposed to this our own age, with its emphasis on human welfare through social controls, and its rather overemphasis on materialism, has seen the painful affliction of the inner life of the spirit. In the words of Tityrus that "We're always too much out or too much in,"[252] Frost engages the readers with the enunciation of this theme, and explicitly enough, extends the telescope and microscope metaphor given in "The Bear." When Tityrus emphasizes that he would, if he were a dictator, allow things to take their course ["...let things take their course..."], and then "claim the credit for the outcome,"[253] he only means to imply that there is a greater possibility of evolving a finer society based on goodwill and innocence if the intellects of man are kept free to grow without any interference or imposition from outside. In other words, men may be treated as Adam in the Garden of Eden, though, as in the best form of democratic Government, their ambition need to be curbed if it happens to take a turn to vault. Though Frost is reticent in commitment which makes him liable for a charge of "spiritual drifting" or "anti-intellectualism," this poem shows that his neutrality is born of responsible speculation, and has little trace of indecisiveness in it. The spontaneity with which he achieves the process of confrontation and extrication almost simultaneously between various contrarieties is evidence enough that Frost is a dynamic equilibrist who can fathom and verify a particular truth profoundly without excluding its opposite. We may take, for example, the theme in "The Armful"—a simple poem that conveys the meaning of this philosophy with a facile spirit. The speaker in the poem goes to get a few things which are as various as "bottles" and "buns" ["Extremes too hard to comprehend at once"], and carries them in his arms making all of those a "whole pile" kept in counterpoised balance against his breast, and trying best to prevent them falling. As he loses balance the "whole pile" crumbles down in the road, and he sits "in the middle of them all," and contemplates "to stack them in a better load."[254] The poem's metaphor of fall is obvious, but what the poet falls into is the event of falling away from achieving a counterpoised balance between extremes of situations. The "whole pile" suggests the accumulated situations of our life. It is further revealed that once we lose balance we land ourselves in confusion, and must have to begin again the very process of marching ahead, in life. This problem of marching ahead engages Frost's attention in "West-Running Brook" with a subtler grasp over the relentless and inexorable flow of existence by time towards decay and death. The young couple who see the brook running west when all other country brooks run east brood over the relevance of this contradictory situation, and, significantly enough, find it to be the very symbol and sign of all that we include in "time, strength, tone, light, life, and love." Between the two the female, being the more responsible partner in the creative process for whom constancy of love is more important than anything else, is sharper in reacting to this scene of contradiction. She strikes the key-note to the discussion by reviewing the situation intuitively: "It must be the brook/Can trust itself to go by contraries/The way I can with you—and you with me."[255] But the brook as the symbol of a polarized tension of contrarieties assumes a greater mystery as the wife perceives the white foam which is the point where the stream reverses its onward flow, and is thrown back on itself.

> Look, look it's waving to us with a wave
> To let know it hears me.'
>   'Why, my dear,
> That wave's been standing off this jut of shore—'
> (The black stream, catching on a sunken rock,
> Flung backward on itself in one white wave,
> And the white water rode the black forever,
> Not gaining but not losing, like a bird
> White feathers from the struggle of whose breast
> Flecked the dark stream and flecked the darker pool
> Below the point, and were at last driven winkled
> In a white scarf against the far shore elders.)
> 'That wave's been standing off this jut of shore
> Ever since rivers, I was going to say,
> Were made in heaven. It wasn't waved to us.'[256]

With a realism which the male-figures in Frost do always have ["Home Burial"], the husband takes a broader perspective of this natural phenomenon in opposition to his wife's more personal, and rather private reaction. But it is also remarkable to see how the wife's private reaction to love in marriage becomes also meaningful as the general observations on human life made by her husband in response to the brook's symbolic existence progress in the poem. The white wave looking like a bird's "white feathers" symbolizes the innocence of all beginnings. This point becomes rather incisive because of the bird metaphor drawn by the poet. If the brook is a symbol of human life, and like the brook the human life, too, was "made in heaven," then the very process of growth, after the innocence of childhood ends, is like "the dark stream" "flecking" "the darker pool/Below the point...." This point is suggested as the husband, in sharp contrast with his wife's "fancy," launches his argument of contraries, particularly in relation to the brook's own intrinsic resistance to its inevitable rush towards the sea of death:

> It flows between us, over us, and *with* us.
> And it is time, strength, tone, light, life, and love —
> And even substance lapsing unsubstantial
> The universal cataract of death
> That spends to nothingness—and unresisted,
> Save by some strange resistance in itself,
> Not just a swerving, but a throwing back,
> As if regret were in it and were sacred.[257]

[Frost's Italics]

The flow of life is all around us ["It flows between us, over us, and with us"] as a result of which we are perpetually exposed to unlearning our innocence by falling a victim to the process of growth and decay. And so, love may also run miles away from its original, innocent response, and tend to get complicated so as to cause a separation of lovers ["It flows between us/To separate us for a panic moment"]. This flow of life, as Frost views it through the husband's arguments, is inevitably the "universal cataract of death/That spends to nothingness." The pointlessness of such a process fails to be deterministic since we have like the brook, that "strange resistance" in ourselves to get back towards the source—the lost plenitude of innocence. A positive assertion of innocence over the complexities of life, particularly of love and the other things that go along with it, such as "time," "tone," "strength," can give meaning to human existence. Frost's suggestion of a postlapsarian melancholy over a lost Eden is, of course, there ["a throwing back,/As if regret were in it and were sacred"], and his Christian orthodoxy in suggesting our desire to worship God cannot be ruled out as we note "The tribute of the current to the source."[258] However, Edenic loss and a postlapsarian melancholy over it, along with a desire to recapture its "lost centre," must not be viewed only as revelation of Christian orthodoxy in Frost. It should also be considered as an existential process—a need and a requirement to make life "whole beyond confusion." Moreover, it should be noted carefully that in Frost attraction towards and rejection of Eden condition, both in its prelapsarian and postlapsarian implications, are a concurrent factor in a large number of poems, and as such, have its greatest contribution to the evolution of Frost's poetry, though, chronologically speaking, he did not write poems of this kind successively throughout his life.[259] Even when the poems tend to reject the Eden conditions, Frost moves through a process of involvement with and extrication from that condition, in consequence of which the poems gain in perspective. We may take a few such poems, and particularly those which we have not considered till now. A viable poem from this angle is "Stopping by Woods on a Snowy Evening." Though a casual reader of this poem may miss its symbolistic effect, it is obvious that a reader who is absorbed in the broad spectrum of Frost's poetry is capable of feeling that the poet "pretends to be talking about one thing" though he is, in fact, all along "talking about many others."[260] This is done by Frost's use of natural human action as a form of symbolism, and in doing so it demonstrates very successfully how a poem can be meaningful even though it does not use stock symbols which form a part of the private, symbolistic tradition of the human society as a remnant from man's mythic past. The poem's appeal lies in the tension that the poet creates in using words in a particular context with a specific voice-posture that makes the context relevant. The subject-matter of the poem, spoken simply, is the story of a rider who stops for a moment to watch the beauty of a section of woods. Then thinking that to stop there may delay his journey, he decides to go ahead to reach his destination punctually before the bed time. It is the last two lines by their rhetorical device of repetition of similar words in similar sentences that give a new dimension to the poem. In fact, the last lines, moving from a simplistic point, assume a symbolistic pattern because of the life-death tension that is raised there. Frost, then, brings the lines to a point of resolution by his much familiar twist in what has been called the voice-posture even when similar sentences or words are uttered. What is also significant is that such a reduction of meaning is in keeping with the events that have gone before. The situation becomes dramatically forceful as three elements emerge to put their impact on the rider: the woods that belong to the owner, the animal world of the horse, and the mysterious snow that has already begun falling to enwrap "everything" with the chill of death.[261] The poet's emphasis is obviously on that "primal fury of origin" symbolized by the lovely but dark and deep woods which at the advent of winter have started lapsing gradually into a death-like silence—a suspension of its usual activity and a wrench on its charm till spring would be around. This in itself shows the independent existence of the woods that could still be there if no observer would have observed it. Nature is, therefore, the indicator of her own "dark forces" which in the form of death can overpower the things of its own making. And yet, Nature's intrinsic capacity for growth and fertility that enables her to rejuvenate herself lies always there. The essence of the Dionysiac attraction which the rider feels for the woods, and his rejection of its charms must needs be viewed in this light. In fact, the rider does not reject the charm of Nature: what he rejects is the dark forces which underly such beauty, and can devastate man. Therefore, the rider's quipping in the first stanza which is half a "whimsy," and half serious is apt:

> Whose woods those are I think I know.
> His house is in the village though;
> He will not see me stopping here
> To watch his woods fill up with snow.[262]

Since "the utterance is in the present tense," it must be noted that the rider does not view the scene objectively: he is "*in* the scene"[263] [Unger's and O'Connor's Italics], and as such, is a part of the whole process of Nature's growth-decay and decay-growth cycle. Since decay cannot be helped, that is, death cannot be avoided excepting in the form of rebirth, the rider's desire to tap the innocent source of Nature, responsible for her growth and charm, is given more emphasis as he decides to leave the scene before the dark forces of Nature symbolized in the snow overpower Everything. Here is, therefore, the regressus motif in man that takes him in that concept of circular motion of time to Nature's Edenic origin—a "lost plenitude" for man as civilization is seen to have been a process of defiling "virgin land" to set up cities. Thus, the rider's desire to go ahead after a brush with Nature's charm and plenitude in the face of the falling snow ["downy flake"] symbolising the onset of decay is well defined in advance to suggest that a recurring pattern of involvement with Nature and extrication from her "dark forces" can only make him conscious of going ahead with a sense of strength in keeping promises of duty which, without any sense of innocence, would indeed, lose its vitality in becoming merely selfish. Man alone is capable of such a response as he views the flow of time both cyclically and lineally. His superiority to the brute world is thus a proven factor, and Frost explains this in familiar terms as the "little horse" thinks the rider's halt near the wood to be "queer." The brute fails to grasp the rider's ability to make a unified vision of Nature's contrarieties—a vision that makes his journey of life worthwhile, and creative before it ends in death ["And miles to go before I sleep,/And miles to go before I sleep"].[264] "Life to go on living" must contain a philosophic endurance of this kind. However, most people turn naturally to the task of living without even realizing that such a philosophic endurance is necessary to face the sudden appearance of adverse circumstances which may even assume a tragic dimension. A good example of it is "Out, Out —" which, apart from demonstrating the conflict between man and machine, reveals some deeper philosophical questions as a commentary on the nature of life. The poem's parabolic structure is evident in its idiosyncratic quality of instructing the readers by way of implication. The story is, therefore, a means to an end, with its emphasis on a kind of allusive language that signifies something else. It is the story of a boy who, instead of attending to simple diversions of a youthful kind, has taken to the responsible task of turning a saw—a mechanical device to cut wood in particular. This saw is set in a mill situated in a country locality against the mountain ranges of Vermont, and thus marks the slow mechanisation of a basically agricultural society in America—the Hamiltonian concept as opposed to the Jeffersonian ideal if put in a broad perspective. What is emphasized by Frost in the beginning is the restraint that the boy feels for the very simple reason that his task to perform a responsible work functions as a counterforce against his simple and innocent occupations as a young man. Thus, the boy, as Thornton observes, "cannot keep his eyes and thoughts off the mountains."[265] Therefore, the psychological distance from his work marks his unconscious desire to escape it. Since the predicament, for the time being, is rather inescapable, it manifests itself in sowing the seeds of tragedy. The subtle articulation of language in the poem by way of a reference to "Supper," echoing the Biblical "Last Supper," strikes the key-note to this tragedy:

> His sister stood beside them in her apron
> To tell them 'Supper.' At the word, the saw,
> As if to prove saws knew what supper meant,
> Leaped out at the boy's hand....[266]

This boy who was indeed "a child at heart" and who was "Doing a man's work" had his sudden fall from innocence into the complexities of experience as he discovered his hand cut by the saw. It was the "seeing" eye of the boy to which Frost draws our attention to suggest this:

> ...But the hand!
> The boy's first outcry was a rueful laugh,
> As he swung toward them holding up the hand
> Half in appeal, but half as if to keep
> The life from spilling. Then the boy *saw all* —
> Since he was old enough to know, big boy
> Doing a man's work, though a child at heart —
> He saw all spoiled. 'Don't let him out my hand off —
> The doctor, when he comes, Don't let him, sister![267]

[Italics mine]

The loss of his hand would mean the loss of his "boy's will"—free, liberated, and basically innocent. Therefore, he makes all the pleadings so as not to allow the amputation of his hand. As the hand was already gone, the boy's desire was in vain. He gradually collapsed into unconsciousness, and finally died—a death which no one anticipated, and, therefore, "No one believed."[268] In spite of the suggestive metaphor of the title of the poem "Out, out—," echoing Macbeth's speech on life as a "brief candle," Frost, like Shakespeare in the "porter scene" of the drama, does not prove himself to be "the neurotic and paranoid figure of despair."[269] His emphasis is on "Life to go on living:"

> ...And they, since they
> Were not the one deed, turned to their affairs.[270]

The parabolic effect of the poem, as in other poems of this genre, points to "deeper roots," and not merely to "grass roots." Hence, we cannot waive off Frost as a naive philosopher saying that his philosophic commitment was thinly textured. In our technocratic society, Frost's metaphor of the saw may seem rather poor, but it is difficult to deny that the effect of tragedy in causing death and disaster would have been of similar intensity, though of wider dimension, even if the reference were to nuclear war-fare or space exploration. In philosophic terms, the Frostian endeavour to contain the opposites can be explained through the concept of Heraclitean strife or Empedoclesian principle that operates between attraction and discord. However, his contribution lay in giving this philosophy, a humane twist—something that Adam would do as he "died into life," being expelled from the Garden of Eden where the difference between good and evil was strictly defined. In life, unless we are guided by religious orthodoxy, we get our motivations through "opposing goods" rather than through a positive conflict between good and evil, virtue and vice, right and wrong. Here is Frost in "To a Young Wretch":

> But even where, thus, opposing interests kill,
> They are to be thought of as opposing goods,
> Oftner than as conflicting good and ill;

Which makes the war-god seem no special dunce,
For always fighting on both sides at once.[271]

Frost's faith, whether religious or otherwise, is imbued with a humanness. Thus, being more of a humanist than a theologian, it is a pointer that he is indeed a poet of man in the last analysis. Beginning with *A Boys's Will* down to *North of Boston,* and the other volumes of poetry that followed it, we see Frost exploring the thematic possibilities of either man's relationship with external Nature or man's relationship with his own self, indentifying the diverse forces and their interaction. It is only when we come to *A Masque of Reason* published in 1945, and *A Masque of Mercy* published two years after that we see Frost for the first time grappling directly with the theme of man's relationship with God. With a wit and humour that link the two *Masques* with the Jonsonian tradition of organically integrating such basic elements of the genre within the dialogic conflict of the play, we find Frost stepping aside its convention of employing mythological characters, and presenting almost naked "prototypes of human or spiritual personalities, symbolic of established moral ideals, whose set speeches, like those by characters in medieval morality plays, subordinate the dramatic conflict and action wholly to an allegorical dialogue of ideas."[272] The two *Masques,* however, should be rated as poems to which we have our consent of Frost indicated in his letter to Untermeyer.[273] The *Masque of Reason* begins with Job and Thyatire, his wife, awaking from sleep and looking at a strange and queer sight of God "caught in the branches" of The Christmas Tree, without being able to extricate Himself.[274] The irony is implicit. Like Adam who was expelled by God from Paradise, and was subsequently a victim to matter, so also God here has been entangled in matter. This is an ironic treatment of God, particularly in relation to man's devotion to Him which, as we know, has degenerated itself into mere rituals in our organized system of religion. Thus, Frost is evidently satirizing the Old Testament concept of God's revelation in parodying it as "a strange light"[275] only. A further irony is involved in the reference to God's throne which does not have the traditional regality associated with it, but is only a "prefabricated plywood flat." A secular touch is given to the sacred subject as God refers assertively to the role played by Job in changing the old, hackneyed relationship of God to man:

My thanks are to you for releasing me
From moral bondage to the human race.
The only free will there at first was man's,
Who could do good or evil as he chose.
I had no choice but I must follow him
With forfeits and rewards he understood —
Unless I liked to suffer loss of worship.
I had to prosper good and punish evil.
You changed all that. You set me free to reign.[276]

As Yvor Winters puts it, the correct perspective to which these lines need to be put lies in "the Fideistic tradition of New England calvinism..." manifest "in more than one passage in Jonathan Edwards, as well as elsewhere."[277] We find its echo also in the works of Donne, Dryden and Swift. The point that ought to be noted here is the extremely humanizing effect felt by God's reference to man's Adamic free will "Who could do good or evil as he chose."[278] God's role is, thus, one of a wit whose comic spirit enables him to view man both in a detached and concerned manner. In fact, Thyatire, "Job's shrewd and sharp-tongued wife" provides a deep examination of God's relationship with man. With the spontaneity and fierceness of a domestic quarrel, Thyatira's argument and its gossipy touch reduces God to the position of a common man. God's remote abstraction and its religious sanction in orthodox Christianity are greatly exploded by the militant, emancipated and sophisticated social consciousness of Thyatira. Her complaint, comically counterpointed against Job's serious and deeply-felt protestation at God's injustices to man, aptly highlights how it has become increasingly difficult for man, with his Adamic free will, to accept injustice even if it were meted out by God. For example, Thyatira is more conscious of rights and privileges ["Witch-women's rights"],[279] and is all attention when Satan appears "like a sapphire wasp/That flickers mica wings."[280] Thyatira is, thus, the eternal female who, with her emotional and non-philosophical nature, is quickly activated "to know the reason why" God has given a free rope to unjust events that, for no fault of man, smite the human race from time to time:

> All you can seem to do is lose Your temper
> When reason-hungry mortals ask for reasons.[281]

Thyatira's mock-serious banter as in the above lines is meant to supplant the serious theme manifest in the dialogue between Job and God. She rejects all philosophic abstractions that bring forth any universal reason to explain God's unsystematic, and rather unjust treatment of man. This may be highly disturbing to those who believe in the finality of the Mosaic Law based on the Judaic orthodoxy in the Old Testament. What Frost makes of this situation is to indicate that the meaningless and apparantly irrational affliction to which Job has been subjected in spite of his unshakable faith in God has ultimately helped in making us able to evaluate "religious thought" in a new perspective. Frost would, therefore, make God acknowledge His indebtedness of Job in the following lines:

> ...I have no doubt
> You realize by now the part you played
> To stultify the Deuteronomist
> And change the tenor of religious thought.[282]

What should also be noted carefully is the "witty" reply given by God in furtherance of the stand taken by Him to justify His ways with man. That God was "just showing off to the Devil..." would also mean that "the Devil's...God's best inspiration"[283]. It may also signify that insofar as man's relationship with God is concerned he cannot establish any "meaningful moral relationship" without involving himself both with good and evil "including evils inexplicable by human finite reason."[284] This reminds us of the situation in which Adam fell after he was expelled from Paradise. Thereafter, Adam's lot was no less a "trial by existence" than that of Job's, calling for a hard struggle to endure all afflictions. The difference lay, however, in that Adam had an implicit faith in "life." It is Thyatira, if not Job, who gives such an obvious Adamic connotation to Job's sufferings in the following lines:

> Job says there's no such thing as Earth's becoming,
> An easier place for man to save his soul in,
> Except as a hard place to save his soul in,
> A trial ground where he can try himself,
> And find out whether he is any good,
> It would be meaningless. It might as well
> Be Heaven at once and have it over with.[285]

The tone here is not only dry in its irony and quizzicality, but also full of a playful bantering humour. What Thyatira believes in with a seriousness underlying the evident humour is that whatever be man's pathway to truth he must needs shape his destiny in this earth alone which is still his "fate." In this also one clearly deciphers a kind of skepticism about God's ways with man—something of a Faustian catechism of Mephistopheles in Thyatira's evaluation of God's unreason. The answer to this is, of course, given by Frost in his subsequent study of God's ways as we find in *A Masque of Mercy.* The theme therein not only exalts man's reverence for God's unforseen will, but also anticipates man's redemption through God's love that is possible in the face of a terrible, and perhaps a little too unmerited tragedy. However, this theme which obviously smacks of orthodox Christianity in the light of what we can commonly understand from the central features of the New Testament is, as usual, couched in a style of ironic punning and joke reminding us of a Yeats or a Shaw in their later phases. The raillery and mockery do also remind us of a Swiftian kind of parody with a touch of wildness, and perhaps something of "naughtiness." All this goes well with Frost when he chooses to play the role of a parodist while talking of religion in terms of man's failure to maintain a just standard of selflessness so much idealized by the main thrust of the Sermon on the Mount. His contention is that it takes love, or for that matter, Mercy to forgive such a failure. This is all the more necessary since God's injustice is inevitable. The lines that focus on this theme bring in the figure of Christ as an Adamic phenomenon introducing a sort of "break with logic":

> Christ came to introduce a break with logic
> That made all other outrage seem as child's play:
> The Mercy on the Sin against the Sermon.
> Strange no one ever thought of it before him.
> 'Twas lovely and its origin was love.[286]

What should also be of help to man in the face of God's injustice, proved well in the event of Jonah's mission, is man's ability to rely on his own intrinsic "courage" however little it might be. Hence. "...The Saddest thing in life/Is that the best thing in it should be courage."[287] Therefore, Jesse Bel is "right" when she glorifies courage, for "courage is of the heart by derivation,/And great it is..., 'though' ...fear is of the soul."[288]

After Adam's expulsion from Paradise it was obvious that his destiny was cast in a course of uncertainty. Man to-day is, of course, a logical heir to this state of affairs. Frost exploits this theme in some of the severest lines in the *Masque of Mercy* which only appear noble as he, in spite of his Puck-like whimsy, coats the episode in a traditional religious language:

> And I can see that the uncertainty
> In which we act is a severity,
> A cruelty, amounting to injustice
> That nothing but God's mercy can assuage.[289]

To add to this there is also the possibility of our ultimate rejection by heaven, for "Our very best, our lives laid down like Jonah's,/Our lives laid down in war and peace, may not/Be found acceptable in Heaven's sight."[290] The poem is, therefore, an invitation to recognize that no manner of salvation or grace "as defined in the Roman Catholic or the more conservative Protestant Churches"[291] can, in fact, help man fruitfully. The best he can afford to do is to show up his best efforts in the face of life's uncertainty, acknowledging failure in himself and others as a sure factor. He would also do well to be merciful towards injustice done unto him and his fellow brothers as a positive step, as Brower says, "to right the wrong we will inevitably go on doing."[292] This is undoubtedly a good way of salvation for all of us, but what must be emphasized is that man has to "go ahead" to "accomplishment" with the consolation available to him that" "The utmost reward of daring is to dare."[293] In the tradition of Adamism, anyone who is willing to live on the validity of such a postulate is indeed willing to accept "a scheme of uncertified possibilities which he trusts; willing to pay with his own person, if need be, for the realization of the ideals which he frames."[294]

This mood of acceptance of "a scheme of uncertified possibilities" is further explored in "Directive"—a poem that examines the value, valence and validity of turning back in time to reach a point of "wholeness beyond confusion." If most of Frost's poems analysed earlier in this Chapter hold fast to the tension of contrariety forming the basis of a unified vision, this poem appears almost as a testament to his final belief in the role of the poet's unambiguous and calm solemnity of tone. Rejecting, therefore, the traditional tone of Frostian "whimsy," the poem takes the reader much beyond any prescribed stoicism where "human identity" can hold its own bravely in the face of a world that is not only "too much with us," but also, as the poem succinctly puts it, "too much for us." It is worthwhile to note that the poem begins with the word "back," striking thereby the keynote to a process which would enable us to attain an existence that would save us from man's confusing, chaotic, and thing-ridden society. In fact, Frost, both in his poems and in his conversation, has shown a deep concern with the problem of going back to whatever one thinks to be the source in one's life.[295]

Indeed such a preoccupation in Frost places him in a line of tradition in American Literature which veritably reveals that one such source may be the American wilderness itself. Down from Thoreau who delved deep into a realization of this truth by a series of experimentations in his own life to Whitman's celebration of the great "I" against the backdrop of all that is "virgin" in land and forests, we have a series of characters, particularly in American fiction, such as Jake Barnes, Nick

Adams and Ike McCaslin, to name only a few, who, cutting themselves free from all human entanglements and relationships discovered their lost identity in the very "darkness" of the wilderness. Frost, not unlike Melville, had in himself a sense of terror so as not to push himself too far into this "darkness," lest, instead of discovering his lost identity, he would lose himself altogether. Hence, in him we discover a growing need to stick to what we have already stated "the vantage point" between the all-devouring "darkness" of the wilderness and the world of human beings.

However, in this poem alone Frost seems to have thrown this caution to the winds, and it is, we suppose, a final testament to his deeply ingrained belief in the sanctity of the "metaphoric critique of the Golden Age idea"[296] which appears to be an offshoot of the American myth of wilderness. Such a myth is a positive reiteration of the Adamic belief that no matter how civilized, and, therefore, artificial, our century might be, there still lurks large the possibility of realizing Edenic bliss if only we would learn the art of substituting "a world of space for the continuum of time." Places, apart from circumstances and situations in human life can, of course, help overcome any deficiency in man to cope with the problem of this rather difficult substitution which obviously looks like a mystery in metaphysics. Frost's poem leads us on to such a place, and presents a situation where all "comers," provided they have the wisdom gained through worldly experience, can verily attain salvation by a realization of innocence, and an intimation of immortality. The particularities of this quest are brought into focus through the Grail legend and the image of water in the poem. Symbolically speaking, Frost gives a significant twist to the Grail legend as he goes out of the well-known areas of the myth in indicating that the hidden "goblet" is only a "broken" one saved from the children's playhouse. Appearing on the surface to be somewhat like another Frostian "whimsy," the metaphor, however, asserts beyond doubt that we can forever renew ourselves physically and spiritually if only we have the ability to bring the "attitude of play" to our adult life. This will not only keep the "whisper of death" away from the twentieth-century man which obsesses him so often, but also act for him as a positive formative decision to serve as a final answer to his life's "in-load" of disturbance, discord and discomfort.

NOTES

1. See Pearce, *The Continuity of American Poetry,* p. 189.
2. Smith, Virgin Land, p. 15.
3. *Ibid.*, p. 47.
4. *Saturday Review,* (Dec. 19, 1970), 24, 29.
5. Pearce, *The Continuity of American Poetry,* p. 408.
6. Wallace Stevens, "Esthetique du Nal," in Wallace Stevens, *The Collected Poems,* p. 326.
7. See Ernest Earnest, *Expatriates and Patriots: American Artists, Scholars, and Writers in Europe* (Durham: North Carolina Press, 1968), p. vii.
8. See for a comprehensive account of this theme Lawrence, *The Classic American Studies,* Chap. 1.
9. Elaine Barry, *Robert Frost on Writing* (New Brunswick, N.J.: Rutgers Univ. Press, 1973), p. 3.
10. Lawrance Thompson, ed. *Selected Letters of Robert Frost* (New York: Holt, Rinehart & Winston, 1964), p. 385.
11. T.S. Eliot, "Tradition and the Individual Talent," in *Selected Prose,* ed. John Hayward (Harmondsworth: Penguin, 1953), p. 23.
12. Letter to John Erskine quoted in Berry, *Robert Frost on Writing,* p. 100.
13. Letter to The Amherst Student in 1935. Quoted in Berry, *Robert Frost on Writing,* p. 112.
14. Letter to Louis Untermeyer, 10 March 1924. Quoted in Barry, *Robert Frost on Writing,* p. 78.
15. Robert Frost, "Education by Poetry," in *Selected Prose of Robert Frost,* eds. Hyde Cox and Edward Connery Lathem (New York: Holt, Rinehart & Winston, 1966), pp. 44-45.
16. Barry, *Robert Frost on Writing,* p. 25.
17. See Lawrance Thompson, *Fire and Ice: The Art and Thought of Robert Frost* (New York: Holt, Rinehart & Winston, 1942), Chapt. 2.
18. Pearce, *The Continuity of American Poetry,* p. 187.
19. Louis Untermeyer, ed. *The Letters of Robert Frost to Louis Untermeyer* (New York: Holt, Rinehart & Winston, 1963), p. 22.
20. Pearce, *The Continuity of American Poetry,* p. 187.
21. Frost, "The Figure a Poem Makes," Preface to *Collected Poems,* 1939. Quoted in Barry, *Robert Frost on Writing,* p. 126.

22. Frost, "The Constant Symbol," Preface to 1946 Modern Library Edition of Frost's Poems. Published separately in the *Atlantic Monthly* of October 1946. Quoted in Barry, *Robert Frost on Writing,* p. 128.
23. *Ibid.*
24. Letter to Sidney Cox, 19 January 1914. Quoted in Barry, *Robert Frost on Writing,* p. 61.
25. Thompson ed. *Selected Letters of Robert Frost,* pp. 191-92.
26. Barry, *Robert Frost on Writing,* p. 14.
27. Letter to Sidney Cox, 19 January 1914. Quoted in Barry, *Robert Frost on Writing,* p. 62.
28. Lecture to the Browne and Nichols School, 10 May 1915. Quoted in Barry, *Robert Frost on Writing,* p. 143.
29. Shakespeare.
30. Barry, *Robert Frost on Writing,* p. 143.
31. *Ibid.*, p. 144.
32. Robert Frost, "A Visit in Franconia," *Interviews with Robert Frost,* ed. Edward Connery Lathem (New York: Holt, Rinehart & Winston, 1966), p. 13.
33. Thompson, ed. *Selected Letters of Robert Frost,* p. 130.
34. Letter to John T. Bartlett, 22 February 1914, Beaconsfield. Quoted in Barry, *Robert Frost on Writing,* p. 66.
35. *Ibid.*
36. Shumaker, *Literature and the Irrational: A Study in Anthropological Backgrounds,* p. 75.
37. See George Herzog, "Drum-Signaling in a West-African Tribe," in Dell Hymes, ed. *Language in Culture and Society: A Reader in Linguistics and Anthropology* (New York: Harper & Row, Publishers, 1964), pp. 312-29.
38. William G. Moulton, "The Nature of Language," in *Daedalus,* 102, No. 3 (Summer 1973: Language as a Human Problem), 35.
39. Kantak, "Poetic Ambiguity in Frost,"35.
40. Thompson, ed. *Selected Letters of Robert Frost,* p. 361.
41. *Ibid.*, p. 179.
42. *Ibid.*, p. 369.
43. *Complete Poems of Robert Frost,* p. 600.
44. Untermeyer, ed. *Letters,* p. 14.
45. Robert Frost, "The Poetry of Amy Lowell," in the *Christian Science Monitor,* 16 May 1925. Quoted in Barry, *Robert Frost on Writing,* p. 136.
46. Introduction to the Arts Anthology: Datsmouth Verse, 1925. Quoted in Barry, *Robert Frost on Writing,* p. 116.
47. Letter to Louis Untermeyer, Amherst, Mass., 10 March 1924. Quoted in Barry, *Robert Frost on Writing,* pp. 77-78.

48. Untermeyer, ed. *Letters,* p. 14.
49. Quoted in Barry, *Robert Frost on Writing,* p. 78.
50. Frost, "The Constant Symbol," in *The Atlantic Monthly* (October 1946). Quoted in Barry, *Robert Frost on Writing,* p. 130.
51. Frost, "The Figure a Poem Makes," Preface to *Collected Poems,* 1939. Quoted in Barry, *Robert Frost on Writing,* p. 126.
52. Quoted in Barry, *Robert Frost on Writing,* p. 127.
53. *Ibid.*
54. Letter to Sidney Cox, December 1914 [The Gallows]. Quoted in Barry, *Robert Frost on Writing,* p. 68. Frost writes, "I want the unmade words to work with, not the familiar made ones that everybody exclaims Poetry! at."
55. Barry, *Robert Frost on Writing,* p. 29.
56. Quoted *ibid.*, p. 51.
57. Thompson, ed. *Selected Letters of Robert Frost,* p. 182.
58. Barry, *Robert Frost on Writing,* pp. 10-12.
59. Quoted *ibid.*, p. 33.
60. Untermeyer, ed. *Letters,* p. 255.
61. Richard Poirier, *Paris Review,* No. 24 (Summer-Fall, 1959), 109.
62. Breslin, *William Carlos Williams,* p. 102.
63. Letter to Braithwaite quoted in Sergeant, *Robert Frost: The Trial by Existence*, p. 163.
64. Breslin, *William Carlos Williams,* p. 102.
65. Lewis, *The American Adam,* p. 45.
66. Sir Maurice Bowra, *The Romantic Imagination* (London: Oxford Univ. Press, 1950), p. 30.
67. Lawrance Thompson, *Robert Frost* (Minnespolis: Univ. of Minnesota Press, 1959), p. 7.
68. See Sergeant, *The Trial by Existence,* pp. 227 ff.
69. *Ibid.*, p. 212.
70. *Ibid.*, p. 219.
71. Frost quoted *ibid.*, p. 143.
72. Cecil Day Lewis, "Introduction," in Robert Frost, *Selected Poems* (Penguin Books, 1955), p. 15.
73. Quoted in Jean Could, *Robert Frost: The Aim Was Song* (New York: Dodd, Meed & Company, 1964), p. 53.
74. *Ibid.*
75. *Complete Poems of Robert Frost,* p. 131.
76. "Introduction," Cox, ed. *Robert Frost: A Collection of Critical Essays,* p. 2.
77. *Ibid.*, p. 5.
78. Danis Radcliffe, *The Major Themes of Robert Frost* (Ann Arbor: The Univ. of Michigan Press, 1963), pp. 1-2.

79. *Ibid.*, p. 4.
80. *Ibid.*, p. 63.
81. Lynen, The Pastoral Art of Robert Frost, p. 27.
82. Frost quoted Charles. R. Anderson, "Robert Frost, 1874-1963," *Saturday Review* (23 February 1963), 20.
83. Quoted *ibid.*, 19.
84. *Complete Poems of Robert Frost,* p. 5.
85. *Ibid.*
86. Reuben A. Brower, *Constellations of Intention,* p. 74.
87. Lewis, *The American Adam,* p. 27.
88. Brower, *Constellations of Intention,* p. 74.
89. Lewis, *The American Adam,* p. 114.
90. *Complete Poems of Robert Frost,* p. 5.
91. Lewis, *The American Adam,* p. 164.
92. *Ibid.*, p. 94.
93. *Complete Poems of Robert Frost,* p. 5.
94. Eliade, *Cosmos and History,* p. 88.
95. *Complete Poems of Robert Frost,* p. 5.
96. Waggoner, *American Poets: From the Puritans to the Present,* p. 295.
97. *Ibid.* Waggoner goes on to challenge this kind of unsympathetic treatment of Frost in the hands of critics. Commenting on the phrase, "strategic retreat," Waggoner opines: "A general makes a strategic retreat in order to win a later battle, or to get into a position to win the whole war."
98. Lawrance Thompson, *Robert Frost: The Early Years, 1874-1915* (New York: Holt, Rinehart & Winston, 1966), p. xxii.
99. See Frost, "The Constant Symbol," in Barry, *Robert Frost on Writings,* p. 130.
100. Thompson, *Robert Frost: The Early Years,* p. xxii.
101. George W. Nitchie, *Human Values in the Poetry of Robert Frost* (Durham, N.C.: Duke Univ. Press, 1960), p. 77.
102. *Ibid.*
103. Brower, *Constellations of Intention,* p. 184.
104. Thompson, *Robert Frost: The Early Years,* p. 621.
105. This charge is negated in his poem "Escapist [?] Never."
106. Thompson, *Robert Frost: The Early Years,* pp. 397-400.
107. *Ibid.*, p. 311.
108. *Complete Poems of Robert Frost,* p. 22.
109. *Ibid.*
110. Nitchie, *Human Values in the Poetry of Robert Frost,* p. 65.
111. John T. Ogilvie, "From Woods to Stars: A Pattern of Imagery in Robert Frost's Poetry," *The South Atlantic Quarterly,* 58, No. 1 (Winter 1959), 74.

112. *Complete Poems of Robert Frost,* p. 30.
113. *Ibid.*, p. 24.
114. *Ibid.*
115. Quoted in Lathem, ed. *Interviews with Robert Frost,* p. 76.
116. *Ibid.*
117. *Complete Poems of Robert Frost,* p. 41.
118. *Ibid.*, p. 272.
119. *Ibid.*, p. 642.
120. Gerber, *Robert Frost,* p. 132.
121. *Ibid.*, p. 132.
122. John Ciardi, "Robert Frost: The Way to the Poem," *Saturday Review,* 40 (April 12, 1958), 13.
123. Clark Griffith, "Frost and the American View of Nature," *American Quarterly*, 20, No. 1 (Spring 1968), 29.
124. *Ibid.*
125. *Complete Poems of Robert Frost,* p. 48.
126. *Ibid.*
127. *Ibid.*, p. 47.
128. Carson Gibb, "Mending Well," *The Explicator Cyclopedia,* Vol. 1, eds. Charles Child Walcutt & J. Edwin Whitesell (Chicago: Quadrangle Books, 1966), p. 137.
129. Elizabeth Jennings, *Frost* (Edinburgh: Oliver & Boyd, 1964), p. 3.
130. See Dorothy Judd, "Reserve in the Art of Robert Frost," *Texas Quarterly*, 6, No. 2, 60-67.
131. Letters to Leonidas W. Payne, Jr., Nov., Nov. 1, 1927 in Thompson, ed. *Selected Letters of Robert Frost,* p. 344.
132. See Carol Anne Kyle, "Epistemological Dualism in the Poetry of Robert Frost," *Dissertation Abstracts,* 29, No. 7 (January 1969), 2267A-2268A.
133. Virginia Scroggin Stone, "Robert Frost: The Breathless Swing Between Content and Form," *Dissertation Abstracts,* 30, No. 6 (December 1969), 2501A. Stone says that Frost's "comic mask sometimes hid a seriousness not always apparent to the casual reader." See also William Mulder, "Freedom and Form: Robert Frost's Double Discipline," *South Atlantic Quarterly,* 54 (July 1955), 386-93.
134. Sister Vincent Waltz, "The Doubleness of Nature in Robert Frost's Poetry of Paradox," *Dissertation Abstracts,* 29, No. 8 (February 1969), 2727A.
135. *Complete Poems of Robert Frost,* p. 48.
136. Ruth Ann Lewis, "Robert Frost, Poet-Teacher: Three Studies," Dissertation. Univ. of Utah, 1969, p. iv.
137. It echoes Keats's "Ode to Autumn" which also acts on a "principle of reversal," and focuses on the "beauty and bounty" of Autumn—a season that usually suggests "emptiness," the precursor of Winter.

138. *Complete Poems of Robert Frost,* p. 322.
139. Dendinger, "Robert Frost: Popular Image of a Poet," p. 126.
140. Jean-Paul Sartre, "American Novelists in French Eyes," *Atlantic Monthly,* 178 (August 1946), 114.
141. Quoted *ibid.*, p. 119. See also review of "A Boy's Will," in *Poetry,* 11 (May 1913), 72-73. Quoted *ibid.*, p. 19.
142. Yvor Winters, "Robert Frost: Or the Spiritual Drifter as Poet," in Cox, ed. *Robert Frost: A Collection of Critical Essays*, p. 82.
143. *Ibid.*
144. *Ibid.*, p. 81.
145. Dendinger, "Robert Frost: Popular Image of a Poet," p. 71.
146. Wilbur S. Scott, "To Earthward," *The Explicator Cyclopedia,* Vol. 1, p. 145.
147. *Ibid.*
148. *Complete Poems of Robert Frost,* p. 280.
149. Thompson, *Fire and Ice,* p. 107.
150. Nitchie, *Human Values in the Poetry of Robert Frost,* p. 93
151. Sidney Cox, *A Swinger of Birches: A Portrait of Robert Frost* (New York: Collier Books, 1957), p. 26.
152. *Ibid.*
153. *Ibid.*, p. 30.
154. *Ibid.*, p. 31.
155. *Ibid.*
156. *Ibid.*, p. 26.
157. *Complete Poems of Robert Frost,* p. 153.
158. Nitchie, *Human Values in the Poetry of Robert Frost,* p. 7.
159. *Ibid.*
160. David A. Sohn & Richard H. Tyne, *Frost: The Poet and His Poetry* (New York: Bantam Books, 1969), p. 71.
161. Wilson O. Clough, *The Necessary Earth: Nature and Solitude in American Literature* (Austin: Univ. of Texas Press, 1964), p. 191.
162. John T. Hiers, "Robert Frost's Quarrel with Science," *The Georgia Review,* 25, 2 (Summer 1971), 192.
163. Dendinger, "Robert Frost: Popular Image of a Poet," p. 34.
164. Nitchie, *The Human Values in the Poetry of Robert Frost,* p. 83.
165. Lynen, *The Pastoral Art,* p. 289.
166. Stephen E. Whicher, ed. *Selections from Ralph Waldo Emerson: An Organic Anthology* (Boston: Houghton Mifflin Co., 1957), pp. 440-41.
167. Quoted in Could, *Robert Frost: The Aim was Song,* p. 258.
168. *Complete Poems of Robert Frost,* p. 324.
169. Sergeant, The Trial by Existence, p. 232.
170. *Ibid.*, p. 234.

171. Sergeant, *The Trial by Existance,* p. 234.
172. Lionel Trilling quoted in A. Alvarez, *The Shaping Spirit: Studies in Modern English and American Poets* (London: Chatto & Windus, 1961), pp. 167-168.
173. See Could, *Robert Frost: The Aim was Song,* p. 258.
174. Brower, *Constellations of Intention,* p. 128.
175. *Ibid.*, p. 128.
176. *Complete Poems of Robert Frost,* p. 324.
177. Alvarez, *The Shaping Spirit,* p. 174.
178. *Ibid.*
179. Brower, *Constellations of Intention,* p. 81.
180. *Complete Poems of Robert Frost,* p. 24.
181. See Pearce, *The Continuity of American Poetry,* p. 275.
182. *Ibid.*, p. 278.
183. Carl Sandburg quoted *ibid.*, p. 270.
184. Dendinger, "Robert Frost: Popular Image of a Poet," p. 73.
185. *Complete Poems of Robert Frost,* p. 386.
186. Dendinger, "Robert Frost: Popular Image of a Poet," p. 110.
187. *Complete Poems of Robert Frost,* p. 32.
188. *Ibid.*, p. 25.
189. Elaine Barry, *Robert Frost* (New York: Frederick Ungar Publishing Co., 1973), p. 82.
190. *Ibid.*, p. 106.
191. *Ibid.*
192. *Complete Poems of Robert Frost,* p. 30.
193. Alfred R. Ferguson, "Frost and the Paradox of the Fortunate Fall" in Jack L. Tharp, ed. *Frost: Centennial Essays* (Jackson: Univ. Press of Mississippi, n.d.), p. 427.
194. Quoted from Frost in Tharp, ed. *Centennial Essays,* p. 427. See Robert Frost, "Education by Poetry: A Meditative Monologue," *Amherst Alumni Council News,* 4 (March 1941), Supplement, 6-7.
195. *Complete Poems of Robert Frost,* p. 272.
196. Tharp, ed. *Centennial Essays,* p. 438.
197. Edward Connery Lathem, ed. *The Poetry of Robert Frost* (London: Jonathan Cape Ltd., 1972), p. 435.
198. *Ibid.*, pp. 434-35.
199. Thompson, ed. *Selected Letters of Robert Frost,* p. 369.
200. *Complete Poems of Robert Frost,* p. 149.
201. *Ibid.*, p. 288.
202. Tharp, ed. *Centennial Essays,* p. 564.
203. *Complete Poems of Robert Frost,* p. 288.
204. Tharp, ed. *Centennial Essays,* p. 555.
205. *Ibid.*

206. *Ibid.*
207. John T. Conder, " 'After Apple-Picking': Frost's Troubled Sleep" in Tharp, ed., *Contennial Essays,* p. 171.
208. *Ibid.*, p. 179.
209. William Bysshe Stein, "'After Apple-Picking': Echoic Parody," *University Review* (Kansas City, No.), 35, 301 ff.
210. *Complete Poems of Robert Frost,* p. 88.
211. *Ibid.*
212. Frost quoted in Reginald Cook, *Robert Frost: A Living Voice* (Amherst: The Univ. of Massachusetts Press, 1974), p. 307.
213. Frost quoted in Cook, *Robert Frost: A Living Voice,* p. 307.
214. Frost quoted *ibid.*
215. *Complete Poems of Robert Frost,* p. 88.
216. *Ibid.*, p. 89.
217. *Ibid*, p. 25.
218. *Ibid.*
219. Cook, *Robert Frost: A Living Voice,* p. 305.
220. *Complete Poems of Robert Frost,* p. 150.
221. *Ibid.*, p. 329.
222. Thompson, ed. *Selected Letters of Robert Frost;* p. 417.
223. George W. Nitchie, "Robert Frost: The Imperfect Guru," in Tharp, ed. *Centennial Essays,* p. 47.
224. W.H. Auden, "Robert Frost," in *The Dyer's Hand* (New York: Random House, 1962), p. 340.
225. Cook, *Robert Frost: A Living Voice,* p. 308.
226. *Complete Poems of Robert Frost,* p. 52.
227. *Ibid.*, p. 53.
228. *Ibid.*, p. 55.
229. Wilbert Snow, "The Robert Frost I Knew," *The Texas Quarterly,* 11, No. 3 (Autumn 1968), 23. See also the Frost-Snow correspondence in Lawrance Thompson. *Robert Frost: The Years of Triumph* (New York: Holt, Rinehart & Winston Inc., 1970), pp. 656-57.
230. Melville quoted in Cook, *Robert Frost: A Living Voice,* p. 262.
231. *Complete Poems of Robert Frost,* p. 529.
232. See Cook, *Robert Frost: The Living Voice,* p. 263.
233. *Complete Poems of Robert Frost,* p. 396.
234. Cook, *Robert Frost: The Living Voice,* p. 266.
235. *Ibid.*, p. 317.
236. *Ibid.*
237. *Ibid.*
238. *Ibid.*
239. Lathem, ed. *The Poetry of Robert Frost,* p. 444.

240. Cook, *Robert Frost: The Living Voice,* p. 269.
241. Maud Bodkin, *Archetypal Patterns in Poetry: Psychological Studies of Imagination* (London: Oxford Univ. Press, 1934), p. 54.
242. *Complete Poems of Robert Frost,* p. 10.
243. *Ibid.*, p. 193-194.
244. Nitchie, *The Human Values in the Poetry of Robert Frost,* p. 82.
245. *Complete Poems of Robert Frost,* p. 80.
246. *Ibid.*, p. 43.
247. *Ibid.*
248. See for the development of this theme Yvor Winters, "Robert Frost: Or the Spiritual Drifter as Poet," *Sewanee Review,* 56 (Autumn 1948), 564-96.
249. *Complete Poems of Robert Frost,* p. 347.
250. *Ibid.*, pp. 347-48.
251. Lawrence Perrire, "The Meaning of Frost's 'Build Soil,'" in Tharp, ed. *Centennial Essays,* p. 232.
252. *Complete Poems of Robert Frost,* p. 425.
253. *Ibid.*
254. *Ibid.*, p. 343.
255. *Ibid.*, p. 327.
256. *Ibid.*, pp. 328-29.
257. *Ibid.*, p. 329.
258. *Ibid.*
259. See Nitchie, *The Human Values in the Poetry of Robert Frost,* pp. 94ff.
260. John Ciardi, "Robert Frost: The Way to the Poem," *Saturday Review,* 40 (12 April 1958), 13.
261. *Ibid.*, 15.
262. *Complete Poems of Robert Frost,* p. 275.
263. Leonard Unger and William Van O'Conner, *Poems for Study* (New York: Rinehart, 1953), p. 599.
264. *Complete Poems of Robert Frost,* p. 275.
265. Thornton quoted in William S. Doxey, "Out, Out-,"*Explicator,* 29, No. 8 (April 1971), Item 70.
266. *Complete Poems of Robert Frost,* p. 171.
267. *Ibid.*
268. *Ibid.*
269. Cook, *Robert Frost: A Living Voice,* p. 262.
270. *Complete Poems of Robert Frost,* p. 172.
271. *Ibid.*, p. 470.
272. Peter J. Stanlis, "Robert Frost's Masques and the Classic American Tradition." in Tharp, ed. *Centennial Essays,* p. 444.
273. Untermeyer, ed. *Letters,* pp. 333-34.

274. *Complete Poems of Robert Frost*, p. 587.
275. *Ibid.*
276. *Ibid.*, p. 590.
277. Yvor Winters, "Robert Frost: or the Spiritual Drifter as Poet," in Cox, ed. *Robert Frost: A Collection of Critical Essays,* pp. 71-72.
278. *Complete Poems of Robert Frost,* p. 590.
279. *Ibid.*, p. 594.
280. *Ibid.*, p. 603.
281. *Ibid.*, p. 592.
282. *Ibid.*, pp. 589-90.
283. *Ibid.*, p. 600, p. 604.
284. Stanlis, "Robert Frost's Masques and the Classic American Tradition," in Tharp, ed. *Centennial Essays,* p. 452.
285. *Complete Poems of Robert Frost,* p. 600.
286. *Ibid.*, p. 630.
287. *Ibid.*, p. 614.
288. *Ibid.*
289. *Ibid.*, p. 641.
290. *Ibid.*, p. 642.
291. Brower, *Constellations of Intention,* pp. 223-24.
292. *Ibid.*, p. 294.
293. *Complete Poems of Robert Frost,* p. 28.
294. William James, *Pragmatism*: *And Four Essays from the Meaning of Truth* (1907 & 1909 rpt; New Delhi: Eurasia Publishing House Pvt. Ltd., 1975), p. 197.
295. See *Complete Poems of Robert Frost,* p. 5, p. 131, p. 519, for poems entitled "Into My Own," "The Road Not Taken," and "One Step Backward Taken." Sentences in these poems such as "I do not see why I should e'er turn back," "I doubted if I should ever come back" and "But with one step backward taken/I saved myself from going," are highly significant in the evolution of this theme in Frost. See also Theodore Morrison, "The Agitated Heart," *The Atlantic Monthly* (July 1967), 77-79.
296. James P. Dougherty, "Robert Frost's 'Directive' to the Wilderness," *American Quarterly,* 18, No. 2, Pt. 1 (Summer 1966), 208.

5

Williams: "On Native Grounds" Of Edenic Bliss

IN THE previous Chapter we have made an attempt to examine the poetry of Robert Frost in the light of "the Adamic Mode" in American poetry, particularly focusing on Frost's ultimate assertion of a faith, human enough to stand man in good stead. We shall now examine the poetry of William Carlos Williams, putting it under the test of similar critical canons. This will obviously create a common ground to enable us to compare and contrast the poetry of these two major poets of our time.

It was not until the years following the World War II that true recognition came to William Carlos Williams who then assumed a status that was equal to Pound's, and perhaps greater than Eliot's. This came about as a result of a shift in sensibility that gave birth to a whole generation of new poets like Robert Lowell, Robert Creeley, Charles Olson, Robert Duncan, LeRoi Jones, Allen Ginsberg, Gary Snider, and Denise Levertov. It was a literature that sought its sustenance from the native soil of America unlike the literature of the expatriates—Pound and Eliot, for example, who drew heavily on foreign cultures. Walter Sutton, while analyzing the modern revolution in American poetry, indicates how Williams chose to get deeply attached to his native place "resisting Pound's repeated urgings to come to Europe and 'bite off a chunk of it.' "[1] The sprawling, and in a way, unlovely city of New Jersey, inspired the composition of his poems that took "the near, the low, the common," to quote Emerson's words, as their subject-matter. While capturing through language the reality and integrity of objects in their bare physicality, he gave such a twist and turn to the everyday speech of America, "purging and refining it to an unostentatious elegance,"[2] that the completed *poem itself* assumed the stature of an object. This explains why his objectivism should not be considered as the product of a pure objective imagism. Even if it was the bare physicality of New Jersey landscape that he portrayed, the tenacity with which he clung to it showed an element of nostalgia for the Edenic bliss of the region, now lost, but once "kept up beautifully" with natural springs and green vegetation of Nature all around.[3]

Unlike the mythic poet, Williams rejected the concept of the linear, and historical progression of time, and 1909 onwards he would consistently free himself from his Whitmanesque and Keatsian "leanings" in order to write poetry which, born of immediate experiences, would place the readers in a "loving contact with the actual."[4] Though he imitated the style of Keats whom he remembered as a "God," it was Whitman who taught him to cultivate an Adamic self-reliance by rejecting "conventional poetic forms."[5] He took up where Whitman had left by reforming and polishing the loose, and broken, though simple, elements of poetic perception. Whitman's fault lay, as Williams says in one of his essays, in composing so freely that the process of "selection and rejection" which is the test of a great artist failed to work in him with proper justification.[6] This may mean that Williams was a very conscious artist, and was not the "freewheeling" sort of poet he is usually thought to be. In fact, he dedicated himself almost throughout his life to generate a fresh use of language in poetry, particularly the kind used commonly by the Americans. This was an arduous struggle, but it was worth it, and for him there was perhaps hardly any means but through it to carry home his view that "the physical [is] the source of all life."[7] This was how he wanted to revive "his world" just as the American Adam would do to regain the lost paradise of the Old World in the New World Garden of America. All this would only indicate that he was one of those few Americans who believed that a poet is responsible to his locality;

he must not "deny his origins, his age, or any aspect of his local environment."[8] "Everything exists from the beginning,"[9] says Williams, and his apt remark that "the place of my birth is the place where the word begins"[10] has been an oft-quoted line to evaluate him as an American poet. There was also the Dionysiac, and for that matter, the Adamic element in him—the one of "sheer drunkenness" in dedicating himself to art, "to write, write as I alone should write...."[11] Thus, Williams exposed himself to his immediate, local ground, wrestling as he did with its brutal, vulgar and grotesque aspects to present a universal vision of life which would redeem the modern man. This means that there is a necessity of rebirth, or of renewal of feelings, fixing them to "a new order," which, as Mircea Eliade would put it, generally emerges out of reabsorbing "the existing order" into the "formless." Eliade adds that "it must be restored to the primordial unity from which it issued; in other words, it must return to 'chaos..'., to 'orgy..'., to 'darkness.'.., to 'water.'..."[12]

The preceding paragraphs explain in some measure why Williams was at odds with the Poundian preoccupation with the power of "Kulchur," and the Eliotic claim for the power of the myth beyond myth—God—as the redeeming force of our life's predicament. As it appears, the "terms" with which Williams would cope with our "past" were entirely different from those of Pound's or Eliot's. If Pound and Eliot would view the present "as an ironic diminuation of past excellance," Williams would like to show in his poetry—particularly his mature ones after 1913—that "the present is," aesthetically speaking, "an ironic diminuation of its own potentiality."[13]

Nothing explains better than this why Williams was shocked when Eliot's *The Waste Land* was published in 1922:

> To me especially it struck like a sardonic bullet. I felt at once that it had set me back twenty years, and I'm sure it did. Critically Eliot returned us to the classroom just at the moment when I felt that we were on the point of an escape to matters much closer to the essence of a new art form itself—rooted in the locality which should give it

> fruit. I knew at once that in certain ways I was most defeated.[14]

For one reason, to be sure, why Williams felt defeated, was the fact of Eliot's failure to deal with a poem's materials *directly* without translating them into symbols. Williams, on the other hand, remained throughout "the great poet of the *things* of this world,...[communicating] the 'thingness' of these objects without unnecessary embelishments...."[15] Thus, anything that was "living" was that which concerned him. Williams says:

> I want to place a value on everything I touch
> and I want to place the human elements first.[16]

Reasonably speaking, what we have so far said about Williams's growth as a poet establishes him as an Adamic poet for our purpose. First of all is, of course, the way he wrote his first poems in 1909 which have for their subject-matter an affirmation of Adamic innocence and simplicity. Though at this point, Adamic innocence and simplicity were for him "transcendent qualities of 'heavenly birth,' preserved by a precious remoteness from the here and now,"[17] we find that even in his mature poems of the later years where he combines "images of nature with images from one of the other subject categories" to see the objects depicted in their whole existence, he puts a premium by way of contrast or ironic understatement on the primal qualities of "unspoilt freshness" in things. Further, his emphasis on the "human elements" by extending nature's dignity to man's love and its emotion,[18] strikes the key-note to the American Adam's humanistic hopes and presuppositions that have come filtered to our own times *via* "The American Scholar" of Emerson.

We may start for the purpose of this study with a few of Williams's earlier representative poems wherein the later manifesto of identifying himself with the physical locality gains ground with difficulty, though. The difficulty lay in what has been called his increasing impatience with the moral constraints put before him by his parents who wanted him to be "a gentlemen" with a sense of propriety and dignity. Though his

Whitemanesque poems were called by him—"my secret life"[19]—he was in the beginning shaky to choose any of the two alternatives of his life: one guaranteeing a paradise of feeling—spontaneous and free—and the other that would banish him from such a paradise, engendering a rigid sense of duty. He depicted this dilemma in a very beautiful early poem—"Adam"—where the tone and temper that is set is perfectly Adamic. The poem opens with an autobiographical note depicting his father's character, and his "fear of the physical/that/ banishes him from paradise, converting the lush Caribbean Island on which he grew up into a hellish world, filled with terrifying sensual seductions."[20] The theme suggests the eternal conflict between liberation and duty, putting into relief the concept of Adamic freedom as life's redemption. What Williams means by "duty" in this poem is to be understood in terms of slavishness that comes, slowly but gradually when one is afraid of looking at one's feelings and thought without taking them to "old racks of moral consideration." This fear is engendered when one is Puritanic enough, like Willims's father, to deny the thrill of experiencing "primal innocence" in the "sheer act of living." Hence, Adam—Williams's father in this context—"...was driven/ out of Paradise—to taste/the death that duty brings/so daintily, so menacingly,/with such a noble air—/that enslaved him all his life/thereafter—."[21] As a sharp contrast to this the poem, "Eve" opens with unravelling the mystery of "womanhood" putting an emphasis on woman's innocence which is almost "infantile" and "defenseless." The character here is, of course, that of William's mother whose interest in art inspired him. "She seemed an heroic figure, a poetic ideal," says Williams.[22] Her years in Paris where she had been an art student created in her that sense of beauty, in consequence of which the sterile environment of the small town in New Jersey where she lived bewildered her. What is important, as the poem shows, is not her bewilderment but her wild desire. "...to escape and leap into chaos/(where Time has/ not yet begun)."[23] This is how she wanted to "restore" her life to "primordial unity,"[24] because it was by tapping that which is beyond the heavy load of "tripartite time" that she could bring about a happy balance between the various phases of her life—physical, spiritual, mental and moral. Williams's concept of American Poetry did also move in some such line, for he wanted to create new forms out of the formless. "Art," Williams said, "must tap the dark anarchistic elements of the self."[25] This poem, as it goes on to portray the various phases of the character of Williams's mother, "taps the dark anarchistic elements" out of which "the natural colors and shapes"[26] of her personality do ultimately emerge:

I'll give you brandy
or wine
whenever I think you need it
(need it)
because it whips up
your mind and your senses
and brings color to your face
—to enkindle that life
too coarse for the usual,
that sly obscenity
that fertile darkness
in which passion mates....[27]

The last lines are important enough. With the fertility imagery as its "focus" which is explored incisively by Williams in his later works, the poet takes us to a moment, particularly in the context of the "here and now," where we are not supposed to be in the world of the dead "that wasted carcass, crippled/and deformed, that ruined face/sightless, deafened...."[28] but are supposed to be in a living world engaged in recapturing lost Adamic innocence through a process of "rebirth and renewal." It also reveals that what we call "the universal, mythical" can be "discovered in the moment, not imposed upon it."[29]

"The Wanderer," a poem that anticipates *Paterson* is one of his earliest endeavours in depicting the horror of his town that "bewildered" his mother. It suggests by contrast a release of creative powers by comprehending the natural *vis-a-vis* the artificial. A searching reader will also discern its relevance as it informs the manner of "the rebirth of a young poet: his evolution of a new identity and his redefinition of such concepts as beauty and the self."[30] Through a process of initiation carried under the supervision of "a fierce old goddess"[31]—the "female principle" that is further explored in *Paterson*—the poet's quest for roots culminates in "a clarification of life" in a society where our bother is "the separateness of men from one another and from the things of their world."[32] "Advent," the first section of the poem, opens with an invitation to us to experience the Edenic bliss of a landscape the beauty of which is suggested by broad, sweeping images, such as those of "the forest," "the horizon," "the tree tops," "the woods," "the yielding river," and "a great sea-gull...vanishing with a wild cry...."[33] The presence of the fierce old goddess symbolises the female principle which Williams would liken later on in *The American Grain* to the creative, fertile soil of his native land—America, the Golden. She embodies "the principle of guidance" and, in fact, plays a vital role in the manner of Eve in the Garden of Eden to baptize the poet who, we suppose, is a confused Adam in this context whose Whitmanesque query ("How shall I be a mirror to this modernity?") is answered amply by her. The outlines of the answer are a pointer to the main tenets of Williams's *ars poetica* as an American artist. This section's sentimental romanticism is balanced by a counterthrust which comes from the "anti-poetic"—the Broadway scene of "Empty men with shell-thin bodies/Jostling close above the gutter,/Hasting—nowhere...."[34] This is how the dirty city's stinking environs sicken the poet, and he expresses his desire in prayerful terms to be liberated. Liberation would come but through "a new marriage":

> May I be lifted still; up and out of terror, up from before the death living around me...[35]

Instead of fulfilling what the poet prays for, she *does* again, as it appears in the fourth section of the poem, "Strike," take the fumbling poet out into the streets of Paterson. The town's lack of subtlety and delicacy is revealed through a concatenation of images such as those of "flat skulls," "ugly legs," "sagging breasts," "protruding stomachs," "rasping voices" and "filthy habits,"[36] to name only a few suggestive ones. "Abroad," and the sections that follow it show that the protagonist is ultimately at peace with himself and the world around. He urges upon his towns people to act decisively, but the way they are to do so is through a discovery and possession of their own Adamic feelings which they have failed to tap under thc impact of technocratic industrial society:

> Waken! my people, to the boughs green
> With ripening fruit within you!
> Waken with myriad cinquerfoil
> In the waving grass of your minds!
> Waken to the silent phoebe nest
> Under the eaves of your spirit![37]

The poem ends with the fierce old goddess leading the poet to a ceremony of baptization—a bath in the water of "The Passaic, that filthy river."[38] Through filth and all, that is, through a realization of "the here and now," the poet is lifted, liberated:

> Until time had been washed finally under,
> And the river had found its level
> And its last motion had ceased
> And I knew all—it became me.[39]

The poem, however, rests on a very important "feeling" which strikes the key-note to the whole theme:

> But she lifted me and the water took a new tide
> Again into the older experiences,
> And so backward and forward,
> It tortured itself within me....[40]

The immediate experiences are grasped, and there is that "backward and forward" journey for realizing the effects of Nature on one hand, and that of civilization on the other to gain a whole, compact, and morally all-embracing vision of life. Such a vision is possible not because Williams gives us at one point the glimpse of "the boughs green," and the salubrious effects of the Jersey mountains, but because he brings in "the counterforce" and makes the readers see the emptiness of "Faces all knotted up like burls on oaks."[41] Poetry of this type does always sizzle with, what John M. Synge has put, "exaltation."[42] In fact, Ezra Pound's words about Williams are to the point. "Where I see scoundrels and vandals," Pound says, "he sees a spectacle or an ineluctable process of nature."[43] The difference of this kind of poetry from that in the Poundian or Eliotic tradition in "the mythic Mode" is obvious, for Williams insists, as Miss Koch says, "on the uncodified and fresh in experiene as a means of liberating potentiality for great vision."[44] It is in the tradition of what has been called rational humanism with a kind of Aristotelian realism smacking of a Deweyan instrumentalist approach to art and its subject-matter. "The Wanderer," having all this felt seriousness about art, is a significant pointer to the poet's achievement in *Paterson,* for there, as it is here, Williams surrenders himself in a sort of uncompromising manner to "feeling" as the stepping-stone to wisdom. Yvor Winters has put this point in logical terms:

> Any feeling arising from the contemplation of
> an idea, whether moral, metaphysical, or
> religious, appears to him merely sentimental....[45]

The most significant metaphor in "The Wanderer"—one that, perhaps, expresses most inclusively Williams's artistic credo—is the Demeter myth that connects him so closely with "the Adamic Mode" in poetry with its emphasis on recapturing "primal innocence" by "a quest for the roots" in life and Nature. The fierce old goddess of the poem is able to unite all the ages of the world. It is a reference, as Guimond says, to Demeter's wanderings at the time "Kora (Springtime) was lost to the world and Demeter (the earth) disguised her beauty, fertility, and power."[46] The world to-day, with its dirt, filth and beggary, is yet a Garden of Eden, for like Winter hiding the seeds of Spring, its ugliness and squalor hide beauty.[47] The search for beauty is, therefore, a spiritual journey to recapture the essentials—a life-giving rapport between appearance and reality. Thus, America personified in her filth is also America, the Golden. Poetry for Williams was primarily a "discovery of the relationship between actuality and the mind confronting it, discovery of the language that would in turn make that discovery 'true' and communicable."[48] In this lay the ability to create the "only viable poetry of democracy" which, as Tocqueville indicated, is ultimately "the poetry of self" endeavouring to give back to things their uniqueness."[49] There is, of course, a basic difference between Williams's earliest poems, and his later ones which culminated in an artistic meditativeness. While differentiating Williams's achievement from that of Stevens's, Riddel makes the point in clearer terms. Unlike Wallace Stevens who from the very start saw life and Nature with a certain amount of self-consciousness, Williams's vision, particularly in his early poetry, lay in looking at "the world through the eyes of an innocent child" having no awareness that the vision is only "a fiction of his own making."[50] After experimenting with the form and content of *Kora in Hell* Williams, of course, achieved the ability to write meditative poetry till it culminated in his *Paterson.* Even then, from the beginning till end, "discovery" remained the key word in Williams canon. Here is emotion as a process—a kind of stream-of-consciousness in which the Wordsworthian recollection of emotions or delayed report of experience is kept at arm's length as far as practicable. Objects that fall under four image categories—nature, man, urban society, and art—tend to be a part of their local surroundings, and the projected phenomena are barely commented upon. Thus, a poem by Williams often speaks for itself. A categoric survey of the image-pattern in some of the early poems by Williams will show the poet's Adamic perception which was almost like that of Adam's in the Garden of Eden—a natural reaction to its flora and fauna, perceiving them, with eyes that remained innocent beyond the heavy weight of time and history. This is a difficult task indeed, for we who are civilized and sophisticated tend to fail to perceive "the *thingness* of things." Yet our eyes have not lost their innocence forever: they give way to innocent perception in many a moment of our life's conscious and unconscious activities. In "Pastoral,"[51] the poet's observation is one of "astonishment." "The little sparrows" that "hop ingeniously/about the pavement...," quarrel no doubt, but there is a definitive "interest" in them which the poet misses to find in the human world and therefore suggests that, lacking as we do any definitive approach to life, our wisdom is just an apologia for foolhardiness. Not so, of course, is the case of "...the old man who goes about/gathering dog-lime...." He "...walks in the gutter/without looking up/and his trend/is more majestic than/that of the Episcopal minister/ approaching the pulpit of a Sunday." The theme is man's "alienation" or, for that matter, "separateness." Man is alienated not only from his environment as we "shut ourselves in," but also from his fellow beings, in consequence of which he has lost "the kind of innocence" as we find, for example, in "the sparrows" and "the old man" depicted in the poem. Williams draws our attention to the city's "pavement" and the "gutter," but what we call filth, dirt and squalor hide the seeds of innocence. As "These things/astonish me beyond words," the poet is aware that these "simple, separate things upon which the imagination feeds have an integrity and vitality"[52] of their own. However, the objects seized upon by imagination do not, as Breslin says, speak for themselves, though Williams shall attain that "ego-shattering concentration upon physical objects,"[53] as he matures as a poet.

The cycle of seasons, the green vegetation of Nature and her trees, wilderness, sea and sea-gulls, and above all "love" are the themes that crowd these early poems. The importance lies in the sudden thematic or linguistic twist and turn that he often gives to his poems of this period. Beneath all, there is the poet's "ego" that works on to catch the "loose threads"—the loss of innocence, the presence of murder and cruelty, the deplorable lack of liberty. And yet the poems are not romantic in the accepted sense of the term. He gives them a local colour with a tendency to get them rooted to the fierce "actuality" or what Ostrom says "sensuality"[54] of American life in the twentieth century. Through their particularities the poems reach out to strike a note of universal emotions.

Though outwardly structured in a loose manner these poems have an inner balance—a quality that resolves tension of opposing emotions of simple "innocence" on one hand and complex "experience" on the other. Notice, for example, the themes in his "Fire Spirit"[55] and "To Wish Myself Courage."[56] Both poems are thematically interconnected. The poet's question in "Fire Spirit" ("Where shall I turn for comfort?") is suitably answered in "To Wish Myself Courage." He says that old age has its own compensation. With his wisdom, and without "the stress of youth" he would then write a powerful "youth-song." He proposes the kind of predilection he shall have in selecting the theme of the "youth-song":

> On the day when youth is no more upon me
> I will write of the leaves and the moon in a tree top!
> I will sing then the song, long in the making
> When the stress of youth is put away from me.[57]

The loss of youth is lamented upon. It's like a fall from Paradise. However, for Williams Paradise is not lost forever it can be regained through our ability to perceive beauty and innocence in spite of circumstances or conditions that may create barriers. The fertility and rebirth metaphor is invoked:

> But when the spring of it is worn like the old moon
> And the eaten leaves are lace upon the cold earth—
> Then I will rise up in my great desire—
> Long at the birth—and sing me thy Youth-song![58]

The motive for retracing "the path" travelled by him is there in order that, Phoenix-like, he shall almost rise from the ashes of his old age, and recapturing youth's beauty, and its love of life and Nature, he shall compose his great "youth-song." Some of the finest lines on the theme of "innocence" and Edenic bliss are found in "The Death of Franco of Cologne. His prophecy of Beethoven:"[59]

> Precious children, little gambollers! "farlings"
> They might have called you once, "nearlings"
> I call you now, I first of all yearlings,
> Upon this plain, for I it was that tore you
> Out of chaos! It was I bore you!
> Ah, you little children that go playing
> Over the five-barred gate, and will still be straying

Spite of all that I have ever told you
Of counterpoint and cadence which does not hold you....[60]

Even music with its notes "Of Counter-point and cadence..."[61] will not touch the make-believe world of these children. Like Adam's fall from Paradise, their world of make-believe will, of course, soon pass into a complex pattern of living:

For I have seen it! I have seen it
Written where the world-clouds screen it
From other eyes
Over the bronze gates of paradise![62]

Williams juxtaposes the "innocence" of these "little gambollers" with Franco's old age—"a second childhood"—but Franco of Cologne is not without "courage." He will compose his "youth-song," too, for "the soul peers through its tatters." In fact, Franco of Cologne did so. He invented our system of musical notation, over Beethoven.

The sudden twists and turns of language, of what has been called "shifts of weight,"[63] are evident in the early poetry—"a living document of experience":[64]

But love is an oil to embalm the body.
Love is a packet of spices, a strong-
smelling liquid to be squirted into
the thigh. No?
Love rubbed on a bald head will make
hair—and after? Love is a lice comber!
Gnats on dung![65]

To this young American lover in the poem the "innocence" of the world is not lost. The consciousness of a certain kind of freedom from the "cares and anxieties" of a world gone old is discernible:

The world is young, surely! Young and colored like—a
girl that has come upon a lover![66]

Williams takes the "lover" as his mouthpiece and indirectly gives us his opinion on "History" in the context of the American Adam's place in the New World Garden of America. This theme has been more amply enunciated with a tendency towards high meditativeness, in *Paterson.* He, unlike Pound and Eliot who considered history as a "continuancy of universals," believed in what has been called "continuity in change."

The beauty of American flora and fauna deeply touched Williams and in a way, excepting the innovation of a modern form and language, he echoes the nineteenth-century tradition after a Whittier, a Lanier or a Bryant, though, of course, he is not blind to his age's sickness, disease and cruelty as evident from poems like "Death" and "The Raper from Passenack." Koch calls the latter an "ambitious" poem, and draws our attention to the poem's "oblique illumination of the cruel impersonality and primitive superstitiousness of the modern industrial world on whose dingy peripheries"[67] we live just as the "raper" and his "victim" do. This sordid American tragedy, with its underlying elements of "neuroticism of modern sexual behavior"[68] can only happen in a society that is unnatural, impersonal, and "narcotized" by pressures and pulls of "power." If this poem depicts one side of the social panorama of a brutal industrial society, there are others that take us to genuine human feelings, born of naturalness, and innocence in bare Edenic terms:

> As the rain falls so does your love bathe every open object of the world.[69]

To this poem eulogizing "spiritual" love, we have poems in contrast like "Canthara" where the sheer physicality of love, minus its whorishness and brutality as depicted in "The Raper from Passenack," becomes a point of ecstasy, though it may shock those who are uninitiated:

> The old black-man showed me
> how he had been shocked
> in his youth
> by six women, dancing
> a set-dance, stark naked below
> the skirts raised round
> their breasts

bellies flung forward
knees flying!
—while
his gestures, against the
tiled wall of the dingy bath-room,
wished with ecstasy to
the familiar music of
his old emotion.[70]

His Whitmanesque leanings as Adamic "namer" and "cataloguer" are obviously there, but unlike Whitman he feels "a sense of loss"—a modern disease, so to say, which is difficult to diagnose. Notice, for example, his reaction in "The Flowers Alone":

I should have to be
Chaucer to describe
them—
Loss keeps
me from such a catalogue....[71]

Still Williams is, perhaps, one of the most celebrated poets who has taken to the difficult task of "cataloguing" American flora and fauna, giving them a stamp of "individuality." The "names" thus take on different connotations either for the twist and turn of language or for the special manner in which he presents the "background." Here are a few examples:

When over the flowery, sharp pasture's
edge, unseen, the salt ocean
lifts its form—Chicory and daisies
tied, released, seem hardly flowers alone
but color and the movement—or the shape
perhaps—of restlessness...
["Flowers by the Sea"][72]

Now!
the cherry trees
white in all back -
yard—
["The Flowers Alone"][73]

Among blue leaves
the apples green and red

upon one tree stand
out most enshrined.

["Wild Orchard"][74]

This is winter,
winter, winter
leather-green leaves
spear shaped
in the falling snow

["Winter"][75]

by the rain and sun—
The strict simple
principles of
straight branches
are being modified
by pinched-out
ifs of colour, devout
conditions
the smiles of love—
....

["The Botticelian Trees"][76]

Trundled from
The Strangeness of the sea
a kind of
heaven—

["The Sea-Elephant"][77]

The contours and the shine
hold the eye-caught and lying
orange-finned and the two
half its size,...

["Sea-Trout and Butterfish"][78]

If the "flowers by the sea" become a vista of sheer "color and movement,"or the Sea-Elephant looks like "heaven" brought forth from the sea, it is, perhaps, all the more necessary for us to *see* that the natural order is not disturbed! Notice what he says about the Sea-Elephant:

...it's wonderful but they
ought to
put it
back into the sea
where it came from.[79]

Thus, in spite of the brutality of our power-narcotized industrial society, the natural order has to be restored, which is also another way of saying that in the midst of "experience," "innocence" must be given its rightful place. The American Adam's quest for Paradise will continue in the face of all hurdles set up by a society fast decaying in the horrors of industrialism. Williams was, however, no escapist. As revealed in *Paterson* he would very well console himself with a "realization that because the world's decay and degradation were universal there was no need for him 'to move from this place' where he was born. He would despair anywhere."[80] Even when portraying winter as a season whose days "are the desolate, dark weeks/when nature in its barrenness/equals the stupidity of man,"[81] Williams would not forget to sing the glory of Spring. "In the spring I would drink! In the spring/I would be drunk and lie forgetting all things..."[82] though his own "...rooms/are no longer sweet spaces where comfort/is ready to wait...."[83] It is the poet's imagination that confers on him the ability to be aware of the world's excellence beneath all horror. "Without imagination," said Williams, "life cannot go on, for we are left staring at the empty casings where truth lived yesterday while the creature itself has escaped behind us."[84] A poem, Williams would write in 1939, is a certain kind of "creative process" that acts like "a counterfoil to the vague and excessively stupid juxtapositions commonly known as 'reality.'"[85] Its impact is "to revive the senses and force them to re-see, re-hear, re-taste, re-smell and generally revalue the world."[86] Since Williams was about twenty, there has been in him this "resignation to existence," to a mood of acceptance of old age and death as the ultimate destiny of man. His letter to Marianne Moore in 1934 brings out the point in clearer terms. He comments that this feeling was the consequence of "something which occurred once when I was about twenty, a sudden resignation to existence, a despair—if you wish to call it that, but a despair which made everything a unit and at the same time a part of myself...."[87] "Things," he adds in the same letter, "have no names for me and places have no significance. As a reward for this anonymity I feel as much a part of things as trees and stones."[88] This negative aspect was, of course, later on turned into a positive force, as we find, for example, in one of his later poems named "Lear."

Some of the earlier poems of Williams celebrate the necessity of this affinity that human beings must feel to have with their environment, however "local" it may be, for by doing so they can, like a physician working upon a patient, "upon the thing before him," discover the universal in the particular.[89]

An attempt is thereby made to maintain the natural order. Even out of "the destructive elements," of the sewage-water-filled "filthy Passaic," there shall emerge a process of "renewal" or "rebirth,"[90] and the lost Paradise can thus be regained.

"Tract" which is termed by Koch as "perhaps the most memorable poem"[91] in Williams's early period tackles this problem from a different angle which is one of achieving a "ground sense" to steer clear of the rigid demands of "custom" or "tradition."

Between "tradition" and "spirit" there has been certainly a wide gap down the ages of man's evolution as a civilized being. To capture the spirit, therefore, the true feelings of the past are to be rescued. Particularly "the American Past," as Williams said, "had to be 'rescued' and made 'usable' to have its proper, vitalizing effect."[92] It is obvious that Williams was saying this in answer to the call given by some writers like Van Wyck Brooks that the American intellectual has to have a major role to play for building the true future of his country. The American intellectual must "invent a usable past," and his job lay in rescuing the great writers like Thoreau, Whitman and Mark Twain, so that he could "tap through them a certain eternal human tradition of abounding vitality and moral freedom, and so build the future."[93] As we said in the preceding lines, the poem "Tract" is one of Williams's earliest attempts to achieve this state of condition. The archetypal pattern of Edenic myth has its varying degrees of impact on the mind of the modern man. Even a simple act of following a principle that is natural may enable us to have a glimpse of an innocent state of Paradise. In a review of *The Complete Collected Poems of William Carlos Williams,* Yvor Winters writes about Williams that "Any feeling arising from the contemplation of an idea, whether moral, metaphysical, or religion, appears to him merely sentimental...."[94] To Winters this is a defect, but, as he said, Williams's habit of eschewing the sentimental side of our morality, metaphysics or religion made his poems less confusing, and in a way sometimes quite unsentimental in their probe of true emotions. "Tract" as a poem is a true enunciation of this dictum which Williams often followed meticulously. The poet's earthy, "ground sense" which is also a sense of the natural leads him to advise his townspeople to reject the traditional mode of performing a funeral. In fact, he asks them to reject all that ill behoves the very sense of innocence that permeates death when it is natural. In this he avoids sentimentalizing or even philosophizing. He views it in an ordinary, familiar manner like an observer who takes an overview of events taking place all around him. Williams wants that nothing should be done that may smack of unnaturality, for death is natural—an event that takes man to eternal rest in innocence. Notice Williams's proposal:

> I begin with a design for a hearse.
> For Christ's sake not black—
> nor white either—and not polished!
> Let it be weathered—like a farm wagon—
> with gilt wheels (this could be
> applied fresh at all expense)
> or no wheels at all:
> a rough dray to drag over the ground.[95]

If this advice would not be accepted and followed there might occur a kind of mental disharmony between the poet and his townspeople, for the poet believes that a funeral, instead of being exhibitionistic as it often is, must needs reflect the true picture of life in its most realistic situations—"battered, weather-beaten and dragging." Williams's "Gulls" puts forth by means of a metaphor which he later on uses in *Paterson* how as artist his destiny was bound with an order of things that emodies a free and natural spirit. The poem's three gulls, and the eagle that does not attack them work out a mode of parable, the meaning of which lies in a "passionate plea," as Koch notes, "for mutual tolerance between the 'singer' and his 'townspeople.'"[96] Williams's townspeople "have [their] own hymns."[97] But the poet "could not be angry with [them], no matter/how much they outraged true music."[98] Symbolically extended, the gulls and the eagle image suggests the commendable character of those "people in the great world who 'whir' about the poet 'calling, calling!'[99] There is a certain creativity in such people just as "the gulls [that] moved seaward very quietly" have a creativity in their very basic "marriage" to "true music." This music is as harmonious as the poet-singer's message of harmony to his townspeople. The artificiality of the townspeople with their "disharmonious music" is obvious, for such music is "outrageous" as it does not befit the great thematic content of the hymns they are singing ["...they invoked some great protector."][100] Most important of all is the poem's quality of using the symbols in such a manner that the "real purpose" is not obscured. On the other hand, the symbols, particularly the gulls and the eagle ineluctably "lift the world of the senses to the land of the imagination,"and thereby they give a "new currency"[101] to the poet's function as an imaginative artist—the singer *par excellence* whose message is peace, harmony and tolerance, in short, a belief in man's basic innocence:

> You see, it is not necessary for us to leap at each other,
> and, as I told you, in the end
> the gulls moved seaward very quietly.[102]

These are some of the actual values with which Williams as a poet was greatly involved. Thus, he did not hesitate to admonish the later Pound:

> You deal in political symbols instead of actual values, poetry. You talk about things (which you yourself have sufficiently damned in the past) instead of showing the things themselves in action.[103]

With Pound, however, Williams had other affinities. In fact, both of them had a deep-rooted conviction that "pagan impulses" must be freed and brought to the surface in the face of the brutal subversion of "man's best possibilities."[104] The gulls that "come from above the river/and crossed slowly seaward!"[105] stand for man's recurring effort to move toward vaster, more naturally conclusive aims ["seaward!"] from narrow, limited spheres ["came from above the river"]. Williams's townspeople should also move from narrow-mindedness to a broader concept of mutual tolerance. The poem, having a brief explication of the theme in the last three lines ["...it is not necessary to leap at each other..."], is very much unlike Williams's usual poetic habit of providing "a mood with gravity," and making "the meaning of the poem...heard only in its reverberations."[106] Sometimes a line or two in a poem, long or short, help in ascertaining the drift of the theme. As Kenneth Burke puts it, such lines "will throw the reader into an unexpected intimacy with his subject, like pushing open a door and advancing one's nose into some foreign face."[107] He also throws light on this intricate process:

> The process is simply this: There is the eye, and there is the thing upon which the eye alights; while the relationship existing between the two is a poem.[108]

The wording is not only "trim," but also there is a certain amount of "sureness and directness" which inform the novelty of Williams's poems, hysterical though they may sometimes be.

This novelty which may look like carelessness to an untrained reader of modern poetry should not make Williams appear anything like a primitive. There was surely a good deal of craftsmanship in every poem that he wrote. It was almost like what Yeats said that one has to "labour [hard] to be beautiful."[109] This was the labour of a man who denied on one hand being anti-intellectual as he was always conscious of his mind,[110] and expressed on the other an "awareness of the emotional qualities which man needed to appreciate and develop properly 'the new' in art and life."[111] In this, of course, lay Williams's hostility to Eliot's poetic mode. In fact, Williams reiterated unlike the Eliot of *The Waste Land* fame that "our age is rich, not poor." He added: "It is rich in its inheritances for the mind, for the spirit.

It isn't bare. That is why I have battled T.S. Eliot from the first." Further, at the risk of making a fool of himself, Williams has insisted that Eliot "has never known what the deepest knowledge of the world offers." In his own individualistic style Williams challenges the very basis of "the mythic Mode" in poetry when he stresses that no poet should vitiate the good by emphasizing "the stereotype and the dead."[112] It is obvious, therefore, that he took the unprimitivistic stand while rejecting the illustriousness of the past, for, as Mircea Eliade has evidenced for us, a primitivist is he who by his very "archaic nature" does not aknowledge anything "which has not been posited and lived by someone else." Goaded by the greatness of "the dead," the primitive would not permit himself to accept new virtues which we might discover in the face of the squalor, dirt, and horror of the present. Thus, the primitive's life, as it is lived, is a kind of "ceaseless repetition of gestures initiated by others."[113] For such "a formal pattern" of existence Williams had his undoubted abhorrence, however, "attractive" or "beautiful" it might be. And yet, Williams, in his determination to be driven by life, was perhaps one of those few native Americans who revealed, ambivalently though, a certain manner of primitivism in their life and letters in looking for, and imbibing the inherent spirit of life's "rare element."[114] No matter how raw and primeval the virtues of American living might be, they made those their ideal, and accepted the view of forsaking allegiance to the past, particularly to the dead virtues of European culture.[115] This was the manner in which Williams fought most consistently to save *his personality* from getting "strophied." Also, it was something in keeping with what Van Wyck Brooks wrote in 1915 with a big question mark:

> How can one speak of progress in a people like our own that so sends up to heaven the stench of atrophied personality?[116]

Williams was perhaps one of the few who went on to express that to avoid smelling of this kind of "personality stench," one has to fight against the very bedrock of America's Puritanical tradition. He asserted:

> There has not yet appeared in the New World any one with sufficient strength for the open assertion...Nowhere the open, free assertion save in the Indian.[117]

Thus, as Van Wyck Brooks indicated, the American intellectual had to invent "a usable past," and, we suppose, Williams was one of the great pioneers who tapped, through a body of original, inspiring and inspired writings, "a certain eternal human tradition of abounding vitality and moral freedom...."[118] Its vitalizing effect lay, as the depiction of a series of characters in *The American Grain* would show, in the American Adam's recurring attempt to go back to "innocence" that lay hidden at the very "source" of all things. It is possible to recapture this "innocence" in the face of "the calumny that surrounds," and thus it necessitates the discovery of truth—its digging up and naming.[119] In poems like "The Source" Williams tapped this original, creative force in Nature, and also brought about a "poetic form" in which the "object" infiltrates into the "phrase," and the "phrase" is welded in a closer bond to the "object." In fact, Williams at this time (1928) freed himself quite successfully from his "imagistic credo" which, as is well known, was almost a rigorous principle with him around 1917 with his emphasis on the "direct treatment of the 'thing' whether subjective or objective"[120] as is manifest in poems such as "The Old Men," "Chicory and Daisies," "Tract," "Riposte" and "Gulls." Unlike the poems of his "objectivist" period, these poems attempt an explanation of the significance of the "subjects," and thus reveal the poet's intricate attitude toward them.[121] A comparison between "The Old Man"—a poem of the Imagist-free verse period—with "To Waken an Old Lady"—a poem of the "objectivist" period—will suffice to prove this point. Through the enunciation of a natural metaphor which works like an "objective correlative," keeping the poet off the poem's "functional area," Williams makes old age speak for itself in "To waken an Old Lady":

> Old age is
> a flight of small
> cheeping birds

shimming
bare trees
above a snow glaze.[122]

Then, mark, for example, the effect of direct statement and absence of "indirection" in the following lines from "The Old Men":

Solitary old men for whom
we find no excuses—
I bow my head in shame
for those who malign you.
Old men
the peaceful beer of impotence
be yours![123]

The contrast between the two poems is obvious. "To Waken an Old Lady" and "The Old Man" have, of course, the same theme to enunciate, that is, the theme of Adamic innocence and solitude of old men and women whose helplessness in the face of shameless people's malignity may give us cause for concern. Whereas in the former the poet strenuously avoids the personal tone and works through apt metaphors, in the latter the poet builds up a definite moral force to achieve the same effect.

After a brief spell of working to certain theories propounded by others as is seen in some of his early poems in spite of their spontaneity which remains a permanent feature with his poetry, Williams, gradually but steadily, formulated his final sesthetic principle under the impact of Zukofksy's doctrine that reality is objective or external to the mind.[124] This again means that the artist must free himself from his personal feelings, opinions and prejudices while presenting the object of his attention. In "A Note On Poetry" (1937) we come across the following words which serve as some of the best commentaries on Objectivism in the words of Williams himself:

> In my own work, it has always sufficed that the object of my attention be presented without further comment. This in general might be termed the objective method. But all art is sensual and poetry particularly so. It is directly, that is, of the senses, and since the senses do not exist without

> an object, for their employment all art is necessarily objective. It doesn't declaim or explain: it presents.[125]

Such a stand suggests, we suppose, an anti-intellectual trend. To view an object without bringing in personal feelings, and to give it a metaphoric existence of some sorts, seem to have an Adamic implication as it is obviously an attempt to retain a state of innocence in the face of circumstances that make such retention highly difficult. The two poems on old age—"To Waken an Old Lady" and "To Old Men"—may serve our purpose to illustrate the argument. The situation of old men's and old women's helplessness in the face of some "shameless" people's malignity would make it difficult to write a poem on the theme of "innocence of old age" without bringing in our feelings of animosity against those who malign them. And yet to express animosity would destroy, however partially it may be, the total image of innocence of old age which the poet intends to convey to the readers. "To Waken an Old Lady" is thus a more successful poem than "To Old Man" as it views old age from an objectivist's standpoint, and retains for us the total image of innocence of old age ("Old age is/a flight of small/cheeping birds"...). Subtly enough Williams does, however, suggest by means of a few apt metaphors ("....bare trees/above a snow glaze") the idea of helplessness of old people in a malign world. What strikes the readers as original is Williams's persistence in reviving "autochthonous elements" through certain "primordial images" like "birds," "snow" and "trees." These "archetypes," to borrow Jung's word,[126] suggest in their totality and by the very manner in which they have been used the idea of innocence and its natural loss. In case of the old men and women the loss of innocence lies in their helplessness in the face of the malignity of people who are shameless. In poems of this type, and not in those where he directly asserts his ideas, we discover a kind of effortless multiplexity, an efflorescence that does not try to be profound, and yet is naturally so. For the poet words come first. And then ideas are "caught" in the pulsating, vibrating concatenation of words. This is as much true of Williams as it has been with others like Stevens. Emily Mitchell Wallace, while commenting on the "immediacy," the "sensual quality" and "pure observation" of a Williams poem, goes on to add that "any thing that is felt on the pulses is a subject for poetry, if the poet has a 'bitter seriousness' about his technique—"which means saying what he means and not saying what he does not mean...."[127] In fact, even "words will/bite/their way/home," particularly when they are actual, and have "a form of motion."[128] A close attention to this kind of poetic process reveals certain important things for us to note in our evaluation of Williams as a poet in "the Adamic Mode." Adam's encounter with the flora and fauna, apart from his personal experiences, in the Garden of Eden gave him the necessary subjective response not only to feel the affective qualities of all natural phenomena, but also to gather evidences of their nature and meaning.

This enabled Adam to find words for "things" and "experiences" that deeply touched him, that is, gave him a variety of novel subjective responses affecting his personality in totality, and leading him, in a way, to his ultimate expulsion from Paradise. This was the slow but gradual process of what has been called his "dying into life"—his "fortunate fall." One of the greatest literary compositions of this century that portrays in unmistakable terms this episode in the growth of man is contained in Bernard Shaw's *Back to Methuselah*—a drama with Edenic motif. The following lines from it will justify the trend of our argument in the preceding paragraphs even at the risk of stretching a point:

The Serpent. The voice in the garden is your own voice.

Adam. It is, and it is not. It is something greater than me. I am only a part of it.

Eve. The Voice does not tell me not to kill you. Yet I do not want you to die before me. No voice is needed to make me feel that.

Adam [throwing his arm round her shoulder with an expression of anguish] Oh no! that is plain without any voice. There is something that holds us together, something that has no word—

The Serpent. Love, Love, Love.
Adam. That is too short a word for so long a thing.[129]

A close study of this dialogue would reveal the intensity of Adam's subjective response—"the voice" as Shaw puts it—and makes it clear that all that Adam experienced assumed meaningful dimensions through the act of "naming." Such responses were Adamically original, born as they were through a realization of "the changes which events make upon" the mind, and thereby "reveal their identities rather than the mind's own qualities."[130] The cumulative effect of civilization's sophistication has, of course, blunted man's ability for "original responses." Therefore, "objects," "things," and even "experiences" when used as materials by a poet may assume, if the poet is not objective enough, a different animation—a sort of lively and imaginative existence unrecognizable in the context of their true identities. However, a mature Williams poem, other than any of those written in the 1920's, is able to show the opposite, that is, how "objects," "things," and "experiences" keep intact their basic existential identities, and exercise thereby a sort of impact on man even to the extent of changing him.[131] This is in tune with Williams's famous verdict that the poet "is not a moralist" in choice of subject, because for him, while the poem is in the process of creation, the whole world is the province.[132] Also, closely embracing the native things and "descending" to present the objective details of what Pound called "the bloody loam,"[133] the poems gained a sensitivity and a daring, perhaps most consistently attempted in modern American poetry with an inexorable measuring of emotion. This was a feature of excellence in this objectivist approach in comparison with imagism where hints in regard to the manner of the object's relation to "the poet's personal and emotional and intellectual"[134] life remained undepicted. This formal relationship between the object and the subject is important as it helps affix a certain kind of significance to the narration of the details of the poem's images. One may take, for example, two very striking poems of Williams, "The Descent of Winter" and "The Source," written to demonstrate not only his ability to Adamically capture "primal innocence" of "things as things," but also to reveal that in poetry, as in painting of a particular kind, objects, in the manner they are presented, may assume a metaphorical tone. This was achieved, though it's needless to overstretch the point, by conceiving "poems as physical units, as paintings, having as their borders the limits set by space and the instant of perception."[135] For example, the poems in "The Descent of Winter," while forming "physical units" in their own right of existence, are born of the poet's instantaneous perception, and as a whole emphasize the possibility of man re-establishing his lost relationship with Nature—a relationship which, in its frenzy to capture "the new" is almost like the American Adam's "voyage" of discovery, the re-enactment of the "Columbus legend." Notice, for example, the process of re-finding the "old past," and fruitfully redirecting it:

> The very old past was refound
> redirected. It had wandered into himself
> The world was himself, these were
> his own eyes that were seeing, his own mind
> that was straining to comprehend, his own
> hands that would be touching other hands...[136]

Apart from comprehending the world of Nature and man around him, the poet's effort is also directed to purge his heart of "impurities," giving it back its lost innocence and bliss:

> O river of my heart polluted
> and defamed I have compared you
> to that other lying in
> the red November grass
> beginning to be cleaned now
> from factory pollution.
>
> Though at night a watchman
> must still prowl lest some paid hand
> Open the waste slices.
>
> That river will be clean
> before ever you will be.[137]

Thus, the poets's world is created with a choice that is clear and uncomplicated, and the objects that he comprehends affect his personal, emotional and intellectual life ["The world was himself..."] so intensely that they speak for themselves, and succeed in presenting a particular state of mind without elaborate explication or declamation. In all this the poet's Adamic sense to arrest and identify himself with "the primal innocence" of the creative, growing Nature at her "original, essential source" is revealed in order to convey the idea that the artist must return to the earth, and must continue to work and create there. For further evaluation of this point, a comparison with another American poet such as Edgar Allan Poe will be apt. Though Poe's reaction to his surroundings could not be fully appreciated by Williams,[138] it is worthwhile to indicate that whatever Williams wrote of Poe, while evaluating Poe's response to unravel the mystery of "things," "objects" and "experiences" at the very source of their existence, is also applicable to Williams himself: "His greatness is in that he turned his back and faced inland, to originality, with the identical gesture of a Boone."[139] While attempting to tap the sources of "originality," Williams discovered a kind of underlying order in the seeming disorder that pervaded the world of Nature and man:

> I have seldom seen such disorder and brokenness—such a mass of unrelated parts of things lying about. That's it! I concluded to myself. An unrecognisable order! Actually—the new![140]

In Williams's poetry this confrontation with "the new" may sometimes begin by the poet's decision to move to Nature, and may end in his ultimate resolution to establish a new relation with the natural. "The Source," one of Williams's earliest objectivist poems, would serve our purpose to illustrate this point. This poem, while being true to the "objects" or "things" it presents, is an example of the manner in which the second tenet of Zukofsky's objectivist credo ["nature as a creator desire for what is objectively perfect..."][141] is transcribed through poetry in greater neatness—in welding phrase, thought and passion to the poem's objects.[142] Ridding the poem of verbiage, a technique learnt by him from Imagism, Williams succeeds in giving the poem a "structural necessity" and fuses "each image [with] a form in its own right."[143] More important of all is the allowance given by the poet to Nature to act as a "Creator." The poem's images take us from stasis to dynamism. To put it precisely, it is a shift from static Nature to a condition of her organic growth and plenitude. The emphasis is on mutability—the complex voyage through "uncertainty" ["balsams stand uncertainly"] to the dawn of a new life perpetrated in process ["edge of bubbles stirs"]. Incidentally speaking, Williams's poems do not take us, for that matter, to "the traditional spring song world of bounding lambs, gamboling children, gentle breezes and universal fecundity."[144] Moving away from any "literary concept" of Nature, Williams gives us the hard core of all manner of rough, harsh and broken "things," "objects" and "situations" which indeed shake us out of "sheer dumpiness," and awaken us to perceive the scene in all its vividness. And so, the scene assumes meaningful dimensions. The images come in positive concatenation in "The Source." It is "a pasture which begins/ where silhouettes of scrub/and balsams stand uncertainly/On whose green three maples/are distinctly pressed/beside a red barn."[145] The poem begins with an accent on pastoralism no doubt, but "the uncertainty" of its growth into dynamic plenitude has been clearly emphasized in the beginning. Gradually, but steadily enough, the poem, as Part I ends, gathers momentum through highly vitalised images of natural creativity that replace the earlier ones of static simplicity. The sexual overtone of "a triple elm's inverted....triple thighs"[146] indicate the organic growth of lichen, twigs, and leaves. In Part II of "The Source," the poet enters into the dawn of a fresh vision as it were, leaving behind the pasture of few details. He gets carried away by the call of the woods lying beyond—the woods where growth, change, fertility and a sort of bustling activity are rather the rule than an exception:

A spring in whose depth
white sand bubbles
overflows

clear under late raspberries
and delicate-stemmed touch-me-nots

....

the water is cast upon

a stair of uneven stones
with a rustling sound

An edge of bubbles stirs
swiftness is moulded
speed grows.[147]

The imagery of the poem in this section poses a sharp contrast with what has gone before. We are in the woods where Nature, delicate and fluent, conquers morbidity. The spring-water that "bubbles," and "overflows" is "cast upon," "uneven stones" which, instead of checking its "swiftness," help increase its speed ["speed grows"]. Though the poem begins with a sense of cataclysm, it does not declaim "catastrophe" or "end" as such. On the other hand, the spring-water's release from the "rock" suggests the necessity to "uncover" the buried creative principle, both in Nature and man, by releasing imagination from the "Rock."[148] It is obvious, therefore, that Williams is rejecting Eliot's attempt to present the "rock" as the very place where man's imagination must needs be secured for his salvation. Williams's belief that "destruction and creation/are simultaneous"[149] springs from a conviction that man's salvation lies in the "natural order."

The poem's theme, broadly speaking, also suggests the paradox of Adam's Fortunate Fall. Adam's expulsion from Paradise brought him grief and suffering, but at the same time landed him in the cycle of birth and death, loss and gain through which he had a sense of the high value of the life of labour that defines human self. Though Williams may not have intended such a theme, the thematic difference between the two sections of the poem, and the resulting tension make it worthwhile to consider it in that light. It is through dynamism, as suggested in Part II of the poem, where the wilderness with its multifaceted landscape is thought to be our "source," that we can seek our true happiness and find our hope. In Part I Nature is depicted as simple and innocent, but there is uncertainty in her organic growth. In the Garden of Eden Adam, too, was too innocent to see his mind growing till he ate of the apple from the Tree of Knowledge, and was consequently expelled from Paradise. From simple and innocent Nature as depicted in Part I of the poem we are taken to witness in Part II Nature's vitality in fertility, and bustling activity. Above all, there is Williams's Whitmanesque celebration of the "body beautiful" ["profuse body"] and this body "advances/over the stones unchanged."[150] The whole poem suggests that it is through a natural order, and through a "leap into reality" which is a part of the natural order that man can get to the source of his true self. Truly speaking, the poem is an objective commentary on the complexity of human personality—of possibilities of hope in man's fallen condition. The symbolic nature of the woods is given fruther artistic sanction in another poem named "The Jungle" where Williams is able to point to the buried qualities in man's nature by presenting a conventional jungle as "back-drop" against a human character. Koch's analysis of the poem is revealing:

> The true subject is the jungle, that is to say, the jungle of the brown girl's personality.... For example, the "breathless interior" of the wood, "the still weight of the trees" are implicit in the breathless, still "waiting" of the girl, are stressed, in fact, by the sibilant mysteriousness of the lines: "shy, brown, soft-eyed.... Upstairs, Sir," as well as by the weak feminine end-syllable of the last line.[151]

If not in broad and sweeping terms, at least by hints and signs, this poem anticipates the mysteriousness of "the female principle" in *Paterson* in such lines like "tangled with wrist-thick/vines...."[152] Moreover, the operational field of this principle gets fixed as in "The Wanderer" in possessing "the natural" as opposed to "the artificial."

It is clear that Williams got himself free of the "romantic inheritance" with its overtones of "epistemological obsessions" and "seminal metaphors of alienation."[153] Thus, he did not feel the necessity to escape and evade, or to transcend the immediate experience as the Romantics did. Hence, Williams's condemnation of "divorce," and admiration of "marriage." In Williams canon, particularly in *Paterson* "marriage" is depicted as a symbol—a gesture of unification of strength and beauty suggested by the city and wilderness respectively. "The Jungle," where the soft-eyed girl guides the gentleman upstairs, suggests this unification, and presents the mysterious sentimentality of the eternal Eve—the logic, we suppose, behind Adam's fall from Paradise. The process of creation as believed by Williams lies in facundating reality with unreality and the anti-poetic with sentimentality. "The imagination is the transmuter," Williams emphasized. "It is the changer. Without imagination life cannot go on, for we are left staring at the empty casings where truth lived yesterday while the creature itself has escaped behind us."[154] Like Spring so also imagination can renew and make the world of decay, loss, and ruin alive to us, enabling ourselves to possess and retain its best and finest qualities. With our proximity to chaos, the poem itself may work itself out as "a field of action" wherein the poet's unmediated perception of moments of experience, and its fluidity and multiplicity may designate for us a path leading to a mood of acceptance and its underlying hope in affirming the continuance of life.

The winter poems like "These," while showing Williams's "basic faith in the world" however barren and ugly it might be, do also demonstrate his ability to see through "loneliness" and "emptiness," and tap "The source of poetry that/seeing the clock stopped, says,/The clock has stopped/that ticked yesterday so well? and hears the sound of lakewater splashing..."[155] This is how the environment is lifted to expression, "to the stark dignity of entrance" as he writes in "Spring and All." The advent of Spring is not announced with suddenness, nor does he present any abstract idea of Spring. Williams does not want to distance us from the immediate. On the other hand, there is a precise concern with the process of taking us back to the sources of life without attenuating or violating its flexibility. Thus spring came:

> By the road to the contagious hospital
> under the surge of the blue
> mottled clouds driven from the
> northeast—a cold wind. Beyond, the
> waste of broad, muddy fields
> brown with dried weeds, standing and fallen
>
> ....
>
> Lifeless in appearance, sluggish
> dazed spring approaches—
>
> ....
>
> Now the grass, tomorrow
> the stiff curl of wildcarrot leaf
> One by one objects are defined-...[156]

The real nature of Spring, and the objective details at the exact moment of Spring's advent—all this should be presented in order that we see Spring as it is and not as a season that could only be romanticized. Williams's theory in this regard is epigrammatic in its compactness:

> The true value is the peculiarity which gives an object a character by itself. The associational or sentimental value is the false. Its imposition is due to lack of imagination, to an easy lateral sliding. The attention has been held too rigid on one plane instead of following a more flexible, jagged resort.[157]

Elsewhere Williams says that "a poem is a small (or large) machine made of words," and when he says so, he means "that there can be no part, as in any other machine, that is redundant."[158] Not only does Williams believe in possessing the environment in its totality, but also he tries through art to give a new dimension to it by lifting its images of things and persons beyond the decay and abuse which ordinarily afflict them. There should also be an intensity of perception on the part of the artist. In Williams's opinion, it is not what a writer "*says* that counts as a work of art, it's what he makes, with such intensity of perception that it lives with an intrinsic movement of its own to verify its authenticity"[159] [Williams's Italics]. Such a creative process would mean that there can be no violation in the use of words by an imposition of thinking and experience. Hence the poem's existence is like that of an object—something that has its own life in a strange operation of sound and rhythm. To speak it differently, the meaning of the poem lies not in its rhetoric but in the very manner of its intimate and intricate relationship of words. Williams makes an explicit statement on this in *Paterson*: "Not prophecy! Not prophecy!/but the thing itself!"[160] In achieving this, as we have emphasized, Williams's potential "tool" is the word. It must be also made clear that this potential tool called "word" should be used by the poet "as a structuring rather than a structural unit... in the *imitation* rather than the representation of nature"[161] [Woods's Italics]. This is not to say that Nature has only to be imitated in the old Shakespearan sense of holding the mirror on to her. What is needed is active invention as a result of which Nature in enlarged. When the process is existentially complete, "We become nature or we discover in ourselves nature's active part,"[162] as Williams puts it. Again, the "verb to do" is involved in order that Nature is imitated in the sense of discovery. Just as Marianne Moore lifted words almost "bodily from greasy contexts" and removed "the aureoles that have been pasted about them,"[163] so also Williams "de-smudged" words from their "artifactual and associative resonances" to bestow on them a kind of "dynamization" of meaning independently of the facts they name. Thus, words are purified, and are returned to an Adamically innocent, semantically "prelapsarian" state beyond corruption. This would mean, as Miller puts it, that "The word is given reality by the fact it names, but the independence of the fact from the word frees the word to be a fact...."[164]

In this context, that is, the role of words in Williams's poetry, the arguments of Claude Levi-Strauss in *The Savage Mind* (1962) may be examined to enable ourselves to understand it more clearly. Levi-Strauss defines the artist as part engineer and part *bricoleur*. As *bricoleur* he is "a jack-of-all trades"—"a handyman" who carries an additional quality of using "devious means compared to a craftsman." His materials of use are the "residue of human artifacts." As opposed to this the engineer has an altogether different role:

> The bricoleur is adept at performing a large number of diverse tasks, but, unlike the engineer he does not subordinate each of them to the availability of raw materials and tools conceived and procured for the purpose of the project. His universe of instruments is closed and the rules of his game are always to make do with 'whatever is at hand,' that is to say with a set of tools and materials which is always finite and is also heterogeneous because what it contains bears no relation to the current project, or indeed to any particular project, but is the contingent result of all the occasions there have been to renew or enrich the stock or to maintain it with the remains of previous constructions or destructions.[165]

The engineer has, of course, "as many sets of tools and materials or 'instrumental sets,' as there are different kinds of projects."[165a]

As such, the engineer finds his own way out and goes beyond "the constraints imposed by a particular state of civilization while the *bricoleur* by inclination or necessity remains within them"[165b] [Levi-Strauss' Italics]. Therefore, the *bricoleur* would think of the "tools" or the "materials" in strict pursuance of a specific project whereas the engineer can even create his tools or instrumental sets to get the project going. When any poetical language is highly artifactual or residual, that is to say derivative in the sense of being tradition-conscious, the poet is said to be inclined to play the role of a *bricoleur*. On the other hand, his inclination to create new techniques, structural patterns and vocabulary make him an engineer. The myth-maker, and for that matter, a poet like T.S. Eliot, may be considered as the poet-as-*bricoleur*. Eliot's poetry is such by the very nature of its synchronic and diachronic involvement with the "artifactual resonance" of our literature through allusion, allegory, symbolism, etc. As opposed to this, the Adamic poet or the poet-as-engineer would not only "comb out" language to purify it, but also would seize upon "new ways of making poems." Williams, in his refusal to separate art from life, and in his continual search after a new "measure" in American poetry would fall in this category. In this connection William's theory of consciousness needs clarification. To him the American in his ordinary day-to-day activity gets locked up from "true value," and in his mad rush for security he is denied the sweets of original and unique selfhood. Thus, like the citizens of Paterson, he is "unroused," and more or less, wakes outside of his body. Beyond his habitual experiences, he is afraid of any "instinctive venture." Williams writes:

> But the thing he never knows and never dares to know is what he is at the exact moment that he is. And this moment is the only thing in which I am at all interested.[166]

It is the core of our "profuse body," as Williams would describe it in "The Source," that contains the very force of our "renewal." In intense moments when we are conscious of ourselves we can return to that self to see the world and the human life in a new and fresh light. For Williams, history, unlike the view held by Joyce, Eliot and Pound, is not "a linear progression of events." It is "a pattern of eternal recurrence" as a result of which we are forever capable of cutting across the welter of events to reach the centre of genuine individuality. This is to say that we progress from an exposure to mere form in order to seize the substance. To make this possible, every moment has to be treated as "a voyage of discovery"—an opportunity to descend to origins. In the "origins" lies the Edenic Bliss, but this, in the opinion of Williams, must be sought in the home ground, for home is the place to which we continually return. This deisre is something like "melting metal":

> It might better be metal. It is as with other metals, when it is heated it melts. It is when the metal is fluid that the imagination can be said to become active; it is the melting, the rendering fluid of the imagination that describes the mind as entering upon creative work.

> It must be melted to create, fluid, unfettered by anything.[167]

The poem, considered from this point of view, springs from the artist's total existence which includes not only the "anti-poetic," but also "the filthy Passaic"—the repugnant and the chaotic:

> The poem... is an assertion that we are alive as ourselves—as much of the environment as it can grasp exactly as Hellas lived in the *Iliad.*[168]

"The Sun," a poem in the objectivist mode, asserts the eternal and the original aspects of life and Nature. It lifts the environment to expression as we find in Sheeler's or Demuth's painting where the industrial landscape, in spite of its banality and chaos, is given meaning by its recurrent motif to get back to the origins. The poem begins with the poet's contemplation of a beach that is strewn with refuse. He does not present the sea in its grandiloquent design which, as Matthew Arnold said in the "Dover Beach," is the cause of philosophic meditation for poets beginning from Sophocles down to our own time. It is "this modern shore" with its "obscene refuse" that charms Williams. The high tide has left its mark on the sea:

> in the night
> a high tide left
> its mark
> and block of half
>
> burned wood washed
> clean—The slovenly
> bearded rocks hiss—[169]

Instead of Eliot's "mermaids singing each to each," here is the singing of the sea-snail, and the climbing of the Sun to make us relax. The Sun, just as the sea-snail, acts as the eternal healer and purifier of Nature. In other words, we must "go down past knowledge," and have the conviction, and understanding that man can only harm Nature temporarily. Nature can rise to life, Phoenix-like, from the very ashes of man's depredations. The poem ends, therefore, with the theme of innocence, for out of every crisis is born a greater faith in Edenic Bliss. The reference to the "screaming children" with "their delight—/logged/in the penetrable/nothingness..." exemplifies for us the necessity to bring to our adult life the playful mood and innocence of children, so that we can conquer the "nothingness," "obscenity" and "vacuity" of modern life. Like the "profuse body" in "The Source," this poem does also refer lastly to "heavy body."

This emphasis on the physical and the immediate springs from, as we have already stated, Williams's view of creativity which he formulated in answer to that of Pound's and Eliot's. His difference from the Poundian credo, affiliated as it has been with "the mythic Mode" in poetry, is stated in clear, and assertive terms in his "Letter to an Australian Editor":

> I wish only to say that for years we [Pound & Williams] have been of opposite but friendly camps, touching the origin of poetic genius. We parted years ago, he to move among his intellectual equals in Europe, I to remain at home and struggle to discover here the impetus to my achievements, if I found myself able to write anything at all.... He left the States under the assumption that it was mind that fertilizes mind, that the mere environment is just putty and that—assuming one's self great [–] the thing to do in this world is, or was then to go to Europe, which he did.[170]

In spite of this break-away from Pound, it is seen that Pound's influence was almost permanently moulded in Williams's poetry, particularly in its aspect of communicating an attitude of the aesthetic "concern for poetry as direct as speech."[171] Williams of course, put his own emphasis on the "idea of constant return to our origins in the immediate physical world."[172] Compared to the position taken by Pound and Eliot such a "locus," that is to say, the poet's "stance" to fix creative process in the earth and in the body, may appear a little too uncommon, though its potentiality need not be questioned. It is this deeper consciousness lying hidden in the body to which Whitman also drew our attention. Here is Williams whose praise for Whitman was couched in candid terms:

> Whitman's proposals are of the same piece with the modern trend toward imaginative understanding of life. The largeness which he interprets as his identity with the least and the greatest around him, his "democracy" represents the vigor of his imaginative life.[173]

This chaotic improvisation that Williams pleaded was also implicit in the very concept of creative process as we come across in *Kora in Hell* which set the ball rolling for the kind of poetry that we find Williams writing after the 1920's:

> A poem can be made of anything. This is a portrait of a disreputable farm hand made out of the stuff of his environment.[174]

Thus, he rejected the conventional mode of poetic and eloquent subjects, and in the words of Wallace Stevens, balanced "the sentimental" and "the antipoetic." The interaction of these two opposites would focundate Williams's poetry, and would act as a pointer to "that truth, that reality to which all of us are forever fleeing."[175] Stevens's claim that Williams was interested to include the antipoetic as a poetic device made Williams write a reply as a sort of protest. It is to be noted with care, for it makes a good clarification of Williams's poetic stance:

> ...the anti-poetic is not something to enhance the poetic—it's [poetry is] all one piece. I didn't agree with Stevens that it was a conscious means I was using.[176]

Despite Williams's disapproval of "the antipoetic," the term *has* to be applied to his poetry, for Stevens intended, as Guimond argues, to carry home the idea that Williams's use of "the anti-poetic" shows his avoidance of the conventional, or, for that matter, the sentimental stock of subjects.[177] One point has, of course, to be remembered in this connection: whether or not Williams's use of the anti-poetic indicated any sort of nihilism in him. Vivienne Koch would argue that "the recognition of anti-poetic detail does not, as Matthew Arnold thought of Whitman, commit one to nihilism. It may instead preclude a thoroughly non-materialistic, affirmative humanism, even when, as with Williams and Cummings, suggesting pagan rather than Christian views...."[178] Adam's fall from Paradise led him to the curse of earning his bread by the sweat of his brow. This would mean that he dynamized himself to perform his new role well which demanded a closer attention to the details around him for his success, and even, we should say, for his survival. Though it might be argued that Adam, in effect, projected the needs and desires of his own nature as objective qualities of the external world, it must not also be ruled out that the objects of the world were there to express themselves for Adam's seeing. The pagan element is implicit in both the processes. What Williams did was to capture "the thing" by a consistent return to project "the anti-poetic" in his poetry, apart from emphasizing a need, through the themes of his poems, to know the elemental and the natural as the very basis of man's life-force. The unmediated vision of the Adamic poet[179] can alone discover such a world, and "celebrate the power of invention itself."[180] The poems primarily of "seeing" such as "Spring Strains," "Nantucket," "Queen-Ann's-Lace," "Young Sycamore," etc., very much succeed in giving us not only a catalogue of "things" and "objects" in their multi-dimensional existence, but also overtly demonstrate the poet's ability for sharp and precise "discovery." In all that he discovered, Williams gave "the things" a separate, individuated existence beyond the tampering of man, and civilization. In the face of change, the continuity of Adamic innocence in them is also stressed. For example, in "Spring Strains" he exhorts the trees to hold on to their innocent existence against the thrust of a counterforce:

> Hold hard, rigid jointed trees!
> the blinding and red-edged sun-blur—[181]

Williams's imagination is metamorphic in that it takes on the Adamic impluse of joining the "objects" of his discovery in a single strain. In "Spring Strains," it is the Sun ["Creeping energy, concentrated"] that "welds sky, buds, trees," and "rivets them in one puckering hold."[182] In "Nantucket," the "things and objects" seen are "montaged" in such a way as to present innocence in the very cleanliness of their existence:

Flowers through the window
lavender and yellow
changed by white curtains—
smell of cleanliness—[183]

The innocence of the flowers—a subject on which some of the best poems of Williams are built—is intensified in this poem by "the/immeculate white bed" in the end. In fact, "discovery" is a word that strikes the key-note to the whole understanding of Williams's poetry. As Brinnin suggests, this process of discovery is one of "relationship between actuality and the mind confronting it." It is also a "discovery of the language that would in turn make that discovery 'true' and communicable."[184] There is an attempt here to merge language "with the chaotic flux of reality."[185] In that "formal desperation" and "schismatic" will,[186] there is no loss of any implications.[187] On the other hand, implications are more often than not "sweeping." Thus, Williams engages himself keenly, and with a sense of adventure, to gain an "insight into the aesthetic of existence"—an aesthetic of "lifting to the imagination those things which lie under the direct scrutiny of the nose."[188] The most successful ones are those which portray objects of an elemental nature and character. The objects exist in their own individual right, but details of their location and action are put in a manner so as to make the whole poem meaningful. In "The Winds," for example, Williams captures the very spirit of the modern world by cataloguing the objects which are blown away by "the winds of this northern March." The end is sweeping as it emphasizes that the winds do blow away" ...scales from/the mind and husbands from wives."[189] The meaning of the poem lies in a subtle suggestion that "modernity" may fall a victim to the negative forces of Nature, and thereby may engender a spirit of "divorce"—a state of dying "incommuni-cado." Nature's destructive forces not only cause revages to her own innocent objects ["blow the bark from the trees/the soil from the field,"] but also extend the ravages to the human world. And yet, as *Kora in Hell* would insist, there is "No Ritual But fact." It is through a contact with the actual [which we should record at "moments of our enlarged consciousness"] that we can save ourselves. *Kora in Hell* explores this paradox in detail, and exhorting us to meet actuality in proper order, teaches us how to move from "divorce" to "marriage," from "desolation into celebration." Thus, renewal can come by a "defenseless witnessing" of chaos: [190]

> ...an infant landscape of shimmering
> ash and flame and we, in
> that instant, lost,
>
> breathless to be witnesses
> as if we stood
> ourselves refreshed among
> the shining fauna of that fire.[191]

It presents no difficulty to translate the theme into Adamic terms. Adam's fall which was an instant loss was "fortunate," for Adam had a sense of more positive values of life which came to him through the process of loss ["as if we stood/ourselves refreshed among/the shining fauna of that fire"].

Till we come to a clarification of Williams's development as a poet after the late 1930's, some more important features of his earlier poetry need to be emphasized. Some of the poems, particularly the ones that celebrate faith in love as the redeeming force in human life, do anticipate, in effect if not in depth, his significant contribution to American poetry in *Pictures from Brueghel and Other Poems*. Among the earlier poetry the simplex but effective ones are "The Trees" and "Rain" where love is freed from "blockage," and is "released" to find its niche in the bosom of man instead of remaining in classical myth:

> There were never satyrs
> never maenads
> never eagle-headed gods—
> There were men
> from whose hands sprung
> love
> bursting the wood—
>
> Trees their companions...[192]

The Adamic poet's belief in men is restored, and "love" is celebrated "against the heaving contra-bass/of the dark ...," as he puts it in another poem, "Trees." In "Rain" love is equated with the pouring rains:

> and nothing
> comes of it but love
> following
> and falling endlessly
> from
>   her thoughts[193]

Thus, love is also restored to Nature, for like the pouring of rains it falls "...endlessly/from/her thoughts." What strikes us as unique is the manner in which the feelings and thoughts are welded into the phrases and words:

> There is something to say and one says it. That's writing. But to say it one must have it alive with the overtones which give not a type of statement but an actual statement that is alive...[194]

Sometimes Williams employs the city—its vastness and swift movement—as a fitting background to the dream of love:

> —a dream
> we dreamed
>   each
> separately
>   we two
> of love
> and of
> desire—
> that fused
> in the night—
> in the distance
>   over
> the meadows
>   by day
> impossible—
>   The city
> disappeared
>   when
> we arrived—[195]

The regular beat and the syncopated verbal stress make the whole poem a model of mobility itself, suggesting the perpetually kinesthetic nature of the city's life. Against this overpowering vastness and swiftness Williams places the dream of love—its aspiration and despair. By drawing our attention to the various hateful forms of love, Williams says to us that "There is no end/ to desire—." In fact, the emphasis here is not on the City of Desire, but on the heavenly City of Love where life is in perpetual happiness. The poem suggests through the depiction of love's degeneration that love and innocence must go together. If love degenerates into whorishness, eating and drinking, the City of Love disintegrates, and it is man's fall from Paradise. In "Young Love" the poet conceives of love even among the "broken pieces of the city—." The scene is enacted in the hospital:

> beds, beds, beds
> elevators, fruit, night-tables
> breasts to see, white and blue—
> to hold in the hand, to nozzle[196]

The image of water as the symbol of soul's purity is brought in to suggest the permanence of "young love":

> Clean is he alone
> after whom stream
> the broken pieces of the city—
> flying apart of his approaches
>
> but I merely
> caressed you curiously
> fifteen years ago and you still
> go about the city, they say
> patching up sick school children.[197]

This is how love is conceived, different in its intensity at different times, and different also as an experience for different people. Koch draws our attention to this treatment of love's paradox in Williams's poetry:

> The paradox of love's compulsion... is that it is
> a dream, more than a little false, "a dream of love'

> toward which we move, a dream, moreover, we have each made for ourselves 'separately.'[198]

Koch expounds this point with reference to Shakespeare's *A Midsummer Night's Dream* and *The Tempest* where the "dream of love" is like the bubble of water that blows at the touch of reality.[199] And so, love, for each one of us is a "private vision of a private wholeness," the common quality being its inclination to disintegration at the touch of reality. It is like Paradise, but all lovers, like Adam must be banished from it.

Whether it is a poem on love or anything else, the technique that Williams employed in the late 'Thirties in composing a poem would anticipate the structural patterns and poetic diction of his later poetry. In 1935 he writes to Marianne Moore:

> There is a good deal of rebellion still in what I write, rebellion against stereotyped poetic process—the too meticulous choice among other things. In too much refinement there lurks a sterility that wishes to pass too often for purity when it is anything but that. Coarseness for its own sake is inexcusable, but a Rabelasian sanity requires that the rare and the fine be exhibited as coming like everything else from the dirt. There is no incompatibility between them.[200]

He did not, therefore, discriminate between the beautiful and the ugly. To him, and to his poetic world the whole panorama had to be lifted to expression:

> What do you think beauty is, since you speak so glibly of the beautiful? You think it's a partial thing, something here against something 'ugly' there. Impossible. It's the whole thing at once. Or nothing.[201]

To capture the beautiful, he must turn to his own country, and this was, as it were, in answer to D.H. Lawrence's address in 1920 to the readers of the *New Republic* with the words: "America, Listen to Your Own." Lawrence's exhortation to recognize and embrace "the black demon of savage America, the aboriginal spirit" had nothing of the romantic facileness of spirit. It was " a mysterious, delicate process," and the American Adam had to shake off his fixation upon a dead past, as Lawrence put it.[202] With a new extension of life, Williams undertook his "descent" into the real America which lay hidden between "the murdered Red America and the seething white America."[203] Considered in this light, the poem "To Elsie" is, by far, the most important of all his earlier poems, and echoes, in a smaller and concentrated canvas, the central and indulging idea of *Paterson.*

"To Elsie" focuses on three of Williams's major concerns as an artist, that is, "a despoiled America, the alienated and self-alienating human condition and the ravished Eden of the imagination."[204] What he wanted to do was to address himself to the problem of creating a poetic world which would be self-sufficient in recapturing the Edenic bliss in an unravished "sensual actuality" remaining in its native state of innocence. The poem begins with an open avowal to embrace the real America ["The pure products of America"] which lay in the despoiled beauty, simplicity and innocence of her mountain folks. The poet despairs that they "go crazy," and take to "sheer lust" of adventure:

> devil-may-care men who have taken
> to rail roading
> out of sheer lust of adventure—
> and young slatterns, bathed
> in filth from Monday to Saturday[205]

A descendant of the Jackson Whites of northern New Jersey, Elsie—Williams's half-mad maid—is the symbol of this degradation to which the simple peasant folks of America subjected themselves in their mad rush for success through adventure, and purposive action:

> to be tricked out that night
> with gauds
> from imaginations which have no
> peasant traditions to give them
> character
> but flutter and flaunt[206]

The familiar rags-to-riches myth of success in the pioneering America, and the gradual evolution of her technocratic society would ravish the imagination of the Americans, but the effect is one of nightmare and demonology, and fall from paradisiacal bliss. The fall occurred as the aspirations of the Americans were not "fed by an organic relation to the physical environment."[207] The whole theme is brought out vividly through the character of Elsie ["voluptucus water/expressing with broken/brain the truth about us—"]. The national desire for easy success and quick wealth which ultimately led to industrialization did not only spoil the Edenic bliss of "isolate lakes and/valleys," but also was ungainly, and was the cause behind the rise of a cheap culture:

> her great
> ungainly hips and flopping breasts
> addressed to cheap
> jewelery
> and rich young men with fine eyes.[208]

The dehumanization of America is brought forth through images of dirt and filth:

> as if the earth under our feet
> were
> an excrement of some sky
> and we degraded prisoners
> destined
> to hunger until we eat filth.[209]

And yet, as suggested by Williams, the separation from "the real sources of life" can be efficaciously obviated through imagination. It is this faculty of our mind which can enable us to continue our search for Paradise which is here and now hidden underneath the dirt and filth:

> While the imagination strains
> after deer
> going by fields of goldenrod in
> the stifling heat of September.[210]

The last lines of the poem, with the image of a driverless car, signify the American avarice, greed, and limitless desire to dominate Nature in a mad rush for worldly success and power:

> No one
> to witness
> and adjust, no one to drive the car.[211]

Breslin brings out the different threads of this symbol effectively:

> The pure products of America *have* gone crazy: abstracted, swift-moving, brutal. The driverless car is another modern version of Pluto, god of avarice and rape, the mythic embodiment of man's dream of dominion.[212]
>
> [Breslin's Italics]

It is Elsie, however,—the woman, and the fecundatory element in life's evolution—to whom our attention is primarily drawn. The driverless car symbolizes, more or less, Elsie's alienation from the environment, and to a major extent, her own self-alienation, too. Thus, the ideals of civilization are neglected. This recalls the voice of the woman writer in the prose correlative to *Paterson.* Her utter loneliness and desolation and her failure to come to terms with herself signifies the American indifference to "sensitive awareness" and "sensuous delicacy" in a mad rush for wealth and power. All that is good, and should not be spoilt, is often associated with the female principle in Williams's writings. As D.H. Lawrence put it in his review of *In the American Grain:*

> The author sees the genius of the continent as a woman with exquisite, super-subtle tenderness and recoiling cruelty.[213]

Like so many of Williams's poems, "To Elsie," does not, of course, present a solution to the shift of consciousness in the American mind which has made brutality and violence a substitute for the traditional innocence and simplicity. It gives us the tension in inviting us to watch the clash of opposing sensibilities. Some of the poems such as "Light Becomes Darkness" are Adamic in an almost straightforward way. They inform the condition of actuality through graphic images which enable us to know the loss, but loss is also viewed as a new sense of value—a milestone in our arduous process of evolution as man. Thus, the ancient myth has given way to a modern myth for good or bad, and again the difference between good and evil is just thin, so that it is difficult to know whether light is darkness or darkness is light. In other words, the seeds of grace may very well lie in sin! Williams pinpoints the fact that "destruction and creation/are simultaneous," and "The decay of Cathedrals/is afflorescent/through the phenomenal/growth of movie houses/whose catholicity is/progress...."[214] If the traditionalist says that this "progress" is only a death-trap, the Adamic Williams has his answer:

> Woe is translatable
> to joy if light becomes
> darkness and darkness
> light, as it will—[215]

This is moral neutrality moving cyclically, and it reducers all differences to a tentative projection of the "ego" governed by circumstances only. A poem, conceived in the light of such considerations, becomes what Williams himself has said, the embodiment of "the active 'I am,'" and not of "the passive 'to be.'"[216] The emphasis of Williams as an artist was to clarify culture and tradition by reasserting things through his intelligence and emotion. He wrote to Horace Gregory:

> If, as I believe and keep always before my eyes, if art is a transference—for psychic relief—from the actual to the formal, and this can only be achieved by invention, by rediscovery, by reassertion by the intelligence and the emotions in any and every age—and if the grand aspect of this living drive is, what it occurs, a culture, then, I say, our chief occupation as artists singly and jointly should be the clarification of form, new alignments, in our own language and culture.[217]

And so, the actuality of his poetic world does not obviate but validates the dictum that what we call our knowledge of the objective world may have its own illusions. By giving us actuality Williams's intention was to stress the point that actuality may very often differ from reality even though the two may appear seemingly identical.[218] This necessitates our yielding to the moment, to "the cry of its occasion" by a simple surrender to the forces of Nature. This may be a form of self-obliteration, but through it a greater self-awareness is likely to emerge. A certain amount of flexibility of imagination is also necessary, and in this arduous process "things," objects" and "situations," are viewed in their relatedness only. The poem "St. Francis Einstein of the Daffodils" is an enunciation of this mental process—a process which was also the cause behind Adam's fall from Paradise. If Adam's mind would not have been subjected to the arduous struggle called the flexibility of imagination he could have turned a deaf ear to the voice of the Serpent or the advice of Eve. The poem is composed on the first visit of Einstein to the United States in the Spring of 1921. It begins with an invocation of America as the "Sweet land"—the land of liberty. What is important is that Einstein's presence in the United States is not only the starting-point of his own freedom, but also the beginning of an intensified form of free and unfettered spirit which is equalised with the advent of Spring. Einstein's Theory of Relativity proved that man and Nature are the same, and their lost contact could be re-established without transforming their nature. What Einstein proved scientifically was a part of the religious credo of St. Francis whose love for men and Nature was so intense that he would have men, birds, and animals come together. Hence, Williams gives Einstein the name of St. Francis Einstein. Einstein himself was the very image of Nature at her sweetest:

> Einstein, tall as a violet
> in the lattice-arbor corner
> is tall as
> a blossomy peartree.[219]

The full blossom of the daffodils indicate the onset of Spring, but to the daffodils, too, there has come a new freedom, for Einstein, keeping up the tradition of St. Francis, has proved their relative equality with man:

> Freedom
> for the daffodils!
> —in a tearing wind
> that shakes
> the tufted orchards—.[220]

The process of loss, that is to say, the human failure to understand the new camaraderie in basic equality, has been emphasized through the image of the "tearing wind/that shakes/ the tufted orchards—." In 1941 Williams wrote that "The poem alone focuses the world." Moreover, poetry is "practical and comprehensive and cannot be the accompaniment of other than an unfettered imagination...."Any limitation will only kill it:

> "We seek as far as we are American to take in the difficult...the GOLD of it no matter how the ornament is shaped or what may be the purpose to which it seems to be put. To reject the spurious... To reveal the rare and the curious relationships which are the mind's true business."[221]

The poet as the alchemist takes Einstein, the discoverer of the Theory of Relativity, as a symbol in order that he will be capable of revealing "the curious relationships" existing between man and Nature—a bond which has been unfortunately forgotten, but need to be remembered with a fresh energy of human imagination. This shows that some of the primitive values which are rather passional in nature need to be expressed again. But unlike the mythic poet, Williams chooses to reject mythological symbols, and makes use of images from actual experience. Understood from this angle, the image of the Negro gardener who, by his tender care, helps blossom the flowers in the garden becomes relevant. He represents the basic tenets of Einstein's Theory of Relativity which, by emphasizing the new identity of the daffodils, have given the flowers their real liberty. The symbol of the dead cat is a mythical fertility rite, and through its rebirth, for the cat is supposed to have nine lives, it helps the flowers and fruits in the garden to grow in Spring. Thematically speaking, the poem is an Adamic effort not only to reiterate the eternal bond that man has with Nature, but also to take into account the fact of its loss as we view Nature oftentimes in a different light without understanding her relative equality with men. The objectivistic predilection is clear-cut in the manner of the poem's composition. The poem is free of declamations or lyric outbursts with its usual repetitions and tangential statements.

Williams's objectivism, as Sutton says, "has sometimes been mistaken as a purely objective Imagism: an effort to copy or imitate.... physical objects in nature."[222] Precisely speaking an objectivist poem by Williams is a "thing" of words invented by the poet himself in the process of determining the nature of his perception:

> His chief commitment, accordingly, is to the reality and integrity of the poetic objects rather than to the physical reality of its 'subject,' even though this physical reality is important to him both in itself and as a stimulus or inspiration to his work.[223]

This creative process involves the making of objects in the very form of poetry, and assigning them a niche in the poetic world in order that the work of science with its engineering talent can be furthered, and intelligence can survive in its confrontation with reality. And so, in such poetry there is a very conscious attempt to avoid perception where senses are rather seductively led to accept things by mere "sensuous intrigue."[224]

It should be carefully noted that in most of the objective poems of Williams the tendency is to leave things almost in a state of suspended animation as a result of which the reader is inclined to fill up the vacuum by bringing in symbolic association. Coming as they do at the end of such poems, a feeling is created, which, of course, varies from individual to individual in its intensity, that the process of perception has not had its point of culmination. Hence, the total metaphor is liable not only to open up the reader's speculation, but also to invite the reader to undertake such a venture. "To block it in the interest of objectivist purity," Sutton says, "would be a too interested and limiting response."[225] One may, for example, scrutinise a poem like the "Young Sycamore." Williams has something in his mind that he must tell us as the opening lines suggest:

> I must tell you
> this young tree
> whose round and firm
> trunk between the wet

pavement and the gutter
(where water
is trickling) rises
bodily.[226]

The diaphoric method to establish a metaphor by juxtaposing "things," "objects," and "situations" is employed. The significance lies, however, in studying the total pattern of juxtapositions. That the tree cannot lose its bodily beauty just because it is sprouting up from the gutter, or that the gutter cannot be considered ugly as the sprouting tree gives it a pattern of beauty, is a major concern for the poet himself. This has to be taken into consideration apart from the suggestive way in which Williams makes the poem end. It is, of course, evident that the poem closes all on a sudden keeping the reader almost suspended for the time being in a vacuum, and asking rather too much of him to understand the metaphor, if not in his own way, at least in accordance with the pattern of juxtapositions of detailed description that has gone before. The tree thins away to a mere "it," and the whole attention is concentrated on:

but two
eccentric knotted
twigs
bending forward
hornlike at the top.[227]

Since it is the climactic point that seethes with a "heat" of its own, it is not unwarranted if we feel the inkling of certain association of ideas in regard to the hornlike twigs to which the tree has lastly boiled down. Firstly, it is not unlikely to say that the tree must be linked with the animal world, and gain its new identity in relative equality. Secondly, it is plausible to connect it "with a primitive animistic but distinctly human view of nature."[228] Thus, the poem viewed in this light, assumes an Adamic tone as it gives us an insight into man's plundering of the natural landscape ["this young tree.../between the wet/ pavement and the gutter"], and then invites us to view Nature as having a close tie with animal and human world ["till nothing is left of it/but two/eccentric knotted/twigs/bending forward/

hornlike at the top"]. The poem is, therefore, an effort at making good our loss in being expelled from Paradise by asking us to recreate in our mind an animistic, but essentially humanistic view of Nature. Sometimes the poet may ask us to plunge ourselves directly into the creative forces of Nature only to discover that complete immersion is suicidal. Notice the opening lines of "The Sea":

> The sea that encloses her young body
> ula lu la lu
> is the sea of many arms—
> the blazing secrecy of noon is undone
> and and and
> the broken sand is the sound of love.[229]

Here are "primitive passional values" which need to be accepted. It should form a part of our modern consciousness, so that we regain at least partially through the poem's creative process a sense of our lost relationship with Nature—primal and innocence. The sea is first perceived by Williams as symbolic of love, and this is captured by the tilting, hypnotic voice of the sea. Then the sea is represented as symbolic of death, too:

> The flesh is firm that turns in the sea
> O la la
> the sea that is cold with the dead man's tears.[230]

As the tension between the concept of love and death comes to a climax ["la lu la lu/but lips too few/assume the new—marruu"],[231] we are lastly given to understand that the sea is the place that dissolves all tensions ["underneath the sea where it is dark/there is no edge/so two—"].[232] Thus, the poem is a symbolic extension of the precept that a total surrender to the forces of Nature may be suicidal for modern man, though he should have to return time and again to the paradise of her hypotic and enchanted spell for a renewal of his spirit against the deadening effect of civilisation.

Williams based his working philosophy about Nature on a sense of neutrality. But if we deeply analyse, it would be found that this neutrality is imbued with a "double vision" based on a knowledge of the ambiguities of human life itself. The centrality of this attraction for the sea lies in Williams's Dionysiac sensuality very much unlike J. Alfred Prufrock's sterilised response of "attenuated intellect"[233] ["I do not think that they will sing to me"]. Again, what gives rise to the poem's tension is the Apollonian "resilience of feelings"—a means of resisting the attraction. Thus, the poem is both prelapsarian and postlapsarian in its Adamic overtones.

Its super-subtle implication reveals the American Adam's mode of compromise which, it might be stated, lies in a polarised pull of strength—one engendered by Nature, and the other by civilization.

As Ostrom has pointed out, Williams's use of metaphor is rather sparse, and whenever he uses it, he makes sure that the metaphor emerges through establishing "an order of things as things."[234] The poet's observent eye is in search of the things, and he presents the things in their uniqueness, and the meaning of the poem emerges from the special pattern of juxtapositions of details. Ostrom comments on this feature as follows:

> Only the direct statement of whatness contains within its sensuality—in addition to all the associational implications we can possibly want—the indispensable purely denotative knowledge of the thing as thing: the denotative fixes the poem's world in the presentness of actuality.[235]

Since as men we act within the limitations of our senses, it is desirable that we present a formulated structure of actual things on the basis of which we can safely undertake the task of studying the world and understanding it. Hence, neither the poet nor his poetry can or should escape the world. What the poet should avoid, and must escape to give his poetry the stamp of reality, is illusion. With "a gift of sanity," Williams concretizes the physical world in order. And, unlike Wallace Stevens, with whom he has other affinities, Williams does not escape the pressure of actuality by means of that counter-pressure called the ideal order of the poem. On the other hand, a poem by Williams takes actuality as its material, and gives the material an order through which the reader can grasp "the underlying reality." One of the well-known poems of Williams that follows this principle almost to the letters is "The Red Wheelbarrow." The sheer physicality of the object's existence as indicated in the poem and its juxtaposition with "rains" and "chickens" strike us as unique. Excepting as an observer who says "so much depends," the poet is not a part of the poem's scene, for what he says is chiefly meant for the reader on whose reaction to the things juxtaposed the meaning of the poem entirely rests. Again, the discursiveness of the opening line is a positive invitation to the reader to seek out the meaning. Approaching the poem thus, we may start with the red wheelbarrow itself as a "thing" belonging to the world of machine—a product of civilization. But civilization, to survive, must maintain its, ecological balance. The poet would, therefore, bring in the other factors necessary for such a survival—"rains" and "chickens" which, in the words of Sutton, stand for "the natural forces of fertility," and "animal life"[236] respectively. This gives a new dimension to the scene as a whole which signifies that without an inter relationship and close interaction between the forces of civilization, natural forces of fertility and animal life, a source of human fertility, too, it is impossible to conceive of the continuance of man on this planet. What Williams has done is to draw our attention to the uniqueness of the thing itself—the red wheelbarrow. He has juxtaposed details of its situation in order to enable us to conceptualize the whole data into experience.[237] If civilization is the product of man's knowledge, it must be borne in mind that such a knowledge must not be divorced from all that is natural, beginning from the forces of Nature down to human fertility, and the animal world. Knowledge is not its own end, and, therefore, it must exist relatively, so that it does not become, as it was with Adam, a curse, and the very cause of his fall from Paradise. Just as in his poem "Pastoral," so also in this poem the poet's imagination feeds on simple, separate things. For the poet as well as to the reader, the difficulty may lie in being able to "relate them coherently one to another."[238] Hence the discursiveness of the opening lines. But the very fact of its discursiveness has also given us scope to annotate a meaning out of the collection of images.

Much more than what we find in such poems as the one discussed above, the later poetry of Williams, to which our attention needs now be drawn, makes Williams's objective vision of experience rather more compact. In this he is part of a tradition made alive by such writers and philosophers as Hazlitt in England, Theophile Gautier and the Parnassians in France, and Schopenhauer in Germany. In fact, Schopenhauer's concept may be briefly and attentively studied by the following citation from his writings, so that we understand Williams's later poetry all the better:

> [If a man] ceases to consider the where, the when, the why, and the whither of things, and looks simply and solely at the *what* if, further, he does not allow abstract thought, the concepts of reason, to take possession of his consciousness, but, instead of all this, gives the whole power of his mind to perception, sinks himself entirely in this, and lets his whole consciousness be filled with the quiet contemplation of the natural object actually present, whether a landscape, a tree, a mountain, a building, or whatever it may be, inasmuch as he *loses* himself in this object...then that which is so known is no longer the particular thing as such; but is the idea, the eternal form....[239] [Schopenhauer's Italics].

The emphasis is clearly on "intensity of perception." Like all aestheticist poets, Williams's "concern for exact meaning is actually a part of the belief that poetic language has the power of a logos that immediately reveals the poet's encounter with bare reality and bare beauty."[240] The verification of the poem's authenticity, then, lies in the movement of the poem itself which is intrinsic. Intensely perceiving the original object or situation, and discovering the appropriate and exact language to embody it, makes the poem an object—a thing-in-itself with its own life.

What Hazlitt meant by "imitation" is also applicable to this process, for "imitation" can make the object, however "displeasing in itself," a source of recurrent pleasure. Any "close and continued contemplation of the object" can open up through "suggestiveness" an area of "new ideas" and "new properties."[241] The objectivist's credo lies in having an "earthy taste" in either portraying human subjects or testing objects of the world. To this he adds "a background of psychological austerity" as a result of which the poet as objectivist runs the risk of becoming "an isolated figure defying the universe."[242]

Williams's more consistent allegiance to the theoretical manifesto of objectivism in the late 'Thirties makes his later poetry highly articulated art-pieces in comparison with his earlier poetry. In spite of this difference from most of his earlier poems the one thing that gives the whole spectrum of Williams's poetry a common quality is their fidelity to capture the universal through the particular. Williams would write in 1939:

> I can produce, if I am able, universals of general applicability. If I succeed in keeping myself objective enough, sensual enough, I can produce the factors, the concretions of materials by which others shall understand and so be led to use—that they may the better see, touch, taste, enjoy—their own world *differing as it may from mine.* By mine, they, different, can be discovered to be the same as I, and, thrown into contrast, will see the implications of a general enjoyment through me[243] [Williams's Italics].

What should also be noted carefully is the poet's habit of going to the universal through the momentarily particular. In fact, the universal is discovered in the moment. Neither being imposed upon, nor being embedded in any particular place, this sense of the universal is conveyed as though he feels that everything exists from the beginning. This shows that the movement of the poems is more or less circular, and before we go forward the poet asks us to go back, as a result of which these poems become, in the words of Breslin, "an *experience* of recurrence"[244] [Breslin's Italics]. The method in these poems is rather a greater tightening of the diaphoric combination of "objects," "things," and "situations" as we found in "The Red Wheelbarrow." The possibility of a metaphor lies in the manner of juxtapositions, and the spaces in between one detail and another may create a poetic field with context and association. But here too, as in the case of "The Red Wheelbarrow," the reactions of different readers are likely to vary from one another in accordance with their differing experiences of life.

One of the chief obstacles to the success of the poems in this mode lies in the possible failure of the reader to connect the images juxtaposed for finding a viable meaning out of them. One may look into the poet's "operational tactic," for example, in "The Red Wheelbarrow." It has been pointed out that the red wheelbarrow as a metaphor for simplicity rests on the very end-stopped rhythm of the poem itself. But Nowottny raises an objection which indicates the possibility that the reader may not react in the very way as intended by the poet himself. He states his opinion on the poem's simple rhythms conveying a metaphor for simplicity in the following lines:

> If the line and stanza endings were nullified by reading out the poem, to some one who had never seen it on the page, as though it were continuous prose, the poem would lose its point.[245]

This objection, we suppose, does only prove in surer terms the contention of Williams that in the last analysis all "poetry of distinction" must rest on "formal invention." In fact, Williams makes this idea the very basis of composition of most of his later poetry:

> There is no poetry of distinction without formal invention, for it is in the intimate form that the works of art achieve their exact meaning, in which they most resemble the machine, to give language its highest dignity, its illumination in the environment to which it is native.[246]

What should also be noted carefully is that in a Williams poem, [particularly his later ones] it does not matter what the line says, though it may be a beautiful line. Since the poet "makes a poem," he must accept "words as he finds them interrelated about him and [should compose] them—without distortion which would mar their exact significances—into an intense expression of his perceptions and ardors [so] that they may constitute a revolation in the speech that he uses."[247] In other words, the verification of the poem's "authenticity" lies not only in its "intensity of perception," but also in its "intrinsic movement."[248] This movement has also to be governed by the character of the speech from which the words arise, so that the effect is one of "beauty, what in a single object resolves our complex feelings of propriety."[249] Hence, in the Olympian realm of poetry, there are no frustrations, for the poet "lives in a world of the imagination where there is nothing but truth and beauty."[250] Williams expands this idea further, and asserts the acceptance of Freud's theory that the "poem is a dream, a daydream of wish fulfillment." Again, the poem's subject-matter is more or less based on "phantasy":

> We may mention Poe's dreams in a pioneer society, his dreams of gentleness and bliss.... Yeats's subject matter of faery. Shakespeare—the butcher's son dreaming of Caesar and Wolsey. No need to go on through Keats, Shelley to Tennyson. It is all, the subject matter, a wish for aristocratic attainment—a 'spiritual' bureaucracy of the 'soul' or what you will.[251]

This "spiritual bureaucracy of the soul" is a unique achievement in Williams whose "objectivism" was not static. He followed "an objectivist progression: the expansion of the image, as contemporary object-incident, to become (through historical focus) a voiced comment on a natural or a human order."[252] The tension lies in a magnetic pull between one mass of things against another. Beneath it lies the concept of a life that "sucks, curls, bulges, rattles, grips, swells, bursts."[253] Above all, there is that primary and primitive urge to get down to the very source—the beginning of the beginning where colours, shapes, patterns and designs, in their interaction with the human world, stand out bold, free and liberated, untarnished by the smudges of tradition or culture. Much earlier than the 'Thirties, Williams had consciously dedicated himself to the task of reconciling some very prosaic subject-matters such as "money," "commerce," "Marketplace"—in fact, "the whole armamentarium of the industrial age"[254]—to the task of poetic expression in the most idealized language possible.[255] It would not be out of place to mention here that the artistic credo that governed Williams's fictions such as *White Mule* and *In the Money* did also work as the very fulcrum on which his poetry stood. It was however, in his later poetry, including his *magnum opus Paterson*, that this credo came to a climax in his "closeness" to material that stirred "in him a sensibility of springtime" which by its very nature became "the source of a new poetics."[256] Adam's decision to eat the apple in the Garden of Eden brought him his expulsion from Paradise no doubt, but the whole event must be viewed as a situation of elation created by a continuous exposure, and "closeness to the object." The Adamic poet functions in certain situations that very much correspond to this "process" as a result of which there is in his poetry not only a "perception of facts," but also a deep "feeling of them." Williams went a step ahead of this as he very consistently attempted to keep his descriptions, and the details thereof "instinct with natural piety." There was also a "virile tenderness" about it, made "alive with sensory detail recreated in language that is swift, bare, tonic, and elated by its closeness to object."[257]

In such an approach to poetry, Williams's position lay in sharp contrast with a host of other poets such as Frost, Sandburg, Robinson, Masters and Vachel Lindsay. Frost would look at the New England landscape, but hardly under the surface. Sandburg would celebrate industrialized Chicago, but mainly in relation to its scenes without unravelling the underlying meanings. Robinson and Masters would consider people from a romantic view-point touching psychology while avoiding the social implications. Vachel Lindsay would sing the evangel's song exposing himself to capture the subtleties of real American folk pieces. But it was Williams who thought himself as the leader to break the ice in our times to accelerate post-modern poetry by beginning to look and record "the import of the scene in his time, and the cumulative meaning back of the object as symbol."[258] Behind this lay Williams's unique "receptivity to the new" — a quality of mental thrust which he so much eulogized while evaluating the characters of men like Boone, Rasles, and Burr *In the American Grain*. Such men had "all their senses waking," and they appreciated with love and affection anything that was away from the beaten track of civilization and culture in its strangeness, novelty, and in its basic difference from the commonplace. In the real sense of the term, this act was indeed "moral: to be *positive*, to be peculiar, to be sure, generous, brave—TO MARRY, to *touch*—to *give* because one HAS ... to create, to hybridize, to crosspollenise,—not to sterilize, to draw back, to fear, to dry up to rot"[259] [Williams's Italics]. In this declaration the poet is inclined to yield like Adam "to that which is essential in his sense of himself in his world."[260] Pearce calls this "the extreme formulation of the 'new mode'"[261] by which he means to categorize the second parallel frontier of modern poetry beset on talent engaged in the "ritual" of creating an individualist tradition.[262] The aim was not only to record the poem's "cry of its occasion," but also to establish a democracy of sensibility "...to reconcile/ the people and the stones"[263] by means of "metaphor." This poetic preoccupation, put forth in his poem "A Sort of a Song," culminated in the composition of *Paterson*. What he achieved through an elaborate and extensive symbol in *Paterson* is done in this poem through succinct metaphors. The poem begins with the snake metaphor. The snake that initiated Adam's fall must "...wait under/his weed."[264] With an emphasis on inventive potentiality the poet would recapture the lost innocence:

> and the writing
> be of words, slow and quick, sharp
> to strike, quiet to wait,
> sleepless.[265]

Man's life is "a broken rhythm" because he is so hopelessly detached from Nature, and because he has lost his primal relationship with her "objects," "things," and "situations." What Williams wanted to do was to re-establish this relationship by first of all rejecting the orthodox Christian vision of the world ["a woman's world,/of crossed sticks, stopping/thought"],[266] and then to rely on his own mind's inventiveness as poet to formulate the decision that "A new world/is only a new mind."[267] "A Sort of Song" gives us the significance of this new world through the metaphor of the saxifrage. The old world's orthodoxy is suggested by a reference to the snake metaphor. Williams means to suggest that we cannot affirm our identity as man by dissociating ourselves from the "rocks," by merely invoking the Christian myth of Adam's fall in sin. On the other hand, our reconciliation with the "physical world," that is, our "origins," will enable us to release from ourselves "a creative power" which, like the "saxifrage" beautifying the "rocks," shall beautify our life with a lift towards ecstasy. And the ideas are not imposed on experience. Williams takes us to a different world of rumination where ideas are not only conditioned by "things," but also spring from the things themselves. The attitude is Whitmanesque:

> As long as the states continue to absorb and be dominated by the poetry of the Old World, and remain unpublished with autochthonous song, to express, vitalize and give color to and define their material and minister to them distinctly, so long will they stop short of first-class Nationality and remain defective.[268]

When this process of absorption is defective in Williams, his works suffer as they are "broken to such an extent that they are difficult to penetrate."[269] When he is in his best form, "Williams creates the impression of a ruminating mind, quick with an elemental strength in the *act* of generating thought"[270] [Breslin's Italics]. We do not, then, simply come across certain "perceptive moments," but are considerably jolted from our stupor as common readers to recognize "a moment of discovery." This formed a natural, appropriate, and distinctive world of its own, recognizable at its threshold by any sensitive reader. In this there was a basic harmony with settings, and an inherent obedience "to laws of sensibility that are seldom relaxed."[271] This was the new world created by Williams in most of his later poems, and this world was so structured as to affirm the conviction that "the here and now is timeless."[272] It is a tiresome game if the reader or the critic endeavours to pinpoint conclusions and summations in these poems, because there is a breathless attempt by the poet himself to grasp the immediate, and the particularized reality of flitting experiences, so that in stead of statements or tenets one only comes across "pragmatic vision continually energized by action and reaction."[273]

The "birth" of this vision is sometimes "catastrophic" as Williams world like to suggest in one of his later poems named "Catastrophic Birth" where, apart from making his usual foray into the world of immediate perceptions, he gives us certain attitudes and convictions which are Adamic in their implications. All "revelations" are like the process of birth, and therefore must have something "violent" about it that need not be rejected but should be accepted as the basic "creative urge." It is also the harbinger of "change" that is "compact":

> Fury and counter fury! The volcano
> Stand firm, unbending. The chemistry
> shifts. The retort does not fracture.
> The change reveals—change
> The revelation is compact.[274]

"Change," in the words of Williams, is a "revelation" and what it reveals is the opening of "new ways beyond all known ways."[275] This was not merely a commitment to sentimentalism, but a pattern of belief based on certain intrinsic qualities of the Adamic poem which imperceptibly transforms the human self, shaving it free in all its brutal, violent, and yet subtle significance of existence. This would necessitate that the self is conceived in the image of the American Adam, and it could go a long way in getting away from tradition, orthodox religion, and the overpowering sense of the past—the connotations of the masters who formulated it. This may be a cause to worry, but Williams is optimistic as he believes that "Peace is reborn above the Cinders":

> The laboratory announces officially that
> there is no need to worry. The cone is

subsiding, smoke rises as a funnel into
the blue unnatural sky—The change impends!
A change stutters in the rocks....[276]

If an Eliot would trace the "progressive revitalization of the practice of poetic art" to not only "the general loss of the sense of tradition, but to the specific loss of direct symbolic transformation as a method of perception,"[277] Williams would go the opposite way in concluding that the discipline of poetry must come from within the human self dedicated to the "credo of change":

There is nothing in literature but
change.... I'll write whatever I damn
please, whenever I damn please and as
I damn please and it'll be good if the
authentic spirit of change is upon it.[278]

This "authentic spirit of change" qualifies the poet to continually renew and even violently refresh his "self" in the act of writing poetry. Williams has given us the clue to this creative process in the following lines which, broadly speaking, indicate the "radical innocence" of the poet whose work is a separate world imaginatively conceived to invigorate the common day-to-day world of man:

Imperceptibly your self shakes free in all
its brutal significance, feels its subtle
power renewed and abashed at its covered
lustihood breaks to the window and draws
back before the sunshine it sees there as
before some imagined figure that would be
there if—ah if—But for a moment your
hand rests upon the palace window sill,
only for a moment.[279]

In other words, a poem written according to this prescription entails upon the poet the ability to take off his mask as opposed to the role of the mythic poet who puts on a mask by surrendering his self to a life-style projected by culture, history, orthodoxy and tradition. Unlike Henry Adams or Eliot, Williams believed in an endless possibility in which the American ego could discover its own "potential for creativity." In this there was no commitment, as in Pound, to an anti-individualistic or anti-democratic connotation of the self. In individualism lay the seeds of grace—of "Springtime" with which Williams not only equated himself, but also thought that he was the "incarnated self of Springtime."[280] Notice, for example, his opinion on "disgrace" which frees itself from the concept of original sin, and indirectly emphasizes the Percephone myth of Springtime rising from Hell:

> Only he who had been confined
> in disgrace underground is rescued alive
> and he knows nothing more of it than to
> stand and curse the authorities who left
> him there so long without food and liquor while
> they were digging him out.[281]

This is how Williams discovers his own "shape-shifting form" as poet-protagonist. Everyone also is only a projection of his own self with its subtle power to renew itself in the face of crisis:

> Rain will fall. The wind and the birds
> will bring seeds, the river changes its
> channel and fish re-enter it.[282]

In such poetry "there is no distinction...without formal invention, for it is in the intimate form that works of art achieve their exact meaning...to give language its highest dignity, its illumination in the environment to which it is native."[283] In a 1950 letter, Williams wrote that "The poem embraces everything we are," and endeavours to communicate a "total culture" by asserting "that we are alive as ourselves...."[284] This assertion naturally leads the poet towards the grasping of the environment in its totality. By a subtle art of articulation the poet would, then, pull to-gether all isolated observations and experiences, and make them profound enough.[285] Unless the poet is rooted to the details of his locality, he will not be capable enough to fathom the profundity, and may very well fail to discover the universal in the particularities concerned. In fact, what we call wisdom or knowledge is known to have begun with our exposure to actuality. It is like Adam getting initiated into an experience of knowledge by deciding to eat the apple in the Garden of Eden which, speaking in scientific terms, remains an outcome of the reaction of the human senses exposed continually to "objects," "things," and "situations." This is also another way of reaching back to the roots, to the origins of an environment. As an American artist it was Williams's prime desire to conceive "the possibility, the sullen, volcanic inevitability of the *place*," and to cultivate the desired willingness "to go down and wrestle with its conditions."[286] [Williams's Italics]. The artist's success lies in surrendering or "succumbing" not only to the beautiful, but also to the sullen, the degraded, the vulgar and the grotesque. This way the poet as artist shall be able to discover "Yourselves! Within yourselves."[287] It becomes then the *via media* to know the truth:

...Tell
me if you do not see there alive!
a creature unlike the others, something
extraordinary in its vulgarity,
something strange, unnatural to
the world, that suffers the world poorly,
is tripped at home, disciplined at
the office, greedily eats money—
for a purpose: to escape the tyranny
of lies....[288]

Technically speaking, the poetic form here is conditioned by the generation of a powerful imaginative force where the details of the narrative exist "as equals in a side-by-side relation," and do not form any pattern in "a linear sequence."[289] Thus, the "tragic and foolish" lie together, "unrecognized,/...without a tongue."[290] this is almost like the physician's "unsqueamish acceptance" of all details of any particular fact. Williams whose profession as a doctor gave him a "clinical perspective" often considers even human beings as "natural objects." He emphasized their pull between social and physical perspectives. Characters who are moulded in this line are found in his fictional works such as *A Voyage to Pagany*, but in his poetry, too, the same approach is conspicuous wherever or whenever the occasion to refer to or analyze human personality arises. Notice, for example, his belief that we can be refreshed by a knowledge of our own embattled self that looms large on the "edge of doom":

> ...For you are merely
> distracted, not relieved in the blood,
> deadened, defeated, stultified.
> But this! is new ....[291]

If this is the human self, says Williams in "Writer's Prologue to a Play in Verse," then "no other speech than poetry"[292] can reveal its complications:

> ...Yourself the thing
> you are, speechless—because there is
> no language for it, shockingly revealed.[293]

The language of such poetry will be, of course, "in the terms you know," and not only it can, but also it "must break through everything." It is the nakedness of truth, "the extraordinary truth" about the "ordinary people" to which Williams would like to take us. With its sense of glory in sheer nakedness of descriptions that reveal "those curious transactions, seldom/heard but in the deadest presentations/now respectfully unnaturalized,"[294] this poem is Adamic in its sentiments. The undercurrent of social commentary in this poem ["This play/is of a woman and he her lover, all/mixed up, of life and death and all..."][295] may smack of a characteristic personal quirk for being non-ostentatious in its rugged simplicity. But what impresses a reader most is Williams's consistent effort to reveal "pioneer virtues," and his ability to cultivate a love for the same with a sense of Adamic innocence. He would often expose certain ugly features of the American character if they violated those virtues at any level of life. "Burning the Christmas Greens," while revealing the utilitarian motive of the American even in matters of religion, points to a time when the growing secularization of the American society and its peculiar paradoxioality may have given rise to a fascination with violence which has even substituted religion in being "recreant." The Christmas, ceremonially speaking, is associated with certain rituals. One of it is to bring branches cut from green trees such as "the coarse holly," "the balsam," and "the hemlock" in order to use them for decoration. What distresses the poet is the pretentiousness behind all this "gentle and good" functioning of certain traditional obligations and expectations in regard to religion. The whole fascination for green branches which, ethnically speaking, goes back to the American preoccupation with the wilderness, acts as a sort of stumbling block as the Christmas time ends:

> ... All this!
> and it seemed gentle and good
> to us. Their time past
> relief! The room bare! We
>
> stuffed the dead grate
> with them upon the half burnt out
> log's smoldering eye, opening
> red and closing under them.[296]

This only indicates that the American sense of religion, with growing sophistication and pleasure-seeking values, has lost its vitality in general. If religion is an offshoot of culture, "the burning of the Christmas greens" is a glaring evidence that the Americans, in their mad rush for material prosperity with individualism functioning as a value, have lost track of the important place that the wilderness has occupied in American history insofar as human activity in America is concerned. Religion apart, Williams would stress man's prelapsarian rapport with Nature's "green"—something that the modern man must re-establish in the face of the mad rush of technocratic society:

> ....
> Green is a solace
> a promise of peace, a fort
> against the cold (though we
> did not say so) a challenge
> above the snow's
> hard shell. Green (we might
> have said) that, where
> small birds hide and dodge

and lift their plaintive
rallying cries...[297]

The enumeration of the common things which is done here is only a testimony that we must "own" those "to live again/ and be in love and/ all its quickening pleasures...."[298] This may have become difficult to achieve for a good deal of Americans whose infatuation with exaggerated notions of masculinity have given them that fascination with violence. However, violence in itself is not destructive if it can give rise to a new life of promise with the prospect for a better world:

Violence leaped and appeared.
Recreant ! roared to life ...[299]

While indirectly hinting that "Violence is as American as cherry pie,"[300] it also does emphasize the creativity of "violence" by exhorting us to see in the United States the best hope for the revolutionary revival which will significantly expand the scope of individual freedom throughout the whole world. Notice, for example, Williams's emphasis on a life born anew and afresh out of "the shining of fauna of that fire":

....
an infant landscape of shimmering
ash and flame and we, in
that instant, lost,

breathless to be witnesses,
as if we stood
ourselves refreshed among
the shining fauna of that fire.[301]

In fact, Williams himself notes a predisposition to violence with its dark undercurrent in the American psyche throughout his *In the American Grin.* This resembles Lawrence's earlier stand as expressed in the *Studies in Classic American Literature* that it would be a mistake on the part of the Americans to overlook their violent behaviour. Such a behaviour is an outcome of such conditions as the frontier experience, racial and ethnic animosities, a revolutionary tradition which supports and sanctions violence and helps create a pervasive distrust of authority in addition to rapid industrialization and urbanization which uproots people and tends to devastate the American social fabric by weakening inter-personal ties.

Williams—"the Adam of the contagious hospital" as Pearce puts it[302]—discovers for himself, and for us, too, the canker of violence ravaging man's Eden. Indeed, Adam's eating of the apple in spite of God's positive directives to the contrary is a form of violent action in consequence of which Adam was banished from Paradise. Even then, as we have already noted, such an act initiated him to play the game of life in the face of all its grim realities in which, paradoxically enough, lay the very secrets of emerging as a hero—triumphing even in defeat. The poem "In Chains" emphasizes this point in different terms. It makes us aware that "...when we have no choice/ but to bend..."[303] to the "designs" of "villainies" and violence of "black-guards and murderers" who rule the roost in this world, we can, however, learn from such a helplessness of ours the glorious lesson of love which can "...rise out of its ashes if/we water it, tie up the slender/stem and keep the image of its/lively flower chiseled upon our minds."[304] This again is another way for the poet to vindicate his own love of life, particularly of the immediate, "phenomenal world"[305] around him. He writes in 1956:

> I've always wanted to fit poetry into the life around us because I love poetry. I'm not the type of poet who looks only at the rare thing. I want to use the words we speak and to describe the things we see, as far as it can be done.... Poetry should be brought into the world where we live and not be so recondite, so removed from the people. To bring poetry out of the clouds and down to earth I still believe possible.[306]

This Adamic sense of being rooted to the ground from which we sprang acts as the very source of Williams's strength as a poet. He writes in "The Cure" that others [perhaps he means Pound and Eliot] by virtue of their dedication to a consciously formulated principle of art, have lost track of their identity with "the unfathomable ground" which could act as the source to inspire poetry of a different sort where "words match the act" and thus come together to become a whole, integrated creative process: [307]

> ....
> Let them write then as they may and
> perfect it as they can they will never
> come to the secret of that form
>
> interknit with the unfathomable ground
> where we wake daily and from which
> among the rest you have sprung
> and opened flower-like to my hand.[308]

This draws our attention to Williams's credo that the poet must develop an unfailing commitment to the local and the commonplace. The theory that poetry should not be based on specific materials only, but by and large, may take anything such as the land at our feet and use it, was a conviction that Williams held as far back as 1919 while advising his fellow poets. He would write:

> The American must work toward a present, a local necessity. This necessity is precisely the same as that which animated Athens, Rome or whatever other locality you wish to name, present day London among the rest: Each man uses what he *has* for his constructions[309] [Williams's Italics].

From this point of view, all manner of conventional ordering of experience may appear abstract, and even "empty-souled" as dried husks. In this there is no insistence on returning to the age-old truths of tradition and culture to find an answer to the confusion and anomaly inherent in the realisation of the meaning of all experience as we find it to be in our day-to-day life. On the other hand, it is the moment of experience that is espoused, since the beginning lies in "the present" as it contains not only everything but also "the seed of all life."[310] Thus, without enclosing or formalizing the moment, the later poems demonstrate time and again Williams's consistent attempt to put the readers inside immediate experience. Beneath this concern with the expanded moment, one discovers Williams's exhortation to the modern writer to get rid of any "distinction" of rigid and tight form. It is the "profusion" and "accumulation" of details which, even in spite of their fragmentariness, may create a poetic field that is multidimensional in portraying actuality.[311] Obviously enough there is in Williams a certain amount of restlessness in grasping the "hard core of beauty" which in every moment of experience begins to reveal itself in unusual shapes and unexpected places. Falling from Paradise, here is the Adam who has left behind the dreams of Adamic bliss only to discover that life is full of ironies, that even "The movement of benediction/ does not turn back/the cold wind."[312] And yet, there is that inherent satisfaction and realization that Adam's contact with actuality "...is all," and must be considered as "a celebration of the light."[313] Such a contact means "to take in the difficult...the GOLD of it no matter how the ornament is shaped or what may be the purpose to which it seems to be put."[314] In this "alchemy," facts are so transmuted that their "rare and curious" qualities are discovered.[315] Again, the poem is "... made of/particulars..."[316] There is, moreover, a feeling of "...something/immediate, open" which is "...waking/centrifugal, centripetal"[317] as though it were Adam's innocent, but classic attempt to take stock of "...holiness/to be found in braver things."[318] In the poem "An Eternity" Williams, while invoking his dead Mother to stage a return from the world of the dead, is hinting that like the human soul there is a definite paramountcy in "the soul of things/that makes the dead moon shine."[319] The revelation of "the soul of things" is sometimes startling as in "To All Gentleness." There the poet concludes by looking at "...a profusion/of pink roses bending ragged in the rain,"[320] that just as "the rose puts out its thorns,"[321] so also it is often quite natural a way to find that innocence or, for that matter, gentleness may very well survive because of violence:

> Not the girth of thigh, but
> that gentleness that harbors all violence,

the valid juxtaposition, one
by the other, alternates, the cosine, the
cylinder and the rose.[322]

This truth is hardly realized because "the moment is lost; without us, the/Completion, the learned moment. The gates/ opened, it also falls sway,/unrecognized!"[323] Williams is probably hinting here at the "visionary and impalpable Now..." which as Hawthorne had remarked in a different but relevant context "...is nothing."[324] And yet, Williams is hopeful enough to capture "the Now" purged of accretions of the past. Like Gide he found it extremely "difficult to cope with the shadowless fragmentations of the immediate scene."[325] Consequently, he was forced to take that difficulty as his poem's "field of action." In this lies the poet's conviction as demonstrated in the poem "To All Gentleness" that reality does not contain any incompatibilities or dichotomies. Nothing is ugly, or, for that matter, ungentle because it is "anti-poetic." In fact everything is part of the world's beauty and "gentleness." It would be, therefore, an example of "ignorant dissociation" if we thought the "pink roses" as beautiful and poetic, and dismiss the "milkweed" as ugly and "anti-poetic." Truly speaking, "milkweed" as a flower can "premise" all flowers including the "pink roses":

The flower is our sign.
Milkweed, a single stalk on the bare
embankment (and where
does the imagination begin?

Violence and
gentleness, which is the core? Is
gentleness the core?)

Slender green
reaching up from the sand and rubble (the
anti-poetic they say ignorantly, a
dissociation)

Premising the flower,
Without which, no flower.[326]

Without stressing a dichotomy between the poetic and the "anti-poetic" which would only show the reaction of "a split mind," Williams grasps reality as "the phase" which is "supreme" in itself. He goes on to expound the thesis that all seeming dichotomies like that between the high and low, ugliness and beauty, violence and gentleness or the poetic and "anti-poetic" are part of the "longer arc, upgrade or downgrade."[327] Arguing in a similar vein it would not be out of place to mention here that the dichotomy between sin and virtue is also difficult to draw, except theoretically. It is our everlasting dilemma whether sin or virtue should be attributed to "the occasion or the men":

> ....Is it the occasion
> or the man? Take an apple and split it
> between the thumbs. Which is which?[328]

Whether Williams perceives "the milkweed" or "the pink roses" it makes no difference to him, because as a poet his perceptions enable him to impute to each man or thing that he sees "a vital sense of its own existence, a fateful self consciousness."[329] In such circumstances it is difficult to say whether he sees or knows, perceives or cognizes. If it is a form of "naturalism," it is also an outcome of his fascination with the "anti-poetic." And this, as stated by Wallace Stevens[330] as early as 1954, is Williams's pre-condition to defining "separateness" in Adamic terms. It shows that Williams had a kind of "lover's reverence" for the particulars of his environment. Not merely the beautiful, loving and gentle should exist in poetry and in life, but for their very existence and survival it is also necessary to be aware of "the counter force" that stems from violence, ugliness and the "anti-poetic." Oftentimes the juxtapositions were so sudden that the effect of alternation was rather traumatic in being highly violent, contracted and unexpected. In the earlier poems as in "The Wanderer" the extremes were treated as opposites, but as we read his poems of the 1950's with their "anti-poetic" subjects we have a feeling that these subjects perhaps possess more positively lasting values, and they aren't there only to act as "prerequisites to the presentation of the beautiful or pleasant."[331] On the other hand, there is a meditative and gentle treatment in juxtaposing the extremes of reality, in consequence of which "they become seasons of the same process in the pattern as well as the theory of his poems."[332] Notice, for example, the following lines from Williams's poem "Venus Over the Desert" whose Adamic undertone clearly conveys its message of "fortunate fall":

> ....Sin you call it,
> but there cannot be cold unless the heat
> has bred it, how can you know otherwise?...[333]

The values emanating from this so-called "deformed subject-matter" are couched in positive terms, and appear to be as convincing as the values of any "opposite camp" buttressed by Christianity's condemnation of sin that led to Adam's fall:

> If I do not sin, she said, you shall not
> walk in long gowns down stone corridors.
> *There is no reprieve where there is no falling off.*
> I lie in your beds all night, from me you wake and go about your tasks. My flesh clings to your bones.... [Italics Mine][334]

Without being cut off from his source of experience, Williams intends to recognize that "all things go back to the ground."[335] Therefore, there is a justification in saying: "There is no reprieve where there is no falling off...." Relying on diction rather than prosody, he suggests this "ground-ward thrust" by means of a few concrete verbs such as "falling," "lie" and "clings."

His objectivist technique taught him accuracy and succinctness which remained a permanent feature with his poetry. However, it is worthwhile to mark that at the close of his concern with objectivism, most of his later poems, without excluding subjective reaction, dealt with "the essentially unchangeable conditions of human insight and human blessedness."[336] This brings us to the much-debated question of the place of ideas and emotions in poetry. We may also remember in this connection the arguments with which John

Crowe Ransom and Frank Kermode jibbed at Eliot's notion of a dissociation of sensibility, Ransom regarding it as a well-known division implicit in the minds of civilized man, and Kermode considering that Eliot desired so much for a unification of thought and feeling that he mistakenly projected it into the earlier poets whom he sought to emulate. We have to say that the question of liking or disliking Eliot's "phrasing" does not rise, because what Eliot did was only to describe an evident historical fact. Clearly enough the unified sensibility tends to have disappeared in English poetry after the Age of Reason set in. What the Elizabethan and Jacobean poets aimed at achieving was no doubt some form of interplay of thought and feeling but in actuality, it had better be described as a development of the thought through concrete images. Though Ransom's opinion is true that abstraction is bound to raise its ugly head as a culture advances and gets sophisticated, it is also equally true that there have been some periods in human history as the Sixteenth and early Seventeenth centuries in England testify when poets have been more or less successful in fusing ideas and emotions by producing a literature which neither smacks of dry didacticism and over-rationalization nor of irresponsible and self-indulgent emotion. The beginnings of modernism are also associated with the felt need for a poetry of this kind.

Considered against this background, we discover in Williams his early alliance to a traditional style in the Keatsian mould which slowly but steadily gave way as he engaged himself in the great task of evolving his own variety in which things, ideas, emotions, scenes and experiences had their peculiar go in a unified sensibility—something that attempted to bridge the Cartesian rift in reality. Trained in imagism and objectivism which taught him to find forever an anti-dote to generalization, platitude, and empty rhetoric, Williams was the master craftsman who gave us in his later poems "undivided reality"—reality not yet separated out into its intellectual and emotional components. In such poems words without being just ideas even in their thinnest abstractions point to a concrete world, connecting it with experience through an association of emotions and values. This is an obvious change from his prior preoccupation with following in his poetry the dictum "No ideas but in things!" Though delicate, and sometimes suddenly pregnant with meanings, Williams's poems on "things" were for most readers "flat." Comparing, for example, "The Red Wheelbarrow" with any of the later poems such as "The Yellow Flower," "The Desert Music," "The Pink Locust" or "Asphodel, That Greedy Flower," we are evidently struck with a new style that breathes fresh air. The changed circumstances of Williams's life in the 1950's—his recovery from a near fatal illness—did obviously contribute to the making of a more personal kind of poetry. In his *Autobiography* (1951) Williams, time and again, persuades us of his essential innocence, honesty, and tenderness. Considered in this light, the poetry of the 1950's reveal a certain ability in Williams to resolve his self-divisions, though this also may have been the reason behind his losing much of his earlier capacity for self-criticism.[337] However, the period saw his poetry palpably throbbing with a new kind of energy as it maintains the balance between his public and private life brilliantly. This is also to say that there was an "even interplay" of quantitative and qualitative values in his poetry. Notice, for example, the following lines from one of his later poems "Approach to a City":

> Getting through with the world—
> I never tire of the mystery
> of those streets: the three baskets
> of dried flowers in the high
> bar-room windows, the gulls wheeling
> above the factory, the dirty
> snow – The humility of the snow that
> silvers everything and is
>
> trampled and lined with use – yet
> falls again, the silent birds
> on the still wires of the sky, the blur
> of wings as they take off.[338]

Williams's accomplishment in these lines is to maintain, as in some of the best writings of our time, a proper tension between the claims of the city and the life-giving energies of the god of the fields and the forest. The juxtapositions are evident enough ["...three baskets of dried flowers in the high/bar-room window," "...the gulls wheeling/above the factory"] to suggest that Williams does not partake of the Whitmanesque tendency to sing the miracles and mysteries of all living things only by putting "to scorn all machinery." Measurable by objective yardsticks, the industrial landscape in the poem which belongs to a world that is public does not lose its mystery. Nor does the poet's "approach to the city" result in any decision to get away from its unreality. On the other hand we find that unlike Wordsworth who chooses the scene of a fine London morning in his poem "Westminster Bridge" to focus the city's beauty, Williams chooses no particular time to find out that the city too has its "silver linings" which give it the tinge of Nature. Williams shows Nature's humility, and also her capacity for revitalizing herself when a crisis is over ["...the humility of the snow that/silvers everything and is/trampled and lined with use—yet/falls again..."]. Whether in the form of "gulls wheeling above the factory," "the silent birds" flying over "the still wires," or the flags moving in "the heavy air" against "a leaden ground," Nature forever enters secretly the civilized man's portals of sophistication and science. All such occasions enable the poet to refresh himself "for there is small holiness/to be found in braver things."[339] Not only is this an attempt by the poet to reunite the dissociated sensibility, but also it is his Adamic self-defense against an obvious fall in the human values—a threat to art, religion, and philosophy in our time when everything is subsumed under scientific measurement and description. The poem is Williams's humble, but, we should say, brave attempt to indicate that "the human dimension" cannot be allowed to be swallowed up by positivism and its spatio-temporal world. It is also to be stressed that the poet's inventiveness or his "transposing sensibility"[340] is capable enough to free beauty from captivity. Williams achieved this by providing "aesthetic salvation" that "frees the consciousness to an awareness of the supreme importance of the nameless spectacle."[341] Marianne

Moore was right in noting Williams's ability to realize an intrinsic value in "things others never notice."[342] Such delineations, as Wallace Stevens would argue, may be labelled as "rubbings of reality."[343] To our mind, Williams took this up as a source of "variety" in his art, making it relevant to a representation of the local present, and its human concerns. Of course, he believed in the beginning that the poet "lives in a world of the imagination where there is nothing but truth and beauty."[344] Frustrations and heartbreaks are kept away from this "Olympus." Such a view of poetry, Williams argued later, which allows a subject-matter as a wish fulfilment for "aristocratic attainment—a 'spiritual' bureaucracy of the 'soul'..."[345] is irrelevant in the context of the new requirements of an art in an industrial age ruled by money, commerce and the marketplace. As such, the poem's language may not be beautiful, for the poem is no longer the poet's expression of "phantasy" through "dreams of gentleness and bliss." In fact, as Murray Krieger points out, the poem, "Far from remaking itself into a sufficient and integral word..." insofar as its language is concerned, proclaims "its insufficiency," and "instead of at once encompassing and constituting its object, it acknowledges the inevitable gap between itself and all that it would be and say."[346] Here are a few lines from Williams's poem "Two Pendants: for the Ears" which will verily prove the point under discussion:

My thoughts
are like the distant smile of a child
who will (never) be a beautiful woman
like
the distant smile of a woman who
will say:
—only to keep you a moment
longer. Oh I know I'm a stinker
but
only to keep you, it's only
to keep you a few moments.[347]

What Williams does here is to avoid giving any conclusive picture of the nature of "his thoughts," because he takes us more uncertainly from one simile to another. He does not, therefore, expand any single simile, but goes on to present a series of similes, so that the description of "his thoughts" take on a mysterious colour. If "his thoughts" are "like the distant smile of a child who will be a beautiful woman," it is also "like the distant smile of a child who will *never* be a beautiful woman." By telescoping the two opposing similes into each other, the poet not only heightens the facts that human thoughts are mysterious, but also proclaims the inevitable insufficiency of language which fails to give any conclusive account of the object of its description. However imperfect this process may be, it is the poet's only means of grasping reality. And in this "imaginative process," as Pearce puts it, lies "our humanity."[348] In the words of Wallace Stevens, the supreme need of the poet is to master the composition of "The Poem of the mind in the act of finding/ What will suffice."[349]

Williams tried to achieve this mastery by playing the role of the American Adam along with his usual role as poet taking in his stride the whole frontier of human sensibility. It enabled him to make that difficult plunge all the way from innocence to experience. As an artist, particularly as we find him in his later poetry, Williams preserved in his own "world of the imagination" all that was splendorous, beautiful and desirable in the face of deformity, pain, disease, decay and death.

At the same time he was also not oblivious of the artist's relationship with those aspects of life which are evil because he was convinced that much things shall exist in life inevitably.[350] For Williams, just as it was for Wallace Stevens, the final condition for the acceptance of reality was the acceptance of evil not known in itself, but rather experienced imaginatively in pain. This "poetic stance" would subsequently lead Williams not only to get obsessed by the plight of the poor whose pain he imaginatively felt during the depression years, but also to recognize that "Life is not to run off into dream..."[351] but to require for itself "a Rabelasian sanity" to exhibit "the rare and the fine...as coming like everything else from the dirt."[352] He would thus write that "a green truck/dragging a concrete mixer" through the street could emit "the clatter and true sound/of verse."[353]

Considered in this light, *Paterson*, to put it metaphorically, is like a beautiful flower that is born of dirt and filth. Its composition marked the very culmination of all that Williams stood for in his formulation of a tangible poetic theory. Though Williams's poetic theory may lastly lead us to justify the composition of *Paterson*, it is worthwhile to appreciate the poem itself that tells more about the truth of poetry than the whole spectroscopy of his critical canon could ever hope to do. Between subject and object, that is, ourselves and the world of the poem, there is the poem itself that acts as a mediating agency. *Paterson*, like all good poetry, is "the cry of its occasion," and the occasion that energized its creation is already a part of the history of American Literature. When *The Waste Land* came out in 1922 in *The Dial*, Williams, like a good many Americans who believed in the redemptive power of their own country, felt utterly cheated:

> It wiped out our world as if an atom bomb had been dropped upon it and our brave sallies into the unknown were turned to dust.[354]

To Williams in particular the whole thing "struck like a sardonic bullet":

> I felt at once that it had set me back twenty years, and I'm sure it did. Critically Eliot returned us to the classroom just at the moment when I felt that we were on the point of an escape to matters much closer to the essence of a new art form itself—rooted in the locality which should give it fruit. I know at once that in certain ways I was most defeated.[355]

Accomplished craftsman as he was, Eliot could have revived the world without being "antipathetic to that which would have been required of him to be a first-rate American poet—or, rather, to write a first-rate American poem."[356] Refusing to assert that the poem is a social instrument which ought to embrace us in our totality, Eliot paralleled the past in terms of the power of myth and religion, and referred man to its sanctimony as a maans of salvation. For Williams, however, the task lay in a different mould. Though it was a unique feature to have attempted to discover "a workable metric" for lifting the environment to expression, gaining insight into a new and total culture, the fact remains that Williams took his cue from the Whitmsnesque tradition that broke with English prosody to create an "open style." Whereas in *The Waste Land* historical materials as part of myth and religion are fitted into a theocentric pattern objectively worked out by Eliot, *Paterson* as an answer to such a situation asserts a scheme of things that emphasizes man's "rootedness" to the place where he actually is. Thus, everything is restored to the process of nature, and objects are not only perceived metamorphically, but also are given their due place in a democratic order that does not separate them from their surroundings. This may have given cause for concern to a good many critics in their attempt to find out any organization in the poem. For example, Randall Jarrell is vociferous enough in bringing his charge of "Organization of Irrelevance" insofar as the poem's unity of tone is concerned:

> Such organization is *ex post facto* organization: if something is somewhere, one can find some Good Reason for its being there, but if it had not been there would one reader have guessed where it should 'really' have gone?[357]

However, in spite of a good deal of accidental matter contained in *Paterson* that makes it a difficult reading filled with boredom, the poem could be better approached through a response to its subtle "play of voices" by rereading it often.

In the late 1930's Williams in his poems, short-stories, novels, and plays had already articulated himself to fulfil the artist's difficult task of quickening and elucidating, fortifying and enlarging the life about him by making it eloquent. Considered in this light, *Paterson*, in the manner it is committed to "articulate the intractable," is a brilliant attempt to communicate "a total culture" by lifting "an environment to expression." The poem asserts that "we are alive as ourselves—as much of the environment as it [the poem] can grasp."[358] Being Adamic in tone there is no moral consideration in this as it bids us to believe that man is the measure of all things. In the face of the religious implication of man's fall from Paradise, Williams, while rejecting a world conceived by orthodox Christianity ["a woman's world,/of crossed sticks, stopping/thought"], believes in the possibility of the birth of a new world—a world that is deeply associated with the growth of a new mind ["A new world/ is only a new mind"].[359] *Paterson* brings this extremely articulated notion of a new world to eminence. "Thus the physician," says Pearce, "having spent a long life healing others, now finally heals himself."[360] What is of greater significance from the point of view of this study, Williams as "Adam—the Adam of the contagious hospital, of the world that is *Paterson*—magicks himself into believing that he has never left Eden."[361] The belief lies in a quest for postlapsarian innocence.

Williams believed also that the modern writer must accumulate in his work of art all kinds of detail in profusion however fragmented those may be, and should sacrifice any aspiration on his part to achieve the distinction of a neat, and tight form. This is because it was Williams's conviction that the Americans "need to build up a mass, conglomerate may be, containing few gems but bits of them—Brazilian brilliants—that shine of themselves, uncut as they are."[362] The emphasis is, therefore, on the "act of creation" itself, and not on the "finished product," that is, a technically perfect work of art founded on the pattern of certain well established rules—traditionally tested and classically validated. Thus, *Paterson* begins with a bang—"*a reply to Greek and Latin with the bare hands*" [Williams's Italics],[363] and with its sprawling and thick texture and multidimensional quality takes the readers to mysterious areas of artistically intense experience. Beneath its variety there are of course some recurrences of tone which open up vistas of meanings fit for thematic studies of the poem. A comprehensive evaluation of *Paterson*, starting with this premise, may very well answer, if not fully, at least partially, the criticism leveled against Williams that "he is wholly incapable of coherent thought," and that "his experience is disconnected and fragmentary."[364] Such an evaluation necessitating an exhaustive analysis is not possible within the limited purview of this study which mainly attempts to focus on Williams's Adamic preoccupation as poet. In all fitness of things, therefore, we may undertake a brief survey of *Paterson* as an Adamic poem only. "A complete little universe" existing "separately" and expressing "the whole life of the poet,"[365] this poem sacrifices narrative action and tends to get concerned with "the internalized experience" of the poet himself confronting certain discreet moments of life. Whereas a mythic poem such as Pound's *Cantos* stands on the edifice of a public mythology, *Paterson* is evidently free from the incursion of such sources that could have supplied it a realistically viable plot. Even, then, the "blocks" of material interspersing the poem in its various divisions and subdivisions cannot be waived off as extraneous. They form a cyclic structure revealing a subterranean system which, for want of any other accommodative term, can be described as Adamic or Edenic, for that matter. It begins with the basic American proposition that in the New World Garden of America, man's allegiance would forever remain dual, and therefore, a little too ambiguous. Thus, the American Adam would embrace ambiguity as the very core of his life-style, and between the call of the wilderness and the fascination of the city he would strive to attain victory by mastering "the syntax of the middle landscape." For example, we can look at Part I of Book I in *Paterson*, and in spite of its fragmentariness discover a unified vision of deep commitment:

> And there, against him, stretches the low mountain.
> The Park's her head, carved, above the Falls, by the quiet
> river; Colored crystals the secret of those rocks;
> farms and ponds, laurel and the temperate wild cactus,
> Yellow flowered...facing him, his

arm supporting her, by the *Valley of the Rocks*, asleep.
Pearls at her ankles, her monstrous hair
spangled with apple-blossoms is scattered about into
the back country, waking their dreams—where the deer
run
and the wood-duck nests protecting his gallant plumage.[366]

The whole scene is Edenic in tone, and is there not only for its own sake, but also to supply the counterforce necessary to provide relief from the violence, crudity and torment of modern city life:

It is the complement exact of vulgar streets
a mathematics calm, controlled, the architecture
mete, sinks there, lifts here.

An incredible
clumsiness of address,
senseless rapes—caught on hands and knees
scrubbing a greasy corridor, the blood
boiling as though in vat, where they soak—

Plaster saints, glass jewels
and those apt paper flowers, bafflingly
complex—have here
their forthright beauty, beside:

Things, things unmentionable
the sink with the waste farina in it and
lumps of rancid meat, milk-bottle-tops: have
here a tranquility and loveliness
have here (in his thoughts)
a complement tranquil and chaste.[367]

The lines, as a part of an "anti-exile poem," draw their energy from the conviction that the modern poet must take his sacramental dip in "the filthy Passaic," that is, must not flee from the crudity of modern life with its loss of traditional religion. On the other hand, he should consider these "limitations" as "opportunities," for he as artist is "the whole man,"[368] and would play the role of what Williams himself says "the compactor" who does not merely "translate the sensuality of his materials into symbols but deals with them directly."[369] It is, thus, a process of expansion into certain new conceptions of the grammar of consciousness in which the passive "to be" is evidently substituted for the active "I am" in Adamic terms.

In fact, the very geographic and historical conditions of the city of Paterson favoured Williams to enable him to write his "epic" in the manner proposed above. The guidebook to New Jersey shows that Paterson is born out of Alexander Hamilton's "vision" of planning a great industrial city at the Great Falls of the Passaic which would preserve the fundamental diversity inherent in the very concept of a Garden State:

> No phrase or nickname can supply an index to New Jersey, for in physical and sociological composition the State is fundamentally diverse. It is often called the Garden State; with equal reason it might be labeled the Factory State, or the Commuter State.[370]

It is, therefore, evident that to write an "epic" on the city of Paterson is to base the narrative technique of the poem on a tension between civilization on one hand and the perceptive, living core of the primordially innocent and beautiful on the other. It is necessary also to caution the reader that the poem's tension with its aesthetic-moral vision, should not be misunderstood as a kind of interpretation of history. If at all history is treated as a part of the theme of *Paterson*, Williams makes it meaningful in a special mythopoetic way. As we know, he wished to make the past alive and important in the present believing very much that the sheer pastness of the past is highly dangerous for culture. For an Eliot the "cunning passages, contrived corridors" of history are dangerous traps for man, and man's "right action" consists in "freedom from past and future also." This is evidently a vision of man in relation to history as contrasting with that of Williams's who contended that the past must be brought to new and meaningful light by the artist's imagination which makes it "present" to us all. *Paterson* would accordingly take us from the old world to the new, and seek "a way of leaving the finished forms of culture" in order to enable ourselves to deal with "the roar, the chaos, of the still-to-be-achieved."[371] In this process the objects that define the historical perspective and geographical contours of the world of Paterson, the city, are sufficiently subjectified, so much so that the shift of emphasis is from "things in itself" to "thing in myself." Thus, Paterson, the city as man, is not only "Dr. Paterson," but is in actuality an extended metaphor that codifies in symbolic terms Dr. Williams's life itself with all his experiences, needs and modes of action in a modern world. This is evidence enough that Williams, the Adamic poet, has created an "alterable myth" in the poem, giving it the stamp of his own private poetic world unlike Robinson Jeffers, Stephen Vincent Benet, Edgar Lee Masters and Hart Crane who, as is well known, turned to historical or folk heroes for their poem's material. In Williams's view, myth "is not a look toward the past, but, as for the Greeks, the self-image of an area's culture...."[372] Ideally speaking, *Paterson* satisfies this definition to a large extent and acts as a sort of poem which contains for the readers a "built-in psychic balance that neutralizes the pressures of actuality and preserves sanity..." in its "broadest acceptability and utility."[373] For example, the very scene in the poem which shows the city of Paterson engaged in a "lovers' embrace" with the Garrett mountain signifies how "psychic balance" can be fruitfully maintained by the modern man if he succeeds in achieving a happy union of mind and body. It also represents a marriage of civilization with the wilderness—a theme successfully explored in Williams's *In the American Grain* to suggest that the American Adam's emergence as a hero lies in his "bold association of wild and cultured life."[374]

What is of particular significance in Edenic terms is that Williams goes on to recreate in an artistically viable manner a graphic scene with primitive and prehistorical overtones evoking in the readers a desire for mythic *regressus*. His achievement lies in enabling us to get imaginatively transported to primordial times in order that we re-live man's "formless experience" as Adam lived it. The Passaic River with its falls, and the surrounding slabs of rocks and gnarled trees contribute to the communication of that unique experience. Symbolically speaking, the scene's "import" lies in the basic polarities of human experience suggested by the juxtaposition of "rocks" and "waters." If the "rocks" signify man's preoccupation with force, terror and violence, the "waters," that is, the "spray" and "tumult" that fill the "void" with a beautiful sight and sound represent "creative force."[375] This again reiterates Williams's view that "The poem embraces everything we are."[376] In fact, *Paterson* is intended to find "an image large enough to embody the whole knowable world" around the poet. Williams adds with emphasis that "The longer I lived in my place, among the details of my life, I realized that these isolated observations and experiences needed pulling together to gain 'profundity.'"[377] Therefore, he took the city of Paterson as his "case" to work up the poem.

As he writes in his *Autobiography*, "Paterson as Paterson would be discovered, perfect, perfect, in the special sense of the poem, to have it—if it rose to flutter into life a while—it would be as itself, locally, and so like every other place in the world."[378] Hence, it is in the very disparateness of a poem that one can discover its identity which, like Prospero's island, contains all varieties, defining and influencing one another by a happy coexistence. In 1939 essay entitled "Against the Weather" Williams would state this point in more categoric terms:

> The compactness implies restriction but does not mean loss of parts: it means compact, restricted to essentials. Neither does it mean the extraction of a philosophic essence. The essence remains in the parts proper to life, in all their sensual reality.[379]

Williams is justified in his own scheme of things in *Paterson* that contains sharp opposites to give us a glimpse of life in all its "sensual reality." On one side we see the city with its unreal citizens walking "outside their bodies aimlessly," and on the other we find the Falls animating "a thousand automations."[380] This interaction born of the particularities of the poet's locale gives rise to a "philosophic essence" of universal "import." It lies perhaps in the unintentional pun that the poet may have played on the world "Falls" meaning it to be the one major factor responsible for industrialising Paterson by supplying it the main source of power, and thereby bringing about its "fall" through a loss of love and human communication. However, it is on the symbolic nature of the Falls, and its profound dignity of character that our attention is ultimately focused. It begins with a few selective details taken from local history calculated to act as a sort of commentary on the "primal" beauty, charm, wonder, and curiosity of the Falls.

In fact, Williams would worship "at his shrine in nature, the Passaic Falls with its drop of seventy feet."[381] To him it was a "thing of beauty." At the same time he was also conscious how this waterpower "inspired Alexander Hamilton in 1791 with the concept of 'The Society of Useful Manufacturers' in which Paterson became the prototype of the American industrial community" with a bias for the 'Protestant ethic' of material success."[382] As Kenneth Burke put it, this was an obvious process of confrontation which New Jersey had to have as a kind of "Vestibule" state which the nation had to trample over "on its way to or from New York."[383] Though Williams could envision the social and cultural benefits of Paterson as a self-sustaining city with the level of livelihood of the citizenry raised, he heralded the progress with mixed feelings, and recognized the loss of humanistic ideals. He deeply felt the need for readjusting the power of the machine with a human impulse.

Book I of *Paterson* has this polarized tension between a sylvan ideal on one hand and the modern fact on the other that constantly interferes and violates it. Williams presents a number of episodes to emphasize the rising tension at its most human and natural level. Paterson, figuring as man, states metaphorically his idea of a total, and all-embracing love, but poetess Cress cuts this dream short by writing her first letter of complaint accusing Paterson of mental cruelty through remote and indifferent behaviour. Again, the vibrant, effervescent and primitive passion of the African Chief with his nine wives is set in contrast with the sterile, purposeless and uncertain love of Mrs. Sarah Cumming, a woman who lacks the naturalness of passion that permeates the character of the youngest of the African chief's wives. Charmed with the wonder and curiosity of the Falls, Mrs. Cumming visits the place along with her husband. Their stiff and abstract manners are, thus, parodied when juxtaposed with the life of the African chief and her queens all tense with life and love at its most uninhibited and unsophisticated level. Mrs. Cumming's slipping or jumping over the falls is a fitting closure to her husband's abstract statement: "My dear, I believe it is time for us to set our face homeward."[384] In that statement two points are symbolically stated. Firstly, there was for the Cummings a necessity to make a backward march to reach the very source of natural and innocent love. Hence the significance of the line "...it is time for us to set our face homeward." Secondly, denied this, Mrs. Cumming has really come back full circle to that other source—the innocence of death—a kind of homeward march which, at its most subconscious and romantic level could not be resisted as she was drawn near the edge of the falls hypnotised by its vigorous thrust. Against this natural attraction for the Falls, Williams presents the unnatural, but heroic love of Sam Patch for a demonstration of diving into the Falls. The day he groped for words to make a speech before diving was also the day of his doom. It was, as it were, a failure of communication, of language, to establish contact with Nature in consequence of which his insolence of assertion over natural power brings in his tragic death, reducing his heroism into shreds. Against these figures, the poet juxtaposes the river as a symbol of fecundatory, fertilizing and creative force. Particularly he presents the river's upstream sources which still retain the primal beauty of Nature. What Mrs. Cumming and also the divorced women in Book I falter and fall is a breaking away from natural passion with which love's beginning and its basic innocence are so intimately connected. If love has to flourish, it must begin somewhere, and therefore, in the words of Williams himself "The concept of the beginning of a river is...a symbol of all beginnings."[385] What is of characteristic significance is that the river's sources do also image Mr. Paterson, the poet and prototype of Williams himself, in a mood of artistic creativity energized by an imaginative potency. It is like the mind of Rasles as described in Williams's *In the American Grain* having "a peculiar sensitivity and daring to embrace native things."[386] What should be carefully noted is Mr. Paterson's incapacity for a total "descent" into his environment which is also filled with brutality and tawdriness. He is only like a blossoming flower, fresh and vibrant, for whom everything possesses a "forthright beauty." With this prelapsarian innocence in his creative spirit, he is not able to awake himself to reality. For example, the "Two half grown girls hailing hallowed Easter," and their "unfledged desire, irresponsible, green" keep him in a moment of stasis. Their initiation into the complex pattern of existence with a gradual loss of innocence which with must accompany it could very well challenge Mr. Paternson's awakening to reality.

As a poet Williams himself could learn that "innocence and simplicity...must perish as 'ideas.'" The poet must, therefore, open himself to embrace "the seemingly corrupt and complex" elements of life so that he can discover "the actuality which these ideas have masked."[387] As Book I closes there is a shift of emphasis that takes us from the pure aesthetic world of artistic creativity to the reality of a material, chaotic world. The poet's invention of a language fit for his locality is based on the use of a manifold of local detail which also, apart from describing "the elemental character of the place," gives us the "modern replicas" through an employment of the "anti-poetic." Unlike Eliot and Pound, Williams does not run off "toward the peripheries" in search of "authority," that is, "other centers."[388] This has been, of course, one of the chief objections against Williams who has rather ceremoniously allowed "himself to be rolled under by time, by an excess of detail which could not be brought to focus in a comprehensive 'field.'"[389] Williams refuses to trace back the present "occurrences" to any past, remote or distant origin. The "lost center" with its "authority, presence, [and]... plenitude" is not acceptable to Williams for whom there is a still more joyful invention as he "turns to the local as a centerless center."[390] Thus, everything has to begin all over again. Also, the centre of all beginnings lies hidden in the local, in the primitive rocky cavern behind the Falls, the place of "first beauty." Listening to the Falls, Mr. Paterson must see the primal innocence of all origins, and this must be done by a process of "descent" and "ascent" to clear off all "blockage" set up by history, tradition and culture.

As we see Mr. Paterson's visit to the Garrett Mountain Park, "the rock,/female to the city..." upon whose body this poet and prototype of Dr. Williams himself "instructs his thoughts," we are made to note how man's actions are far removed from the core of Adamically true and pagan exuberance. Even in that sylvan setting women do not appear beautiful. Their beauty is "gross" in its artificiality. It is the "budding tree," and the dog affectionately patted by its master that give Mr. Paterson the counterpoint to this gross materialism manifest in the "eating and drinking" of the city picnickers enjoying a traditional peasant picnic.[391] They appear to have been distanced from "home" like the Homeric wanderer, "blocked from origins by the authority of history, the tradition."[392] "Home" here means "the place where the word begins." It is Williams's intention to get back "home" not only by representing an "overview" of reality, but also through "a process of deconstruction" of language. Such a process palpitates in its own immediacy to the invention of a ground of its own primordial appeal particularly because it endeavours to be distanced from any privileged and perhaps valorized preoccupation with "Word":

> Without invention nothing is well shaped,
> unless the mind change, unless
> the stars are new measured, according
> to their relative positions, the
> line will not change, the necessity
> will not matriculate: unless there is
> a new mind there cannot be a new
> line, the old will go on
> repeating itself with recurring
> deadliness....[393]

As Book II proceeds we find that Mr. Paterson's impotence is intensified, and his anger and fear cause despair in him as a result of which he fails in his creative venture. Even love with its primordially recreative emotions gets reduced to sheer vulgarity as Mr. Paterson marks a pair of drunken lovers engaged in passionless coition:

> She stirs, distraught,
> against him—wounded (drunk), moves
> against him (a lump) desiring,
> against him, bored
>
> flagrantly bored and sleeping, a
> beer bottle still grasped spear-like
> in his hand.[394]

These lines reveal the dangers of stultification of natural passion which needs continual "renewal." Thus, Mr. Paterson's meditative walk upon the female rock enables him to realize what it is to fall, to be blocked, and divorced. His quest for beauty does also end in frustrations. He is yet to realize that "A life that is here and now is timeless."[395] Consequently, Mr. Paterson is driven back into himself comprehending his own memory. But, then, as we come close to the end of Book II we anticipate a change in his conscious perceptions which are also Williams's own artistic credo:

> The descent beckons
> as the ascent beckoned
> of accomplishment
> a sort of renewal
> even
> an initiation, since the spaces it opens are new
> places
> inhabited by hordes
> heretofore unrealized
> of new kinds –
> since their movements
> are towards new objectives
> (even though formerly they were abandoned)

> No defeat is made up entirely of defeat – since
> the world it opens is always a place
>   formerly
>   unsuspected. A
> world lost,
>   a world unsuspected
>   beckons to new places
> and no whiteness (lost) is so white as the memory
> of whiteness.[396]

Williams means to imply that in abandoning oneself to comprehend the compulsive "present" one may take a risky downward movement to the very source of actuality which may "now" be experienced as it lies embedded in one's own being. The immediate moment is, therefore, potential, and the artist must have a freedom consistent with an attentive contact with the here and now. Unlike Eliot who believes that truth lies in some "still-point" beyond myth, language and knowledge, Williams cogitates that all that is elementally true, and, therefore, acceptable is inherently structured in our day-to-day existence. It would be, as Williams had hinted earlier, a movement from "Mathematics to particulars,"[397] and thus would bring about a shape out of Chaos. Gradually we find the poem moving towards the realization of this concept. Even as we see Mr. Paterson going out to visit the Park in a Sunday, he is already trying to lift himself and his environment to expression. It is this that enables him to hear the unspoken language of man—the voice of the Falls which, as Williams observes, is the emerging "new mind" of the place. It only means that Mr. Paterson, and therefore, the poet himself, would "see all" like Eliot's Tiresias, but he shall not "suffer all."[398]

If "No defeat is made up entirely of defeat…" then there is nothing called a lost world, for such a world would unsuspectedly beckon to "new places." Here lies the vital complexity of Williams's version of the "fortunate fall," for it results mainly from an interplay between "ascent" and "descent"—a concept that also brings in the idea of "blockage" and man's ceaseless attempt at its "dispersal." Indeed, Adam's "defeat" and his consequent expulsion from Paradise did only open new spaces for him to begin again, and again.

Books III & IV of *Paterson* take the readers to this process of beginning all over again, of liberating creative spirit lying locked in repression, a failure of language and blockage as Williams would like to put it:

> Jostled as are the waters approaching
> the brink, his thoughts
> interlace, repel and cut asunder,
> rise rock-thwarted and turn aside....[399]

As Book III begins, Mr. Paterson bids a temporary goodbye to the stale summer streets of a city where life does not grow in camaraderie and fellow-feeling, but has its continually persistent run to kill itself in rebuff born of isolation, bereftness and despair. He goes to the library to seek his sanctuary, but in doing so he only articulates his own frustration. His exploration of the past in search of "beautiful thing: /—a dark flame,/a wind, a flood—counter to all staleness,"[400] brings him close to the source of primal energy—air, fire, water—as he reads with a stirring of profound emotional oppressiveness, about the 1902 tornado, fire and flood that devastated the city of Paterson. This marks the beginning of a process of liberation springing out of Mr. Paterson's awareness of violence internalized in his mind as an apocalypse. It is a "catastrophic birth," and in the "ruins" which are only manifest forms of "peace" coming into life through a violent opposition of cosmic forces,[401] Mr. Paterson discovers to regain the "lost ground"—the "first beauty," forever hidden in dirt and filth. The violence referred to is only the violence of creative—the volcanic fury of the origin. The "fecundative principle" which Williams suggested as the principle of art and life in the beginning of the poem through the analogy of Mr. Paterson's embrace with the Garrett Mountain is also the principle of realizing that to regain the plentitude of a lost origin it is not nostalgia that helps, but it is descent into formlessness inhering tawdriness and foulness that takes us to the Beautiful Thing. In Book III the Beautiful Thing appears in the form of a black woman whom Mr. Paterson encounters "in a low bed (waiting)/under the mud plashed windows among the scabrous/ dirt of the holy sheets." Neither dirt nor ugliness—a condition of Fall—has taken away her innocently radiant beauty:

> —for I was overcome
> by amazement of could do nothing but admire
> and lean to care for you in your quietness—
> who look at me, smiling, and we remind
> thus looking, each at the other in silence
>
> You lethargic, waiting upon me, waiting for
> the fire and I
>
> attendant upon you, shaken by your beauty
> Shaken by your beauty
>
> shaken.[402]

There is here no error of Original Sin: it rather shows the mystery of originating violation—the whoring of the virgin.[403] If the poet was important in his failure to respond to his environment and the history of his locality in Book II, Book III shows him setting out in an Odyssey to descend, that is, to "fall" from sophistication, artificiality, fastidiousness along with erudition in order that he touches the very core of the "problematic of history"—the origin recovered in the "nowness of all expression" hidden in the sacrophagus of time at a "centerless center."[404] This happens to Mr. Paterson as he reads about the flood—the wild forces of Nature. The forces take on a symbolic turn as the poet-protagonist reads the numerous mass of books in the library:

> And there rises
> a counterpart, of reading, slowly, overwhelming
> the mind; anchors him in his chair. So be
> it. He turns O Paradiso ! The stream
> grows leaden within him, his lilies drag, so
> be it. Texts mount and complicate them-
> selves, lead to further texts and those
> to synopses, digests and emendations. So be it.
> Until the words break loose or—sadly
> hold, unshaken...[405]

The confusion and chaos are a fertile ground to descend to and the "Paradiso" lies ["O Paradiso!"] in that ultimate utterance enwrapped in mysterious silence:

—to the teeth, to the very eyes
uh, uh
FULL STOP
—and leave the world
to darkness
and to
me.[406]

It is to that state of "uh, uh" [like the Vedantic "OM"] which gives a "FULL STOP" to all chaos in an ultimate silence emerging from sound that the poet must go to seize and reconstitute the original site of expression. Thus, Williams suggests that poetry must ultimately be recognized, insofar as its "origin" is concerned, as a conglomeration of certain kinds of emotion which, for their very irrationality, cannot be touched by any "form of logical definition or analysis...."[407] For Mr. Paterson the ultimate silence that he has captured is an acceptance of the logic of Nature's return to her origin filled with darkness. This is also the darkness of the creative act, and so, for Mr. Paterson it is time to reverse the process of his "descent" to begin afresh:

Degraded. The leaf torn from
the calendar. All forgot...[408]

This is the origin of art, or for that matter, the artistic moment of first expression that must cause the crumbling of fixed modes. Williams satirizes the past, and through it the fixed modes that permeate it:

....There is no recurrence.
The past is dead. Women are
legalists, they want to rescue
a framework of laws, a skeleton of
practices, a calcined reticulum
of the past which, bees, they will
fill with honey.[409]

The end of Book III, with Mr. Paterson's recapturing of the formless moment of creation significantly lost to us in our postlapsarian conditions of life, shows the rejection of the Library as a place of sanctuary. The Library makes Mr. Paterson conscious of "Time" which is "the problematic," for "Time" is also the sign and symbol of man's deprivation of innocence. To put it differently, it is through time that man can measure his lost innocence. Therefore, Mr. Paterson reverses his journey to come back to the Passaic Falls—to the centre outside the tyranny of time. Such a movement is in sharp contrast with classical ideas concerning the concept of the centre. According to it "the center is, paradoxically, *within* the structure and outside it"[410] [Derrida's Italics]. Considered in this light, the Eliotic paradox in the *Four Quartets* is "contradictorily coherent," but Williams's *Paterson* is a demonstration how this paradox can be demystified by stepping aside its myth of "centered structurality." Williams not only challenges the "generic pattern" of history, but undertakes a unique attempt to station himself at a center outside the tyranny of history.[411] Stationing himself at the crossroads of past, present and future, he feels that it is in the chaotic present with its "roar" of immediacy that we can find the source of renewal, of beginning again. Mr. Paterson's return to the Falls after abandoning the Library marks the beginning of this difficult process:

> The past, the future below
> and the present pouring down: the roar,
> the roar of the present, a speech—
> is, of necessity, my sole concern.
>
> They plunged, they fell in a swoon,
> or by intention, to make an end—the
> roar, unrelenting, witnessing
> Neither the past nor the future.
>
> Neither to stare, amnesic—forgetting.
> The language cascades into the
> invisible, beyond and above: the falls
> of which it is the visible part—

Not until I had made of it a replica
will my sins be forgiven and my
disease cured—in wax: la capella di S. Rocco
on the sandstone crest above the old

Copper mines—where I used to see
the images of arms and knees
hung on nails (do Montpellier).
No meaning. And yet, unless I find a place

apart from it, I am its slave,
its sleeper, bewildered—dazzled
by distance. I cannot stay here
to spend my life looking into the past:

the future's no answer. I must
find my meaning and lay it, white,
beside the sliding water: myself—
comb out the language—or succumb

—whatever the complexion. Let
me out ! (Well, go!) this rhetoric
is real![412]

The Adamic poet's rejection of the past, and his desire to liberate himself without falling into its trap are evident here, for the past for him is a sign and symbol of "blockage" or "divorce." Significantly enough, Williams, apart from immersing, and losing himself in the "roar" of the immediate present, does indicate that the poet cannot forget his own self, and its desire for communion with Nature ["I must/find my meaning and lay it, white,/beside the sliding water: myself/comb out the language—or succumb"]. Here is the Whitmanesque emphasis on the "I," and its continuous pleasure springing from a vigorous interaction with the mysterious forces of matter. However, it is with the sheer physicality of the present moment that the poet wants a "marriage" of his mind to renew it, and free it from the deadening effect of the past. There alone lies the "Beautiful Thing," and to possess it one has to reject, as Williams hints, all manner of mediation. Its essence also remains in a certain "defiance of authority" which is its "first definition." Escaping a "subordination to a mediation that stands outside it," "beauty" "reveals the enigma at its center."[413]

In Book IV Williams undertakes the artistic task of touching the core of beauty as he lifts the whole environment into expression. Titling it as "The Run to the Sea," Williams gives us some of the most disturbing details in modern poetry as he follows the Passaic *via* Manhattan down to its fall in the Atlantic—the river's end, and also its origin as the sea happens to be so for all rivers. It is the sea of death "the sea that sucks in all rivers, 'dessled, led/by the salmon and the shad."[414] The danger involved in the elemental forces of brute Nature, a descent to which will not only devastate but destroy man, is symbolically presented through the shark symbol "that snaps/at his own trailing guts, makes a sunset/of the green water."[415] The poet's warning is also there ["Turn back I warn you"]. And yet, "The sea *is* our home whither all rivers/(wither) run"[416] [Williams's Italics]. If the sea is the home, then, man the exile, must seek a homecoming. It echoes the Lawrentian "preparation for death" as we find it, for example, in his poem "The Ship of Death" with its emphasis on a death-birth and birth-death cycle. In the midst of it all lies, of course, the creative principle symbolized in the person of Madam Curie. As the process of "home-coming" starts, life becomes meaningful if we emulate her innocent curiosity. Such a curiosity is no mere nostalgia for a "lost truth," but a desire to discover a design which, instead of being imposed upon Nature, must be only Nature's imitation. Mr. Paterson's creative principle, that is, the persistent, relentless effort to begin from the beginning by discovering the "presence of an absence" is also based on such an imitation.

Thus, in his old age when Mr. Paterson falls into a reminiscence of old acquaintances, the near and dear ones, it is the siren call of the sea that appeals to him most which is in fact the "presence of an absence" of consciousness of the place of his origin while he lives:

the nostalgic sea
sopped with our cries

> Thalasa! Thalasa!
> calling us home.[417]

Williams goes on to add that though the sea is our home, it "draws us in to drown" with "losses and regrets."[418] And yet, the sea is also the sea of birth—a view not only sanctioned by religious orthodoxy, but also verified and proved true by the Darwinian theory of Evolution:

> Listen!
> Thalasa! Thalasa!
> Drink of it, be drunk
> Thalasa
> immaculate: our home, our nostalgic
> mother in whom the dead, enwombed again
> cry out to us to return.[419]

The sea is, therefore, not a "tomb," but a "womb"—a recreative process from which all life shall emerge. This is suggested as *Paterson* observes that "...among brown fronds/and limp starfish" "seeds float in."[420] Mr. Paterson's swim in the sea is, therefore, symbolic of that complete "immersion" in or "descent" into the "source" which every artist must undertake to "renew" his art and thereby find the "seeds" of his creativity. As suggested by Williams himself, "The ocean of savage lusts in which the wounded shark smashes at its own tail is not our home. On the contrary, it is the seed that floats to shore, one word, one tiny, even microscopic word, is that which can alone save us."[421] The search for "presence," as conceived by Williams, is an abandonment of the "vertical project" which language "as abstracts of universal ideas" may undertake. Moreover, a poem's language must also be the "perpetual articulation" of the artist's desire to discover "primordial relations."[422]

What the poet-protagonist does in *Paterson* is the discovery of such "primordial relations" of language—its essential innocence lost in course of time. It thus becomes the articulation of a language freed from the received forms of what has been called "vertical" literature.[423] As Mr. Paterson swims in the sea he is not swept away by the turbulence of the sea. This suggests communication and contact with the "origin," the "source" that throws back the flotsam of "weeds, bearing seeds." With this in his grasp, Mr. Paterson floats ashore. The "seeds" he has brought must "take root in new ground where a new beginning must germinate." It means that the artist's totality of experience lies in the "innocence of origins" which has to be embraced in full so that his desire to "begin again" is fructified.[424] The "sea of blood" is rejected, for it is the home that forever gives us its nostalgic call for traditional unity born of the authority of history.[425] Consequently, Mr. Paterson heads inland "toward Camden where Walt Whitman, much traduced, lived the latter years of his life and died."[426] The process is thus reversed from "ascent-descent" to "descent-ascent." With the "seed" of creativity in his grasp which must be planted in new ground other than the "source" from which it has come up, Mr. Paterson's moving inland is suggestive of the dilemma of the artist as the "archetypal wanderer" for whom the quest for "beginnings" is an eternal process of "going back" and "moving forward"—backward to innocence from experience, and forward to experience from innocence.

Book V of *Paterson* is the culmination of that artistic process with which the poet-protagonist of the earlier books gets so deeply involved. Being the aesthetic recreation of the local detail, it retrieves the presence, the wholeness of time forever. In doing so the poet takes us to the pantheon of the artists and poets who in the very totality of their experience form and provide a *locus*.

As a coda or epilogue[427] to the earlier books, this section of *Paterson* aims at achieving an artistically harmonious affirmation of the motifs, events, and episodes that form the structure and texture of Books I-IV. Thus, Mr. Paterson's visit to the Garrett Mountain—the principle of harmony between the male and the female principles—as we find it in Book II is artistically affirmed in Book V through Audubon's archetypal wanderings through deep and dark wilderness covering three American states till he finds the wounded unicorn:

Audubon (Au-du-bon), (the lost Dauphin)
left the boat
down stream
below the falls of the Ohio at Louisville
to follow
a trail through the woods
across three states
northward of Kentucky...

He saw buffalo
and more
a horned beast among the trees
in the moonlight
following small birds
the chicadee
in a field crowded with small flowers
...its neck
circled by a crown!
from a regal tapestry of stars!
Lying wounded on his belly
legs folded under him
the bearded head held
really aloft.[428]

The wounded unicorn symbolizes the artist's quest for returning Nature to her primacy beyond Civilization and History. Though "the wounded beast lies down to rest," the poet emphasizes its "regality," a quality of innocence beyond death ["We shall not get to the bottom: death is a bottom"][429] which has been eternally arrested in art like Keats's Urn. If in Book III Mr. Paterson's mind is purged of the deadening effect of the past that enables him to "release" his creativity from "blockage," in this book he is able to speak of The Cloisters, and its tapestries narrating the hunt of the unicorn as an artistic process transcending time. Williams creates his own personal myth in making the unicorn stand for the purity and innocence of artistic imagination, and thus gives it an Adamic imprint, freeing it from its usual allegory in orthodox Christianity:

It is the imagination
which cannot be fathomed

It is through this hole
we escape....[430]

In its spiral-like structure Book V of *Paterson* arrests the continuum of time by making the end turn back into a beginning just like Yeats's gyres reversing themselves:

The (self) direction has been changed
the serpent
its tail in its mouth
"the river has returned to its beginnings"
and backward
(and forward)
it tortures itself within me
until time has been washed finally under:
and "I knew all (or enough)
it became me."
—the times are not heroic
since then
but they are cleaner
and freer of disease
the mind rotted within them
we'll say
the serpent
has its tail in its mouth
AGAIN![431]

The process of beginning and ending, and then ending to begin again is, therefore, an eternal one. It is like the dance that reverses to turn upon itself and the flower that hedges the tapestries in. Time finally stands still just as Mr. Paterson moves backward and forward in a cyclic process. The act of memory is, therefore, an eternal beginning and ending, and in this circularity alone time can be transcended. The "fall" into time's historicity is thus arrested, and more so, when love's innocence in old age is also recreated through imagination as in "Asphodel, that Greeny Flower: "

As I think of it now,
after a lifetime,
it is as if
a sweet-scented flower

were poised
and for me did open.
Asphodel
has no odor
save to the imagination
but it too
celebrates the light.
It is late
but an odor
as form our wedding
has revived for me
and begun again to penetrate
into all crevices
of my world.[432]

This is how man's search for his origins goes on forever. Williams's concern with the "fallen" state of man lies in viewing "factical existence" as a "falling *from* primordial authentic temporality"[433] [Heidegger's Italics]. His role lies in the paradox of demystifying the existing myths to create a "primary myth" which is, in fact, not a myth, but an idea that coincides with things. In this he is not thrown into the sheer historicity of things, because his Adamic naming, or his process of recovering innocence starts with the first premise of "doing violence to the very things he loves"[434] by lifting them to an artistically viable plane in order to reveal the ground wherein the origin of his own historicity lies.

NOTES

1. Walter Sutton, *American Free Verse: The Modern Revolution in Poetry* (New York: A New Directions Book, 1973), p. 119.
2. *Ibid.*
3. Guimond, *The Art of Williams Carlos Williams: A Discovery and Possession of America,* p. 5.
4. Breslin, *William Carlos Williams: An American Artist,* p. 12.
5. *The Autobiography of William Carlos Williams* (New York: Random House, 1951), p. 53.
6. *Selected Essays* (New York: Random House, 1954), p. 230.
7. Breslin, *William Carlos Williams: An American Artist,* p. 4.
8. Guimond, *The Art of Williams Carlos Williams: A Discovery and Possession of America,* p. 21.

9. William Carlos Williams, *The Great American Novel* (Paris: Contact, 1923), p. 9.
10. William Carlos Williams, *A Voyage to Pagany* (New York: The Macaulay Co., 1928).
11. *Autobiography,* p. 51.
12. Mircea Eliade, *Myth of the Eternal Return: Cosmos and History,* p. 88.
13. Guimond, *The Art of William Carlos Williams: A Discovery and Possession of America,* p. 53.
14. *Autobiography,* pp. 174-75.
15. Joel Osborne Conarroe, "William Carlos Williams's *Paterson:* Substance and Structure," Dissertation, New York Univ., 1966, p. 5.
16. Quoted in Vivienne Koch, *William Carlos Williams* (Norfolk, Conn.: New Directions, 1950), p. 263.
17. Breslin, *William Carlos Williams: An American Artist,* p. 11.
18. Wagner, *The Poems of William Carlos Williams,* p. 23.
19. William Carlos Williams, *I Wanted to Write a Poem, ed.* Edith Heal (Boston: Beacon Press, 1958), p. 8.
20. Breslin, *William Carlos Williams:* An American Artist, p. 6.
21. *CEP,* p. 371.
22. *I Wanted to Write a Poem,* ed. Heal, p. 16.
23. *CEP*, pp. 375-76.
24. Eliade, *Myth of the Eternal Return: Cosmos and History,* p. 88.
25. Guimond, *The Art of William Carlos Williams: A Discovery and Possession of America,* p. 26.
26. "Introduction," in Rosenthal, ed. *The William Carlos Williams Reader,* p. xxiii.
27. *CEP,* p. 377.
28. *Ibid.* p. 378.
29. Breslin, *William Carlos Williams: An American Artist,* p. 79.
30. *I Wanted to Write a Poem,* ed. Heal p. 26.
31. Breslin, *William Carlos Williams: An American Artist,* p. 21.
32. Pearce, *The Continuity of American Poetry,* p. 338. Pearce categorizes this as an Adamic theme.
33. *CEP*, p. 3.
34. *Ibid.* p. 5. The lines echo Eliot's "City of dreadful day" populated by automatons [W.L. 60-63]. For further clarification of this point by Williams in *Paterson,* see Guimond, *The Art of William Carlos Williams: A Discovery and Possession of America,* p. 17.
35. *CEP,* p. 6.
36. *Ibid.*, p. 7.
37. *Ibid.*, p. 8.
38. *Ibid.*, p. 11.
39. *Ibid.*, p. 12.

40. *Ibid.,* p. 11.
41. *Ibid.,* p. 7.
42. See John M. Synge, *Poems and Translations* (Dublin: Maunsel & Co. Ltd., 1911), pp. 3-4.
43. Ezra Pound, "Dr. Williams' Position," *The Dial,* 85 (Nov. 1928), p. 398.
44. Koch, *Williams Carlos Williams,* p. 262.
45. Yvor Winters, "Poetry of Feeling," *The Kenyon Review,* 1, No. 1 (Winter 1939), p. 104.
46. Guimond, *The Art of Williams Carlos Williams: A Discovery and Possession of America,* p. 15.
47. *Ibid.,* p. 17.
48. John Malcolm Brinnin, *William Carlos Williams* (Minneapolis: Univ. of Minnesota Press, 1963), p. 7.
49. Joseph N. Riddel, *The Clairvoyant Eye: The Poetry and Poetics of Wallace Stevens* (Baton Rouge: Louisiana State Univ. Press, 1967), p. 13.
50. *Ibid.*
51. *CEP,* p. 124.
52. Pearce, *The Continuity of American Poetry,* pp. 338-339.
53. Breslin, *William Carlos Williams: An American Artist,* p. 54.
54. Alan Ostrom, *The Poetic World of Williams Carlos Williams* (London: Southern Illinois Univ. Press, 1966), p. 11.
55. *CEP,* p. 24.
56. *Ibid.,* p. 32.
57. *Ibid.*
58. *Ibid.,* p. 32.
59. *Ibid.,* pp. 25-26.
60. *Ibid.,* p. 25.
61. *Ibid.*
62. *Ibid.,* p. 26.
63. Brinnin, *William Carlos Williams,* p. 14.
64. *Ibid.,* p. 14.
65. *CEP,* p. 50.
66. *Ibid.,* p. 53.
67. Koch, *William Carlos Williams,* p. 79.
68. *Ibid.*
69. *CEP,* p. 74.
70. *Ibid.,* p. 143.
71. *Ibid.,* p. 90.
72. *Ibid.,* p. 87.
73. *Ibid.,* p. 90.
74. *Ibid.,* p. 88.
75. *Ibid.,* p. 89.
76. *Ibid.,* p. 80.

77. *Ibid.*, p. 71.
78. *Ibid.*, p. 91.
79. *Ibid.*, pp. 72-73.
80. Guimond, *The Art of William Carlos Williams: A Discovery and Possession of America,* p. 8. Also see *Paterson,* II, ii, 93.
81. *CEP,* p. 433.
82. *Ibid.*, p. 229.
83. *Ibid.*
84. *Selected Essays,* p. 213.
85. *Ibid.*, p. 235.
86. *Ibid.*
87. *The Selected Letters of William Carlos Williams,* ed. John C. Thirlwall (New York: McDowell, Obolensky, 1957), p. 147. Hereafter cited as Thirlwall, ed. *Selected Letters.*
88. *Ibid.*
89. Autobiography, p. 391.
90. Guimond, *The Art of William Carlos Williams: A Discovery and Possession of America,* pp. 24-25.
91. Koch, *William Carlos Williams,* p. 19.
92. Williams, *In The American Grain,* p. 219.
93. Van Wyck Brooks, *America's Coming-of-Age.* Rev. edn. (Garden City, N.Y.: Doubleday & Co., Inc., 1958), pp. 85-86.
94. Winters, "Poetry of Feeling," 104-105.
95. *CEP*, p. 129.
96. Koch, *William Carlos Williams,* p. 18.
97. *CEP,* p. 126.
98. *Ibid.*
99. Koch, *William Carlos Williams,* p. 19.
100. *CEP*, p. 126.
101. *Selected Essays,* p. 213.
102. *CEP,* p. 126.
103. Thirlwall, ed. *Selected Letters,* pp. 249 ff.
104. "Introduction," in Rosenthal, ed. *The William Carlos Williams Reader,* p. xxi.
105. *CEP,* p. 126.
106. Brinnin, *William Carlos Williams,* p. 26.
107. Kenneth Burke, "Heaven's First Law," *The Dial,* 72 (Feb. 1922), p. 196.
108. *Ibid.*
109. *See* Williams, "Symposium on Writing," *The Golden Goose,* Series 3, No. 2 (Autumn 1951), p. 94.
110. John C. Thirlwall, "William Carlos Williams' '*Paterson*,'" *New Directions 17* (New York: New Directions, 1961), p. 295.

111. Guimond, *The Art of William Carlos Williams: A Discovery and Possession of America,* p. 241.
112. William Carlos Williams, "Two Letters," *The Golden Goose,* 6, No. 5 (October 1952), p. 30.
113. Eliade, *Myth of the Eternal Return: Cosmos and History,* p. 5.
114. *Autobiography,* p. 360.
115. *Selected Essays,* pp. 140-142.
116. Brooks, *America's Coming-of-Age,* p. 84.
117. *In the American Grain,* pp. 154-155.
118. Randolph Bourne, "The History of a Literary Radical," *The Yale Review,* 8, No. 3 [n.s.] (April 1919), 484. This telling essay is reprinted in *The History of a Literary Radical* (New York: B.W. Huebsch, 1920).
119. Williams, *In the American Grain,* p. 196.
120. Ezra Pound, ed. *Payannes and Divisions* (New York: Alfred A. Knopf, 1918), p. 95.
121. Guimond, *The Art of William Carlos Williams: A Discovery and Possession of America,* p. 34.
122. *CEP,* p. 200.
123. *Ibid.,* p. 158.
124. *See* Louis Zukofksy, "Preface—'Recencies' in Poetry" in Louis Zukofksy, ed. *An "Objectivists" Anthology* (New York: To Publishers, 1932).
125. "A Note On Poetry," *The Oxford Anthology of American Literature,* eds. W.R. Benet and N.H. Pearson (New York: Oxford Univ. Press, 1938), p. 1313.
126. Carl Gustav Jung and Carloy Kerenyi, *Essays on a Science of Mythology The Myth of the Divine Child and the Mysteries of Elusis* (New York: Bollingen Series XII, 1949), pp. 99-100.
127. Emily Mitchell Wallace, *A Bibliography of Williams Carlos Williams* (Middletown, Conn.: Wesleyan Univ. Press, 1968), pp. ix-x.
128. *CEP,* p. 68.
129. Bernard Shaw, *The Complete Plays* (*The Times of India—The Statesman* Associated Newspapers of Ceylon Ltd., 1939), I, 861.
130. Guimond, *The Art of William Carlos Williams: A Discovery and Possession of America,* p. 105.
131. *I Wanted to Write a Poem* ed. Heal, p. 77.
132. *Paterson,* p. 122.
133. Quoted in Conarroe, "William Carlos Williams's *Paterson:* Substance and Structure," p. 41.
134. Zukofksy quoted in Guimond, *The Art of William Carlos Williams: A Discovery and Possession of America,* p. 105.
135. Bram Dijkstra, *The Hieroglyphics of New Speech: Cubism, Stieglits and the Early Poetry of William Carlos Williams* (Princeton, N.J.: Princeton Univ. Press, 1969), p. 64.

136. *CEP,* p. 306.
137. *Ibid.,* pp. 308-309.
138. *In the American Grain,* p. 228.
139. *Ibid.,* p. 226.
140. *The Farmers' Daughters* (Norfolk, Conn.: New Directions, 1961), p. 327.
141. Zukofsky, ed. *An "Objectivists" Anthology,* p. 10.
142. Williams Carlos Williams, "Notes on Norman MacLeod," *Mosaic,* 1, No. 1 (Nov.-Dec. 1934), p. 28.
143. See *Autobiography,* p. 264, and Guimond, *The Art of William Carlos Williams: A Discovery and Possession of America,* p. 101.
144. Breslin, *William Carlos Williams: An American Artist,* p. 63.
145. *CEP,* p. 346.
146. *Ibid.*
147. *Ibid.,* p. 347.
148. William Carlos Williams, *Spring and All* (Dijon: Contacts, 1923), p. 14.
149. *CEP,* p. 266.
150. *Ibid.,* p. 348.
151. Koch, *William Carlos Williams,* p. 74.
152. *CEP,* p. 342.
153. *See* J. Hillis Miller. ed. *William Carlos Williams: Collected Critical Essays* (Englewood Cliffs, N.J.: Prentice-Hall, Inc., 1966), p. 132.
154. *Selected Essays,* p. 213.
155. *CEP,* p. 434.
156. *Ibid.,* p. 241.
157. *Selected Essays,* p. 11.
158. *Ibid.*
159. *Ibid.,* p. 257.
160. *Paterson,* p. 242.
161. Powell Woods, "William Carlos Williams: The Poet as Engineer," in Matthew J. Bruccoli and Joseph Katz, ed. *Profile of William Carlos Williams* (Columbus: A Bell & Howell Company, 1971), p. 80.
162. *Autobiography,* p. 241.
163. *Selected Essays,* p. 128.
164. Miller, ed. *William Carlos Williams: Collected Critical Essays,* p. 11.
165. Claude Levi-Strauss, trans. La Pensee Sauvage, *The Savage Mind* (Chicago: Univ. of Chicago Press, 1968), p. 17.
166. *Ibid.*
166a. *Ibid.,* p. 19.
166b. *Spring and All,* pp. 2-3.
167. *Selected Essays,* p. 308.
168. *Selected Letters,* p. 286.
169. *CEP,* p. 412.

170. Quoted in Breslin, *William Carlos Williams: An American Artist,* p. 45.
171. Brinnin, *William Carlos Williams,* p. 11.
172. Breslin, *William Carlos Williams: An American Artist,* p. 45.
173. *Spring and All,* p. 58.
174. William Carlos Williams, *Kora in Hall: Improvisations* (San Francisco: City Lights Books, 1957), p. 65.
175. *See* Wallace Stevens, "Williams," Preface to Williams's *Collected Poems, 1921-1931* (New York: The Objectivist Press, 1934), pp. 1-2.
176. *I Wanted to Write a Poem,* ed. Heal, p. 52.
177. *See* Guimond, *The Art of William Carlos Williams: A Discovery and Possession of America,* pp.128-129.
178. Koch, *William Carlos Williams,* p. 71.
179. *See* Pearce, *The Continuity of American Poetry,* p. 348.
180. *Ibid.*
181. *CEP*, p. 159.
182. *Ibid.*
183. *Ibid.*, p. 348.
184. Brinnin, *William Carlos Williams,* p. 7.
185. Ihab H. Hassan, *The Dismemberment of Orpheus: Toward a Postmodern Literature* (New York: Oxford Univ. Press, 1971), p. 7.
186. Jacques Riviere quoted *ibid.*, p. 9.
187. Frank Kermode quoted *ibid.*
188. *Selected Essays,* p. 11.
189. *CEP,* p. 349.
190. Thomas Whitaker, *William Carlos Williams* (New York: Twayne Publishers, 1968), p. 120, p. 125.
191. *The Collected Later Poems of William Carlos Williams* (Norfolk, Conn.: New Directions, 1950), p. 18. Hereafter cited as *CLP.*
192. *CEP,* p. 67.
193. *Ibid.*, pp. 76-77.
194. Williams quoted in Whitaker, *William Carlos Williams,* p. 67.
195. *CEP,* p. 384.
196. *Ibid.*, pp. 254-255.
197. *Ibid.*
198. Koch, *William Carlos Williams,* p. 86.
199. *Ibid.*
200. *Selected Letters,* ed. Thirlwell, pp. 155-156.
201. Williams quoted in Guimond, *The Art of William Carlos Williams: A Discovery and Possession of America,* p. 130.
202. *See* D.H. Lawrence, "America Listen to Your Own," in *Phoenix,* ed. Edward D. McDonald (New York: Viking, 1936), pp. 90-91.
203. *Ibid.*

204. Whitaker, *William Carlos Williams,* p. 65.
205. *CEP,* p. 270.
206. *Ibid.*
207. Breslin, *William Carlos Williams: An American Artist,* p. 69.
208. *CEP*, p. 271.
209. *Ibid.*, pp. 271-72.
210. *Ibid.*, p. 272.
211. *Ibid.*
212. Breslin, *William Carlos Williams: An American Artist,* p. 70.
213. Lawrence, *Phoenix,* ed. McDonald, p. 335.
214. *CEP,* p. 266.
215. *Ibid.*, p. 266.
216. *Selected Essays,* p. 197.
217. *Ibid.*, p. 226.
218. *See* Ostrom, *The Poetic World of William Carlos Williams,* p. 17.
219. *CEP*, p. 379.
220. *Ibid.*
221. *Selected Essays,* pp. 243-244.
222. Sutton, *American Free Verse: The Modern Revolution in Poetry,* p. 120.
223. *Ibid.*
224. *See* "An Objectivists' Anthology," *The Symposium,* 4, No. 1 (January 1933), 114-117.
225. Sutton, *American Free Verse: The Modern Revolution in Poetry,* p. 119.
226. *CEP,* p. 332.
227. *Ibid.*
228. Sutton, *American Free Verse: The Modern Revolution in Poetry,* p. 125.
229. *CEP,* p. 275.
230. *Ibid.*
231. *Ibid.*, p. 276.
232. *Ibid.*
233. Breslin, *William Carlos Williams: An American Artist,* p. 74.
234. Ostrom, *The Poetic World of William Carlos Williams,* p. 14.
235. *Ibid.*
236. Sutton, *American Free Verse: Modern Revolution in Poetry,* p. 121.
237. *See* R.A. Durr, *Poetic Vision and the Psychedelic Experience* (Syracuse: Syracuse Univ. Press, 1970), p. 7.
238. Pearce, *The Continuity of American Poetry,* p. 339.
239. *The Philosophy of Schopenhauer,* Modern Library Edition (New York: Random House, 1956), pp. 146-147.
240. L.S. Dembo, *Conceptions of Reality in Modern American Poetry* (Berkeley: Univ. of California Press, 1966), p. 49.
241. Hazlitt quoted in Dembo, *Conceptions of Reality in Modern American Poetry,* pp. 54-55.

242. *Ibid.*, pp. 58, 59.
243. *Selected Essays,* pp. 197-198.
244. Breslin, *William Carlos Williams: An American Artist,* p. 79.
245. Winifred Nowottny, *The Language Poets* (London: Athlone Press, 1962), p. 120.
246. "Author's Introduction (1944)," in *CLP*, p. 5.
247. *Ibid.*
248. *Ibid.*
249. *Ibid.*, p. 4.
250. *Selected Essays,* p. 189.
251. *Ibid.*, pp. 281-282.
252. Ruth Lechlitner, "William Carlos Williams," *Poetry,* 54 (September 1939), p. 332.
253. *Ibid.*, p. 331.
254. *Selected Essays,* p. 282.
255. *Ibid.*
256. Philip Rahv, "Torrents of Spring," *The Nation,* 144 (26 June 1937), p. 733.
257. *Ibid.*
258. Lechlitner, "William Carlos Williams," 329.
259. *In the American Grain,* p. 121.
260. Pearce, *The Continuity of American Poetry,* p. 344.
261. *Ibid.*
262. *Ibid.*, p. 343.
263. *CLP*, p. 7.
264. *Ibid.*
265. *Ibid.*
266. "To Daphne and Virginia," in *Pictures from Brueghel and Other Poems* (London: MacGibbon & Kee, 1963), p. 76.
267. *Ibid.*
268. Whitman quoted in Amy Lowell, "Walt Whitman and the New Poetry," in Francis Murphy, ed. *Walt Whitman* (Harmondsworth: Penguin Books Ltd., 1969), p. 215.
269. Breslin, *William Carlos Williams: An American Artist,* p. 75.
270. *Ibid.*, pp. 75-76.
271. John Malcolm Brinnin, "William Carlos Williams," in Unger ed. *Seven Modern American Poets: An Introduction,* p. 106.
272. Williams quoted *ibid.*, p. 94.
273. Brinnin, "William Carlos Williams," in Unger, ed. *Seven Modern American Poets: An Introduction,* p. 94.
274. *CLP*, p. 8.
275. Ibid.

276. Ibid., p. 9.
277. Elizabeth Drew, *T.S. Eliot: The Design of His Poetry* (rpt. 1970; Delhi: Doaba House Book Sellers & Publishers, 1970), p. 14.
278. Williams quoted in Pearce, *The Continuity of American Poetry,* p. 287.
279. See *Kora in Hell: Improvisations*. Section XIX, p. 2.
280. Williams, *I Wanted to Write a Poem*. p. 29.
281. *GLP*, p. 9.
282. *Ibid.*
283. "Author's Introduction (1944)," *Ibid.*, p. 5.
284. Thirlwall, ed. *Selected Letters*, p. 296.
285. See *Autobiography*. p. 391.
286. *In the American Grain*, p. 225.
287. *CLP*, p. 13.
288. *Ibid.*
289. Breslin, *William Carlos Williams: An American Artist,* p. 132.
290. *CLP*, p. 13.
291. *Ibid.*
292. *Ibid.*
293. *Ibid.*
294. *Ibid.*, p. 15.
295. *Ibid.*
296. *Ibid.*, p. 17.
297. *Ibid.*, p. 17.
298. *Ibid.*, p. 20.
299. *Ibid.*, p. 18.
300. The remark is Rap Brown's. See for an assessment of violence in American history, society and character David Abrahamsen, *Our Violent Society* (New York: Funk and Wagnalls, 1970); Avid Demaris, *America the Violent* (Cowles Book Co., 1970); Alphonso Pinkey, *The American Way of Violence* (New York: Random House, 1972).
301. *CLP*, p. 18.
302. Pearce, *The Continuity of American Poetry*, p. 346.
303. CLP, p. 19.
304. *Ibid.*
305. *Selected Essays*, p. 236. Williams writes: "In every man there must finally occur a fusion between his dream which he dreamed when he was young and the phenomenal world of his later years if he is to be rated high as a master of his art."
306. Williams quoted in John C. Thirlwall, "William Carlos Williams '*Paterson*,'" in *New Directions* 17 (New York: New Directions, 1961), p. 253.
307. *Selected Letters*, pp. 129-130.
308. *CLP*, p. 23.

309. Williams quoted in B. Rajan, ed. *Modern American Poetry* (New York: Roy Pubs., 1952), pp. 189-190.
310. Breslin, *William Carlos Williams: An American Artist*, p. 3.
311. *Selected Essays,* pp. 284-285.
312. *CLP,* p. 22.
313. *Pictures from Baueghel,* p. 181.
314. *Selected Essays,* pp. 242-243.
315. See *Ibid.*, p. 244.
316. *CLP,* p. 33.
317. *Ibid.*
318. *Ibid.* p. 177.
319. *Ibid.* p. 183.
320. *Ibid.* p. 24.
321. *Ibid.* p. 24.
322. *Ibid.* p. 29.
323. *Ibid.* p. 28.
324. Hawthorne quoted in Lewis, *The American Adam*, p. 119.
325. *Ibid.* p. 118.
326. *CLP*, p. 28.
327. *CLP*, p. 26.
328. *Ibid.* p. 27.
329. Pearce, *The Continuity of American Poetry,* p. 338.
330. See Morse, ed. *Opus Posthumous*, pp. 254-257. Stevens accordingly considers Williams a "romantic" poet.
331. Guimond, *The Art of William Carlos Williams: A Discovery and Possession of America,* p. 220.
332. *Ibid.*
333. *CLP*, p. 172.
334. *Ibid.*
335. Williams quoted in Wagner, *The Poems of William Carlos Williams: A Critical Study*, p. 14.
336. Philip Wheelwright, "Poetry, Myth and Reality," in Allen Tate, ed. *The Language of Poetry* (Princeton, N.J. Princeton Univ. Press, 1942), p. 3.
337. See Breslin, *William Carlos Williams: An American Artist,* p. 211.
338. *CLP*, p. 177.
339. *Ibid.*, p. 177.
340. Conarroe, "William Carlos Williams's *Paterson:* Substance and Structure," p. 39.
341. *Ibid.*, p. 13.
342. See Marianne Moore, "Things Others Never Notice," *Poetry* 44 (May 1, 1934), pp. 103-106.
343. See Wallace Stevens, "Rubbings of Reality," *Briarcliff Quarterly*, 11, No. 2 (October 1946), pp. 201-202.

344. *Selected Essays,* p. 189.
345. *Ibid.*, pp. 281-282.
346. Murray Krieger, *Theory of Criticism: A Tradition and its System* (Baltimore: The Johns Hopkins Univ. Press, 1976), p. 211.
347. *CLP*, p. 218.
348. Pearce, *The Continuity of American Poetry*, p. 390.
349. Wallace Stevens, *Collected Poems* (New York: Alfred A. Knopf, 1965), p. 239.
350. See William Carlos Williams, *The Farmer's Daughters* (Norfolk, Conn.: New Directions, 1961), p. 208.
351. *Selected Essays,* p. 88.
352. *Selected Letters,* pp. 155-156.
353. *CEP*, p. 59.
354. *Autobiography,* pp. 174-175.
355. *Ibid.*
356. *See* B. Rajan, ed. *Modern American Poetry* (London: Dobson, 1950), p. 187.
357. Jarrell, *Poetry and the Age,* pp. 238-39.
358. *Selected Letters,* p. 286.
359. *Pictures from Brueghel,* p. 76.
360. Pearce, *The Continuity of American Poetry,* p. 346.
361. *Ibid.*
362. *Selected Essays,* pp. 284-285.
363. *Paterson,* p. 10.
364. Your Winters quoted in Conarroe, "William Carlos Williams's *Paterson:* Substance and Structure," p. 12.
365. Williams quoted in Pearce, *The Continuity of American Poetry,* p. 374.
366. *Paterson,* p. 17.
367. *Ibid.*, pp. 50-51.
368. Alan Ostrom, *The Poetic World of William Carlos Williams* (London: Southern Illinois Univ. Press, 1966), pp. 7-8. *See* also Thirlwall, ed. *Selected Letters,* p. 197.
369. Thirlwall, ed. *Selected Letters,* p. 197.
370. *New Jersey: A Guide to its Present and Past,* American Guide Series (New York: The Viking Press, 1939), p. 3.
371. Louis L. Martz, "The Unicorn in *Paterson:* William Carlos Williams," in John Hollander, ed. *Modern Poetry: Essays in Criticism* (Oxford: Oxford Univ. Press, 1968), p. 349.
372. Ostrom, *The Poetic World of William Carlos Williams,* p. 99.
373. *Ibid.*
374. *Paterson*, p. 21.
375. See *Ibid.*, pp. 16-17.
376. Thirlwall, ed. *Selected Letters*, p. 286.
377. *Autobiography,* p. 391.

378. *Ibid.*, pp. 391-392.
379. *Selected Essays,* p. 198.
380. *Paterson*, p. 14.
381. A.M. Sullivan, "Dr. William Carlos Williams, Poet and Humanist," in Charles Angoff, ed. *William Carlos Williams* (Cranbury, N.J.: Associated Univ. Press, Inc., 1974), p. 38.
382. A.M. Sullivan, "Dr. William Carlos Williams, Poet and Humanist," p. 38.
383. Kenneth Burke, "William Carlos Williams: A Critical Appreciation," in Angoff, ed. *William Carlos Williams,* p. 17.
384. *Paterson*, p. 24.
385. Edith Heal, ed. William Carlos Williams, *I Wanted to Write a Poem* (Boston: Beacon Press, 1958), p. 74.
386. *In the American Grain,* p. 121.
387. Thomas R. Whitakar, *William Carlos Williams* (New York: Twayne Publishers, 1968), p. 34.
388. See *Paterson*, pp. 36-37. Williams suggests the difference by bringing in the bird and fish metaphor "one unlike the other...."
389. Joseph N. Riddel, "*The Inverted Bell: Modernism and the Counter-poetics of William Carlos Williams* (Baton Rouge: Louisiana State Univ. Press, 1974), p. 12 See also Robert Creeley, ed. Charles Olson, *Selected Writings* (New York: New Directions, 1966), pp. 82-83.
390. Riddel, *The Inverted Bell,* p. 13.
391. *Paterson*, p. 73.
392. Riddel, *The Inverted Bell*, p. 34.
393. *Paterson*, p. 65.
394. *Ibid.*, p. 75.
395. *Selected Essays*, p. 196.
396. *Paterson*, p. 96.
397. *Ibid.*, p. 13.
398. Riddel, *The Inverted Bell*, p. 143.
399. *Paterson*, p. 16.
400. *Ibid.*, p. 123.
401. See Jean Starobinske, *The Invention of Liberty, 1700-1789,* trans. Beranard C. Swift (Geneva: Skire, 1964), p. 180.
402. *Paterson*, p. 151.
403. See Riddel, *The Inverted Bell*, p. 170.
404. See Martin Heidegger, *On the Way to Language*, trans. Peter D. Hertz (New York: Harper & Row, 1971), pp. 159-160.
405. *Paterson*, p. 156.
406. *Ibid.*, p. 167.
407. Riddel, *The Inverted Bell,* p. 171.
408. *Paterson*, p. 167.
409. *Ibid.*, p. 169.

410. See Jacques Darride, "Structure, Sign, and Play in the Discourse of the Human Science," in Richard Machsey and Eugenio Donato eds. *The Language of Criticism and The Sciences of Man: The Structuralist* Controversy (Baltimore: The Johns Hopkins Press, 1970), pp. 247-248.
411. *Ibid.*, p. 249. Also See *In The American Grain*, p. 188.
412. *Paterson*, pp. 172-173.
413. Riddel, *The Inverted Bell*, p. 169.
414. *Paterson*, p. 234.
415. *Ibid.*, p. 234.
416. *Ibid.*, pp. 234-235.
417. *Paterson*, p. 235.
418. *Ibid.*, p. 236.
419. *Ibid.*, p. 236.
420. *Ibid.*, p. 235.
421. Thirlwall, ed. *Selected Letters,* p. 292.
422. See Riddel, *The Inverted Bell*, pp. 256 ff.
423. See Roland Barthes, *Writing Degree Zero*, trans., Annette Lavers and Colin Smith (New York: Hill & Wang, 1968), p. 87.
424. See Barthes, *Writing Degree Zero*, p. 258.
425. *Autobiography*, p. 392.
426. *Paterson*, p. 237.
427. Louis Marts, *The Poem of the Mind*, p. 155.
428. *Paterson*, pp. 245-246.
429. *Ibid.*, p. 246.
430. *Ibid.*, p. 247.
431. *Ibid.*, p. 271.
432. "Asphodel, That Greeny Flower," in *Pictures From Brueghel*, p. 182.
433. See Martin Heidegger, *Being and Time*, trans. John Macquarrie and Edward Robinson (New York: Harper & Row, 1962), p. 436.
434. Riddel, *The Inverted Bell*, p. 44.

6
Conclusion

AN ATTEMPT has been made in this book to explore the possibilities of putting in perspective two important poets of our time—Robert Frost and William Carlos Williams—by examining their major poems to see how far they are relevant in relation to "the Adamic Mode" in American poetry. As a literary phenomenon compelling our attention to consider it as a positive and far-reaching critical canon, "the Adamic Mode" in poetry has, as we have noted in Chapter III, certain social and historical implications revealed, by and large, through the works of a large number of poets in America beginning from the Colonial period down to our own age. What is more important, "the Adamic Mode" has also accounted for a recognizable element of continuity in American poetry. In fact, no other poetic mode has a more intense flavour of the native American soil. Robert Frost and William Carlos Williams, as stated in Chapter I had their differences as poets. However, we have brought them together, because their differences within broad similarities, evident in their functioning through a particular poetic mode, serve to illuminate new areas of their identity as poets. After putting forth the proposition that "the Adamic Mode" is a special kind of poetry as opposed to "the mythic Mode," we have attempted to explain its creative process—the imaginative "leap into reality" that defines the poet's self. It is like any other artistic animation dedicated to feelings. But its difference from "the mythic Mode," as we have made it clear, lies in its adherence to basic emotions, and in making such emotions a discipline of art. Further, while making a survey of poets who bear testimony not only to such aspects of "the Adamic Mode" as above, but also to an enunciation of Adamic themes, we have looked into the historical and sociological cycles of the American scene which, broadly speaking, have affected this poetic mode under scrutiny. The separate Chapters on Robert Frost and William Carlos are an effort to find out the basic principles that underly and determine the nature of their poetry. We have let the two studies stand in their own right, and in juxtaposition to reveal by themselves what they will of both poets, though a certain amount of cross reference, comparison, and contrast has been incorporated without unduly overstretching the same.

The differences between the two poets should not, however, obscure their similarities. We would, therefore, propose, while concluding this dissertation, to undertake an evaluation accordingly.

Frost had little or no feeling of affinity with the modern poets whose method of writing often led them to violent structural juxtapositions, and frantic gropings after organizing principles. In this context one can only remember the reservations he had had about some of the greatest poets of our time. When Frost was once asked in an interview by Richard Poirier whether he had any affinity with, say a poet like Wallace Stevens, his answer was rather revealing:

Interviewer: I mean in your reading of him, whether or not you felt any—

Frost: Any affinity, you mean?

> Oh, you couldn't say that. No. Once he said to me, 'You write on subjects.' And I said, 'You write on bric-a-brac.' And when he sent me his next book, he'd written'S' more bric-a-brac' in it. Just took it good-naturedly. No, I had no affinity with him. We were friends. Oh, gee, miles away. I don't know who you'd connect me with.[1]

Frost was, however, quite liberal, rather democratic, in his view that he would not grudge a due appreciation on his part if it could be discovered or felt that *his own* poetry bears an affinity in some manner or the other with the works of any other poet.[2] Therefore, there is for us Frost's immediate critical sanction if our study ventures to bring out his poetry's similarities, apart from its basic differences, with any poet, and for that matter, with that of Williams who no less than Wallace Stevens, dabbled in "bric-a-brac" as a poet. As is well known, "bric-a-brac" could endow poetry with power—"the power," as Kazin put it, "to shape words that open up new realities in the mind...."[3] However, Frost had a distrust of this kind of poetry as opposed to Williams who believed that poetry is not a game which could be played to a set pattern. Of course, Frost never intended to write poetry to a rule. His remark that no poetry should be written with the last line in mind, is, as we know, a stock phrase quoted often by the critics. In an interview by Stanley Kochler, Williams observed that Frost was not "true to the American idiom as [he himself was] trying to be."[4] Even Eliot as Williams condescended made an effort "to record the speech," and "to be true to the American idiom." Eliot, however, did not succeed in finding the way to do it.[5] Williams, we suppose, was a little wrong in evaluating Frost in this light, for it has already been a part of the critical heritage of our time that insofar as Frost's subjects and themes are concerned most of his poems, and particularly his early poems, were American adaptations of the conventional techniques and forms of Romantic and Victorian poetry. Such an observation is not unwarranted, for as far back as March 1915, Ezra Pound, "the poet's poet" in the hierarchy of modern poetry, wrote to his friend Alice C. Henderson that Frost was "Vurry Amurk'n, with, I think, the seeds of grace." Indeed, Frost had sprung from a uniquely American sensibility. Frost would himself testify to it in a famous aphorism: "All literature begins with geography." The early poems of Frost, and even those that he wrote later with an emphasis on "voice-posture" wrung chunks off from the colloquial idiom and simple diction in the American Grain. Critics like Lawrance Thompson and Louis Untermeyer considered Frost's American background as an important factor in the growth of his poetry. "....Frost's entire work is deeply rooted in the American, even in the most vital Puritan, idiom. It is, 'native to the grain,' and yet thoroughly original."[6] He is also "the most American of poets" because of his "characteristically plain utterance" and "the conversational tone of speech" in his poetry.[7] Almost a national poet, Frost had his appeal to Americans in general who, without hunting for symbols which is the business of perhaps sophisticated Freudian critics, enjoyed reading Frost in their own light. In comparison, the appeal of Williams was limited to the sophisticated circles of poets who believed that modern poetry is impossible with direct statement, finished form and explicit sentence. Even if it is stated that Frost's usage of American idiom in poetry is limited, [he hardly used any American slang], it must be reiterated that "the most American trait" in him is his "American-ness,"[8] something which Williams attempted rarely. Frost's handling of the complex contrarieties of life in a simple, artless style, and above all, his mastery in containing the "two-endedness of things" with a shrewd, deliberate Yankee humour, even though the matter was as full of seriousness as the claims of justice and mercy, made him "a king of American culture hero...."[9] What is perhaps the most striking feature of resemblance between the two is the "locativeness" of their art, though, as artists, both of them have reached out to grasp the universal through the particular. A cursory glance at Frost's *North of Boston* or *New Hampshire*, and Williams's *Paterson* will convince us. The famous remark of Williams that a classic is "the local, fully realized, words marked by a place," evoke a special quality in American literature of native books like *Winesburg, Ohio*, *The Country of the Pointed Fires*, and, of course the well-known *Walden* and *The Adventures of Huckleberry Finn*. Both Frost and Williams belonged to this great tradition of "local colorists." Escaping parochialism and provincialism, they asserted the local, and made the region of their stay an "existential choice." Like William Faulkner's Yoknapatawpha County, so also New England, New Hampshire and Paterson became for these two poets microcosms for transcending ideas and feelings in order to merge them in the broad spectrum of universal emotions and thoughts. This recalls the intensity of vision that emerges from a poem by Hardy or a novel like *Wuthering Heights* by Family Bronte where the region is identified with qualities of universal import such as independence, self-reliance, resourcefulness, courage and energy. Robert Frost has himself written: "Because I wrote my novels in New Hampshire/is no proof that I aimed them at New Hampshire."[10] Similarly, writing a letter to Horace Gregory in 1939, Williams describes his attempt to discover "a usable past" in America itself:

> Of mixed ancestry, I felt from earliest childhood that America was the only home I could ever possibly call my own. I felt that it was expressly founded for me, personally, and that it must be the first business in life to possess it; that only by making it my own from the beginning to my own day, in detail, should I even have a basis for knowing where I stood.[11]

His was the belief that by living in a place one can imaginatively possess it. Thus, at a time when writers were in a mood to turn their backs on the New World casting their option in favour of the older, and richer culture of Europe, Williams chose to delve into "the bloody loam" of "murica," as Pound put it. This was an effort to lift the environment to expression, so much so that Pound, just because of Williams's freshness of observation, called him "the observant foreigner, perceiving American vegetation and landscape quite directly, as something put there for him to look at...."[12] The word "foreigner," as we feel, does not imply here the foreign origin of Williams's parents.[12] On the other hand, it means, as Pound must have intended, that Williams's concern was with a clear-eyed, and direct perception of things as if they were being seen by him for the first time. This Daniel Boone of American Literature, as Joel Conarroe put it,[13] made it almost his mission to give fresh names to "things," "objects" and "situations." It was like the American Adam's quest for a fresh identity in the New World Garden of America.

Place, it may be stated, is the only avenue that takes us to perceive the universal: "One has to learn what the meaning of the local is, for universal purposes. The local is the only thing that is universal...."[14] Eliot's negligence [perhaps intentional as he was an "intellectual head"] to look through, and recognize the work-a-day culture of America sprang from a growing dissatisfaction with the concept that no culture can, in a way, stand on its own unless it is pinned down and "bedded in a locality." Williams's quarrel with Eliot originated from this difference apart from others that we have already stated. It was, therefore, more of a literary rivalry, and less of personal jealousy was involved as we perhaps found with Frost whose curt treatment of Eliot is well known. Since Frost's death in 1963, detractors have, of course, noted this "sensitive sense of jealous rivalry," and "have criticized his egotism," making almost a case of "stubbornness, self-distrust, and laziness" in him as a person. The partisans have as well been intensely fervent by keeping his image high in emphasizing "his intense personal loyalty and the great shows of courage in his long struggle for recognition." Both the "stances" must be viewed with reservations. There is no point in the diatribe of the detractors, for Frost's cantankerousness and egotism, as Reginald Cook says, can be attributed to human frailty, and should be taken in that stride only.[15] Furthermore, an overzealous, or what we should say, a compassionate treatment of Frost can only lead to a confusion of critical interpretation of Frost as a poet. To probe it further, one would say that the fact really lay in the bias of the New Criticism of the 1940s in favour of *The Waste Land* of Eliot and the *Cantos* of Ezra Pound. These critics ascribed the merit of originality to Eliot and Pound whereas their treatment of Frost remained callous, and at best evocative only in pointing out some characteristic elements in him. As opposed to this, they were only too happy, clever scholars as they were, to unmask the poetic subtleties in Eliot and Pound in explication *des textes*. Cook would say that "A cultivation of tolerance might better have been urged."[16] He is of the opinion that "while cryptic poetry may test an advanced reader with his guard up while seated in the window 'behind the *Encyclopaedia Britannica*,' the discerningly witty and deceptively simple poet might sharply test the flexibility of the same reader with his guard down."[17]

Like America which is the very marvel of a civilization, Robert Frost is difficult to be discerned in proper perspective. It was obviously the New Critics' disparagement that caused a rankle and hitch in his heart which, over the years, took a sort of personal turn in him. One, of course, does not discover this element of personal rankle in Williams whose main difference with Eliot lay in certain literary convictions regarding what should a modern poet do about his environment. Such convictions lie in the poet's act of possessing the environment whether or not one deserves it, just, as one possesses one's home like one's mother's love whether or not one deserves it:

> The descent beckons
>   as the ascent beckoned
>   Memory is a kind
> of accomplishment
>   a sort of renewal
>   even
> an initiation, since the places it opens are new
> places.[18]

Frost would invite us to a similar situation in "The Death of the Hired Man" where home becomes a "memory of accomplishment," and "a sort of a renewal/even." As though speaking on behalf of the old and dying Silas who is "back," Warren's wife puts the central idea in relief:

> 'Home is the place where, when you have to go there,
> They have to take you in.'[19]

Both to Frost and Williams, home is not, as T.S. Eliot says, "where one starts from" ["East Coker"], nor does place imply that it is "always and only place" ["Ash-Wednesday"], and cannot carry further implication of strength. Silas would not go to his brother's, but in the penultimate stage of his life would return to Warren's only, though he was there a mere "hired man." Even then, his tendency to go back to the origins of his life's experience with the Warrens is generated by a sense of renewal—an initiation into innocence beyond death.

This is not to say that Frost's "poetic locale" was too narrow. It is broad enough. Lloyd Dendinger indeed points out that

Frost's preoccupation with the popular American metaphor of discovering a new Eden[20] has perhaps made him popular with both the folk and serious readers. It was Rutherford that gave to Williams his sense of place which took him from the particular to the universal. To Frost, too, "places are more to me in thought than in reality."[21] His letter to Susan Hayes Ward confirms it further:

> The feeling of time and space is perennially strange to me. I used to lie awake at night imagining the places I had traversed in the day and doubting in simple wonderment that I who was here could possibly have been there and there. .... There is a pang there that makes poetry. I rather like to gloat over it.[22]

When we come to Williams we also find that he believed in what Frost calls "gloating" over places, though Williams made use of his locality quite differently from Frost as he, unlike Frost, would make his imaginative leap into the very banalities of modern life. Williams was determined that his poetry should reveal a "contact" with experience, and as such would be in touch, time and again, with his "locality" which he terms as an "immediate objective world of actual experience."[23] Frost had, of course, a need for this "objective world of actual experience," but he would very consistently, and perhaps from the conventional point of view, avoid to record banalities in his poetry. By an act of possessing the "locality" and recording not only the ideal, but the banal, Williams experimented his "grand design" in poems after poems with the full intention of destroying "the constant barrier between the reader and his consciousness of immediate contact with the world," and to "refine, to clarify, to intensify that eternal moment in which we alone live."[24]

In Williams the focus of a "vision of place" may be taken as the whole American Scene of the twentieth century which he connects, as he does in the book *In the American Grain*, with "a usable past." He was in unique advantage of capturing this broad panorama, even in some of its neglected details, because he chose to spend the major period of his life in New Jersey, a place where the industrial landscape is a record of modern man's victory over Nature. It has already been stated earlier how the pastoral landscape of New Jersey gradually gave way to a growing industrial landscape. This may be kept in mind while going through Williams's concept of "marriage" and "divorce" in *Paterson*—a concept which ultimately leads him to conceive of the city of Paterson as Mr. Paterson and the Garrett Mountains as "Beautiful Thing." In Frost, particularly in his early poems, the locality which gives rise to his experiences and explorations of reality is the white Mountains north of Boston and the Derry Countryside of southern New Hampshire. The later poems, too, bring to the readers certain other specific localities like the Taconic Mountains around Shaftsbury and the Green Mountains around Ripton in Vermont's heartland. Some of the details, as Cook puts it, may strike to a mid-twentieth-century reader of poetry a note of legend.[25] Farmers who have now "electrified fences," "mechanical hay balers drawn by tractors," "unionized factory workers" may look in vain for such details of day-to-day farming life as we come across in "Mending Wall," "The Death of the Hired Man," "The Need of Being Versed in Country Things," etc. The back-country New England, the solitary house, the old cellar holes, the moss-covered gravestones, the tree-choked clearings and a host of other details of farm life in New England and New Hampshire may bring to us melancholy in our contemplation "of decline by defeat and abandonment by default"—the eternal verities of life to which our attention need to be drawn.[26] Williams's *Paterson* does also give us some old historical details which only make meaning when read in perspective, keeping ourselves to the "motif" of the poem as a whole.[27]

Though a Hemingway would emphasize that "unless you have geography, background, you have nothing," it is true, that the prevalence of mere geography in spite of the "dramatic vacuum"[28] that its absence might create cannot give us a guarantee of a sense of place in Literature. What is important is "the special feelings" with which a place is associated. The objects in Williams have their independent identity, and the reader can visualize them by a study of the words used, and in particular, by listening to the rhythms that are employed to convey the sense of the objects. In Frost the birch, the spring pool or the dark woods are "accurately identified," but they would not be what they are without the presence of an observer. This brings out a sharp contrast between Robert Frost and William Carlos Williams. We cannot say that we do not like Williams's "wheelbarrow" because it is red, and is not, for example, green. For Frost, however, there are questions of discrimination. Cook reveals:

> ...while traveling by rail from Boston to New York, he takes pains to notice if the birches he sees are his kind of swinging birches bending to left and right. The spring pools of which he writes while in Michigan, he points out to a Vermont audience, are 'not as full of water as they were usually, right now.' The dark woods in "Stopping by Woods" are alders—"snow falling among the alders," he tells us.[29]

In effect, Frost's discrimination for particular aspects of objects, while being a pointer to what Cook says his "restrained feeling" in regard to place and locality,[30] does also draw our attention to the primitivistic "stance" of considering the external realities of the world from some point of view that is more sentimental than rational. This also accounts for the "smears of mystery" with which Frost's objects have been presented. Thus, when a reader of Frost's poetry comes across the description of "desert places," "dark woods" or "birches" in their particular contexts he tends to tackle their meaning through the symbolic overtones implicit in them. As opposed to this, the objects in the poetic world of Williams are often there for their own sake, and have "a character by itself" to fecundate our mind:

> The true value is that peculiarity which gives an object a character by itself. The associational or the sentimental value is the false.[31]

This is not to emphasize that there was no subjective element in Williams's poetry. Guimond clarifies the point:

> Philosophic objectivism assumes that subjective knowledge needs continually to be connected by objective realities. Similarly the objectivist poets assume that the subjective elements of a poem achieve excellence or perfection to the extent that they are 'created' by natural, that is, by objective realities.[32]

Though it would be an error of criticism to call Frost an Objectivist artist in the Zukofksian sense of the term, it can be profitably assumed on the basis of observing poems such as "Home Burial," "Desert Places," or "Stopping by Woods" that the "subjective knowledge" of the speakers in these poems is engineered by certain "objective realities." In the "Home Burial," the wife's natural sorrow culminating in a frenzy is not as much due to "a flawed" relationship replete with misunderstanding as it is for certain objective realities, that is, living in isolation in the outskirts of civilization, and the burying of their child in the home ground as no help came from anyone. Similarly, the poem "Desert Places" connects the "desert places" of the speaker's mind with the empty, vacuous and deserted landscape in the approach of fall. Again, in the "Stopping by Woods," the decision of the speaker that he has "miles to go" before "sleep," is generated primarily because of the Dionysiac attraction that he feels for the dark woods. Without this "counterforce" there would not have been perhaps the decision to march forward. It would not be out of place to state here that, like Wordsworth, Frost was also employing his imagination "to give the charm of novelty to things of every day."[33] Though Williams intended over and over again to carry home the idea of the artist's "imaginative quota" which enables him to switch over from one thing to another, and to find a bond of common qualities between the subject and the object, it must, however, be remembered that he wrote poetry more from his mind's interaction with "fancy" than from "imagination." It is fancy, no doubt, which can relate different elements in "a diaphoric" combination to bring forth a modicum of meaning.[34] Linda Wagner calls attention to this aspect in Williams's poetry by stressing that even in small poems that take bric-a-brac as subject matters Williams is capable, by a process of meaningful juxtaposition, to tease out a subject good enough for explication.[35] This dominates, to quote Ford Maddox Ford, "the whole fabric of modern art."[36] "The Red Wheelbarrow" is a good example of this creative process in which the meaning of thc poem lies in the specific juxtaposition of objects and the subtle rhythms that give the objects a new dimension, and context of existence. The poem in its simplicity is intended to become an object—the red wheelbarrow itself. There is no "making play," or there is nothing "wild" about the whole thing, though Frost would ask us to realize these two aspects of poetry as important. To him:

> A poem is a thought—felt thing, isn't it? You can make a hyphenated word out of it. More wildness, you know; the wildness comes, must be something wild [in it].... Now the emphasis is on 'making play.' No! I'm going to make the emphasis right in the beginning. Who are we that we should talk about our object. Well, we are troubadours.... The word metaphor comes right in there that will test your agility, your knowledge—way up high! 'with things we trust you already know.' That's the least part of it.[37]

As we have already said, some of the things Frost trusted would appear to be legends in the context of our modern life. In fact, a comparison between Frost and Williams, like the one between him and Wallace Stevens, could only convince us that Frost "borrowed an existing ethos and mythos as the surface of his invention, whereas Williams, not unlike Wallace Stevens, "*invented* the universe about him"[38] [Cifelli's Italics]. This is perhaps the reason why Rosenthal would say that in Williams we find a "keener and more adventurous insight into the aesthetic of existence"[39] which we miss in Frost. Though Frost talks of metaphor ["The word metaphor comes right in there that will test your agility, your knowledge—way up high!"], it is obvious for a reader of Frost's poetry that Frost does not very much believe in single metaphors as he believes in piling up a series of situations, "objects" and "things" which, taken together in the context of the whole poem, assume metaphoric tenor to the extent of becoming symbolic. In Williams, however, a single metaphor may be presented in the beginning, and the poem is constituted by looking into its meaning through a juxtaposition of other details. As the metaphor for simplicity and innocence, the red wheelbarrow is given momentum at the very beginning, and other details only intensify this meaning. But it becomes difficult to understand the dark woods in "Stopping by Woods" as metaphorically significant until the last line is reached where the meaning is clarified by the repetition of the phrase "And miles to go before I sleep." All this would come forth, as in Frost's dramatic monologues and eclogues, through a "voice-posture" in the protagonist of the poem modulated after the necessity of a particular situation. In Williams "the voice-posture" is more or less his own. It is internally generated, and "transcribed to the page from the lips of the poet" himself. It was often a search after "measure" which ultimately gave Williams his mastery over "the triadic foot" as we find in a poem such as "The Descent."[40] In this there is sometimes a single elastic rhythm running from the beginning to end.

In regard to the subject-object relationship in the poetry of Frost and Williams, it is worthwhile if we closely study Frost's "All Revelation," so that we can employ our findings as a sort of commentary on Williams's attitude towards such a relationship as revealed while we analyzed some of his objectivist poems in the last chapter. In "All Revelation" some of the mutually exclusive dimensions in the modern literary mind are, we observe, unified in a balanced manner. Of course, Frost was less concerned with attuning himself to the spirit of his age, as Eliot did, or with formulating an insight into a philosophical system, as Wallace Stevens or Williams achieved. Whereas Williams talks of defenseless exposure to chaos for mitigating the demands of renewing ourselves, Frost shows his affinity to a more balanced view, and while mentioning the possibility of exposure to chaos for renewal, emphasizes the necessity to inform chaos with structure and meaning. All this is possible because there runs a profound relationship between man and his world. Here is Berg to comment on, and what he says may be taken as a general introduction to our discussion:

> The relationship of man and world is so profound, that it is an error to separate them. If we do, then man ceases to be man and the world to be the world. The world is no conglomeration of mere objects to be described in the language of physical science. The world is our home, our habitat, the materialization of our subjectivity. Who wants to become acquainted with man, should listen to the language spoken by the things in his existence. Who wants to describe man should make an analysis of the 'landscape' within which he demonstrates, explains and reveals himself.[41]

Phenomenologically speaking, the landscape assumes its coherence because the artist makes it so by emphasizing certain objects in it in accordance with his subjective inclinations. The object of importance in the landscape that is seen in "All Revelation" is "a ray cathode," and as it is seen with a "mental thrust," its dynamism is evoked, and so it becomes a metaphor for "the act of the mind." By scientifically cognizing "the geode" it is found that the glow in its interior originates from "the cathode ray." The metaphoric significance of "the cathode ray" lies in its affinity insofar as its function is concerned with the very process of human perception. This is suggested by the phrase "A head thrust in." As we come to the third stanza of the poem it is clear that Frost has extended the metaphor of "the geode ray" further to suggest that our mental perception, in its tendency to be excursive, is capable of grasping and shaping the world—the external reality in general. Epistemologically speaking this may be taken as the post-Kantian idea "that the mind is in some part constructive of the world."[42] There are, however, other features of philosophical implication in the poem, as stated in the first stanza ["But where it is it thrusts in from/on what it is it thrusts into…"],[43] which takes us to consider the mind's origins and its "constitutive acts."[44] It is obvious that without limitations to define and measure our won mind we can only ask—"What can of its coming come?"[45] The last stanza gives us the Frostian "strategy" in the face of "alien entanglements." The strategy is applied through a paradox. On one hand, our consciousness enters the world, and thereby constitutes it, and on the other the objects exist as realities independent of mind. Frost maintains a double vision. "All revelation has been ours" no doubt, but quite plausibly, as Frost would say with his ironic humour, they may prove to be "strange apparition of the mind!". Most of Frost's poems, it would appear, are embedded in this "double vision." With this vision as his "safety valve" against the ravages of life Frost himself is, however, committed "to the powers and limits of human consciousness to recreate its world in accordance with the needs and desires of self."[46] In Williams, the poetic act consists in setting a part of the world in a new context. He takes care that the objects exist as self-contained realities, and more or less, his mind unlike that of Frost's, does not determine the poetic world with pre-ideational data of human experience as actually lived. Situating his poems mostly in the modern urban environment, Williams's mind, like that of Wallace Stevens's in our time, is conditioned and perhaps created by his poems. Frost may take a metaphor from actual experience whereas Williams rather devotes a considerable amount of his poetic energy in employing the poem as a vehicle to find or even invent a metaphor. As Weatherhead says, a Williams poem "is a conscious and deliberate process, and frequently the poet is there in the poem supervising it, as it were."[47] As opposed to this in Frost the whole thing starts, as he has said, "with a lump in the throat." As he tackles the images one after another with an "epiphoric" combinations, the whole poem, as it were, becomes a metaphor born out of a situation which has its origin in Frost's deeply "thought-felt" experience. It will be profitable to assess this difference in depth if, for example, Frost's "An Old Man's Winter Night," is compared and contrasted with Williams's "The Red Wheelbarrow."

"An Old Man's Winter Night" is a concentrated drama. The images run into a metaphor, and the metaphor runs into an archetypal symbol, so that the poem is not merely Frost's effort to capture the pathetic features, and lonely endeavours of old age, but also becomes a commentary on certain forces and counter-forces such as light against dark, order against chaos, and life against death. And, so it becomes, more or less, an affirmation and assertion that life continues "living" in spite of the futility of old age—its emptiness and darkness. Metaphors, born out of images, gain momentum in their "epiphoric" combination from the very beginning. After the old man's failure of vision ["...kept his eyes from giving back the gaze"],[48] failure of memory ["...kept him from remembering what it was"],[49] and his dark and empty life ["...looked darkly in at him...in empty rooms"],[50] are stated in clear and simple terms, the poet strikes the keynote to the whole drama of old age in the following lines:

> A light he was to no one but himself
> Where now he sat, concerned, with he knew what,
> A quiet light, and then not even that.[51]

The light that shines now is the old man's spiritual "light" ["A light he was to no one but himself"], and it is likened to the pale light of the moon. Such an analogy is obvious, for the old man "...consigned to the moon, such as she was.../ his snow upon the roof,/His icicles along the wall to keep."[52] It implies the utility, and implicit glory of the moon. Though her light is quiet and subdued, she indeed gives meaning to night. Thus, the old man's spiritual light, his "simple, separating self" gives him his affirmation in life, and in his quiet and retired life, he refuses to be subdued by metaphysical forces. This analysis shows the manner in which the meaning of the poem comes out by piling of images which gain significance as a whole. The process indicates the mind's ability to structure objects in accordance with subjective knowledge. As opposed to this, Williams's technique, manifest in "The Red Wheelbarrow," is highly objective in its very rudiments. The metaphor is one of "simplicity," and the poem is "pure simplicity rendered in a simple manner."[53] The images are ordinary, and refer to real things and each one is analogous to the idea of simplicity. There are only four things in the poem which are juxtaposed with one another: the wheelbarrow, its vividness, its background, and lastly its importance. The "vividness" of the wheelbarrow is suggested by "glazed." Moreover, its background and importance are suggested by "chickens," and "so much depends"[54] respectively. As all these are "diaphorically" combined, the effect is one of an invention of a metaphor. The particularized reality of the wheelbarrow is caught in the poem's rhythm—its end-line pause which is simple. Hence, there is no artificiality involved, and the "object" is caught, as it were, in its native state. It may have been a private experience to Williams, but it is "ordered in a form external to the consciousness that entertained it in a flux."[55]

The difference between Frost and Williams is obvious. The objective realities in Frost are governed by his subjective knowledge, whereas in Williams there is an attempt to capture "the thing itself." In other words, Williams conveys us the experience of the object without structuring it by the inclinations of his artistic self. Williams shares the poetic impulse discovered in such poets as Marianne Moore and Wallace Stevens that the capturing of the native state of things to enable ourselves to get the ideas inherent in them ["No ideas but in things"] is the source of true delight. Even while depicting people, the tendency of Williams, is objective. He gives us "behavioristic, sharply observed, sympathetic and empathetic sketches."[56] These sketches drawn by Williams do not give us "the knowledge of a character that one gets from some of Frost's early dramatic monologues and narratives...."[57] This has obviously led many critics to admire the craftsmanship of Frost, and to express their unwillingness to bracket Williams with him. What should also be noted, as Narasimhaiah says, is Williams's tendency in some of the poems to present matter as almost inert, and dead without transforming them into energy, so that one has a feeling that in him the "emotion of fact" is not converted into "emotion of poetry."[58]

In Frost, the objects are used for the sake of a situation, or for what they represent. Williams, on the other hand, has compelled our attention to discard any mode of assumption about the world which may engender in us an inclination, and even an unwillingness, to look at things for what they are in themselves. We are struck by the simplicity, and innocence of the red wheelbarrow just because it is there in a unique circumstance of its own existence. It is this pattern, and not its utility conceived by man, that strikes us as original. Such a perception has a prelapsarian implication, echoing Adam's seeing of things and objects in the Garden of Eden, unspoilt by man's utilitarian motives. In Williams's poetic process, which is anti-Eliotic, the objects do not present us the possibility of formulating a principle for any emotion. Unlike Eliot's symbolic peach, hotels, oystershells or fog, Williams's red wheelbarrow, rain, and white chickens exist for their sake in the everyday world of man. This is not to say that these typical objects do not "contain implicit extensions of meaning." But what is to be noted is that "these extensions inhere in the realities of the things themselves."[59] Since ideas are important, contends Williams, they must be rooted and must find their life in the native state of objects and their relations in a poem. What Ostrom says in relation to Williams's poetry is apt: "the denotative fixes the poem's world in the presentness of actuality."[60]

The Frostian world, as our analysis of "An Old Man's Wintry Night" has revealed, depends on the emotional significance of "things" and "objects," and this significance is the structuring, the "objective correlative" for the situation that reveals the poem's theme. Each image is a preconceived thread in the evolution of the metaphor which is the whole poem. The structuring that has been given here to the images is postlapsarian, for it is smeared with the mysterious colour of man's rational and emotional reactions, particularly after he was banished from the Garden of Eden.

Our findings at this stage reveal that Frost and Williams are Adamic poets, each different from the other. Frost is postlapsarian, because the old man in "An Old Man's Wintry Night" undertakes his quest for Paradise through loss and pain and futility by asserting the continuance of life as the light that smears darkness. Williams is prelapsarian, because the red wheelbarrow caught in its bare simplicity records a state of condition that is perpetually innocent. The process of recapturing this in the form of the poetry is also a quest for Paradise.

Because of this sharp difference in technique, the appeal of Frost and Williams to the Americans had its strange variation. If Robert Frost read his poetry to packed audiences, and had almost become a national hero, it was not strange to understand why it was considered in Washington in 1952 that offering the chair of poetry to Williams would be an outrage,[61] why "very few people in Rutherford know anything about Bill's writing,"[62] and why he had a limited circle of admirers confined to poets, ladies, and the kinds.[63] It should not be, however, concluded that Williams's impact was not deeply felt. When Robert Frost combined in him the position of the "official bard of the administrative establishment and the fireside poet to the American people,"[64] Williams had his share of life's prizes. It was particularly because of certain rising waves of art like the Beats of San Francisco, and because of the American "predilection for the 'divine average.'"[65] His abiding contribution to American poetry lay in influencing a select group of poets who wanted to form like him a vision out of the hard, artless things of day-to-day life in America. Such a man would not "mourn wildflowers bulldosed into the ditch/for homes with families ..."[66] whereas Robert Frost could write in his "Tuft of Flowers":

> But he turned first, and led my eye to loose
> At a tall tuft of flowers beside a brook,
> A leaping tongue of bloom the scythe had spared
> Beside a ready brook the scythe had bared.[67]

It is a happy, though queer, coincidence that both Frost and Williams have been compared by some critics with D.H. Lawrence. To emphasize the main points of such a comparison is but to focus on the similarities as well as the differences between Frost and Williams. While evaluating Frost's poetry in an occasion that celebrated the eighty-fifth birthday of the poet.

Lionel Trilling took the current critical opinion by surprise when he ventured to compare Frost with Lawrence. Particularly the reply of Mr. Adams to Trilling's speech testified to it. Frost himself would also not appreciate it, and was "utterly at sea" as he confessed to it in an interview.[68] Frost whose ideals were embedded in an intense humanism might not have liked a comparison with D.H. Lawrence whose "sexual monism" was well known and would be, more or less, an anathema to be kept at an arm's length by the traditionalist Frost. However, Lionel Trilling's mention of Lawrence was well-intentioned in that it aimed at bringing out those salient features in Frost's poetry which approximated to Lawrence's exhortation in *The Classic American Studies* that the American artist must slough off the old European consciousness to formulate a new radicalism based on Nature and Man as they are actually interrelated in the American soil. Trilling emphasized that the Frostian world is populated with characters who are "isolated... lightning-blasted ... tied down and calcined to life," so much so that "each in his own way" has been reduced "to some last irreducible core of being." This was a form of reaction, it must be stated, against "the post-Renaissance humanism of Europe,"[69] for Frost's humanism, in its basic delineation, lies in man's attempt to remain in pastoral tie with Nature with an awareness of the ambiguities of life. Furthermore, there is in him a search for a truth that evolves from an Adamic faith in purity, simplicity, and innocence which must thrive, and be contained in our knowledge of the contrarieties of life. Characters that embody these qualities can be mentioned as examples from a good number of Frost's poems to substantiate Trilling's view that D.H. Lawrence's deliberations on what American Literature should be can bear fruitfully on an evaluation of Frost's poetry. These characters invariably live on the outskirts of civilization, and like "heroes in space" undertake their quest for a deep human identity in the context of man's relation with man, and with Nature. One of the points which Tilling only hinted in passing that the characters affirm their "separateness and isolateness" of themselves,[70] could have been further explored to bring the analogy with Lawrence a little closer. The indefatigable manner in which the Frostian characters maintain their "separateness and isolateness"—a choice which gives rise to the tension in their life—calls our attention to certain elements of the human self defined in Freud's *Psychoanalysis and the Unconscious.* It is the "vital self" to which Lawrence draws our attention. It is the "individual unit of consciousness and being which varies at the conception of every higher organism." It is like "a germinating egg" that grows "on and on to the strange and peculiar complication in unity which never stops"[71] till the individual dies. Bedient puts it in clearer terms:

> This 'peculiar complication' is indeed complex. In part, it consists of two contrary impulses: one reactive and separative and culminating in the 'I': the other sympathetic and connective and culminating in the sense of the Infinite—that 'great being' of which the self is defined as a 'unit.' For the rest, the complication consists in the dual activity of the mind and the senses.[72]

In a number of poems which have been analyzed earlier, particularly "Into My Own," "Dream Pang," "Apple-Picking" and "Directive," man's knowledge of the contrarieties and the ambiguities of life, with his quest for bliss in the very centre of life's confusion, does indeed make us aware of the mysterious functioning of the Lawrentian "vital self." Even in the *Masques* we discover the duality of the "vital self" in the separative-connective nature of Job's relationship with the Infinite—that "great Being" called God. Furthermore, it is worthwhile to note that though Frost, with some manner of his orthodoxy and Puritanism, would not have appreciated Lawrence's "sexual monism," his poem "The Subverted Flower" makes a very near assertion of the fact that sex is the essence of a man's and a woman's "being," and is like a sway of darkness which, paradoxically enough, enables us to emerge free and liberated to view the Soul's light. That Frost was highly conscious of the sexual imagery of the poem is obviously explained when, on being asked by a lady to tell the meaning of the poem, he quipped "Frigidity in Woman." Some of the lines reveal the erotic imagery in plain and understandable terms:

> She was standing to the waist
> In goldenrod and brake,
> Her shining hair displaced.
> He stretched her either arm
> As if she made it ache
> To clasp her—not to harm;
> As if he could not spare
> To touch her neck and hair.[73]

It was her social inhibitions, or as Frost put it her "frigidity," that might have made her shrink from the total experience of sex. And again, if chastity is only the lack of opportunity, it may be stated that "her mother's call/From inside the garden wall" made perhaps all the difference to her. The poem's carnal imagery is highly suggestive:

> A hand hung like a paw,
> An arm worked like a saw
> As if to be persuasive,
> An ingratiating laugh
> That cut the snout in half
> An eye become evasive.[74]

The yearning for the Lawrentian love as the "democracy of touch"—a love of and for body—is given free reins in the dialogues of the poem:

> 'It is this that had the power'
> ....
> 'If this has come to us
> And not to be alone—'
> ....

The consciousness of "organic romance," to use again a Lawrentian term, moulds the girl's reaction to the sexual urge of the boy, and is suggested through the flower imagery in the poem:

That the flower had done but part,
And what the flower began
Her own too meager heart
Had terribly completed.

Thought Frost did not write another poem of this kind, even one poem such as "The Subverted Flower," with its intensity of sexual experience, suggests that Frost as an artist was not oblivious of the fact that man and woman could have a glimpse of their own being in immersing themselves in that nameless world of "phallic mystery." The "quick of all her plasm" having been touched, the girl in the poem is born a woman, though the process is not complete firstly because of her traditional and social inhibitions, and secondly because of the opportunity that came her way but did not materialize itself for obvious reasons. We would not suggest that Frost composed this poem with the concept of Lawrentian "organic romance" in his mind, but it would not be out of place if we emphasized that such a concept was at least known to him.

In Williams, the knowledge of this concept is more consistent, and he gives evidence in his life and letters that he had eagerness to establish personal and emotional contact with D.H. Lawrence, the man and artist. In this he differs largely from Frost who did not even use the word 'sex' in his poetry as evidenced from the *Concordance to the Poetry of Robert Frost*.[75] The similarity between the attitude of Frost, and Williams does, however, lie in what each of them did to contribute their mite in creating a literature that might be true to the basic instincts of the New World Garden of America. In analyzing their approach to "objects," "things" and "situations," we have seen their basic difference, though both of them are Adamic poets insofar as the effect of their writings is concerned in general.

Williams's reaction to rise to the occasion of the exhortation in Lawrence's "America Listen to Your Own" to slough off the European past, and to create a national literature true to the spirit of America, has gained attention in our earlier discussion. The point to dilate upon here is to find out briefly the working of the

Lawrentian poetic credo, and his concept of "sexual monism" in Williams. Lawrence's review of *In the American Grain* strikes the key-note to such a study:

> The author sees the genius of the
> continent as a woman....[76]

Lawrence emphasizes that the exquisitely "super-subtle" and tender creature will "demand of men sensitive awareness, sensuous delicacy, infinitely tempered resistance."[77] Beginning from "The Wanderer" *via* such poems as "Love Song," "To Elsie," "Portrait of a Lady," "Rain," "A Marriage Ritual," "The Sea" down to *Paterson*, Williams invites us to share his view of man and woman—the male and female principles—as organically melting into each other to structure the unity of life. Notice, for example, the sexual overtones in the lines stated below:

> And we swerved clamorously downward—
> 'I will take my peace in her henceforth!
>
> ("The Wanderer")[78]

> ...Ah, yes—below
> the knees, since the tune
> drops that way, it is
> one of those white summer days,
> the tall grass of your ankles
> flickers upon the shore—
>
> ("Portrait of a Lady")[79]

> So spread
>   the words
> Far apart to let in
>   her love
> And running in between
>
> ("Rain")[80]

> the stain of love
> is upon the world:
>
> ("Love Song")[81]

> Once
> anything might have happened
> You lay relaxed on my knees—
> the starry night

spread but warm and blind
above the hospital—

("Young Love")[82]

...her great
ungainly hips and flopping breasts

addressed to cheap
jewelry
and rich young men with fine eyes

("To Elsie")[83]

The sea that encloses her young body
ula lu la lu
is the sea of many arms—

("The Sea")[84]

The scene's the Park
Upon the rock
female to the city
—upon whose body Paterson instructs his thoughts

(*Paterson*)[85]

—the leg raised, verisimilitude
even to the coarse contours of the leg, the
bovine touch! The leer, the cave of it,
the female of it facing the male, the satyr—

(Priapus!)[86]

With the lonely implication, goatherd
and goat, fertility, the attack, drunk,
cleansed.

(*Paterson*)[87]

All this as quoted above, with their incisive erotic imagery, points to the Lawrentian "reality of peace" that issues from "organic togetherness" of sexual congress—the strange, invisible "quest for identity." Thus, invoking the Lawrentian credo of sex we have been able to trace similarities, however ill-connected those might be, between Frost and Williams. It is again Lawrence's poetry, we believe that would very well enable us to point to striking dissimilarities insofar as the form of Frost's and Williams's poetry is concerned. Like Lawrence, both Frost and Williams had also a kind of empathic responsiveness to trees and flowers. Being a "sensibilist," and to a major degree an "environmentalist," Frost's botanic interest has been well stressed. A similar concern can also be marked in Williams:

> It is a pleasure for me now to think of these things, but especially of the flowers I got to know.... The slender neck of the anemone particularly haunts me for some reason and the various sorts of violets.... My curiosity in these things was unbounded—secret certainly.[88]

Both of these poets acted, as it were, to reawaken themselves to undertake the American pioneer's adventure to sense the beauty of the New World Garden, keeping themselves at a vantage point in the borderland between Civilization and Nature. It was a process of repossessing the world that they confronted in the eyes of the American Adam. What should not also be lost sight of is the tension that both have felt, as Frost's "Stopping by Woods" and Williams's "The Sea" show, that man for his survival in civilization must not only resist the Dionysiac attraction for a total surrender to Nature, but also return time and again to her hypnotic charm to renew himself.

In regard to poetic technique, or its form, Frost differs sharply from that of Lawrence's, and via Lawrence from that of Williams's. It has something to do with form in craftsmanship. Cook's judgment on Frost reveals the point, and tends to place him in the classical perspective:

> Frost obviously took advantage of the moods for the inception of his poetry, but he is in the Horatian tradition, and consequently observation, mental agility, the recollected and contemplated, and the continual self-surprises he explained were the incremental rewards of skillful practice in a highly self-disciplined art.[89]

In describing the poet's relationship to his craft, Frost would pinpoint "form," and explain it by the metaphor of an athlete—, preferably the "baseball pitcher who feels either in or out of form, as the case may be, on any given day."[90] When Frost is in his form, his language gains force from precise expression. This allegiance to discipline made him rather very uncomfortable while talking about the practitioners of loose and limp lines in poetry. These poets not only relaxed in an invidious manner the prescriptive rules of art, but also sometimes vulgarized their material to the extent of creating indiscipline and confusion. And his deprecation of free verse as playing tennis "with the net down" explains the whole point. Frost's approach to form was rather empirical, and bears little relationship with the Platonistic terms of mimetic theory that mirrors such abstractions as the Idea, the One, or the Form of Forms. Inductively thinking of form, Frost explained the impulse behind it as "just the desire to take whatever comes to hand—whatever is in front of you—and shape it."[91] Neither reproducing an archetype nor imitating an idea, he emphasized form as "making" which means "shape" that "has something to do with the consistency of parts."[92] The shift of emphasis is presumably on what Cook says "the parts of the structural method of organization in the poem: metrical beat in line and stanza, rhyme, idiom, and tone (with its implied tempo, pitch, and accent)."[93] In addition to this, he captured the "overtones of the national in the local, of the universal in the national."[94] This differs sharply from the Lawrentian emphasis on poetry as "the cry of its occasion" where form is governed by the mood of the moment. Lawrence also keeps the switch on to receive vibrations from the deeper recesses of his mind—the unconscious, and the sub-conscious. And, his mixing of autobiographical elements in his poetry made it further complicated in a manner so as to create a wide gap between his experience, and its public communication. Some poems like "The Ship of Death," for example, would exploit archetypal ideas to give Lawrence's intimate experiences a validity in abstractions which remain somewhat like a "closed chamber" to those who do not have similar experiences. Frost hardly partook of anything of this in principle, though "The Subverted Flower," thematically speaking, is the nearest thing that he attempted to equalize an "erotic credo" attempted by Lawrence himself throughout his novels, and in some of his poems also such as "Love on the Farm" ["And down his mouth, comes to my mouth! and down/ His bright dark eyes come over me, like a hood/Upon my mind: his lips meet mine, and a flood/ Of sweet fine sweeps across me, so I drown/Against him, die, and find death good"].[95] When one comes to Williams, it is marked that his poetry's form comes very much nearer to that of Lawrence's not only in its sensibility in revealing a "phallic consciousness," but also in its attempt to employ the poem as a vehicle for "the cry of its occasion." Consequently, Williams, unlike Frost, does not bother much about the traditional method of organization in a poem, though it would be highly unfair to state that he had no knowledge of it, nor did he attempt it in any poem. In fact, a poem such as "Self-Portrait" does not thrive merely on the Whitmanesque "barbaric yawp" but rests on employing rhyme, alliteration, and other traditional modes of poetic diction. If Robert Frost would say that every education in poetry must start with Mother Goose,[96] Williams seemed to have taken pleasure in almost demonstrating what he meant by writing a poem such as the one entitled "When Structure Fails Rhyme Attempts to Come to the Rescue." Though "Structure" and "Rhyme" are given symbolic significance here in representing the horse's diminishing "body" and its "dreams" respectively, Williams is, in fact, relying on such internal rhymes as "phlegm,/ahem!," "veins/ matches," "the bars—beggars"[97] to convey the theme instead of taking to his usual structural pattern where the homespun, natural and conversational style, with a voice that is "folksy" and "vernacular," gives an impression that what he records is only a process of working through his materials. In short, the wonder of it lies in its "artful artlessensss,"[98] or in its carefully chosen carelessness. On the contrary, the Frostian style is more akin to the classical tradition. Frost, it is well known, called himself a Synecdochist which in itself shows his allegiance to traditional matters concerning poetic diction—the meter, the metronome, and the Iambic. Even "tension" which meant so much to the New Critics was viewed by Frost as a "jargon"—a "cant":

> Now there. Now you talk about tension a lot. That's part of that jargon, that cant of literary criticism. Everything's tension, tension, tension. That kind of jargon makes one sick anyway. But if you want to talk about tension, here's tension right away between the meter and the rhythm; and

> if the tension breaks it's love that makes the song, it's got to be a tension that holds—sometimes a very big strain, in that one, 'Let me not to the marriage of true minds.'[99]

We have, of course, explored the working of tension in Frost's poetry, but what we find in the above quotation is a record of Frost's inclination towards a classical mastery over poetic diction. Williams was rather inventive in attuning himself to the metronomic "triadic foot" which he experimented in his love-lyric "Asphodel, That Greeny Flower." Through this he ventured to break down old poetic diction, and like Lawrence he went through the visibility of human experience to capture "the subconscious 'urge of life that is within.'" And to "make a new world"[100] to his poetry, he was not given any hunch to surrender himself to the task of lifting to expression the physicality of "things" and "objects" through which we must formulate our vision of the world. It is even striking, as in Lawrence, that Williams views his own life, and also the life of the people around him in its own right only.

Attention may now be drawn to the individual poems of Frost and Williams, which, in spite of their formal and structural differences, in their shift of emphasis in the use of poetic diction, incidentally evoke either a similar situation viewed differently, or echo similar phrases, imagery or metaphor in the face of a basic difference in the treatment of an identical theme. This would not mean that there was any conscious imitation of such factors by both of them. It may have been only a consequence of their belonging to a particular milieu. And if literature is the record of that milieu through a common language that captures human experience, either flitting or permanent, such similarities are bound to occur. With Frost and Williams these similarities, of course, highlight their differences all the more, for they utilized them to evoke different responses, though in some cases, as in our examination of Frost's "An Old Man's Winter Night" and Williams's "The Red Wheelbarrow," we have seen that the aim was similar, that is, to explore the world of man through "things" and "situations."

We may begin with two of the earlier poems of Frost and Williams. The poems are Frost's "Home Burial" and Williams's "The Dead Baby." The two poems centre round the death of a child. Both Frost and Williams strike the same note of innocence in portraying the character of the child. For Williams the dead child is "a white model of our lives/a curiosity—/ surrounded by fresh flowers."[101] The same freshness of its character is also emphasized when Frost draws our attention to "the fresh earth" from the "baby's grave."[102] Both poets put an accent on the word "fresh," and by doing so reveal the inherently simple innocence of the child. If it is "fresh earth" for Frost, it is only "fresh flowers" for Williams. What is even significant is the ability in Frost and Williams to study the characteristic difference of nature between the father and the mother of the dead child. If the father shows an ability in practical mindedness, and understands the mystery of life and death in reasonable terms, the mother views the whole thing with surcharged emotions, and is beyond consolation. Frost writes:

> '...What was it brought you up to think it the thing
> To take your mother-loss of a first child
> So inconsolably—in the face of love.'[103]

Williams does also capture a similar "voice-posture" in the father's deliberations:

> The mother's eyes where she sits
>   by the window, unconsoled—
> have purple bags under them
>   the father
> tall, well spoken, pitiful
>   is the abler of these two—
>
> Sweep the house clean
>   here is one who has gone up
>   (though problematically)
> to heaven, blindly
>   by force of the facts—
> a clean sweep
>   is one way of expressing it.[104]

What should be noted is the striking similarity between the poets in conveying the sense of the continuity of life while capturing the pretense of other people's sympathy who go their own way. If in Frost they are friends making "pretense of following to the grave,/But before one is in it, their minds are turned/and making the best of their way back to life,"[105] in Williams they come as friends no doubt but they are "...the curious/holiday seekers,"[106] for whom the personal grief of the parents may touch them in passing, but makes no meaning. This recalls a situation as we find, for example, in the end of Hemingway's *Old Man and the Sea* where the tourist woman notes the handsome tail of the great fish reduced to skeleton, but bothers the least to know anything of the old man's tragic struggle.

Though the two poets talk of the eternal verities of life in a tone that is similar, the difference lies in the background and the consequent atmosphere that is created. Frost's "baby" died in a place that is in the outskirts of civilization, and burying the baby in the home ground was a necessary corollary to the conditions of isolation and helplessness that prevailed there. In Williams's poem the baby dies in the hospital. Help comes in the way of the father and mother, and it is more than a routine affair:

Hurry up! Any minute
    they will be bringing it
    from the hospital.[107]

This difference would also highlight the way of life that the two poets led. Frost chose to remain in continual "isolation" in the outskirts of civilization whereas Williams had to remain in Rutherford for his medical practice. Also his sense of "isolation" is, more or less, the one that usually comes from "self-alienation" of the modern man in metropolis. But it is not to say that Williams did not feel the spell of Nature. It has already been referred that he felt a certain kind of sense of loss in his nostalgic contemplation over the gradual vanishing of the pastoral landscape of New Jersey. His residence itself was at the edge of Rutherford, and was at a site nearer to the sea. He felt lonely, as it were, if he was not in close communion with Nature—her trees, flowers, plants and animals. As he confesses, it was one of his motifs in *Paterson* to diminish the distance between past and present by imaginatively mastering a knowledge of the familiar sights and sounds of *Paterson*, the city, through a recollection of Kipp's Woods.[108]

With this in our mind, we may now compare Frost's "Desert Places" with Williams's "Man in a Room," and also make the comparison more relevant by bringing in citations from other poems of Frost and Williams which may enlighten the points made. Frost's "Desert Places" begins with the description of a barren and desolate landscape in Winter, and goes on to emphasize the corresponding loneliness of the speaker. The landscape symbolizes not only his own loneliness as viewed externally, but also his "mind's vacuous barrenness in some of its areas" which are as terrifying as the landscape outside. In fact, the speaker's discomfort lies not so much in confronting a terrifying Nature as in realizing that his own mind is as bad a "desert place" as the deserted, stark and bald landscape of Winter he confronts. It is the memory of this that indeed scares him, and he is rather afraid of looking directly into his own self. Just as the speaker in Frost's poem can realize the stark horror of his own mind by objectively projecting himself through an actual experience, so also the speaker in Williams's poem is able to know his own desolation by discovering an identity between himself and the objects in his own room. However, he consoles himself by a memory of a pastoral landscape ["Nor ditch-pool, nor green thing. Colour of flower,/Blood-bright berry none, nor flame-rust/Or leaf, nor pink gall-sting or stem…"][109] and feels its contrast with the starkness of objects in his room ["Bed, book-backs, walls, floor,/Flat pictures, desk, clothes-box, litter/Of paper scrawls…"].[110]

Both Frost and Williams are Emersonian in the sense that they are rather reluctant to look directly into the self. They attempt their self-exploration in an objective manner, avoiding mere introspection and subjectivity. In other words, their knowledge of the self comes through the objects of the world, and through their "dance with its persons, places, and things."[111] It is obvious that Frost's method in conveying the metaphor of loneliness and terror is epiphoric as he piles the images one after another to gain momentum, whereas the approach of Williams is diaphoric since he juxtaposes the images either from memory, or from actuality, and keeps a "verbal space"[112] that is, a kind of "language of silence" between them which can only be understood by the readers in finding the meaning through the context.

The consolation of the protagonist in Frost's "Desert Places" lies in that he cannot be scared by Nature's "empty spaces" as he had gained enough courage in realizing the terror of his "own desert places." In comparison, the protagonist in Williams's poem is able to feel the emptiness of his own mind as he views the banality of the objects in his room. However, he is relieved in finding an affinity between himself and "The flower-white tree which is in blossom with "petals, dew-wet" in spite of the fact that the petals are under the continuous assault of the raving wind. An element of violence appears to have been, therefore, suggested through the image of the "Torn petals," but such a fact only gives courage and faith to the observer who need not bother about the incursion of loneliness and violence into his life. Like the tree affirming its existence in continued blossoms in spite of the violence done to it, he too, must affirm his life in the face of its loneliness, emptiness and violence. Thus, "isolation" becomes heroic because there is always "the perilous ordeal of the quest for the ultimate experience."[113] The observations of the speakers in Frost's "Desert Places" and Williams's "Man in a Room" may equally border on the perilous, but there are no exaggerations involved in that. The complexities of the life of the speakers in both the poems are only another sure sign that they shall not tire themselves out in their quest for simplicity and innocence. Louis Zukofksy asserts the very same thing in propounding his thesis that a man who has faced complexities, that is to say, loneliness, terror and violence has the capacity "to return the world to simplicity again." He justifies the point by a passage from *Raquel Heline Rose:*

> It is in complexities that appear finally as one person that the good of a life shows itself—ringing all together to return the world to simplicity again...like a good picture; a sharp differentiation of good from evil—something to look at end to know with satisfaction, something alive—that has partaken of many things, welcoming them indiscriminately if they seemed to have a value—a colour—a sound to add still more to the intelligent, the colourful the whole grasp of feeling and knowledge in the world.[114]

As in "Man in a Room," so also in his poem "The Desert Music," Williams confronts chaos and vacuity, but what is significant is that his encounter with this human condition becomes for him the very source of his inspirations, energy and conviction in the power of imagination. Consequently, life is "seen not so much as issuing from death as leading to it: and it is this intense awareness of 'desert places' that summons the imagination and awakens its equally intense music of survival."[115] In Frost and Williams, therefore, there is this affirmation to survive in the face of terror, violence, loneliness and desolation which form the very fabric of man's existence on this planet to be sure. Frost confronts the same terror in "Come In" ["Almost like a call to come in/To the dark and lament"],[116] but he has his "safety valve," too, to guard against it—his ironic humour, and "double vision" ["But no, I was out for the stars:/I would not come in"].[117] In some other poems of Frost such as "The Wind and the Rain," the dreary landscape itself has its seeds of grace ["Flowers in the desert heart/contrive to bloom/On melted mountain water led by flume/To wet their feet"].[118] While comparing Frost's "Desert Places" with Williams's "Man in a Room" one finds that the diction used by Frost is an "extension" of metaphor to convey the mind's "desert places" whereas Williams employs the method of "precise intention" and "varied play of connotation,"[119] to enable the readers to have a similar awareness of "things," "objects," and "situations" that tend to get interacted with our experience of life and Nature. Familiar themes such as "death," "terror," and "loneliness" had an appeal for both the poets. These themes have occasioned in them a poetic insight to enable them to look through the surface of life. Under such circumstances, the readers, as Zukofksy has put it, have also their little roles to play, and in that process they become "something of a poet" themselves. It does not mean that we "contribute" to the poetry, but it has certainly that pleasant surprise to enable us to find ourselves the subject of the "energy" of the poems.[120]

Frost's "Into My Own" and Williams's "The Ordeal" give us some such pleasant surprise. We discover in those poems something of our own quest of a highly individuated order of existence so eccentric perhaps in its intensity that it may cause concern in the minds of those who love us. Frost takes the "dark trees" as the symbol for the mysterious quest of the poem's speaker who is unable to resist their Dionysiac spell. He prefers to "steal away," and get lost in "their vastness."[121] This, for the speaker, is a way of establishing contact with the primordial entities of life. It is also his means to explore the possibilities of realizing the permanence of Truth [equated with love]—an abstraction of which he had only a flitting experience while living his ordinary day-to-day life in society. In fact, his quest would not change him at all. On the other hand, his near and dear ones who are invited by the speaker to follow him would only be all the more convinced if they met him in that trackless woods that he had been better rooted to the eternal verities of life. In Williams's poem the protagonist's quest is a search of human desire, and is, therefore, symbolically related by the poet to "the winding flame"—"the Hell-flower" that shall consume all.[122] The flame metaphor has an obvious suggestion of love reduced to lust, and brings in the association of that "other fire of asceticism of St. Augustine and Buddha."[123] This theme of burning in Eliot's "Four Quartets" culminates in "a vision of the rose of love in the tradition of Dante,"[124] and is, therefore, based on a Christian-mystical plane, but what we find in this poem of

Williams is a very realistic depiction of the same theme as it avoids the religious myth, and uses a "primary myth" based on an idea coexistent with things. In Frost's poem the story of the man lost in the woods takes on a parabolic turn, and is obviously meant as a kind of invitation to others to unravel his mystery. Williams, on the other hand, does not intend any such invitation to others. What he wants is that the man must recover himself from his "descent" into Hell, and be back in society "unchanged,"[125] so that after his experience of "the winding flame" of desire which was rather "predestined to disman him,"[126] he would settle down to the innocent pursuits of life. Whether we associate it with the strange love for being lost in the wilderness or with that complex phenomenon of a man's love reduced to a pursuit of lust, in both poems human desire implies an operation of Adamic "free will." This may not be congenial to a large number of people who love us and whose lives are based on simple occupations recommended by society at large.

Frost once said, "My poems...are all set to trip the reader head foremost into the boundless."[127] This voyage "into the boundless" has for its basic working premise a desire to engage the immediate, perceptual world around him as "the spirit's alchemiciana."[128] This process may often lead to an intense realization of the roots of knowledge and truth. Both Frost and Williams examine the theme in "The Bear" and "The Fool's Song" respectively. To Williams, "truth," a concomitant of Frost's "Knowledge," is like a free "bird." Like Frost's "bear," it must not also be caged in. For both the poets, the cage metaphor serves to highlight the factor that a pursuit of truth and knowledge lies in a free play of the human spirit, and cannot be merely bogged down to the Library or the Laboratory. The polarized tension of opposites in Frost's poem pertaining to the "sedentary" man on one side, and the "peripatetic" man on the other can be related to a parallel situation in Williams's poem ["...I had the bird in the cage" as against "...when the bird was flown from the cage."][129] Again, Frost's embittered satire in saying man "A baggy figure"[130] is the same as Williams's saying that he who sings "Heigh Ho! Truth in a cage"[131] is indeed a fool.

From a sense of liberation of the human spirit to a simple love of Nature revealing itself in a botanic interest in, and a Dionysiac attraction for trees, flowers and leaves, the cry is not far enough in Frost and Williams as poets. We have already discussed Frost's love of the same and the symbolic turn that he gives to them in his poetry whether he treats them singly, in a group, or in the manner they appear in the wilderness. For illustration, one may turn to a study of his poems like "Birches," "Christmas Trees," "Flower-Gathering," "Leaves Compared with Flowers," "Maple," "Rose Pogonias," "Stopping by Woods on a Snowy Evening," "The Tuft of Flowers," "A Young Birch," etc. In Williams's poetry we also discover a wide preoccupation with trees, flowers and leaves. Such a preoccupation may result in a simple observation or may turn the observation into metaphysics, or may even enunciate Williams's own poetics in terms of the observation. If on one hand the shape of the tree may stand for masculine energy, its blossoms on the other may remind us of feminine beauty. In "The Botticellian Trees"[131a], for example, the trees symbolize the "poem's alphabets," and their leaves symbolize the "tune of a song" in which the poem throbs with life. All taken together it is "the smiles of love" which the trees stand for. In "The Tree" we find Williams calling them "the bastards" for the very manner in which they "thrash and scream/ guffaw and curse"[132] as the wind blows and rains drop. In "The Flowers Alone" the tone again shifts to a deep appreciation of "the coral/peach trees melting/ the harsh air—/ excellence/ priceless beyond/all later/fruit!"[133] The emphasis here is not on the rich harvest of peach fruits that the tree might bring, but on the beauty, and excellence of the tree itself as an object "priceless/beyond/all later/ fruit!" In comparison, Frost's "After Apple-Picking" reveals that the harvester's wakeful dream is even filled with "Magnified apples" that "appear and disappear,/ stem end and blossom end...."[134] While highlighting the plenteous harvest of apples, the poem's situation does ultimately form a symbolic pattern signifying life as activity—its desire and the nature of its outcome. Williams's "The Flowers Alone" is, however, first of all a picture poem arresting the very image of the trees as objects of innocence excellent in their own way. The poet admits at the beginning that it is this loss of innocence ["Loss keeps/me from such a/catalogue—"][135] that fails him in truly cataloguing the trees. The poet's observation centres round the fact that trees can possess a certain "priceless excellence" in themselves, which has to be noted irrespective of any considerations of "all later/fruits!"[136] Thus, human beings who run after "fruits"—the outcome of their actions—may find life a forced existence ["And now, driven, I/go forced to/another day—"].[137] Both poems make the trees and their blossoms a symbol of life. If Frost's poem takes us to a broader area to consider the basic nature of life as it is lived in all times, Williams's poem is more symptomatic of a sense of rootlessness and dispossession that inheres modern life. On the whole trees play a very significant part in moulding the philosophic content in some of the more popular poems of these two poets. Notice, for example, Frost's "Birches" where the poet associates the trees with man's heavenward desire. A similar notice is struck in Williams's "Della Primavera Transportata al Morale" in which the poet likens the upward thrust of a tree with the soul's contemplation to merge in God:

> The soul, my God, shall rise up
> —a tree.[138]

In fact, Williams has said in "The Avenue of Poplars" that "He who has kissed/a leaf/need look no further—."[139] Frost's "A Prayer in Spring" and "Sycamore" take us much deeper into such an area of feelings, stating the theme in clearer terms:

> Oh, give us pleasure in the orchard white,
> Like nothing else by day, like ghosts by night;
> And make us happy in the happy bees,
> The swarm dilating round the perfect trees.
> ....
> For this is love and nothing also is love,
> The which it is reserved for God above

To sanctify to what far ends He will,
But which it only needs that we fulfil.
["A Prayer in Spring"]

Zacchous he
Did climb the tree
Out Lord to see[140]
["Sycamore"]

Frost's habit of sneaking away into the woods, unnoticed and undiscovered, particularly when he was a poet-in-residence, has been already mentioned in Chapter IV. Almost a similar habit in Williams did continue throughout his life. It started with his childhood and early teens:

> It was an unconscious triumph all day long to just be able to get out of doors and into my personal wild world...flowers and trees were my peculiar interest. To touch a tree, to climb it especially, but just to know the flowers was all I wanted.[141]

That this interest in Williams was life-long is testified by his son Williams Eric:

> There was always a wet newspaper or a burlap-wrapped bundle of wild things in the car when he and mother returned from a trip. Ferns, moss, wild orchids, ginger, trillium, wild violets in variety, trailing arbutus, wild geraniums.... There was a daily ritual arm-in-arm circuit of the yard, usually early in the morning before leaving for the hospital, as he and mother inspected and planned the plantings. They shared a love of growing things...the garden was major item of activity and conversation at our house.[142]

In both poets this inclination for the country things had very little of what should be said about the unsophisticated simplicity of a countryman like the Aryshire Burns. When it comes to Frost, whether we talk of his life in Derry, Franconia, New Hampshire, South Shaftsbury, Ripon of Vermont, he did indeed resemble an Emersonian Poet Farmer trying to strike a deeper level of speculation in regard to his experience of Nature's flora and fauna. Williams went, we should say, a step ahead when he formulated a very important part of his poetics as we find it signified in that single but telling sentence in *A Novellette*: "Words on a par with trees." Later on he would get excited as he referred to this sentence as "penetrant" and "powerful."[143] The metaphor lay in giving the same kind of "ardent attentiveness" to words as he gave to trees while writing poems. If this was so with Williams, in Frost, too, we have sometimes a very "darksome" view about the trees as we find, for example, in "The Sound of Trees" and in "Tree at my Window." In such lines as "let them think twice before they use their powers...,"[144] one senses "an implication of a darksome anthropomorphic plot in which he and the trees are involved...."[145] This feeling, one should say, is "the converse of his love of trees and yet [a] part of it...."[146] The same is also more or less true of Williams who calls the trees "bastards" when he depreciates ["The Tree"], and "priceless" ["The Flowers Alone"] when he appreciates.

Particularly, when both poets face the landscape of the city it is interesting to note how they bring in pastoral imagery to keep the poem's tension balanced. We may compare two short poems by the poets for a brief analysis to reveal this point. It may also be indicated that such a balance helps pacify any violent feelings that might be roused in us while considering for ourselves the city's degradation or fall from innocence. The city as a *locus* of attention is, of course, not central in Frost. If Frost is known as the poet of the country side, Williams can very well be named as the poet of the city. While referring to the city Frost's tone is not often appreciative. Sometimes he is even condemnatory as in "A Masque of Mercy" where we find a bitter remark that "The City is admittedly an evil...." In "Christmas Trees" the stranger from the city is "A stranger to our yard, who looked the city...." The city street is again "Abysmal" ["The Lost Follower"] or has the "saddest" feature about it ["Acquainted with the Night"]. Moreover, it is the city that "seems intoppling from a height" ["The Fear of Man"], and is perhaps built on an "insecure rock pedestal" ["A Masque of Mercy"].[147] This is evidence enough to reveal Frost's attitude towards the city in addition to his own personal way of life which was, so to say, a kind of silent affront against the city mode of life. Of course, Frost did not sufficiently develop in any particular work this theme of opposition of the country to the city. This has been a major complaint by Williams himself when he reviewed "A Masque of Mercy":

> We have at the beginning an opposition of country to city though I don't think this theme is sufficiently developed as the story goes on – the bookstore being in the country to which from the city Jonas fled.[148]

In one of his more well-known poems namely "Acquainted with the Night" we find Frost making his "strategic retreat" from the city. Passing beyond "the saddest city lane," he "outwalked the furthest city light."[149] The beauty of the poem lies, as discussed earlier in Chapter IV, on the evocation of certain pastoral images. Thus, Frost's poem acquaints us with a quest for Edenic bliss beginning with a meaningful flight from a city. In comparison, Williams's poem entitled "Flight to the City" takes the city as a point of attraction, its excitement being a testimony to might and mass and beauty and to the raw pursuit of excellence. The city, Williams means to convey, has its beauty, too. But unfortunately its perpetual mobility blunts most people's sensibility, so much so that there is "Nobody/to say it—"[150] "The Easter stars" do also shine above the city's flashing lights. The poet's metaphor intensifies the pastorality of this image by signifying that the "shining" stars are like "coronal of the black."[151] The "skyscrapers" are like "a crown for her head with/ castles upon it…"[152] Such lines do obviously evoke the romantic mystery of the Middle Ages—its castles and knights and adventures. By a subtle manipulation of imagery that unifies the pastoral sensibility with that of the city's sensibility ["…skyscrapers/filled with nut-chocolates/dovetame winds—"].[153] Williams draws our attention to the intrinsic beauty of the city. For him the city is not merely "the labyrinth of human collectivity" or just a place that happens to be "the classical opposite of the temple in the poet's mythological landscape," but it becomes, in course of the poet's interaction with its events and experiences, the very place of the poet-wanderer's "invention."

Having been the epitome of the act of "*Grunding*" [grounding or founding], and, mythologically speaking, having been built for man's protection against "the giants and other outlaws," the city is forever man's "place of gathering" where he can suitably "attempt to recover his original lost ground, the ground abandoned or lost" as a result of "his initial act of violence," that is, the way Cain repeated his father's "violation."[154] As opposed to this, Frost's critique of the city is significantly based on the American myth of wilderness. The poet's desire in "Acquainted with the Night" to "out walk the furthest city light" is, by and large, a subtle examination of this myth in its simplest terms. Frost feels that the world of innocence can still be recaptured even though the distractions of an industrial era are "too much for us."[155] This is particularly possible with the American, for he as American born and brought up in the ideological tradition set up by a whole generation of people such as Crevecoer, Franklin and Jefferson is capable of recreating "a time made simple by the loss/Of detail...."[156] The flight from the city is for Frost an effective way of going "back" in time to respond to that condition of innocence which helps form character in an achievement of identity and creation of value in a quasi-frontier environment. This involves a sense of "freedom." It is also an obvious outcome of one's exposure to a pastoral environment. In fact, such a sense of "freedom" is ingrained in a sense of "departure" defining one's own self, as Frost would like to put it. The person thus involved, it must also be noted, "looks backward, not forward"[157] while departing. It is moreover a form of individuality in the moulding of which society hardly exists as a factor conditioning the relationships of man. Notice, for example, the manner in which Frost disposes of his encounter with "the watchman on his beat."[158] Suggesting that such encounters are only intrusions into a "one man's world" just as it happens to be, for example, when the buck in "The Most of It" appears in the scene all on a sudden, Frost in this poem curtly dismisses "the watchman on his beat." Passing by the watchman, Frost would express an "unwillingness to explain" his credentials to him. This is indicated by the timely dropping of his eyes. Such an "aloneness" is for Frost a condition of strength which perhaps enables him best to discover his Adamic self—his existence as a simple, separate person for whom "time was neither wrong nor right," but only an extended possibility to recapture his "lost origin" in all its "primal innocence." In the midst of a world that is too much for us, Frost was fond of being pre-occupied with the idea of re-establishing contact with our "lost origin," and worked it out in some of his wall-known works like the "Directive," and the *Masques*. In the two *Masques* the question is whether conventional religion is enough or it can only be valuable if "something original has been contributed to it...,"[159] whereas in the "Directive," we suppose, Frost admirably tackles a greater problem – the one of going back to whatever one believes in one's heart to be the "source." Such a "source" may be discovered in locating the "goblet"—a symbol of lost innocence. In Williams's *Paterson*, the poet-protagonist's adventure takes him also to the primal origins of life and art. What is important is that even a closeness to foulness—"the filthy Passaic"—is a moment opportune enough for Williams to unravel the mystery of the "first beauty" lying hidden in the very process of disintegration that may even release forces to build a new world. The persistence of the attempt lies, as in Frost, in being "whole again beyond confusion." It is the affirmation of an Adamic self-definition enabling the poets to accept a principle of innocence in the face of man's fall from Paradise the stamp of which is evident, we suppose, in the savagery of contemporary society.

All that we said is ample evidence to enable us to conclude that not unlike a whole generation of poets answering the call of an Emerson, and following a pattern of humanistic credo set apace by a Whitman, the two poets under scrutiny in this study have undoubtedly taken American poetry to a plane liberated enough to sing the intrinsic glory of man and the "things" of his world. If for Williams the Adamic preoccupation lay in the utterance of his concept that there are "no ideas but in things," for Frost all "love of things" was ultimately a form of "duty," and all that was "real was turning to words" in his poetry in the face of every limitation posed by history and tradition.

NOTES

1. *Writers at Work: The Paris Review Interviews*, Second Series (London: Secker and Warburg, 1963), pp. 17-18.
2. *Ibid.*
3. Alfred Kazin, "Introduction," *Writers at Work: The Paris Review Interviews.* Third Series (London: Secker & Warburg, 1967), p. ix.
4. *Ibid.*, p. 14.
5. *Ibid.*
6. Thomson, *Robert Frost*, p. 41.
7. Louis Untermeyer, *Robert Frost: A Backward Look* (Reference Department: The Library of Congress, 1964), p. 2.
8. A conversation between Robert Frost and a group of students at Bread Loaf, July 1962, quoted by Peter J. Stanlis "Robert Frost's Masques and the Classic American Tradition," in Tharp, ed. *Centennial Essays,* p. 442.
9. G.W. Nitchie, "A Momentary Stay Against Confusion," in Cox, ed. *Robert Frost: A Collection of Critical Essays,* pp. 174-175.
10. *Complete Poems of Robert Frost,* p. 206.
11. Quoted in Miller, ed. *William Carlos Williams: A Collection of Critical Essays,* p. 29.
12. His mother was of French and Spanish origin, and his father who did not want to relinquish his own British citizenship would not rather permit Williams to become an American.
13. *See* Joel Conarroe, *William Carlos Williams Paterson: Language and Landscape* (Philadelphia: Univ. of Pensylvania Press, 1970), p. 2.
14. Quoted *Ibid.*, p. 12.
15. See Cook, *Robert Frost: A Living Voice*, p. 4.
16. *Ibid.*, p. 5.
17. *Ibid.*
18. *Paterson*, p. 96.
19. *Complete Poems of Robert Frost*, p. 53.
20. Lloyd Dendinger, "Robert Frost The Popular and the Central Poetic Images," *American Quarterly*, 21 (Winter 1969), p. 804.
21. Thompson, ed. *Selected Letters of Robert Frost*, p. 122.
22. *Ibid.*, pp. 41-42.
23. *Selected Essays*, pp. 33-34.
24. *Spring and All*, pp. 1-3.
25. Cook, *Robert Frost: A Living Voice*, p. 17.

26. *Ibid.*
27. See *Paterson*, p. 126.
28. Cook, *Robert Frost: A Living Voice*, p. 20.
29. *Ibid.*
30. *Ibid.*
31. See *Selected Essays,* pp. 11-12.
32. Guimond, *The Art of William Carlos Williams: A Discovery and Possession of America,* p. 102.
33. See A. Kingsley Weatherhead, *The Edge of the Image* (Seattle: Univ. of Washington Press, 1967), p. 102.
34. See Philip Wheelwright, *Metaphor and Reality* (Bloomington: Indiana Univ. Press, 1962), pp. 76-ff.
35. See Wagner, *The Poems of Williams Carlos Williams: A Critical Study,* p. 40.
36. Quoted in Hugh Kenner, *Gnomon* (New York: McDowell Obolensky, 1958), p. 146.
37. Frost quoted in *Robert Frost: A Living Voice,* pp. 60-61.
38. Edward Cifelli, "Ciardi on Frost: An Interview," in Tharp, ed. *Centennial Essays,* p. 489.
39. M.L. Rosenthal, *The Modern Poets: A Critical Introduction* (New York: Oxford Univ. Press, 1960), p. 113.
40. See *Writers at Work,* Third Series, pp. 10-11.
41. J.H. Van Den Berg, *The Phenomenological Approach to Psychiatry* (Springfield: Charles C. Thomas, 1955), p. 32.
42. Frank Lentrichhia, "Robert Frost and Modern Literary Theory," in Tharp, ed. *Centennial Essays*, p. 317.
43. *Complete Poems of Robert Frost,* p. 444.
44. Lentrichhia in Tharp, ed. Centennial Essays, p. 318.
45. *Complete Poems of Robert Frost,* p. 444.
46. Tharp, ed. *Centennial Essays,* p. 330.
47. Weatherhead, *The Edge of an Image,* p. 116.
48. *Complete Poems of Robert Frost,* p. 135.
49. *Ibid.*
50. *Ibid.*
51. *Ibid.*, p. 135.
52. *Ibid.*
53. Weatherhead, *The Edge of the Image,* p. 110.
54. *CEP.*, p. 30.
55. R.P. Blackmur, "D.H. Lawrence and Expressive form," *Form and Value in Modern Poetry* (Garden City, N.Y.: Anchor Books, 1957), p. 256.

56. Randall Jarrell, "Introduction," *Selected Poems of William Carlos Williams* (New York: New Directions, 1969), p. xii.
57. *Ibid.,* pp. xii-xiii.
58. See C.D. Narasimhaiah, "William Carlos Williams," *Literary Criterion,* 10, No. 3 (Winter 1972), pp. 55-67.
59. Ostrom, *The Poetic World of William Carlos Williams*, p. 21.
60. *Ibid.,* p. 14.
61. *Writers at Work,* Third Series, p. 22.
62. *Ibid.* p. 19.
63. *Ibid.*, pp. 28-29.
64. Stanley Kunitz, "Frost Williams, & Company," *Harper's Magazine,* 225 No. 1349 (October 1962), p. 100.
65. Narasimhaiah, "William Carlos Williams," p. 56.
66. Paul Engle, "William Carlos Williams, " *Vertical Files,* American Studies Research Centre, Hyderabed.
67. *Complete Poems of Robert Frost* p. 32.
68. See, *Writer at Work,* Second Series, p. 25.
69. Lionell Trilling, "A Speech on Robert Frost: A Cultural Episode," in Cox, ed. *Robert Frost: A Collection of Critical Essays,* p. 157.
70. *Ibid.*
71. Lawrence quoted in Calvin Bedient, *Architects of the Self: George Eliot, D.H. Lawrence and E.M. Forster* (Berkeley: Univ. of California Press, 1972), p. 126.
72. *Writers at Work,* Second Series, p. 25.
73. *Complete Poems of Robert Frost,* p. 453.
74. *Ibid.,* p. 454.
75. See Edward Connery Lathem, ed. *Concordance to the Poetry of Robert Frost* (New York: Holt Information Systems, 1971).
76. Lawrence, *Phoenix,* p. 335.
77. *Ibid.*
78. *CEP,* p. 4.
79. *Ibid.* p. 40.
80. *Ibid.* p. 75.
81. *Ibid.* p. 174.
82. *Ibid.* p. 253.
83. *Ibid.* p. 271.
84. *Ibid.* p. 275.
85. *Paterson,* p. 57.
86. *Ibid.* p. 74.
87. *Ibid.*

88. *The Autobiography* p. 10. See also "Introduction," in *The William Carlos Williams Reader,* p. xxiii.
89. Cook, *Robert Frost: Living Voice,* p. 222.
90. *Ibid.*
91. Quoted *Ibid.,* p. 220.
92. Quoted *Ibid.*
93. *Ibid.*
94. *Ibid.*
95. D.H. Lawrence, *Selected Poems* (1950; rpt. London: Penguin Books, 1954), p. 14.
96. See Cook, *Frost: Living Voice,* pp. 164-165.
97. *CLP*, p. 79.
98. Sherman Paul, *The Music of Survival: A Biography of a Poem by William Carlos Williams* (Urbana: Univ. of Illinois Press, 1968), p. 48.
99. Frost quoted in Cook, *Frost: A Living Voice,* p. 155.
100. Rosenthal, *The Modern Poets: A Critical Introduction,* p. 160.
101. *CEP*, p. 113.
102. *Complete Poems of Robert Frost* p. 72.
103. *Ibid.* p. 71.
104. *CEP,* p. 113.
105. *Ibid.*
106. *Complete Poems of Robert Frost,* p. 72.
107. *CEP,* p. 113.
108. Paul, *The Music of Survival*, p. 49.
109. *CEP,* p. 37.
110. *Ibid.*
111. Paul, *The Music of Survival,* p. 26.
112. See the Chapter on William Carlos Williams in Carry Nelson, *The Incarnate Word: Literature as Verbal Space* (Urbana: Univ. of Illinois Press, 1973).
113. Glanco Cambon, *The Inclusive Flame: Studies in American Poetry* (Bloomington: Indiana Univ. Press, 1963), p. 76.
114. Quoted in Louis Zukofksy, *Prepositions: The Collected Critical Essays of Louis Zukofksy* (New York: Horizon Press, 1967), p. 43.
115. Paul, *The Music of Survival,* p. 95.
116. *Complete Poems of Robert Frost*, p. 446.
117. *Ibid.*
118. *Ibid.,* p. 449.
119. Zukofksy, *Prepositions,* p. 139.
120. *Ibid.,* p. 31.

121. *Complete Poems of Robert Frost*, p. 5.
122. *CEP*, p. 23.
123. B. Das, "The Love Ethic in a Permissive Society," *The Indian Association for English Studies, Proceedings of the XXI Annual Session* (Bhubaneswar: The Utkal Univ. Publication at Goswami Press, 1970), p. 30.
124. *Ibid.*
125. *CEP*, p. 23.
126. *Ibid.*
127. Frost quoted in Cook, *Robert Frost: The Living Voice*, p. 279.
128. Wallace Stevens quoted *Ibid.*, p. 279.
129. *CEP*, p. 19.
130. *Complete Poems of Robert Frost*, p. 348.
131. *CEP*, p. 19.
131.a.*Ibid.*, pp. 80-81.
132. *Ibid.*, p. 66.
133. *Ibid.*, p. 90.
134. *Complete Poems of Robert Frost*, p. 88,
135. *CEP*, p. 90.
136. *Ibid.*
137. *Ibid.*, p. 91.
138. *Ibid.*, p. 63.
139. *Ibid.*, p. 280. In Frost we have a large number of references to the significant part played by the "leaves." Green leaves in the "Tree at my Window" have a greater profundity than the talks of men ["Not all your light tongues talking aloud/could be profound."] In "Reluctance" leaves are "creeping and scraping," and in "Bereft" they are "hissing and striking." In "Leaf Treader" "They spoke to the fugitive in my heart as if it were leaf to leaf." See *Complete Poems of Robert Frost*, pp. 318, 43, 317, 388.
140. *Complete Poems of Robert Frost*, pp. 17, 439.
141. *Autobiography*, p. xii.
142. Eric quoted in Emily Mitchell Wallace, "The Forms of the Emotions… the pointed Trees," in Charles Angoff ed. *William Carlos Williams* (New Jersey: Associated Univ. Press, Inc. 1974), p. 22.
143. *Imaginations*, p. 294.
144. *Complete Poems of Robert Frost*, p. 303.
145. Sergeant, *The Trial by Existence*, p. 279.
146. *Ibid.*, p. 279.
147. See *Complete Poems of Robert Frost*, pp. 132, 324, 539, 625.

148. William Carlos Williams, "The Steeple's Eye," review of Frost's "A Masque of Mercy," in *Poetry*, 72 (April-September 1948), p. 39.
149. *Complete Poems of Robert Frost* p. 324.
150. *CEP*, p. 244.
151. *Ibid.*
152. *Ibid.*
153. *Ibid.*
154. Riddel, *The Inverted Bell*, p.75. *See* also Martin Heidegger, *An Introduction to Metaphysics*, trans., Ralph Mannheim (New York: Anchor Books, 1961), pp. 54-56. Angus Fletcher, *The Prophetic Moment: An Essay on Spencer* (Chicago: The Univ. of Chicago Press, 1971), pp. 11-34. C. Kerenyi and C.G. Jung, *Essay on a Science of Mythology*, trans. R.F.C. Hull, Bollingen Series (New York: Harper Torchbooks, 1963), p. 14.
155. *Complete Poems of Robert Frost*, p. 451.
156. *Ibid.*, p. 451.
157. Pearce, *The Continuity of American Poetry*, p. 277.
158. *Complete Poems of Robert Frost*, p. 451.
159. Morrison quoted in Berry, *Robert Frost*, p. 126. The originality lies in Paul's way of defining God's mercy not as an act of forgiving sins or failures but as His acceptance as a free gift of the best sacrifice that man has to offer. "...May my sacrifice/Be found acceptable in Heaven's sight," in *Complete Poems of Robert Frost*, p. 642.

Select Bibliography

WORKS BY ROBERT FROST & WILLIAM CARLOS WILLIAMS

Frost, Robert, *A Boy's Will*. New York: Holt, 1915.

____. *North of Boston*. New York: Holt, 1915.

____. *Mountain Interval*. New York: Holt, 1916.

____. *New Hampshire: A Poem. With Notes and Grace Notes*. New York: Holt, 1923.

____. *West-Running Brook*. New York: Holt, 1928.

____. *A Further Range*. New York: Holt, 1936.

____. *A Witness Tree*. New York: Holt, 1942.

____. *A Masque of Reason*. New York: Holt, 1945.

____. *A Masque of Mercy*. New York: Holt, 1947.

____. *Steeple Bush*. New York: Holt, 1947.

____. *In the Clearing*. New York: Holt, 1962.

____. *Collected Poems of Robert Frost*. New York: Holt, 1930.

____. *Selected Poems*, ed. Robert Frost with introductory essays by W.H. Auden, Cecil Day Lewis, Paul Engle and Edwin Muir. London: Jonathan Cape, 1936.

____. *The Pocket Book of Robert Frost's Poems*, ed. Louis Untermeyer. New York: Pocket Books, 1946.

____. *The Poems of Robert Frost*. New York: The Modern Library Edn., 1946.

____. *Complete Poems of Robert Frost*. New York: Holt, 1949.

____. *The Poetry of Robert Frost,* ed. Edward Connery Lathem. London: Jonathan Cape, Ltd., 1972.

____. *The Letters of Robert Frost to Louis Untermeyer*, ed. Louis Untermeyer. New York: Holt, 1963.

____. *Selected Letters of Robert Frost,* ed. Lawrance Thompson. New York: Holt, 1964.

____. *Interviews with Robert Frost,* ed. Edward Connery Lathem. New York: Holt, 1966.

____. "Education by Poetry: A Meditative Monologue." *Amherst Alumni Council News*, 4 (March 1931), Supplement, pp. 6-7.

____. "Introduction" to *King Jasper* by Edwin Arlington Robinson. New York: Macmillan, 1935.

____. "Introduction" to *A Swinger of Birches: A Portrait of Robert Frost.* New York: New York Univ. Press, 1957.

____. "Introduction" to *New Poets of England and America,* eds. Donald Hall *et al.* New York: Meredian Books, 1957.

____. "Vocal Imagination." Lewiston (Maine*) Evening Journal*, 5 May 1925, p. 8.

Williams, William Carlos. *The Autobiography of William Carlos Williams.* New York: Random House, 1951.

____. *The Collected Earlier Poems of William Carlos Williams.* Norfolk, Conn.: New Direction, 1951.

____. *The Collected Later Poems of William Carlos Williams.* Revised Edition, Norfolk, Conn.: New Directions, 1963.

____. *The Complete Collected Poems of William Carlos Williams, 1906-1958.* Norfolk, Conn.: New Directions, 1938.

____. *Paterson I-V.* Norfolk, Conn.: New Directions, 1963, Originally Published in Single Vols., New Directions, 1946, 1948, 1949, 1951 & 1958.

____. *Collected Poems. 1921-1931.* Preface by Wallace Stevens. New York: The Objectivist Press, 1934.

____. "America, Whitman, and the Art of Poetry." *The Poetry Journal,* 8 (Nov. 1917), pp. 27-36.

____. "An Essay on *Leaves of Cross.*" *Leaves of Grass: One Hundred Years After,* ed. Milton Hindus. Stanford, Calif.: Stanford Univ. Press.

____. "An Approach to the Poem." *English Institute Essays, 1947.* New York: Columbia Univ. Press, 1948.

____. "The New Poetical Economy." *Poetry,* 44 (July 1934), pp. 220-25.

____. "A Note on Poetry." *The Oxford Anthology of American Literature,* eds. W.R. Benet & N.H. Pearson, New York: Oxford Univ. Press, 1938.

____. "A Note on the Art of Poetry." *Blues,* 1, No. 4 (May 1929), pp. 77-79.

____. "Objectivism." *Encyclopaedia of Poetry and Poetics,* ed. Alex Preminger. Princeton: Princeton Univ. Press, 1965.

____. "Ah Extraordinary Sensitivity." *Poetry,* 60 (Sept. 1942), pp. 338-40.

____. "Faiths for a Complex World." *American Scholar,* 26 (Fall 1957), pp. 453-57.

____. *Spring and All.* Dijon: Contacts, 1923.

____. *A Voyage to Pagany.* New York: The Macaulay Co., 1928.

____. *Selected Essays.* New York: Random House, 1954.

____. "An Objectivists' Anthology." *The Symposium,* 4, No. 1 (January 1933), pp. 114-17.

____. "Notes on Norman Macleod." *Mosaic,* 1, No. 1 (Nov.-Dec. 1934), pp. 27-28.

____. "The Steeple's Eye." Rev. of Frost's "A Masque of Mercy," In *Poetry,* 72 (April-Sept., 1948), pp. 33-41.

____. "Symposium on Writing." *The Golden Goose, Series,* 3, No. 2 (Autumn, 1951), pp. 89-96.

___. "Two Letters." *The Golden Goose,* 6, No. 5 (Oct., 1952), pp. 30-32.

____. *In the American Grain.* Norfolk, Conn.: New Directions, 1956.

____. *Kora in Hell: Improvisations.* San Francisco: City Lights Books, 1957.

____. *I Wanted to Write a Poem.* ed. Edith Heal. Boston: Deacon Press, 1958.

____. *The Farmers' Daughters.* Norfolk, Conn. New Directions, 1961.

____. *Pictures from Brueghel and Other Poems.* London: MacGibbon & Kee, 1963.

____. *Imaginations,* New York: New Directions, 1970.

OTHER WORKS CONSULTED

Abrahamsen, David. *Our Violent Society.* New York: Funk and Wagnalls, 1970.

Aldrich, Charles Roberts. *The Primitive Mind and Modern Civilization.* London: Kegan Paul, Trench, Trubner & Co. Ltd., 1931.

Allen, Gay Wilson. *Walt Whitman Handbook.* New York: Hendricks House, 1962.

Alvarez, A. *The Shaping Spirit: Studies in Modern English and American Poets.* London: Chatto & Windus, 1961.

Anderson, C.R., ed. *Centennial Edition.* Baltimore: The Johns Hopkins Press, 1945.

Anderson, Charles R. "Robert Frost 1874-1963." *Saturday Review,* 23, Feb. 1963, pp. 17-20.

Auden, W.H. "Robert Frost," in *The Dyer's Hand.* New York: Random House, 1962.

Barlow, Joel, *The Columbiad: A Poem,* Vol. I. Philadelphia: C & A Conrad & Co., 1809.

Barry, Elaine, *Robert Frost.* New York: Frederick Ungar Publ. Co., 1973.

___. *Robert Frost on Writing.* New Brunswick, N.J.: Rutgers Univ. Press, 1973.

Barthes, Roland. *Writing Degree Zero,* trans. Annette Lavers and Colin Smith. New York: Hill & Wang, 1968.

Beaver, Harold, ed. *American Critical Essays: Twentieth Century.* London: Oxford Univ. Press, 1959.

Becker, Carl. *The Heavenly City of the Eighteenth Century Philosophers.* New Haven: Yale Univ. Press, 1932.

Bedient, Calvin. *Architects of the Self: George Eliot. D.H. Lawrence and E.M. Forster*. Berkeley: Univ. of California Press, 1972.

Berg, J.H. Van Den. *The Phenomenological Approach to Psychiatry*. Springfield: Charles C. Thomas, 1955.

Blackmur, R.P. "D.H. Lawrence and Expressive Form," in *Form and Value in Modern Poetry*. Garden City, N.Y.: Anchor Books.

Blum, John M., *et al. The National Experience: A History of the United States*. New York: Harcourt, Brace & World, Inc., 1963.

Bode, Carl, ed. *The Great Experiment in American Literature.* New York: Frederick A. Praeger, Publishers, 1961.

Bode, Carl, *et al.* eds. *American Literature,* Vol. I, II, III. New York: Washington Square Press, Inc., 1966.

Bodkin, Maud. *Archetypal Patterns in Poetry: Psychological Studies of Imagination.* London: Oxford Univ. Press, 1934.

Bourne, Randolph. "The History of a Literary Radical," *The Yale Review,* 8, No. 3 [n.s.] (April 1919).

Bowra, Sir Maurice. *The Romantic Imagination.* London: Oxford Univ. Press 1950.

Bradbury, John M. *The Fugitives: A Critical Account.* Chapel Hill: Univ. of North Carolina Press, 1958.

Bradley, Phillips, ed. Alexis de Tecqueville, *Democracy in America.* Vols. I & II. New York: Alfred A. Knopf, 1963.

Bradley, William Aspinwall, *William Cullen Bryant.* New York : The Macmillan Co., 1905.

Breslin, James, E. *William Carlos Williams: An American Artist.* New York: Oxford Univ. Press, 1970.

Brinnin, John Malcolm. *William Carlos Williams.* Minneapolis : Univ. of Minnesota Press, 1963.

____. "William Carlos Williams," in Leonard Unger, ed. *Seven Modern American Poets: An Introduction*, 1967; rpt. Allahabad: A.H. Wheeler & Co. Pvt. Ltd., 1971.

Brooks, Van Wyck. *America's Coming-of-Age*. Rev. edn. Garden City, N.Y.: Doubleday & Co., Inc., 1958.

____. *Scenes and Portraits: Memories of Childhood and Youth.* New York: E.P. Dutton & Company, Inc., 1954.

Brower, Reuben A. *The Poetry of Robert Frost: Constellations of Intention.* New York: Oxford Univ. Press, 1963.

Burke, Kenneth. "Heaven's Frost Law." *The Dial.* 72 (February 1922), pp. 94-98.

____. "William Carlos Williams: A Critical Appreciation," in Charles Angoff, ed. *William Carlos Williams*. N.J.: Associated Univ. Press, Inc. 1974.

Cambon, Glanco. *The Inclusive Flame: Studies in American Poetry.* Bloomington: Indiana Univ. Press, 1963.

Cargill, Oscar. *Intellectual America: Ideas on the March.* New York: Macmillan & Co., 1941.

Carpenter, Frederic I. *American Literature and the Dream.* New York: Philosophical Library, 1953.

____. "The American Myth": Paradise (To Be) Regained." *PMLA*, 74 (1959), pp. 599-612.

Chari, V.K. *Whitman in the Light of Vedantic Mysticism*. Lincoln: Univ. of Nebraska Press, 1964.

Charvat, William. *Origins of American Critical Thought. 1810-1835*. Philadelphia: New York: A.S. Barnes & Co., Inc., 1961.

Ciardi, John. "Robert Frost: The Way to the Poem," *Saturday Review,* 40 (12 April 1958), pp. 13-15, 65.

Clark, William Smith, ed. *Lowell: Essays, Poems & Letters*. New York: The Odyssey Press, 1948.

Clough, Wilson O. *The Necessary Earth: Nature and Solitude in American Literature*. Austin: Univ. of Texas Press, 1964.

Conarroe, Joel. *William Carlos Williams' Paterson: Language and Landscape*. Philadelphia: Univ. of Pennsylvania Press, 1970.

____. "William Carlos Williams's *Paterson:* Substance and Structure." Dissertation. New York Univ. 19.

Cook, Reginald L. "Frost on Frost: The Making of Poems." *American Literature,* 28 (March 1956), pp. 62-72.

____. *Robert Frost: A Living Voice.* Amherst: The Univ. of Massachusetts Press, 1974.

Cowley, Malcolm. *Exile's Return: A Literary Odyssey of the 1920s.* New York: The Viking Press, 1951.

Cox, Hyde & Edward Connery Lathem, eds. *Selected Prose of Robert Frost.* New York: Holt Rinehart & Winston, 1966.

Cox, James M., ed. *Robert Frost: A Collection of Critical Essays.* Englewood Cliffs, N.J.: Prentice Hall Inc., 1962.

Cox, Sidney, *A Swinger of Birches: A Portrait of Robert Frost.* New York: Collier Books, 1957.

Condor, John T. "'After Apple-Picking': Frost's Troubled Sleep," in Jack L. Tharp, ed. *Frost: Centennial Essays.* Jackson: Univ. Press of Mississippi, n.d.

Commager, Henry Steele, *The American Mind: An Interpretation of American Thought and Character Since the 1880s.* New Haven: Yale Univ. Press, 1950.

Cowan, Louise. *The Fugitive Group: A Literary History.* Baton Rouge, Ls.: Louisiana State Univ. Press, 1959.

Crevecoer, J. Hector St. John de. *Letters from an American Farmer.* 1782; rpt. New York: Fox, Auffield & Company, 1904.

Cyclopaedia of American Literature (1855), Vol. II. New York: Charles Scribner, 1866.

Dahlburg, Edward. *The Sorrows of Priapus.* Norfolk, Conn.: New Directions, 1957.

Dahlstrom, Carl Enoch. *Strindberg's Dramatic Expressionism. 1930;* rpt. New York: Arno Press, 1978.

Das, B. "The Love Ethic in a Permissive Society," in *The Indian Association for English Studies, Proceedings of the XXI Annual Session.* Bhubaneswar: The Utkal Univ. Publication at Goswami Press, 1970.

Davenport, Jr., F. Garven. *The Myth of Southern History: Historical Consciousness in Twentieth-Century Southern Literature.* Nashville: Vanderbilt Univ. Press, 1967.

Degler, Carl N. "The Sociologist as Historian: Riesman's *The Lonely Crowd.*" *American Quarterly* 15, No. 4 (Winter 1963), pp. 483-97.

Demaris, Avid. *America the Violent.* Cowles Book Co., 1970.

Dembo, L.S. *Conception of Reality in Modern American Poetry.* Berkeley: Univ. of California Press, 1966.

Dendinger, Lloyd Nash. "Robert Frost: Popular Image of the Poet." Dissertation. Louisiann State Univ., 1966.

____. "Robert Frost: The Popular and the Central Poetic Images." *American Quarterly,* 21 (Winter 1969), pp. 792-804.

Derrida, Jacques. "Structure, Sign, and Plays in the Discourse of the Human Sciences," in Richard Macksay and Eugenic Donate, eds. *The Language of Criticism and the Sciences of Man: The Structuralist Controversy.* Baltimore: The Johns Hopkins Univ. Press, 1970.

Dijkstra, Bram. *The Hieroglyphics of New Speech: Cubism, Stieglitz and the Early Poetry of William Carlos Williams.* Princeton N.J.: Princeton Univ. Press, 1969.

Donoghue, Denis. *Connoisseurs of Chaos: Ideas of Order in Modern American Poetry.* London: Faber & Faber, 1965.

Dougherty, James P. "Robert Frost's 'Directive' to the Wilderness." *American Quarterly,* 18, No. 2, pt. 1 (Summer 1966), pp. 208-209.

Doxey, William S. "Out, Out—." *Explicator,* 29, No. 8 (April 1971), Item 70.

Drew, Elizabeth. *T.S. Eliot: The Design of His Poetry.* 1970; rpt. Delhi: Doaba House Book Sellers & Publishers, 1970.

Dudden, Arthur, P. "Nostalgia and the American." *Journal of the History of Ideas,* Oct.-Dec. 196, pp. 512-513.

Durr, R.A. *Poetic Vision and the Psychedelic Experience.* Syracuse: Syracuse Univ. Press, 1970.

Earnest, Ernest. *Expatriates and Patriots: American Artists. Scholars, and Writers in Europe.* Durham: North Carolina Press, 1968.

Eliade, Mircea. *Myth of the Eternal Return: Cosmos and History* trans. Willard R. Trask. Princeton, N.J.: Princeton Univ. Press, 1971.

____. *Myth and Reality* trans. Willard R. Trask, New York: Harper & Row, 1963.

____. *Images & Symbols: Studies in Religious Symbolism,* trans. Philip Mairet. New York: A Search Book, 1969.

Eliot, T.S., ed. *Ezra Pound: Selected Poems.* London: Faber & Faber, 1928.

____. *Selected Essays.* New York: Harcourt Brace, 1960.

____. "Tradition and the Individual Talent" in John Hayward, ed. *Selected Prose.* Harmondsworth: Penguin, 1953.

____. "The Poetry of W.B. Yeats." *Southern Review,* 7 (Winter 1941), pp. 442-454.

——. *Selected Prose,* ed. John Hayward. 1953; rpt. Harmondsworth: Penguin Books Ltd., 1953.

____. "'Ulysses' Order and Myth," *The Dial,* 75 (Nov. 1923), pp. 380-383.

Emerson, Ralph Waldo. *Essays*. New York: Carlton House, n.d.

——. *Essays: First and Second Series.* New Delhi: Eurasia Publishing House (P) Ltd., 1972.

____. *English Traits, Representative Men, Other Essays.* 1908; rpt. London: J.M. Dent & Sons Ltd. New York: E.P. Dutton & Co., Inc., 1951.

Engle, Paul, "William Carlos Williams." *Vertical Files,* American Studies Research Centre, Hyderbad.

Epsey, John Jenkins. *Ezra Pound's Mauberlev: A Study in Composition.* London: Faber & Faber, 1955.

Faber, Doris. *Robert Frost: America's Poet.* Englewood Cliffs, N.J.: Prentice-Hall, Inc., 1964.

Fedler, Lillian. *Ancient Myth in Modern Poetry.* Princeton, N.J.: Princeton Univ. Press, 1971.

Ferguson, Alfred E. "Frost and the Paradox of the Fortunate Fall," in Jack L. Tharp, ed. *Frost: Centennial Essays.* Jackson: Univ. Press of Mississippi, n.d.

Fiedler, Leslie A. *An End to Innocence: Essays on Culture and Politics.* Boston: The Beacon Press, 1955.

Fletcher, Angus. *The Prophetic Moment: An Essay on Spencer.* Chicago: The Univ. of Chicago Press, 1970.

Foerster, Norman. *Nature in American Literature.* New York: Macmillan, 1923.

____. *American Critical Essays: XIXth and XXth Centuries.* London: Oxford Univ. Press, 1930.

Frank, Waldo, ed. *The Collected Poems of Hart Crane.* New York: Live right Inc. Publishers, 1933.

____. *The Rediscovery of America: An Introduction to a Philosophy of American Life.* New York. Charles Scribner's & Sons, 1929.

Freud, Sigmund. *General Introduction to Psychoanalysis*, trans. Joan Riviere. New York: Washington Square Press, 1952.

____. *Civilization and its Discontents*, trans. Joan Riviere. New York: J. Cape & H. Smith, 1930.

Gasset, Ortega Y. *The Revolt of the Masses,* trans. anon. London: G. Allen & Unwind, Ltd. 1932.

Gerber, Philip L. *Robert Frost.* New York: Twayne Publishing, Inc., 1966.

Ghiselin, Brewster. *Creative Process.* New York: The New American Library, 1955.

Gibb, Carson. "Mending Wall." *The Explicator Cyclopedia,* Vol. I, eds. Charles Child Walcutt & J. Edwin Whitesell, Chicago: Quadrangle Books, 1966.

Gilman, William H., et al. *Journals & Miscellaneous Notebooks of Ralph Waldo Emerson.* Cambridge, Mass.: Harvard Univ. Press, 1964.

Goodheart, Eugene. *The Cult of the Ego: The Self in Modern Literature.* Chicago: The Univ. of Chicago Press, 1968.

Gould, Jean. *Robert Frost: The Aim Was Song.* New York: Dodd, Mead & Company, 1967.

Grant, Douglas. *Purpose and Place: Essays on American Writers.* New York: St. Martin's Press, 1965.

Griffith, Clark. "Frost and the American View of Nature." *American Quarterly*, 20 No. 1 (Spring 1968), pp. 21-37.

Guerin, Wilfred L., et al. *A Handbook of Critical Approaches to Literature.* New York: Harper Row, 1966.

Guimond, James. *The Art of William Carlos Williams: A Discovery and Possession of America.* Urbana: Univ. of Illinois Press, 1968.

Hassan, Ihab H. *The Dismemberment of Orpheus: Toward a Postmodern Literature.* New York: Oxford, Univ. Press, 1971.

____. "The Idea of Adolescence in American Fiction." *American Quarterly,* 10, No. 3 (Fall 1958), pp. 312-324.

____. *Radical Innocence: Studies in the Contemporary Novel.* Princeton: Princeton Univ. Press, 1961.

Heidegger, Martin. *Being and Time,* trans. John Macquarrie, and Edward Robinson. New York: Harper & Row, 1962.

____. *An Introduction to Metaphysics,* trans. Ralph Manheim. New York: Anchor Books, 1961.

____. *On the Way to Language,* trans. Peter D. Herts. New York: Harper & Row, 1971.

Herzog, George. "Drum-Signaling in a West-African Tribe" in Dell Hymes, ed. *Language in Culture and Society: A Reader in Linguistics and Anthropology.* New York: Harper & Row, Publishers, 1964.

Hiers, John T. "Robert Frost's Quarrel with Science." *The Georgia Review,* 25, 2 (Summer 1971), pp. 182-205.

Hoffmann, Daniel G., ed. *American Poetry and Poetics.* New York: Doubleday, 1962.

Horton, Rod W. and Herbert W. Edward. *Background of American Literature Thoughts.* New York: Appleton-Century-Crofts, Inc., 1952.

James, William. *Pragmatism: And Four Essays From the Meaning of Truth.* 1907 & 1909 rpt; New Delhi: Eurasia Publishing House Pvt. Ltd., 1975.

Jarrell, Randall. "Introduction." *Selected Poems of William Carlos Williams.* New York: New Directions, 1969.

____. *Poetry and the Age.* New York: Vintage Books, 1953.

Jefferson, Thomas. *Notes on the State of Virginia,* ed. William Peden. Chapel Hill: Univ. of North Carolina Press, 1955.

Jennings, Elizabeth. *Frost.* Edinburgh: Oliver & Boyd, 1964.

Johnson, Thomas H. *The Complete Pomes of Emily Dickinson.* Boston: Little, Brown & Co., 1960.

____. *Emily Dickinson: An Interpretative Biography.* Cambridge: Harvard Univ. Press, 1966.

Jones, Howard Mumford, and S.I. Hayakawa, eds. *Oliver Wendell Holmes: Representative Selections.* New York: American Book Co., 1939.

Judd, Dorothy. "Reserve in the Art of Robert Frost." *Texas Quarterly,* 6, No. 2, pp. 60-67.

Jung, Carl Gustav and Caroly Kerenyi. *Essays on a Science of Mythology: The Myth of the Divine Child and the Mysteries of Flusis.* Middletown, Conn., Wesleyan Univ. Press, 1968.

Kantak, V.Y. "Poetic Ambiguity in Frost." *Western Humanities Review,* 28, No. 1 (Winter 1974), pp. 31-46.

Kazin, Alfred. "Introduction," in *Writers at Work: The Paris Review Interviews.* Third Series. London: Secker and Warburg, 1967.

Kenner, Hugh. *Gnomon*. New York: McDowell Obolensky, 1958.

____, ed. *T.S. Eliot: A Collection of Critical Essays*. Englewood Cliffs, N.J.: Prentice-Hall, 1962.

____, *The Pound Era*. Berkeley: Univ. of California Press, 1972.

Kerenyi, C. & C.G. Jung. *Essay on a Science of Mythology*, trans. R.F.C. Hull, Bollingen Series. New York: Harper Torchbooks, 1963.

Koch, Vivienne. *William Carlos Williams*. Norfolk Conn.: New Directions, 1950.

Konvitz, Milton R. Rev. of *The Myth of the Machine: The Pentagon of Power,* by Lewis Mumford, in *Saturday Review,* 19 Dec. 1970, pp. 24-29.

Krieger, Murray. *Theory of Criticism: A Tradition and its System*. Baltimore: The Johns Hopkins Univ. Press, 1976.

Krueger, Thomas A. "The Historians and the Edenic Myth: A Critique." *The Canadian Review of American Studies,* 4, No. (Spring 1973), pp. 3-18.

Kuklick, Bruce. "Myth and Symbol in American Studies." *American Quarterly,* 24 (October 1972), pp. 435-450.

Kunitz, Stanley. "Frost, Williams, & Company." *Harper's Magazine,* 225, No. 1349 (October 1962), 100.

Kyle, Carol Anne. "Epistemological Dualism in the Poetry of Robert Frost." *Dissertation Abstracts*, 29, No. 7 (January 1969), 2267A-2268A.

Lanier, Mary D., ed. *Poem of Sidney Lanier*. New York: Charles Scribner's Sons, 1906.

Lathem, Edward Connery, ed. *Concordance to the Poetry of Robert Frost* New York: Holt Information Systems, 1971.

Lawrence, D.H. *Studies in Classic American Literature*. London : Heinemann, 1964.

____. *Selected Poems*. 1950; rpt. London: Penguin Books, 1954.

____. "America Listen to Your Own," in *Phoenix*, ed. Edward D. McDonald. New York: Viking, 1936.

Lechlitner, Ruth. "William Carlos Williams." *Poetry* 54 (Sept. 1939), pp. 326-35.

Leland, Godfrey. *Sunshine in Thought.* New York: C.T. Evans, 1862.

Lerner, Max. *America as a Civilization: Life and Thought in the United States Today.* New York: Simon and Schuster, 1957.

Levi-Strauss, Claude. *The Savage Mind,* trans. La Pensee Savage. Chicago: Univ. of Chicago Press, 1968.

Lewis, Cecil Day. "Introduction," in Robert Frost, *Selected Poems.* Harmondsworth: Penguin Books, 1955.

Lewis, Ruth Ann. "Robert Frost, Poet-Teacher: Three Studies." Dissertation. Univ. of Utah, 1969.

Lewis. R.W.B. *The American Adam.* Chicago: Univ. of Chicago Press, 1955.

Locke, John, "An Essay Concerning the True Original, Extent and End of Civil Government: Second Treatise on Civil Government," in *Social Contract: Essays by Locke, Hume and Rousseau,* "Introduction" by Sir Frnest Barker. New York: Oxford Univ. Press, 1960.

Lovejoy, Arthur, O., et al. *A Documentary History of Primitivism and Related Ideas.* Baltimore: Johns Hopkins, 1935.

Lowell, Amy. "Walt Whitman and the New Poetry," in Francis Murphy, ed. *Walt Whitman.* Harmondsworth: Penguin Books Ltd., 1969.

Lowell, James Russell. *The Complete Poetical Works.* Cambridge Edition, Boston: Houghton Mifflin Co., 1897.

Lynen, John F. *The Pastoral Art of Robert Frost.* New Haven: Yale Univ. Press, 1960.

Lynn, Kenneth S. *The Dream of Success: A Study of the Modern American Imagination.* 1955; rpt. West Port, Conn.: Greenwood Press, Inc., 1972.

Madden, David. "True Believers, Atheists and Agnostics", in *American Dreams, American Nightmares,* ed. David Madden. Carbondale: Southern Illinois Univ. Press 1970.

Malinowski, B. *Magic. Science and Religion.* New York: Doubleday & Co. Inc., 1955.

Martz, Louis. *The Liberal Tradition in America: An Interpretation of American Political Thought Since the Revolution.* New York: Harcourt, Brace & World, Inc., 1955.

____. "The Unicorn in *Paterson:* William Carlos Williams," in John Hollander, ed. *Modern Poetry: Essays in Criticism.* Oxford: Oxford Univ. Press, 1968.

Marx, Leo. *The Machine in The Garden: Technology and the Pastoral Ideal in America.* New York: Oxford Univ. Press, 1964.

Mathiessen, F.O. *The Responsibilities of the Critic.* New York : Oxford Univ. Press, 1952.

____. *American Renaissance: Art and Expression in the Age of Emerson and Whitman.* Delhi: Oxford Univ. Press, 1973.

Matthews, Fred. "The 'Myth' and 'Value' Approaches to American Studies." *The Canadian Review of American Studies,* 3, No. 2 (Fall 1972), pp. 112-121.

May, Henry F. *The End of American Innocence.* New York: Alfred A. Knopf, 1955.

Mazzaro, Jerome. *William Carlos Williams: The Later Poems:* London: Cornell Univ. Press, 1973.

Miller, J. Hillis, ed. *William Carlos William:* Englewood Cliffs, N.J.: Prentice-Hall, Inc., 1966.

Miller, James E. Jr. *Walt Whitman.* 1962; rpt. Allahabad: A.H. Wheeler & Co. (P) Ltd., 1971.

Miller, Perry, *The New England Mind: Seventeenth Century.* Cambridge: Harvard Univ. Press, 1967.

____. *The Raven and the Whale: The War of Words and Wits in the Era of Poe and Melville.* New York: Harcourt, Brace & Co. 1956.

____. *The New England Mind: From Colony to Province.* Cambridge, Mass.: Harvard Univ. Press, 1953.

Morse, S.F., ed. Wallace Stevens, *Opus Posthumous*. New York: Alfred A. Knopf, 1957.

Moore, Arthur K. *The Frontier Mind: A Cultural Analysis of Kentucky Frontiersmen*. Lexington: Univ. of Lexington Press, 1957.

Moore, Marianne. "Things Others Never Notice." *Poetry*, 44 (May 1934), pp. 103-106.

Morrison, Theodore. "The Agitated Heart." *The Atlantic Monthly*, July 1967, pp. 72-79.

Moulton, William G. "The Nature of Language." *Daedalus*, 102, No. 3 (Summer 1973), pp. 17-35.

Muilenberg, James. "Adam and Second Adam," in *A Handbook of Christian Theology*. New York: Living Age Books, 1958.

Mulder, William. "Freedom and Form: Robert Frost's Double Discipline." *South Atlantic Quarterly*, 54 (July 1955), pp. 386-393.

Munson, Graham. *Making Poems for America: Robert Frost*. Chicago: Encyclopaedia Britannica Press, 1962.

Murdock, Kenneth. *Handkerchiefs from Paul*. Cambridge: Harvard Univ. Press, 1927.

Musgrove, S. *T.S. Eliot and Walt Whitman*. New York: Haskell House Pubs. Ltd., 1970.

Narasimhaiah, C.D. "William Carlos Williams." *Literary Criterion*, 10, No. 3 (Winter 1972), pp. 55-67.

Nash, Roderick. *Wilderness and the American Mind*. New Haven: Yale Univ. Press, 1967.

Nelson, Carry. *The Incarnate Word: Literature as Verbal Space*. Urbana: Univ. of Illinois Press, 1973.

New Jersey: A Guide to its Present and Past. American Guide Series. New York: The Viking Press, 1939.

Niebuhr, Richard. *The Kingdom of God in America*. New York: Harper & Brothers, 1937.

Nitchie, George W. "Robert Frost: The Imperfect Guru," in Jack L. Tharp, ed. *Frost: Centennial Essays*. Jackson: Univ. Press of Mississippi, n.d.

——. "A Momentary Stay Against Confusion," in James M. Cox, ed. *Robert Frost*: A Collection of Critical Essays. Englewood Cliffs: Prentice-Hall, 1962.

——. *Human Values in the Poetry of Robert Frost.* Durham, N.C.: Duke Univ. Press, 1960.

Noble, David W. *The Eternal Adam and the New World Garden : The Central Myth in the American Novel since 1830.* New York: George Braziller, 1968.

——. *The Paradox of Progressive Thought.* Minneapolis: Univ. of Minnesota Press, 1958.

Norton, C.E., ed. *Letters of James Russell Lowell.* New York: Harpers & Brothers, 1894.

Nowottny, Wilfred. *The Language Poets,* London: Athlone Press, 1962.

Noyes, Russell, ed. *English Romantic Poetry and Prose.* New York: Oxford Univ. Press, 1956.

Ogilvie, John T. "From Woods to Stars: A Pattern of Imagery in Robert Frost's Poetry." *The South Atlantic Quarterly,* 58, No. 1 (Winter 1959), 64-74.

Olson, Charles. *Call Me Ishmael.* San Francisco: City Light Books, 1947.

——. *Selected Writings* ed. Robert Creeley. New York: New Directions, 1966.

Ostrom, Alan. *The Poetic World of William Carlos Williams.* London: Southern Illinois Univ. Press, 1966.

Parks, E.W., ed. *The Essays of Henry Timrod.* Athens: Univ. of Georgia Press, 1942.

Parrington, Vernon Louis. *Main Currents in American Thought: An Interpretation of American Literature from the Beginnings to 1920.* 3 Vols. in 1. New York: Harcourt, 1937.

Paul, Sherman. *The Music of Survival: A Biography of a Poem by William Carlos Williams.* Urbana: Univ. of Illinois Press, 1968.

Pearce, Roy Harvey. *The Continuity of American Poetry.* Princeton, N.J.: Princeton Univ. Press, 1961.

Pearson, Norman Holmes. "Williams, New Jersey." *The Saturday Review,* I (Autumn 1957), p. 36 —.

Perrire, Lawrence. "The Meaning of Frost's 'Build Soil'," in Jack L. Tharp, ed. *Frost: Centennial Essays.* Jackson: Univ. Press of Mississippi, n.d.

Pinkey, Alphonso. *The American Way of Violence.* New York: Random House, 1972.

Poirier, Richard. *Paris Review,* No. 24 (Summer-Fall 1959).

Pound, Ezra. *Pavannes and Divisions.* New York: Alfred A. Knopf, 1918.

——. *Personae: The Collected Shorter Poems.* New York: New Directions, 1926.

——. "Dr. Williams' Position," *The Dial,* 85 (Nov. 1928), pp. 395-404.

Pradhan, Narinder Singh. "Edenic Themes in Modern American Drama." Dissertation. University of Utah, 1972.

Quinn, Arthur Hobson, ed. *The Literature of the American People: An Historical and Critical Survey.* New York: Appleton-Century-Crofts, Inc., 1951.

Quinn, Sister M. Bernetta. *The Metamorphic Tradition in Modern Poetry.* New Brunswick, N.J.: Rutgers Univ. Press, 1955.

Radcliffe, Denis. *The Major Themes of Robert Frost.* Ann Arbor: The Univ. of Michigan Press, 1963.

Radhakrishnan, S., trans. *Bhagavadgita.* London: George Allen & Unwin Ltd., 1967.

Rahv, Philip. *The Myth and the Power House.* New York: Farrer, Straus & Cirous, 1965.

——. "Torrents of Spring." *The Nation,* 144 (26 June 1937), p. 733.

Rajan, B., ed. *Modern American Poetry.* London Dobson, 1950. New York: Roy Pubs., 1952.

Ranchan, Som P. *Walt Whitman and the Great Adventure with Self.* Bombay: Manaktalas, 1967.

Ransom, John Crowe. *Poems and Essays.* New York: Vintage Books, 1955.

Reed, Henry B. "The Haraclitan Obsession of Walt Whitman," *The Personalist,* 15 (April 1934), pp. 125-136.

Riddel, Joseph N. *The Inverted Bell: Modernism and the Counterpoetics of William Carlos Williams.* Baton Rouge: Louisiana State Univ. Press, 1974.

——. *The Clairvoyant Eye: The Poetry and Poetics of Wallace Stevens.* Baton Rouge: Louisiana State Univ. Press, 1967.

Riesman, David, *et al. The Lonely Crowd: A Study of the Changing American Character.* New Haven: Yale Univ. Press, 1950.

Rosenmeir, Jesper. "New England's Perfection: The Image of Adam and the Image of Christ in the Anti-nomian Crisis, 1634 to 1638." *The William and Mary Quarterly,* 26 (Spring 1953), pp. 361-362.

Rusk, Ralph L., ed. *The Letters of Ralph Waldo Emerson,* Vol. IV. New York: Columbia Univ., Press, 1939.

Rosenthal, M.L. *The Modern Poets: A Critical Introduction.* New York: Oxford Univ. Press, 1960.

——. ed. *The William Carlos Williams Reader.* New York: A New Directions Books, 1966.

Sanford, Charles L. *The Quest for Paradise: Europe and the American Moral Imagination.* Urbana: Univ. of Illinois Press, 1961.

——. "An American Pilgrim's Progress." *American Quarterly,* 6, No. 4 (Winter 1954), pp. 297-310.

Santayana, George. *Character and Opinion in the United States.* New York: George Braziller, 1955.

——. "The Genteel Tradition in American Literature," in *Winds of Doctrine and Platonism and the Spiritual Life.* New York: Harper & Brothers, 1957.

Sartre, Jean-Paul. "American Novelists in French Eyes." *Atlantic Monthly,* 178 (August 1964), pp. 114-118.

Schmitt, Peter J. *Back to Nature: The Arcadian Myth in Urban America.* New York: Oxford Univ. Press, 1969.

Scott, Wilbur S. "To Earthward," *The Explicator Cyclopedia,* Vol. 1, eds. Charles Child, Walcutt & J. Edwin Whitesell, Chicago: Quadrangle Books, 1966.

Schorer, Mark. "The Technique as Discovery." *Hudson Review* 1 (Spring 1948), pp. 67-87.

——. *The Literature of America: Twentieth Century.* New York: McGraw-Hill Book Company, 1960.

Sequeira, Isaac. *The Theme of Initiation in Modern American Fiction.* Mysore: Geetha Book House, 1975.

Sergeant, Elizabeth Shepley. *Robert Frost: The Trail by Existence.* New York: Holt, Rinehart and Winston, 1960.

Shaw, Bernard. *The Complete Plays.* The Times Index — The Statesman Associated Newspapers of Ceylon Ltd., 1939.

Shumaker, Wayne, *Literature and the Irrational: A Study in Anthropological Backgrounds.* Englewood Cliffs, N.J.: Prentice-Hall, Inc., 1960.

Smidt, Kristian. *Poetry and Belief in the Work of T.S. Eliot.* London: Routledge and Kegan Paul, 1961.

Smith, Grover. *T.S. Eliot's Poetry and Plays: A Study in Sources and Meaning.* Chicago: Univ. of Chicago Press, 1956.

Smith, Henry Nash. "Virgin Land Revisited." *Indian Journal of American Studies*, 3, No. 1 (June 1973), pp. 83-90.

——. *Virgin Land: The American West as Symbol and Myth.* Cambridge: Harvard Univ. Press, 1950.

Smith, John E., ed. *The Works of Jonathan Edwards* Vol. 2. 1843; rpt. New Haven: Yale Univ. Press, 1959.

Snow, C.P. *Variety of Men.* London: Macmillan , 1967.

Snow, Wilbert. "The Robert Frost I Knew." *The Texas Quarterly,* 11, No. 3 (Autumn 1968), p. 9-48.

Sonh, David A. & Richard H. Tyne, *Frost: The Poet and His Poetry*. New York: Bantam Books, 1969.

Spencer, B.T., *The Quest for Nationality*. Syracuse: Syracuse Univ. Press, 1957.

Spiller, Robert E. *The Cycle of American Literature: An Essay in Historical Criticism*. New York: The Macmillan Company, 1955.

Stanford, Donald E., ed. *The Poems of Edward Taylor*. New Haven: Yale Univ. Press, 1960.

Stanlis, Peter J. "Robert Frost's Masques and the Classic American Tradition," in Jack L. Tharp, ed. *Frost: Centennial Essays*, Jackson: Univ. Press of Mississippi, n.d.

Starobinske, Jean, *The Invention of Liberty, 1700-1789*, trans. Bernard C. Swift. Geneva: Skira, 1964.

Stedman, Edmund Clarence & Ellen Macay Rutchinson, eds. *A Library of American Literature from the Earliest Settlement to the Present Time*. Volume II. New York: Charles L. Webster & Co., 1890.

Stein, William Bysshe, " 'After Apple-Picking': Echoic Parody." *University Review*, Kansas City, No. 35, pp. 301-6.

Stevens, Wallace, "Williams," in William Carlos Williams, *Collected Poems, 1921-1931*. New York: The Objectivist Press, 1934.

——. "Rubbings of Reality." *Briarcliff Quarterly*, 11, No. 2 (October 1946), pp. 201-202.

——. *Letters of Wallace Stevens*, ed. Holly Stevens. New York: Alfred A. Knopf., 1966.

——. *The Collected Poems of Wallace Stevens*. New York: Alfred A. Knopf, 1957.

——. *Poems by Wallace Stevens*. New York: Vintage Books, 1959.

Stroller, Leo. *After Walden: Thoreau's Changing Views on Economic Man*. Stanford, Calif.: Stanford Univ. Press, 1957.

——. "Thoreau's Doctrine of Simplicity." *N.E.Q.*, 29 (Dec. 1959), p. 457-8.

Stone, Virginia Scroggin. "Robert Frost: The Breathless Swing Between Context and Form." *Dissertation Abstracts*, 30, No. 6 (December 1969), 2501A.

Sullivan, A.M. "Dr. William Carlos Williams, Poet and Humanist," in Charles Angoff, ed. *William Carlos Williams*. Carnbury, N.J.: Associated Univ. Press, Inc., 1974.

Susman, Warren I. "The Useless Past: American Intellectuals and the Frontier Thesis, 1910-1930." *Bucknell Review*, 11 (March 1963), p. 1-20.

——. "History and the American Intellectual: Uses of a Usable Past." *American Quarterly*, 16, No. 2, Pt. 2 (Summer 1964), p. 243-263.

Sutton, Walter. *American Free Verse: The Modern Revolution in Poetry*. New York: A New Directions Book, 1973.

Synge, John M., *Poems and Translations*. Dublin: Maunsel & Co. Ltd., 1911.

Tate, Allen, "Emily Dickinson," in Fgbert S. Oliver, ed. *American Literature*, 1890-1965. New Delhi: Eurasia Publishing House (P) Ltd., 1970.

The Oxford Anthology of Americna Literature, eds. W.R. Benet and N.H. Pearson, New York: Oxford Univ. Press, 1938.

The Philosophy of Schopenhaur, Modern Library Edition. New York: Random House, 1956.

The Complete Poetical Works of Whittier, Cambridge Edition. Boston: Houghton Mifflin & Co., 1894.

The Complete Poetical Works of Oliver Wendell Holmes, Cambridge Edition. Boston: Houghton Mifflin & Co., 1922.

The Complete Poetical Works of Long Fellow, Craige Edition. Boston: Houghton Mifflin & Co., 1922.

Thirlwall, John C. "William Carlos Williams' 'Paterson'," in *New Directions 17*. New York: New Directions, 1961.

Thompson, Lawrance, *Fire and Ice: The Art and Thought of Robert Frost*. New York: Holt, Rinehart & Winston, 1942.

——. *Robert Frost.* Minneapolis: Univ. of Minnesota Press, 1959.

——. *Robert Frost: The Early Years, 1874-1915*. New York: Holt, Rinehart & Winston, 1966.

——. *Robert Frost: The Years of Triumph*. New York: Holt, Rinehart & Winston Inc., 1970.

——. "Robert Frost" in *Seven Modern Poets*, ed. Leonard Unger. 1967; rpt. Allahabad: A.H. Wheeler & Co. Pvt. Ltd., 1971.

Thoreau, Henry, *A Week on the Concord and Merrimack Rivers*, ed. Walter Harding. New York: Holt, Rinehart & Winston, Inc., 1963.

Townlye, Rod. *The Early Poetry of William Carlos Williams*. London: Cornell Univ. Press, 1975.

Unger, Leonard and William Van O'Conner. *Poems for Study*. New York: Rinehart, 1953.

Untermeyer, Louis, ed. *Complete Poems of Edgar Allan Poe*. New York: The Heritage Press, 1943.

——. *The Poetry and Prose of Walt Whitman*. New York: Simon & Schuster, 1949.

——. *Robert Frost: A Backward Look*. Reference Department: The Library of Congress, 1964.

Valery, Paul. *The Art of Poetry*, trans. Denise Folliot with an Introd. by T.S. Eliot. London: Routledge & Kegan Paul, 1958.

Waggoner, Hyatt. *American Poets: From the Puritans to the Present*. Boston: Houghton Mifflin & Co., 1968.

Wagner, Linda Welshimer. *The Poems of William Carlos Williams: A Critical Study*. Middleton: Wesleyan Univ. Press, 1964.

Wallace, Emily Mitchell. "The Forms of the Emotions...the Pointed Trees," in Charles Angoff, ed. *William Carlos Williams*. New Jersey: Associated University Press, Inc. 1974.

——. *A Bibliography of William Carlos Williams*. Middleton, Conn.: Wesleyan Univ. Press, 1968.

Walter, Rush. "The History of Ideas in Europe: An Essay in Redefinition," *The Journal of American History*, 51, No. 4 (March 1965) 599-614.

Waltz, Sister Vincent. "The Doubleness of Nature in Robert Frost's Poetry of Paradox." *Dissertation Abstracts*, 29, No. 8 (February 1969), 2727A.

Warren, Robert Penn. "Pure and Impure Poetry." *Kenyon Review*. Spring 1942, pp. 228-254.

Weatherhead, A. Kingsby. *The Edge of the Image*. Seattle: Univ. of Washington Press, 1967.

Weber, Brom, ed. *The Complete Poems and Selected Letters and Prose of Hart Crane*. New York: Anchor Books, 1966.

Wheelright, Philip. "Poetry, Myth, and Reality," in Allen Tate, ed. *The Language of Poetry*. Princeton, N.J.: Princeton Univ. Press, 1942.

Whicher, Stephen E., ed. *Selection from Ralph Waldo Emerson : An Organic Anthology*. Boston: Houghton Mifflin & Co., 1957.

Whicher, George Frisbie. *This Was a Poet: Emily Dickinson*. New York: Charles Scribner's Sons, 1938.

Whitaker, Thomas. *William Carlos Williams*. New York: Twayne Publishers, 1968.

Whitman, Walt. *Specimen Days*. Philadelphia: David McKay, 1883.

Winters, Yvor. "Poetry of Feeling." *The Kenyon Review* 1, No. 1 (Winter 1939), 104-107.

——. "Robert Frost: Or the Spiritual Drifter as Poet." *Sewanee Review*, 56 (Autumn 1948), pp. 564-596.

Woods, Powell, "William Carlos Williams: The Poet as Engineer," in Matthew J. Bruccoli and Joseph Katz., eds. *Profile of William Carlos Williams*. Columbus: A Bell & Howell Company, 1971.

Writers at Work: The Paris Review Interviews, Second Series. London: Seeker and Warburg, 1963.

Wyllie, Irvin G. *The Self-made Man in America: The Myth of Rags to Riches*. New York: The Free-Press, 1954.

Zukofksy, Louis. *Prepositions: The Collected Critical Essays of Louis Zukofksy*. New York: Horizon Press, 1967.

——. "Preface — 'Recencies' in Poetry," in Louis Zukofksy, ed. *An "Objectivists" Anthology*. New York: To, Publishers, 1932.